The Hunter's Rifle

The Hunter's Rifle

Hunter's Information Series™
North American Hunting Club
Minneapolis, Minnesota

The Hunter's Rifle

Copyright© 1988, Clay Harvey

Library of Congress Catalog Card Number 88-061127
ISBN 0-914697-15-3

Printed in U.S.A.
6 7 8 9

The North American Hunting Club
offers a line of hats for hunters.
For information, write:
    North American Hunting Club
    P.O. Box 3401
    Minneapolis, MN 55343

Contents

Acknowledgments

The Hunter's Rifle is destined to become a modern classic comparable to the well-known works of O'Connor, Carmichel and Gresham. The efforts of the author combined with the behind the scenes work of the NAHC staff have made this a work really worth the time to read.

Thanks to: NAHC Executive Vice President Mark LaBarbera, Managing Editor Bill Miller, Associate Editor Dan Dietrich, Member Products Manager Mike Vail and Special Projects Coordinator Linda Kalinowski.

Steven F. Burke, President
North American Hunting Club

Photo Credits

Photos in this book were provided by the author. In addition to examples of his own talent, he has included photos from Rick Jamison and a variety of firearms manufacturers. Also included are photos by Leonard Lee Rue.

About The Author

Clay Harvey was born and reared in Fayetteville, North Carolina, where he began squirrel hunting with his dad at age seven with a Daisy BB rifle. The squirrel population did not suffer greatly.

He attended Methodist College for a couple of years, majoring in contract bridge, then decided academia was not for him and joined the Army, where he served three years. Stationed in Korea in 1967-68, he pulled ambush patrols on the DMZ, but saw no action. During this overseas stint he began his first competitive period, entering and winning at such diverse sports as pistol shooting, Olympic-style weight lifting, and ping pong.

After returning from Korea, he was stationed at Fort Bragg, where he tried out for the XVIII Air Borne Corps pistol team and made the cut. He traveled all over the southeastern United States, firing .22s and .45s for Uncle Sam. A few years later, he entered powerlifting competition and took a few turns at action-style combat handgun tourneys. He did well in both.

Clay has hunted in Virginia, Alabama, Missouri, South Carolina, Ohio, West Virginia, Colorado, Idaho, Wyoming, Montana, Arizona, Nebraska and New Mexico, as well as his native North Carolina. When asked how many big game animals he has slain, he said: "I'm not sure; I didn't begin keeping records of game kills until a few years ago. However, I recently went

through my notebook covering the last four years. The total for big game animals only was 59 during that period.''

His list of credits in the journalistic field is extensive, and includes *Guns & Ammo, Petersen's Handguns, Petersen's Hunting, Shooting Times, Guns, Gun World, Handloader's Digest* and the *Guns & Ammo Annual*, not to mention various anthologies and nearly all the Harris titles. He is currently a contributing editor to the prestigious *Gun Digest*, serves the same function for *Guns Illustrated*, and in the past has been listed on the mastheads of both *Handloader* and *Rifle* magazine, and wrote a column for *Gun Digest Hunting Annual*. Clay was contracted by Pachmayr to author a monograph on the .38 Special.

His first book, *Popular Sporting Rifle Cartridges*, was published by DBI in the summer of 1984. It was offered as a featured-alternate selection by the Outdoor Life Book Club; its first printing sold through quickly.

The book has been esteemed by Clay's peers. Rick Jamison, of *Shooting Times*, plugged it in his reloading column; Dave Petzal reviewed it favorably in *Field & Stream*, as did the August *American Rifleman*. Pennsylvania gun scribe Bob Bell lauded it in print; John Wooters of *Petersen's Hunting* mentioned it in *Guns & Ammo*; Finn Aagaard cited it in *American Hunter*. Noted firearms expert Massad Ayoob penned in the May 1988 issue of *Gun World* magazine an article on the .30-06 versus the .308 Winchester. In it he had this to say: "The argument is perhaps best addressed in the excellent book, *Popular Sporting Rifle Cartridges*, a DBI title. It's written by Clay Harvey, whom I respect as one of the most learned and logical rifle experts of our day, right up there with Jim Carmichel (of *Outdoor Life*). Harvey is able to balance his twin personae of true rifle aficionado and practical field rifleman...." That same level of expertise, concise writing and glint-in-the-eye amusement is obvious in his newest effort, *The Hunter's Rifle*. In fact, we at the North American Hunting Club think it may well set a new standard among books on guns and hunting.

Clay Harvey lives in North Carolina, with his wife Barbara and their brand-spanking-new son Chris.

Dedication

This book is for my wife, Barbara, from whom shines the light of my days.

Foreword

The first time I saw Clay Harvey's writing, I was assistant editor at *Rifle* and *Handloader* magazines. I was impressed by the obvious honesty of the reporting and even more by his writing style. I later learned that it was Clay's first manuscript submission. That was 15 years ago. Since that time I've had the opportunity to hunt with him from the Colorado canyons to the North Carolina coastal woods.

Some have taken more game than Clay, but I know of no one who gains more worthwhile knowledge from each harvest. Clay examines, measures, weighs and carefully records each technical detail. He makes notes about feelings, reactions and perceptions. If he writes that an elk shot seven years ago weighed 682 pounds and was taken at 197 paces, you can bet he not only paced it off, but recorded the date, time, distance, weight and a lot of other details in a notebook at the time. He examines wound channels and goes to lengths to recover bullets, all in the quest of knowledge. First-hand knowledge.

He's equally observant and open-minded about guns and cartridges. If he writes that a pump is faster than a semi-auto or that the standing position is more accurate than offhand, you can believe it. Clay doesn't guess about such things. He tries it under controlled conditions, and many times.

Anyone who watches him shoot knows Clay shoots a *lot*, and it shows in his writing. He writes from his own experience yet he's not too proud to quote the experience of others if he respects their word. You don't find many writers doing that, and it's refreshing.

Perhaps Clay's greatest asset is his unique ability to write about the technical and mundane and make it interesting. He can do it like no other. He'll make you laugh. He'll have you choking back tears.

For example, as I write this I've just finished the lead-in to Chapter Six, the black bear chapter, where Clay takes a unique approach to writing about the hunting and killing of a huge black bear. He presents the essence of the hunt with an intense level of awareness and sensitivity, not only from the hunter's viewpoint, but from the quarry's. Clay's observations of his hunt have a perception that will touch you. He conveys an immense pride at having succeeded in his objective, yet a sensitivity and respect for the bear that only a hunter knows. You'll relate to Clay's writing because it's real and from the heart. Through his account you'll not only see and hear, you will feel.

While all this might sound like so much puffery to get you to buy this book, such is emphatically not the case. I mean what I say. When *you* read his words and absorb his feelings, you'll identify with what I've said. And I'll wager that you'll be looking for more of his writing.

—Rick Jamison
NAHC Member
Sutton, Nebraska

Preface

It all started back in 1951. An elderly neighbor tossed out about 30 copies of something called *The American Rifleman*—all from the late '20s and early '30s.

Since then, I've read just about every gun periodical, book or reference I could get my hands on. Unfortunately, somewhere around the late '60s I discovered a fly in my heretofore smooth splotch of gun grease. The articles I was reading were getting dull, duller and dullest. Seemed like I'd read them all before. It struck me that the people who were penning those pearls of gun-writing prose (for the third or fourth time around) didn't possess enough practical gun experience, pride, professionalism or style to make them worthy of the title "gunwriter."

Harsh words, I admit. However, there are a lot of you guys who will read that last paragraph and smile knowingly.

This is where your author Clay Harvey enters the picture. It's my opinion that Clay doesn't just *write* articles about guns and hunting; he metaphorically *paints* those subjects. And he does it with the pride, professionalism and style of a man who urgently cares about every word he writes.

There's a lot of personality in Clay's writing, and he doesn't leave you longing for a conclusion. In the event you don't know it (or haven't guessed), Clay's also a man of opinion who isn't hesitant to share his views with his readership. In my experience, that's a rarity shared by only the best writers in the business.

As an outdoor writer/editor, I've spent the past 15 years reading scores of manuscripts, most of them poor, some fair and too damn few fit to print. After awhile, a truly great gunwriter stands out immediately. Clay is one of those stand-out authors—a writer's writer, if you will.

Like everyone else in this crazy game, Clay fell upon some tough times a few years ago and decided to get out of gunwriting. After a year or two, he changed his mind much to the general good of the gun/hunting publishing business.

Frankly, I can't imagine a world without the words of Clay Harvey. He's just too damn good at it. How good? One nationally known editor told me, "He won't last in the gunwriting game. He's too good. Look for him to surface in New York, Hollywood or on the Best Seller List."

Obviously, I agree.

Know that what follows is vintage Clay Harvey. Sit back, get comfortable and let your mind walk down the path Clay will paint for you. If by some chance that path veers toward New York or Hollywood and I'm not around to say it, drop Clay a line and tell him Bob Anderson said, "I told you so!"

Robert S.L. Anderson
Associate Editor, *Gun Digest*

Introduction

As you might have guessed from the title, this is a book about rifles. For hunting. Hunter's rifles.

It is also about cartridges, because the two are inextricably interwoven—but cartridges for hunting, not benchrest competition or silhouette toppling. This tome is for the hunting rifleman, written by a hunting rifleman.

To be brutally honest, if a hunter wants only to gather meat, he would be best served not by a rifle at all, but by a 12 gauge shotgun with three or four extra barrels. He could then take all feathered critters, and use the same barrels for small forest dwelling edibles such as tree squirrels and cottontails. Simply by switching to a slug barrel, he could take cleanly any animal on this continent—and most of those on any other as well—so long as the range was kept to 100 yards or less.

But, alas, the fun would have been removed, at least so we riflemen feel. For us it isn't the taking of game that truly matters, but how we take it; how far, how deftly, how memorable the shot. Besides, one can't always get within shotgun slug range of a wary whitetail buck, not to mention a bull elk or bighorn ram! A cow perhaps, or a ewe, or a bear cub not wise to the ways of man. But sometimes we have to stretch out to 200 yards—occasionally more—to take the animal we want, not simply the first one we spy within range.

And then there are those times, even at shotgun distances, when we can see only part of the animal. Precision is needed to hit a baseball-sized throat patch on a partially screened whitetail. Shotguns seldom have such precision. And then there's the recoil question: 12 bore slug loads kick, and there is simply not an equivalent return in range and power to justify absorbing such punishment. In fact some shooters, many shooters, can't take the pounding dished out by a slug load and shoot creditably.

With the rifled arm, the shooter can tailor his gun and load to specific requirements, including such important considerations as range, recoil, bullet performance and accuracy. The shotgunner can select the size of his gun and its barrel length. But so can the rifleman, with even more flexibility. If he reloads his own slug loads, he could exercise some control over the recoil, but to tame it noticeably will lessen the already limited ranging potential of the smoothbore.

All things considered, the rifle is the gun for the serious hunter. The bow, handgun and shotgun are tools for close range. Beyond 100 yards they are in all but a few instances inferior to the properly chosen rifle. This book is devoted to matching the rifle and the cartridge to the job at hand. Let's get on with it.

1

Weighing The Rifle/Cartridge Relationship

Choosing a hunting arm involves two separate but interwoven facets: the rifle and the cartridge. The selection of each deserves careful deliberation if you intend to have a pleasant and productive relationship with your gun.

In the beginning, it's best to decide what cartridge fits your needs, develop a list of possibles and then see what rifles are built around it.

Sometimes, there may be a specific action type (lever action, pump, turnbolt, semi-auto or single shot—maybe even a double if you want something really unusual) that you lean toward, simply because you like it. If that's the case, your cartridge choices may be limited.

Let's look at an example. Suppose you are enamored of old Western movies. You grew up on a diet of TV shows featuring Wyatt Earp and Bat Masterson. If so, you may think the only gun for you is a lever-action carbine, similar to the ones on the movie screen. They might include the Marlin 336 or 1894 carbines if you're not a stickler for details; a Winchester Model 94 or even a Model 92 if you seek authenticity. Although there are special runs from time to time, the most commonly available chamberings for such levers are the .30-30 Winchester, .35 Remington and .44 Magnum. If you look carefully, you might find a used .32 Winchester Special, .25-35 WCF (Winchester Centerfire), .32-40

There is nothing wrong with favoring a particular type of rifle, like this hunter's "cowboy gun", but you need to accept the idea that this choice will limit the cartridges from which you can choose.

WCF, .38-55 WCF or similar old-timer. You may come across a current issue .375 Winchester, .44-40 WCF, .45 Colt, .307 Winchester or .356 Winchester. Marlin chambers the .444 Marlin and the antideluvian .45-70 Government. Even the fine little 7-30 Waters is around, although not in carbine form. The shorter Winchester Model 92 came reamed to .25-20 WCF, .32-20 WCF and .38-40 WCF; rumor has it that a well-known company is thinking of reintroducing some of these.

Considering this list, it may seem that you have plenty of loads from which to choose. At first glance, that is the case. However, when versatility is a factor, not many are really good loads. For small-game hunting, all but the little .25-20 and .32-20 are far too strenuous if you plan to eat what you kill. Conversely, none of these are the ticket for long-range varminting; they have neither the velocity necessary to flatten trajectories and initiate rapid bullet

Cartridges for some of the traditional lever actions include (left to right): 7-30 Waters, .30-30 Winchester, .307 Winchester, .35 Remington, .356 Winchester, .44 Magnum, .444 Marlin and .45-70 Government.

blow up nor the accuracy required to hit small targets way out yonder.

Moving up to medium-sized game at moderate ranges, you'll find most of the above mentioned cartridges able to handle the chore, but eliminating the .25-20, .32-20, .38-40—yes they have killed plenty of deer, but they never were much count at it—likewise the .25-35, .32-40 and .38-55. Besides, you won't be seeing many of these rifles *or* cartridges on dealers' shelves; they're becoming collectors' items.

What you will likely find among the classic-style leverguns are the .30-30, .35 Remington, .44 Magnum, .444 Marlin and the .45-70, with an occasional 7-30 Waters, .307 Winchester, .32 Special, .356 Winchester or .375 thrown in. These are all fine deer rounds, and most will work on black bear and wild hogs. A few will take elk and moose cleanly at moderate ranges, and two or three—if stoutly handloaded—will handle the biggest stuff on this continent out to perhaps 200 yards.

But they won't reach out across a sage flat to deck a pronghorn buck 400 yards away; they won't do double duty on ground hogs or prairie dogs in July, hitting the little critters out where they live;

few, very few, will shoot into one inch, many of them not even two inches at 100 yards. Further, the rifles that handle these rounds are not really suited for scope sights, except for the rare Monte Carlo combed variation. They *will* accept a scope, but they aren't really *suited* for scope use. Sometimes their trigger pulls leave something to be desired. In short, if you're a ''cowboy gun'' addict, you'd better learn to Injun up on your game!

Let's take the pendulum to the other extreme. Suppose you're a Vietnam vet who cut his teeth on the M16, and any rifle that doesn't wear military fatigues and sport a 20-round mag. sticking out its bottom just doesn't light your fire. Well, if the .308 Winchester cartridge suits you, you can buy several military-style arms to take it, and they will do a fine job in the field. However, if you find such guns too heavy and unwieldy for hunting, you're out of luck. The light, handy little M16 comes only in .223 Remington, and the .223 ain't no deer cartridge.

An alternative for the military rifle enthusiast is the Ruger Mini-Thirty. With soft-point ammunition, the short 7.62 x 39mm—for which the Ruger is chambered—will do a credible job on whitetail deer out to maybe 150 yards. That's the same range the .30-30 works best within, so the 7.62 x 39 is sort of a latter-day .30-30 carbine, at least in application. It's short, light, pleasant to shoot, boasts adequate deer-slaying ballistics, exhibits moderate accuracy and its price won't break the bank. For the military-oriented hunter who doesn't care to tote nine or so pounds of gun over hill and dale, the Mini-Thirty is about the only alternative.

These examples illustrate why it's best to choose your cartridge first, rather than the gun or action type. The rifle helps the shooter direct the bullet. But the cartridge/bullet combination is what does the work and downs the game.

Working from the ballistic end of the rope then, how can our prospective rifleman arrive at his tool? Like so: Suppose our nimrod has perused the factory ballistics sheets and soul searching tells him that he seldom seeks game larger than whitetail deer or pronghorn. Further he surmizes that most of his ammo is expended on such vermin as rockchucks or prairie dogs, and decides on something like a .243 Winchester.

Fine. What action types can he choose from? All of them: pump, turnbolt, lever, single-shot and semi-auto. (We'll delete the double rifle from any future discussion because it's too esoteric.)

And brand? Everyone makes boltguns, from importers like Parker-Hale, Sako and KDF, to such old-line companies as

Deciding on a cartridge first, like the popular .243 Winchester will allow you to choose from a variety of rifle brands and models. Here the .243 is shown chambered in the Weatherby Fiberguard, a Remington auto and a Remington pump. It can also be had in single-shot and lever action configurations.

Winchester (U.S. Repeating Arms Co.), Remington, Ruger and Browning. Savage turns out leverguns in .243. Ruger and Thompson/Center peddle single shooters. Remington fabricates several grades of trombones and Browning sells autoloaders. Naturally, this list is not complete. It merely shows how unlimited the field is for such popular cartridges as the .243 Winchester.

If our budding rifle buyer wants a deer, black bear and caribou rifle, he might decide on something bigger. If he's not a handloader and wants something potent, he might opt for the trusty old .30-06 Springfield. Except for the lever action which only Winchester and Browning have built, all the other action types can be had in .30-06.

Of course, not all cartridges are as popular as the .243 or .30-06. If a gent desires a .284 Winchester, for example, he'll have to save up his shekels for an Ultra Light Arms Company Model 20, or perhaps a Shilen or KDF semi-custom item. No popular-priced .284 is currently produced, more's the pity. It's an excellent round.

And thus do we see that while the choosing of a rifle/cartridge duo for hunting is no impossible task, it cannot be undertaken lightly if a truly suitable arm is the intent. But can actual harm be done if misjudgment occurs? Can we actually be so far off base that a missed opportunity—or worse, a wounded animal—might befall us? Yes. Yes, indeed.

My pet example of having the wrong setup at the right time came in 1978 while deer hunting in deep woods. It involves, naturally, one of the most impressive bucks I've seen. If he had been a spike, this misadventure would not haunt me so.

Winchester had just introduced a new cartridge for their popular and beloved Model 94 lever-action carbine, hoping to assuage the pessimists who proclaimed the .30-30 underpowered, even for whitetail. Dubbed the .375 Winchester, the nascent offering boasted a 200-grain soft point factory load at a claimed 2,200 feet per second (fps), for a whopping 2,150 foot pounds of muzzle energy. That's the same muzzle speed quoted for the 170-grain .30-30 factory load. But with a bullet much larger in caliber, and 18 percent heavier, those numbers mean close to 20 percent more energy.

For elk at close range, there was a fat 250-grain soft point at a listed 1,900 fps and 2,005 foot pounds—definitely no long-range number, but at 100 yards it would dig deep into elk meat while delivering a 1,500 foot-pound blow. That may not be awesome power, but it's no love tap, either.

So there I was, sitting against a tree with this shiny new Model 94 Big Bore in my lap. It was late in the afternoon, nigh dark in fact, and the gloom was deepening. I looked down at my rifle, all decked out with a Lyman receiver sight and big white front bead sight, and began to have second thoughts. Would there be enough light left in the day to use those iron sights if a buck sashayed my way?

I found out soon enough.

A hollow *boom* echoed my way from a corn field off to my right rear. Then another. And another! I heard buckshot ripping through the foliage aft of my position, then thwacking into tree trunks. I pulled in my landing gear, trying to stuff all of myself behind that pine tree and avoid any perforation of my tender skin.

And then a new sound. A galloping sound. A four-legged *galloping sound!*

I bit off my right glove, spat it out, climbed to one knee, faced in the direction of the onrushing deer, brought my gun up to port arms. Then waited, looking for horns.

Here he came! Wide through the chest, running straight at me, sides protuberant as a steer's, horns *out past his ears*, by golly. Heart went *thumpety-thump*; stomach tied itself into a knot. I thumbed back the hammer.

He was running straight at me. Good. I wouldn't have to worry about lead; just aim right at that muscular chest and touch one off.

Okay. Now! Up came the gun, like lightning. But by the time I had the butt at my shoulder, he had braked with both front legs and turned 90 degrees to my right. Instantly. Now I had a swinging broadside shot. With little light and less time, I looked for that broad front bead. I couldn't find it. At all. There simply wasn't enough light left for it to reflect back to my eye. Like a duffer, I tossed a wild shot that is probably still going.

I went back to where the buck had changed directions so abruptly. Paced from there to where my right glove lay in the leaves; 40 *feet.*

I'd missed a broadside shot at a running buck at 40 feet! No matter that I couldn't see my sights; I should have known better than to hunt with a peep sight under conditions of fading light, given a choice. I had a choice; a whole rack full of scoped rifles. My mistake. I had been caught with the wrong outfit at the right time.

More examples spring to mind. My pal Rick Jamison, hunting and reloading editor for *Shooting Times* magazine and a North

You might get along with the wrong hunting rifle set-up until you're confronted with a real moment of truth. A whitetail buck who's headed for new territory won't offer a second chance because you picked the wrong rifle or the wrong cartridge for the situation.

This hunter used a rig similar to the one the author had when he botched the chance on the biggest whitetail he's ever seen. In this hunting situation, this was the right choice.

American Hunting Club member, was at one time fooling around with an ancient 1886 Winchester chambered to .40-65, an old black-powder load with the trajectory of a nine-year-old tossing a medicine ball. As luck—or poor planning—would have it, Rick chanced upon Ol' Mossyhorn himself. I don't recall whether the buck ran out of sight first, or whether Mr. Jamison's cupboard ran dry, but the buck was not reduced to venison on that occasion.

"If I had been carrying a scoped bolt action," Rick lamented, "that old boy would be on my wall right now." I believe him. Rick may not be as good looking as me, but he can sure shoot!

Years and *years* ago, I chanced to go whitetailing with a gent I knew only casually. We each sat a stand in the early hours, but come lunchtime decided to still hunt a thicketed bedding area. So full of brambles was this spot that even the rabbits wore chaps.

We eased into the jungle about 40 yards apart. Within seconds our only means of determining each other's whereabouts was by sound. I maneuvered myself through perhaps 50 yards of the clinging vegetation when a burst of rustly sound assaulted me from my right front, between me and my partner. Something large and four-legged was beating a hasty departure.

"He'll fire any time," thought I. Not a shot did I hear. After a few moments, I moved on.

An hour later, my crony and I met up at a clear-cut. He was so covered with briars he looked like two porcupines wrestling.

"Did you hear that deer get up?" he queried.

I nodded.

"See him?"

I shook my head.

"Big buster. Wide rack, six points, heavy neck. In the rut."

"Why didn't you shoot?"

He looked down at his rifle, a scoped Model 70 Winchester chambered to 7mm Remington Magnum. The man was not happy.

"This long barrel kept catching hold of every vine, briar and tree limb I stumbled past. Scope got so tangled up once, I had to cut the stuff loose from it with my skinning knife. I'd fought so long and hard, just getting through that mess, that I was arm-weary when that buck jumped out of his bed. I doubt I could have got on him with a six-pound 20-bore double, let alone this heavy thing."

Wrong gun at the right time.

Which reminds me of a hunt on which I invited an Army buddy on, back when I was shooting daily for the XVIII Air Borne Corps. The only rifle my friend had at his disposal was a seedy old .30-40 Krag he'd bought for 40 bucks at a pawn shop. He'd killed a spike the week before, hunting out of a tree stand deep in the forest. Range? Fifty steps. He allowed as how his old smokepole was one helluva deer slayer.

We went to Bladen County and hunted adjacent to a run of soybean fields. *Big* soybean fields. The only deer he spotted that day were a small buck and a doe feeding at the far end of one of those fields. Range? He guessed maybe 350 yards. If he had been toting a scoped .30-06, there'd have been fresh liver on the table that night. He shot for the rifle team and could do right well. Plus, he could judge range. But most importantly, he knew the limitations of his rifle and wisely passed up the shot.

Nearly 20 years ago I hunted regularly with a fellow named

The 7mm Mag. is not a brush gun. It doesn't shoot like one, and in most cases it certainly doesn't carry like one. Here Rick Jamison surveys some 7-Mag. country.

Though some hunters look on the .44 Mag. as a no-account when it comes to hunting rifle calibers, it is a proper choice in the right hands in the right hunting situation. Here it is chambered in the easy-carrying, light-kicking Ruger .44 Carbine.

Troy Picket. Troy hunted deer about like the rest of us go to work: kind of regular like. He owned two centerfire rifles. One was a Ruger .44 Carbine, the sporter version as I recall, now quite rare. The other was a trusted and accurate Ruger Model 77 turnbolt reamed to 6mm Remington. He let the terrain choose the rifle. When he strolled into the woods, he toted the .44 shorty; while overseeing the fields, the 6mm lay across his knees.

The last year I hunted with him, Troy decked two bucks. One was slain as it was rapidly departing a soybean field, hit with the fifth shot, at perhaps 400 yards. The second buck was dropped at around 75 yards if my memory serves, with the .44 in the woods. Neither buck required a finisher. Good examples of the *right* gun at the right time.

Aside from topography, there are other aspects to picking a gun/cartridge combo. Shooting experience is one. If you're a once a year shooter, then .30-06-level recoil is likely to induce a flinch unless you are stalwart indeed. Those folks who practice with their rifles year long, either through off-season varminting or just good old-fashioned "target shooting," should be capable of handling the .270, .30-06 group with reasonable precision, although magnum recoil levels might leave them cold.

Further muddying the creek are special considerations such as the age of the gunner. A 12-year-old boy simply can't handle the rearward punch that an experienced and more solidly built man can; neither can the arthritic bones of the average septuagenarian. Both extremes require a mild stroke at the buttplate. Likewise the normally-experienced distaff hunter, unless she works nights at the local roller derby rink.

Of course, mitigating circumstances abound. Some early-teen youngsters have been shooting centerfire rifles for years, or perhaps competing in trap or skeet. Ditto the lady shooters, not to mention some active 70-year-olds. Under such circumstances, the recoil of a .270 Winchester—even if fired from the prone position, which intensifies recoil sensation—would not be unnerving, and accurate shot placement should be expected.

And then there are the folks in the shooting game with both feet. They burn up handloaded ammo at a rate that makes the component companies grin gleefully. For them, hunting is merely an extension of their shooting interests. There is little I can offer these enthusiasts, except perhaps some experiences they haven't partaken of as yet, or maybe corroboration of something they have discovered on their own, but that seems to run against the common "wisdom" in our beloved shooting sport.

Of course, a few died-in-the-wool shooting buffs don't apply their logic quite as fruitfully as they might when it comes to choosing hunting loads, cartridges and rifles. Many of them put too much stress on accuracy, often at the expense of important attributes like rifle portability, bullet design or external ballistics. Believe me, it is more important to achieve all the power your rifle can safely deliver so long as it is not at the total expense of "hunting" accuracy than it is to strive for quarter-sized, 100-yard groups fired from a bench rest.

Don't misinterpret this. Accuracy *is* important. For some types of hunting, it is one of two key ingredients. But seeking *unusable* precision all too often becomes obsessive, and the gunner chases after it for no good reason, having found already sufficient accuracy for any hunting purpose. Avoid that trap and you should fare well. Future chapters will discuss this matter in more detail.

One final point about rifle selection: some guns are simply easier to shoot well than others. How so? What makes the difference you ask? Aside from choosing a rifle having sufficient intrinsic precision, the most important factor is trigger pull quality. Alas, in these litigious times, most rifles come out of their factory cartons with pulls ranging from fair to atrocious. If your selection boasts a mediocre trigger, take it to a gunsmith. Period.

Choice of a hunting rifle is a personal thing. As long as it is a legal firearm and you can make it perform satisfactorily in the field, then no one has a right to question your choice.

Secondly, a rifle should balance well, and have a comb height commensurate with the sighting system. If you can't get a good "cheek weld," then it is doubtful that you will manage to hit much. And if you do, you'll do so *in spite of* your gun, not because of it. Should you be talented enough to do good shooting with a poorly-stocked rifle, think how well you'll do with one that fits!

Finally—and inarguably—we all shoot better with a gun that doesn't hurt us. It's that simple. Some shooters can overcome the bugaboo of excessive recoil, or become used to it if it's not truly painful. Nonetheless, if the gun *hurts* you when it goes off, it will take all your concentration just to do a mediocre job with it, let alone an excellent one. Think about that when you are considering the purchase of one of the .30 caliber magnums or larger.

2

Take The Fits
Out Of Judging Rifle Fit

Rifle "fit" means different things to different folks. When addressing the subject, I consider all of the physical qualities that make a hunting gun shootable, especially under adverse conditions. When a long-range target gunner bellies down at the range, he requires a fit that would be a decided hindrance to a hunter except under isolated circumstances; ditto the metallic silhouette competitor.

"Fit" includes such individualized considerations as stock size and shape at both the buttstock *and* the forend, comb height in relation to the sights, pitch, weight, balance and other design properties which affect the dynamics of a rifle. Most of these have a direct influence on perceived recoil, which is a gremlin that can never be ignored. No one can gaze into a crystal ball and tell you what rifles will suit *your* physique and shooting style, but you can learn to judge better what you're looking for in rifle fit.

The Stock

We'll start at the butt end of the rifle, which is the more important of the two stock sections when considering shootability. In matters of recoil *only*, longer and straighter is better. A long, straight stock helps to nullify felt recoil, at least so far as your shoulder is concerned. To your face it's another matter entirely,

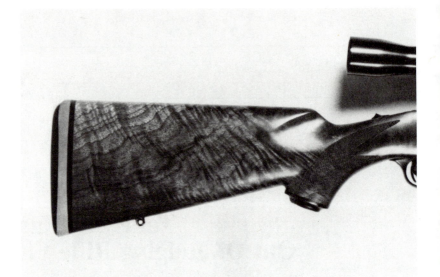

A long straight comb like on this Ruger 77 helps cut down on felt recoil at the shoulder. It does, however, increase the slap the gunner gets in the jaw.

but most folks are more adversely affected by a painful blow to the shoulder than one to the cheekbone.

Assuming *moderate* recoil levels, in every aspect of hunting rifle stock design a shorter length of pull is better—for several reasons. When most of us look at a hunting rifle for the first time, it is either at a gun store or inside a hunting buddy's house. In either case, we will probably be wearing less bulky clothing than we will be while hunting, unless the quarry is a varmint of some description or we plan to hunt in a very warm climate. Thus, the rifle that feels *just right* when we toss it to shoulder while wearing shirtsleeves will likely turn out to be a bit long when we are decked out in hunting garb. It doesn't take much cold weather clothing to measure a half-inch. A half-inch in length of pull is extremely noticeable when a quick first shot is essayed.

Now, if *all* of your hunting is done from a stand, and you *always* have plenty of time to nestle up to your rifle, making little adjustments as you do, then you might get by with most any length of pull. However, if the only shot you get next season is a fleeting one at a big buck and you snarl the heel of your comb in your armpit, don't blame the Red gods; they gave you a chance!

Excessive stock length can produce other difficulties. I took a shot at a pronghorn buck last season from an awkward position. I was sitting, trying to lean around an obstruction as the little prairie goat looked straight at me from 400-450 yards. My partner fired; I thought I saw the buck jerk at the shot. Assuming he had hit—and since I'd been told by our guide to back him up—I fired.

"Boom!" went my 7mm-08.

The liquid "plop" of the bullet drifted back on the wind. The pronghorn ran off.

I reached for the bolt while keeping an eye on the buck. In my awkward posture and heavy coat, I could barely reach the bolt knob! I said a bad word and groped for the handle, found it and muscled it up with a couple of fingers. That's not the way to jack a bolt handle!

Through a combination of grit and determination, I managed the task. But it took five times as long as it should have, or *would* have if my stock had been shorter. We got the job done on the pronghorn, but it wasn't the neatest of jobs. It did however, teach me something I'd never have learned at the range or sitting in an armchair back home. *Shorter is better!*

Too short *isn't* better. If the stock fit places your thumb under your nose, as on an old Springfield '03 or SMLE Jungle Carbine, said nose is going to take a battering. And if your brow gets a bit chummy with the scope's ocular bell, your forehead will get tenderized when you touch off a shot. But that's a story we'll get to shortly.

Comb Height

Comb height is important. Very important. Most hunters have no idea of just how important it is. If they did, there would be no market for "see-through" scope mounts.

The main purpose for the comb of your rifle is to place your shooting eye *exactly* in line with your aiming device, quickly and consistently every time you shoulder your gun. Common sense, right? If you want to connect at long range, you will need a firm "cheek weld." What's a cheek weld? Solid contact with the stock.

That's easy, just jam the old puss down on the wood, right? Sure, if your comb and sight plane match up. If they don't, you'll either be looking over or under the sights when you attain your weld. Neither will do much good.

Try taking a snap shot at a bouncing ball with a rifle whose comb doesn't coincide with the sight line. Some hunting rifles, from Germany in particular, require a jaw like a donkey's in order

This is a perfect illustration of the folly shown in the products of some European gun makers. The comb of this rifle is obviously intended for iron sights, as it is quite low. Thus, when a scope is mounted, the gunner must put her lower jaw against the stock instead of the proper, fleshy part of the face below the right eye.

to obtain cheek weld while simultaneously peering through a scope sight!

But not all combs are too low. Iron sights, being substantially lower than a scope's centerline, necessitate more drop to the stock to be used properly. Thus some of the previously mentioned European rifles are as ideal for iron sight usage as they are ill-suited to scope sighting.

The unfortunate part of all this is that the fellow who wants a specific rifle has no control over its suitability for various sighting systems as it comes from the box. Bear this in mind when you are looking through the iron sights mounted on a factory rifle, marveling at how well the gun fits you. When you mount a scope, suddenly it won't fit anymore!

The thing to look for in a rifle which you plan to scope is a comb height that makes it difficult to scrunch your face down to

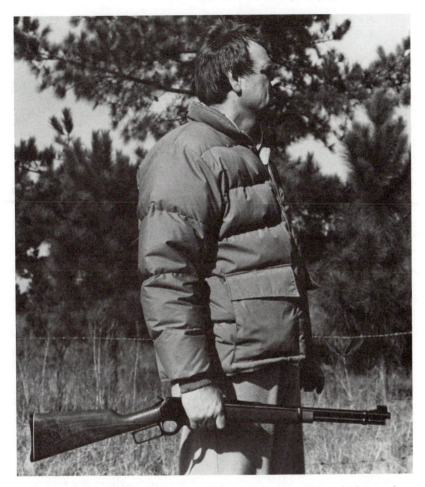

Iron-sighted rifles like this Marlin 336-T require a generous drop to the buttstock or the shooter will look over his sights when he is in a hurry. Note how low the heel of the stock is relative to the top edge of the receiver.

see through iron sights. Conversely, should you intend to utilize open sights or an after-market aperture unit, the comb height should be comfortable with the sights that come on the gun.

Stock Pitch

Stock pitch is more difficult to understand than the easily measured length of pull or easily seen comb height. While pitch is measurable, *the resulting figure is not readily useable.*

Basically, the stock pitch is the relationship of the bore's

Roy Weatherby may not have invented the Monte Carlo rifle stock, but he did more to popularize it than anyone else. This is a Weatherby Mark V, complete with the traditional Weatherby humped-back buttstock.

centerline to the angle of the buttplate. This angle affects felt recoil, the agility with which the rifle seems to jump to the shoulder, and how firmly a rifle's buttplate clings to your shoulder—particularly when firing from an awkward position.

Unless you intend to alter the pitch of your rifle by having a gunsmith hack away at your stock, forget about pitch. Go by the seat of your trousers; if a gun "feels" right at your shoulder from a *variety* of shooting positions, the pitch is likely correct for you. Should you desire to make an adjustment, strive to increase the shoulder contact area. Decreasing it will exacerbate the effects of recoil. Seek the expertise of a gunsmith who knows stock design, then get a second opinion.

Weight

Facts first: The heavier a firearm is, the less it recoils with a given load. The heavier it is, the less you will see your body's tremors when you peer through the scope. The heavier it is, the more securely it will nestle into a sandbag rest when you benchrest test it. The heavier the barrel, the greater the likelihood that it will digest many different loads with acceptable accuracy. The heavier the barrel, the slower it will heat up when firing rapidly or repeatedly.

Equally factual: the heavier a rifle is, the more tiring it is to carry. The heavier a rifle barrel, the more ill-balanced the gun will be. The heavier a rifle, the more tiring it will be to hold steadily in a standing position.

Now, which of these items is of most importance to you? How should I know? I know what is most important *to me*, especially in a hunting gun: within limits, the less weight, the better. Since good stock design can assuage felt recoil to a marked degree, and since highly effective muzzle brakes are offered by a plethora of firms, I'm an addict of light guns. Additionally, I avoid magnum rifles unless I need them (not often), and besides, I can't get any of my hunting buddies to tote my rifle around for me. I like real light guns. How light? Six to six and a half pounds scoped, slung and loaded, if given my druthers. Not more than seven and a half in a big-game rifle of standard chambering unless only stand hunting is my intent. Varmint rifles are, of course, an exception.

Remember, your hunting firearm will be carried more than it will be shot. *A lot* more! If you are too arm-weary to swing Ol'Betsy into line when that big bull quits his bed, you aren't going to eat much elk meat.

But, you shout, light guns kick a fellow to pieces! They won't group, and they walk their shots all over the paper. Well? Don't they? If you choose wisely, no. They don't.

A properly-bedded lightweight bolt action will shoot right along with a heavier gun in the big-game fields, where few shots are fired. In my experience, they will hold their zero just as well, assuming proper bedding and—if possible—a synthetic stock.

As you'll see in the next chapter—when we'll be looking at specific rifles—some lightweight numbers shoot so accurately it's scary. Ultra Light Arms Company, of Granville, West Virginia, is a prime example. ULA rifles are the lightest you can buy, with most Model 20s weighing around *five* pounds. Yep, five pounds (without sights, sling or ammo, of course). And oh, how they'll group.

There's no need to dwell on it now, but here's a preview. Not one of the five ULA Model 20s I've tested has failed to print under 1¼ inches for five-shot strings at 100 yards. One of them went *just over one-half inch*, and two more will stay under an inch.

But, you say, ULA rifles are more expensive than I can afford. How do some of the less-expensive lightweight rifles group? Very well, thanks. I've thoroughly tested all six chamberings in which the Remington Model Seven is available; all would print 1¾ inches

A tall gent like Bob O'Connor can well handle a rifle with 22 inches of barrel. For brush hunting though, and for more abbreviated gunners, a shorter barrel is preferred.

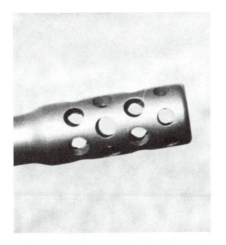

This is a muzzle brake installed on a .338 Magnum rifle by Ultra Light Arms Company. This device vents gasses in all directions, which makes it seem as though the muzzle is held in a vice. The result is restricted muzzle rise and recoil. Just what you'll want on a large caliber, lightweight gun.

or less, despite the catalogue heft of only 6¼ pounds. I recently tried a new U.S. Repeating Arms Company (Winchester brand name) Model 70 Winlite in .300 Winchester Magnum. Averaging 1.18 inches for several five-shot strings with factory ammo, it came within a whisker of being the most accurate magnum rifle I've ever tested. It weighs but seven pounds.

I could go on, but there is little need. The fact is, light rifles will shoot accurately.

Okay, you agree, so they group well off the bench. Aren't they much tougher to hit with in the field? Not so's you'd notice. I've hunted with Ultra Light Model 20s for two years in several chamberings and have taken turkey, deer, pronghorn, groundhogs, prairie dogs and black bear with 'em. I've never missed a shot because I was too wobbly or unsteady, or because I had insufficient confidence to pull the trigger when I was supposed to. I've hunted in wind, rain, snow and sleet—taking shots as they came. I've decked critters clear out to 450 yards or so, and popped them at 65. ULAs never let me down. Although I sometimes let *them* down.

The point is, light weight in and of itself will not cost you game if your hunting arm is stocked correctly for *you*, and is adequately accurate. Obviously, ULA rifles meet both criteria for me. In spades.

Balance

Balance is an important aspect of rifle fit, though it is seldom mentioned in print. Some shooters like a rifle to be a bit muzzle

This hunter's pet deer slayer is a Remington-built Mohawk bolt action in 6mm Remington. He obviously follows the belief that in such terrain, shorter is better.

heavy, especially for offhand shooting. And those who like the prone position often hail weight in front balance as the only way to go.

Snap shooters—such as whitetail still hunters who believe in a quick accurate first shot while standing in an off-balance position—espouse the virtues of a rifle balancing "between the hands." Such a rifle is neither muzzle nor butt heavy, but centers its weight and mass just in front of the trigger guard. It makes for a gun that mounts quickly, swings smoothly and seems to weigh less than it actually does. "Dynamic" is the word you'll hear when rifle balance is being hashed about, particularly as it relates to rifle fit.

So, what it boils down to is, "You pays your money and you takes your choice." *You* have to be the final arbiter of what kind of balance you want in your hunting rifle.

This is an Ultra Light Arms Model 20 with the author's first turkey. Note how the camouflaged stock and dulled finish help the gun blend with the background. ULA is, in the author's opinion, the finest hunting rifle available today.

Forend

Most gunners seem to think that the forward half of the stock is unimportant. Tain't so, McGee. When a rifle is held correctly, the leading hand aids its swing on a moving target. The forward hand takes much of the sting out of a heavy-recoiling rifle, assuming the gunner is savvy enough to take a firm grip out there. In tight-sling shooting from offhand or kneeling, that up-front mitt combines with the sling to enable the rearmost hand to concern itself with trigger pull, not rifle steadiness. It works well when you know how to do it.

Thus, a hand-fitting and hand-*filling* forend is a major factor in the equation. So what shape should a forend have? Let's see. Do this: cup your left hand. (Your right, if you're a southpaw.) What kind of profile does the pocket formed between your thumb and fingers show? Mine looks sort of pear-shaped. So I choose a pear-shaped forend. Simple enough. Choose a forend that fits and feels good in your hand.

Two other criteria enter the picture: length and thickness. If

One of the advantages of a light, well-balanced rifle—like the Weatherby Fiberguard .243 the author is carrying—is that it allows you to freeze in one position over long stretches of time without fatigue.

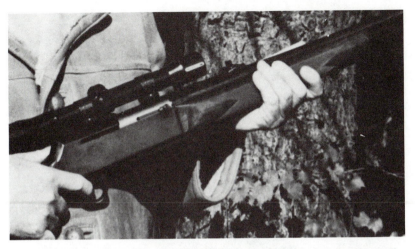

A proper forend shape is that which fits the hand—rounded or pear-shaped. For this hunter, the Browning BAR has the right configuration.

you have large hands, the forend of your rifle should be thick, to fit that ham of a hand. If your mitts are small, then a slender forend is what you want; no mystery here. Ditto for length; if you wear a 36-inch sleeve, then a "normal" forend will crowd you a mite. The rest of us can get by with what the factories provide, just as long as we watch the front sling swivel. If it crowds your hand, it'll bite you in recoil.

Eye Relief

Eye relief is the distance between your eye and the rearmost (ocular) bell of your rifle scope—or of the *rear* element of an iron-sight system. Unless you intend to mount a peep sight on the upper tang of your rifle, forget eye relief as it applies to iron sights. If you *do* use a tang-mounted aperture sight, be extremely careful, especially when shooting uphill.

There are several things to consider when you are after sufficient eye relief—"sufficient" being defined as that distance necessary to keep you from getting whacked on the noggin by the scope.

First, you should buy a rifle scope with a pretty long eye relief, which is listed numerically in any scopemaker's catalogue. Now, don't go *too* far, purchasing one of the handgun scopes with an eye relief designed for use at arms' length! Normal eye relief for a hunting-rifle scope runs from as little as 2.5 inches up to a

Although the author's wife can handle the weight and length of this Model 70 acceptably, she finds it a bit cumbersome. Too much weight out front! Shorter and lighter, within reason, is almost always better in a hunting piece.

whopping 5.3! I like as much as I can get without giving up something equally important.

Second, if you can get by with a rifle having moderate recoil, that means you can skimp a bit on the eye relief without endangering your forehead unduly. Or you can tone down the kick of a heavy caliber through the use of a muzzle brake, straight stock or longer than normal length of pull. Of these four choices, I'd tend toward a muzzle brake. Better yet, simply avoid the hard-kicking cartridges. Given *no* such options, you'll want as much eye relief in your scope as you can get.

Finally, if your scope and mount system will allow it, mount your scope as far forward as is practical while still being able to see the full field of view. You'll find to your chagrin that sometimes

A proper eye relief for a rifle without extremely heavy recoil is shown here. This hunter has mounted the scope to take advantage of the full field of view; note the relation of his eye to the scope's ocular bell. If the scope were farther forward, he would have to crane his neck too much for quick, comfortable shooting. If it were more to the rear, he would likely get cracked in the eyebrow under recoil.

your choice of rifle and scope won't jibe, or that your mounting system offers insufficient latitude to place the scope where you need it. Ain't life grand?

The moral is to take several factors into consideration when deciding on your rifle/scope/mounting system, not just what you like the looks of, or the price of, or what the pimply-faced salesman in the store *tells* you to buy.

A final tip for you lanky, long-necked fellows. Once you get that scope installed on the deck of your hunting gun and hie off to the range with a couple boxes of ammo, resist any impulse to "crawl" the stock. Keep your face as far back as the scope's built-in eye relief will let you. Should the stock be too short, have a gunsmith lengthen it a bit. If you pay no heed to this advice, sooner or later you'll have a notch in your eyebrow to show for it.

Summing Up Rifle Fit

Summing up, here's the gist of this chapter on gun "fit." 1) Lighter is generally better, within limits. 2) A straight stock will soothe recoil a bit, as will an extended length of pull. However...3) a too-long stock will eventually get you into trouble, so except in the matter of recoil shorter is generally better. 4) Buy a gun whose balance *you* like, one that feels right to you.

Most importantly, match the comb height to the sights that you'll use on the gun. Don't compromise. See-through mounts are a compromise. Select *one* sighting system and stick with it; learn to use it; get comfortable with it. If you like iron sights, fine. Same goes for a scope. Except in rare circumstances, choose one system and stay with it.

3

Today's Hunting Rifles

A side from considerations of caliber, the most pressing choice the hunter has to make is action type. Each action has strengths and weaknesses, and it's up to the hunter to put on his thinking cap to decide just what he needs for *his* type of hunting. The basic centerfire rifle actions, in order of popularity, are: bolt action, lever action, semi-automatic, pump and single-shot. (The position in sales of these last two is an educated guess, not only mine, but industry people as well. Nonetheless, we all may have erred.)

Let's take a close look at the various actions, sorting the grain from the chaff.

Bolt Actions

Unquestionably the best seller among centerfire rifles, the turnbolt design has a long list of attributes and a mere sprinkling of negative aspects. Foremost among the good points is accuracy.

Two cases in point. I am currently testing a pair of disparate turnbolts, one varmint rifle and one big game gun. The varminter is a Remington Model 700-V, intended for use on fox. Chambering is .223 Remington, the same cartridge we used in Vietnam. Tested with several different factory loads one stood out quite clearly: Federal's little 40-grain hollow point "Blitz." It scored an aggregate, consisting of four five-shot strings, running .4961-inch at 100 yards. Yep, *under half an inch* with factory ammunition in an untuned rifle with out-of-the-carton trigger pull, bedding and an inexpensive scope set at only 5x! Impressed? I was.

That is the best performance I have ever received from any rifle—including expensive benchrest guns—with factory ammunition, for an average, not simply an occasional fluke group. In fact, the gun may actually do better. Scope adjustments were made after shooting the third string, the final group ran .7343 and was strung horizontally. None of the other three clusters evidenced any stringing tendencies, and the largest measured .4843. That horizontal spread may have been caused by scope adjustment backlash, and not by the gun or ammo. Still, a sub half-inch four-string group average is phenomenal.

Would any other action type duplicate this feat? Not in a million years. Oh, it's within the realm of *possibility* with a match grade military autoloader, but I'd pay to see it done. There may be a Ruger Number One or Browning single shot somewhere that might manage it with select handloads, but I'd pay to see that, too. Frankly, I doubt there are many *turnbolts* that could replicate those four groups.

The second rifle I've been working with is an Italian boltgun imported by Kassnar. It goes under the sobriquet Churchill Highlander, and is a moderately priced gun of its type, particularly since it boasts cut checkering, a hinged steel floorplate with release in the guard bow, a rubber buttpad, sling swivel studs, a crisp trigger and excellent workmanship.

My svelte Italian is reamed to .30-06 and topped with a Kassnar 4x Vistascope, itself not a high-ticket item. Only two loads were included in the range session: Federal's 125- and 180-grain pointed soft points. Why such a reliance on Federal ammunition? Simple: Federal ammo almost always outshoots every other brand. Note I said almost always; *not* always. *Federal, quite truthfully, is the first stuff I try in most any gun.*

The result of my cursory and preliminary testing showed the 125-grain load the better of the two, so far as precision was concerned. The four-group average ran 1.20 inches. Since I've never shot a .30-06 sporter that would group under 1.10 inches, I consider that accuracy level to bode well for my Churchill.

Would any other action type in a comparable caliber have equaled that? Maybe. The most accurate automatic I've tested would do so; none of the others, and there have been quite a few, would come close. I have fired one or two single-shot Rugers that

Remington 700V in .223 was exceptionally accurate.

would print around 1¼ inches for five-shot strings. Close, but no cigar.

Before you cry foul, saying that these two rifles are not representative, let me head you off. They *are* representative of their peers, albeit on the tight side. For example, the least accurate Remington 700-V I ever tested (a .308 Winchester) would still go inside three-fourths of an inch at 100 yards, and it had a split stock! A 6mm Remington managed .625 with little difficulty, and a 7mm-08 Remington 700-V went into .690 for six groups. A .223 belonging to a friend fired two strings into .44 inch on one occasion, me shooting one group and he the other. I have no idea what that gun would hold for an average, but I suspect it wasn't much over half an inch. So, my current 700-V turnbolt is the best I have tested extensively, but not by much.

And the Churchill? In my experience with .30-06 boltguns, which has been considerable, most will go from 1⅛ inches to 1⅝ inches with their best loads, firing at least three five-shot strings at 100 yards. As you can see, my Highlander fell right into that bracketing, though admittedly on the low end. Thus, while it may well turn out to be the most accurate ought-six I have ever owned, so far it is merely on the "good" side of average.

Not *all* bolt actions shoot well. However, more turnbolts shoot accurately out of the box than any other action type, not excluding single shots. I expect any quality-built boltgun to print under two inches at 100 yards with good ammo. Those with extremely light barrels (.50 inch at the muzzle) do well to group 1¾ inches, though many will go under 1½. Most magnums of .30 caliber or less will manage sub 1½-inch strings with selected fodder. Generally, the .270 Winchester, 7mm-08 Remington, .284 Winchester and all the varmint/deer calibers (.243, 6mm Remington, .250-3000 and .257 Roberts) should print around 1¼ inches. They will frequently (with the lone exception of the Roberts) ease inside an inch. Varmint chamberings go under an inch, even in sporters.

Such levels of accuracy are not often attained by actions other than turnbolts, with the exceptions I'll note further on. So, if extreme precision is what you're after, and particularly if you are a reloader, the boltgun is the way to go.

So what else does the bolt action offer? The following: availability in a variety of configurations, weights, prices, brands and chamberings; strength; simplicity of takedown for cleaning; powerful camming power to seat and extract oversized, corroded or otherwise disreputable ammo; excellent gas-handling capability in

Though turnbolts are usually touted as exceptionally accurate, sometimes this is not the case. The Savage Model 340 shown here would do no better in the author's tests than a lever action in the same .30-30 chambering.

case of a ruptured primer or case failure; compatibility with any kind of bullet shape; style and grace.

Let's look at each of these in detail. First, market saturation. Let's face it, nothing comes close to the boltgun when it comes to variations in configuration and chamberings. *Nothing.* If you want a repeating rifle reamed to the .338 Magnum, it will be a bolt unless you turn up a Browning BAR semi-auto. If you plan to pursue pachyderms in Africa with a .458 Winchester, and want an affordable rifle that fires more than once, the turnbolt is your only choice. You'd like a magazine-fed .257 Weatherby Magnum for pronghorn chasing? Buy a Weatherby Mark V. The ancient and honorable 7 x 57 turn you on? Unless you are content with a single shot, the bolt action's the gun for you.

At a fast count, the current edition of *Gun Digest* shows 90 different bolt action centerfires, counting different models within a product line, and there are some guns that weren't listed! If we count synthetic-stocked permutations as different rifles, the tally exceeds 100.

Know how many sporting self-loaders there are? Three, counting only those commonly available in big-game calibers.

There's another one reamed to small-game/plinking rounds, and a couple imported versions I've never seen on dealers' shelves.

How about levers? Not including special issue or commemorative guns (which come and go year after year), I count 12, with several of those in marginal big game chamberings like the .44-40. For all practical purposes, the hunter has but four different makes of lever actions, assuming he might want to shoot a deer past 100 yards or so.

Pumps? One. Single shots? Six, counting the esoterica.

There are more bolt actions than all the others *combined*. And that's good for you; it gives you a broad choice in price, purpose, cartridge availability and gun "fit."

Next, we'll look at strength, one of the most touted but least important advantages attributed to the turnbolt. How can strength be less than critically important, you ask? Well, since all factory ammo is loaded within standard industry pressures that are safe in all sound guns originally factory-chambered for said loads, unless you are a *reckless* handloader, your gun is strong enough. If you *are* a reloader, you should stoke your ammo to the same pressure ceiling as the factories, unless of course you are more experienced than they and have better pressure-testing equipment. There are a few instances where it is considered acceptable for the experienced handloader to exceed the factory working pressures of specific cartridges. Nonetheless, the reloader should still work within a pressure limitation that a good modern semi-auto, Remington pump and Savage or Browning lever action could digest with equanimity.

If you were being paid by someone to test overloaded ammunition routinely, under laboratory conditions, then you would likely want to cuddle up to a strong modern turnbolt, or maybe a Ruger Number One. But more than likely, you're not being paid to do so, and if you were, you would be too smart to hunt with such ammo.

The upshot of all this is that whatever advantage a turnbolt has in strength over a modern lever action, pump, single shot or semi-automatic is of little or no consequence. That extra strength is merely the safety *margin*, a danger zone in which you should hope never to find yourself.

Ease of takedown for cleaning is a more practical benefit offered by the turnbolt. I suppose the Marlin lever actions are fairly uncomplicated to a mechanically-inclined individual, and the Ruger .44 carbine is not beyond the ken of such a gent. But taking down a Browning BAR would reduce me to fits of tears and whimpering; the Winchester 94 leaves me scratching my head; the Remington pumps and autos are best left to gunsmiths; Ruger's Number One I won't even contemplate.

But give me a couple of proper-fitting screw drivers and I'll reduce my Model 70 or Remington 700 or Ruger 77 or Browning A-Bolt to a lapful of parts in a minute or two. What's more, I can dry 'em off, clean 'em, oil everything that needs it and put the whole thing back together in short order. All by myself. Without leftover parts

Another important characteristic of the turnbolt—camming power—is no myth. When you need to shove an ill-fitting case home, and there's a big buck shoveling turf behind him because you muffed your first shot, a boltgun is the one to have. Your auto will heave to a halt right quick. A lever will toss in the towel. Ditto any pump I ever shot. But not the ol' turnbolt. If that ratty cartridge will go in the chamber *at all*, the powerful camming power of that big, strong, heavy bolt will offer the needed impetus.

And yank it out! Assuming a properly fitted and designed extractor, that brass will *give* when you raise up a bolt action's handle. Now, most self-loaders are pretty competent in the extraction department, and only one levergun I've shot had a tendency to leave a case in the chamber from time to time. But by and large, the bolt action is a bit more reliable when it's time to pull the spent case out of the breech.

And should a case or primer let go, perish the thought, most turnbolt designs will channel the fiery gas where it won't do much harm, if any. Not so with all sporting autoloaders, pumps and some levers.

The bolt-action configuration lends itself to any type of bullet shape, which enables the hunter to avail himself of the ballistic properties of sharp-pointed spitzers for down-range punch and a flat trajectory. Should he desire a blunt-prowed bullet, he can simply switch. It's not so easy with some of the other actions, most notably traditional levers like the Winchester Model 94 and the Marlins, and the handy little Ruger .44 Carbine. These tubular-magazine guns require a very bluff-nosed projectile indeed, to keep from setting off the cartridge just ahead as they all crowd together in the magazine. A sharp-pointed bullet can act just like a firing pin, denting the primer of another cartridge sufficiently to make it go off. When that happens, things get right lively.

Such leverguns as the Browning BLR and the long-lived

The exceptional camming power of the typical turnbolt will shove a case home when a lesser action will not. Plus, that long side-spring extractor will yank it out again! That's a Kimber Model 84 in .223; note heavy extractor, front locking lug, thick receiver walls for strength.

Savage 99, not to mention the scarce Winchester 1895 and its Browning counterpart, have always handled any bullet shape desired. Each of these boasts either a box-type magazine or a Mannlicher-Schoenauer-style spool or rotary magazine. Both arrangements work as well with spitzer bullet loads as any boltgun's cupboard.

A rifle with a box-type magazine can handle safely such pointed bullets as the one at the right, while those utilizing a tubular magazine must use flat or round-nosed bullets like the one on the left. Regardless of point shape, never use a full-jacketed bullet in a tubular magazine.

The Remington series of pumps and autoloaders use a detachable box, as does Browning's BAR. Naturally, the single shot rifle can accept any kind of bullet shape, since it has no magazine. Thus, the turnbolt isn't the *only* type of action that will handle pointed bullets, but it's still an asset.

Finally, we come to style. Some bolt actions are absolutely gorgeous; others would cause a gargoyle to blanch. The same can be said of all the other actions as well. Nonetheless, many, many shooters feel that the turnbolt is the most elegant rifle of all. I concur with that assessment.

To my eye, the handsomest factory rifle ever built is the current-production Winchester Model 70 Featherweight. Another beauty is the Ultra Light Arms Model 20, if you can accept a synthetic-stocked rifle as being handsome. A good specimen of the Remington Model 700 Classic looks nice, especially in a 22-inch-barreled version with no sights. Ruger's Model 77 International is attractive, cute, exotic, lovable; their plain-barreled M77 Ultra Light is no eyesore. Sako's Classic was right up there with the best, only a touch below the Model 70 Featherweight.

The Ultra Light Arms Model 20, shown here on a prairie dog hunt in .22-250, is author's aesthetic pick among the synthetic stocked boltguns.

Kimber's Big Game Rifle and Model 84 are so nice they bring tears to my eyes. Matter of fact, aside from a few military rifles, one or two commercial items and some odd European sporters, it's hard to come up with a truly ugly turnbolt.

So how about the other action types? Well, the Ruger Number One is quite distinguished looking—more attractive than some bolt actions—it doesn't keep me awake nights. The Browning 1885 and Thompson/Center Model TCR '87 are comely, but inspire me not to lust. But then, I'm no avid single-shot fan, except possibly for the Sharps—now *there* is a looker. Big upright, deliciously curved hammer; color-case hardened receiver; burl walnut... I take it back, there *is* one single shooter that fans my flame.

Pumps? Only the long-dead Remington Model 141 had any character at all, so far as appearance goes.

Among the autos, the BAR is the only looker, and it gets high marks. I like it as much as many bolt actions, perhaps because its profile resembles that of a fine turnbolt. There's that straight comb, bereft of the dreaded Monte Carlo influence; the full, well-rounded forearm; the clean, unpretentious trigger guard. Also handsome is the little Ruger International .44, long since cashiered. Fortunately I have one, and often sit up nights admiring it.

And the levers. The little cowboy in me dotes on any Winchester lever action, and particularly the Model 92 and 94

The author's choice as the handsomest factory rifle ever built is the current issue Winchester Model 70 Featherweight carried by this hunter.

Remington's Model 700 Classic, issued but once a year in a limited run, is one of the author's favorite lookers.

Ruger's Model 77 Ultra-Light is a good-looking little gun, to the author's reckoning.

Aficionados of boltgun beauty like the author mourn the passing of the Sako Classic from Sako's line.

Kimber turns out as handsome a bolt action as anyone could desire. The one shown is a M84 Super America. Is that a gorgeous stock?!! Is that a gorgeous mouflon ram?!!

For single-shot fans, the Ruger Number 1 in the International version will turn a few heads.

To the author's way of thinking, the only pump rifle with any cosmetic character is the long-dead Remington Model 141.

The Browning BAR is the best-looking auto, to the author's mind.

Many of today's riflemen, who grew up on serial westerns, find the Winchester Model 94 to be the most attractive lever gun.

variations—a legacy from my childhood days watching "oaters" at the local cinema, no doubt. Although I admire the Savage 99 and Browning BLR mightily as tools, their looks do not inspire me to song. (Their accuracy and function are another story.)

To recap: the turnbolt is the most popular action, the most accurate, the strongest, the easiest to break down for cleaning and maintenance, has the greatest capacity for feeding and extracting suspect ammunition, handles errant gasses with facility, is the most cosmopolitan in its taste for differing bullet styles and, to many, is the most attractive rifle in the woods. So what? you ask. Are all these things *really* that important? To be frank, most aren't.

"Blasphemy!", boltgun admirers shout. So let's discuss it.

As I mentioned earlier, unless you are a foolhardy reloader or shoot surplus ammo of indeterminate age and safety, the modern single shot, pump, auto or lever has all the strength required. The days when gun writers, store clerks and some component suppliers suggested that a handloader could improve on his rifle's performance simply by adding a few more grains of powder are over. Thank goodness. Thus, a bolt action's strength has become pretty much academic. Remember, the *brass case* is the weak link in most instances, not the rifle.

The vaunted accuracy that we boltgun lovers tout is there all right. That and 50 cents will get you a cup of coffee. Here's a bulletin: 99.9 percent of *all* centerfire rifles produced, at any price, anywhere, will outgroup 99.9 percent of the guys who shoot them. You doubt? Can you shoot five shots, all day, every day, into three inches at 100 yards? From a field position? I can't. I can *some* days, from *some* positions, most notably prone. But I can't do it every day, on demand, five shots straight. Maybe you're a better shot than me; lots of folks are. But most aren't.

Okay, so when I'm really clicking I can print three inches from a solid field position, assuming I'm not under stress, cold, irritable and that I have no time limit like that imposed when a big buck has just lowered his haunches in preparation for making himself scarce. Of all the hundreds of rifles I have tested in the past 20 years, only a handful were incapable of grouping five shots in three inches, day after day, group after group, with their favored ammo.

The point is that you do not require a one-inch or even a two-inch rifle to place a careful bullet into a deer's lungs at hunting ranges. (Varmint hunting is a different matter entirely.) And the least accurate rifles—with one exception—are the traditional leverguns, most of which are chambered for short to moderate range cartridges anyhow. And at such distances, a six-inch group is all that's needed. Given some attention to load selection, the classic levers will cut that with little sweat. The Marlins in particular will usually group under 2½ inches at 100 yards, which translates to five inches or a bit more at 200 yards (the practical limit of the "brush" cartridges for which the Marlins are chambered), assuming no wind and a good rest.

So the advantage in accuracy enjoyed by the bolt action rifle is rarely of any consequence in the field, and then can be taken advantage of only by a good shot firing from a very steady position. For most hunters—including quite experienced and competent ones—any action type at all will have all the accuracy necessary, *assuming attention is devoted to finding a load the gun likes.* Hunters who won't undertake the trouble and expense required to ascertain their rifles' best loads should take up knitting.

Oh, in case any of you long-range fanatics are raising your hand to be heard, let me head you off at the pass. Except under survival conditions or in dealing with a rabid or otherwise dangerous animal, no unwounded big game animal should *ever* be shot at past 350-400 yards, and then only under perfect conditions at a known range with select equipment. The fact that a turnbolt 7mm Magnum might be *capable* of grouping inside six inches at 500 yards, whereas a similar autoloader could not, is irrelevant. No healthy animal should be fired upon at such a distance. Period.

Popularity is an important aspect of a boltgun's persona. It enables a broad choice in the marketplace. However, the other actions are adequately represented in various price ranges and option packages. Anyone who chooses intelligently should not be handicapped by his choice.

As I pointed out earlier, the simplicity of takedown is an important advantage of the turnbolt. That's one of the reasons it is my action of favor, especially for hunting under severe weather conditions.

The ability of the bolt action to seat and withdraw from its chamber recalcitrant ammo is, again, a viable reason to buy one. Nonetheless, if you renew your supply regularly and purchase good quality stuff, it is doubtful that you will run afoul of a problem except perhaps in inclement weather. Keep your loads dry and clean! I must admit that for hunts in distant places, I tend to pull a turnbolt from the rack. When I hunt deer on the back 40, or over the weekend a mere 100 miles from home, I don't concern myself.

The upshot is that if you give a bit of thought to your rifle while hunting, keeping it decrudded and unrusted and dry, and maybe lubricated if it isn't too cold or dusty, and do as much for your ammunition, and take your gun once a year to a competent gunsmith for a *thorough* cleaning and inspection, you can pretty much hunt with whatever you want.

Before we delve into the specific bolt action models, let me cover a claim that at one time was advanced in favor of the bolt action: a crisp trigger pull.

Today, with lawsuits lurking around every corner, firearms manufacturers have copped out on us shooters so far as trigger-pull quality is concerned. The bolt action has suffered the most. Today (in most instances, but not all), the gun buyer is as apt to find a Browning BAR, Winchester 94 or Marlin 336 with a reasonably good trigger pull as he is a Browning A-Bolt or Winchester Model 70. Fortunately, some turnbolts have fully adjustable triggers and careful gunsmithing by a *knowledgeable* person can rectify the situation.

With the exception of a couple of leverguns and a single shot, action types other than the bolt are not so amenable to trigger tuning. In fact, most of them should not be trifled with. It thus behooves the prospective buyer to travel some distance if necessary to visit a well-stocked gunshop where he can examine and dry fire several examples of the rifles he is interested in. If said dealer is reluctant to let you pick and choose from his stock, travel some more. In my opinion, having an arms dealer order you a gun sight unseen to save you a few bucks is going about the firearm acquisition business bassackwards.

Turnbolts You Can Buy Today

Let's examine a few specific turnbolts. We'll go alphabetically, covering guns available in both varmint and big-game chamberings that seem to be sufficiently secure in the marketplace so as not to disappear before you can find one.

Browning. Browning's turnbolt offering is built in Japan, unlike the famous F.N.-actioned rifle the company sold for many years until its price became prohibitive. The lamented F.N. turnbolt was of typical Mauser design, and a very high-quality item. Almost as good, in fact, as the current A-Bolt. Incidentally, the old style Browning short-action rifles were built on the superb Finnish Sako short and medium-length actions, not F.N.

Both the A-Bolt and the "High Power" (as it was catalogued) are impeccably made, have cut checkering, hinged floorplates, good wood, an excellent external finish on lumber and metal and are quite stylish. The High Power wore a long Mauser side-spring extractor, a bolt guide rib, a pivoted Mauser-type ejector and bolt release, and was as heavy as a badger wearing combat boots. The A-Bolt has a short claw extractor with almost as much bite as the Mauser style, a plunger ejector that works every bit as positively, albeit with less finesse, and a cartridge depressor to enable a three-lug bolt body that is lightweight and strong. It also boasts a short 60 degree bolt rotation. The High Power and other two-lug actions require a 90 degree bolt articulation. The A-Bolt's bolt release is in the same location as the High Power's, at the left rear of the receiver. The elder rifle had a pivoting safety at the right rear

A Browning A-Bolt in .270 Win. was used to take this spike buck.

of the action, just aft of the bolt handle; the A-Bolt's safety is a sliding button on the tang. The newer gun is as handsome as its progenitor, maybe more so, with its more nearly classic style. And it's lighter in most chamberings.

Unique to the A-Bolt (and the short-lived BBR) is an X-shaped follower spring, which precludes any tipping of cartridges in the magazine. Works, too. The A-Bolt can be had in glossy or matte finish, camo stock, a stainless steel version, and is now offered with a synthetic handle, too. The High Power came in one configuration—two, if you count a heavy-barrel option as a separate version.

I have fired extensively 10 A-Bolt rifles to date. All printed under 1½ inches with their pet ammunition, sometimes with several loads, and that's for three or more five-shot strings at 100 yards from benchrest. Three of the 10 grouped *under an inch*, and nine were reamed to deer-capable calibers, not varmint numbers. Know how many other rifles—regardless of price—I've tested that could match that record? None. Not one. Every brand of turnbolt (or any other action type) that I have tried at least six examples of has provided one or more that would not group into 1½ inches or less. *Every* brand. Except the Browning A-Bolt. If I had to bet the egg money on a single, popular-priced, sporter-weight rifle, with accuracy as the deciding factor, and had to choose one *out of the box*, the A-Bolt would get my vote.

How about function? Just fine. I have had very few failures to feed or eject with an A-Bolt, and I test all rifles by feeding ammo from the magazine as I fire them, not chamber loading them one at a time. The safety button is smooth and crisp, but (sob!) not silent. And it locks the bolt handle in place! Bolt articulation is slick and positive, and the distinctive bolt knob is attractive and comfortable to use.

So what's not to like? Cosmetically, only one item: the trigger is gold plated. Ugh. Practically, only two items: the floorplate is jiggly and sometimes rattles, and the trigger pull is not adjustable. I know; there *is* an adjustment according to the catalogue. So take one and ''adjust'' it; see if it makes one whit of difference in the pull weight.

No gun is perfect. But, the A-Bolt comes pretty close.

Interarms. Aside from Britain's Parker-Hale, the Interarms Yugoslavian-fabricated traditional (read Model '98 type) Mauser action is the only one still imported into the U.S. as a *new* firearm. As on the F.N. Brownings, there is a typical Mauser extractor, ejector, bolt stop, trigger-guard assembly and bolt shroud. These add up to an action that features controlled round feeding (which means the cartridge feeds up under the long claw extractor as it rises from the magazine box, not snapping in at the last moment of bolt closure), which is beloved by reactionaries everywhere. And then there are the Mauserphiles who maintain that only a long side-spring extractor can be relied upon to yank a stuck case out by its shorthairs. I find this interesting, and wonder at length why virtually all the armies in the world feel that they can rely on the short-claw extractor in their automatic weapons. Oh, well. What do they know?

For what it's worth, I have had just as many problems with feeding and ejection from the Mauser system as from most of the modern types of turnbolt. In fact, I have had *more* ejection problems from the Mausers than from any plunger-ejector iterations, and I've shot far fewer Mausers than the latter. The Garand-Style plunger ejector is not without its faults, but reliability is not one of them. Workmanship on the Interarms Mark X rifles is not quite up to that of many modern domestic boltguns. The metal work is a giant step behind even the most mundane military Model '98, although the Mark X is said to be of superior metallurgy. I don't know for certain, so we'll take the word of those who so opine.

The Mark X is adequate in the accuracy department, though I have never tested a sample—save for one unusually good 7mm Remington Magnum—that was a real bell ringer. Functioning has been spotty in the magnum chamberings, at least in my experience, and ejection is not exactly vociferous in my current Mark X custom-built .35 Whelen unless I slam the bolt back with the force of an NFL line-backer hitting a tackling dummy.

All things considered, if you are sold on the controlled-round feed, Mauser-type extraction system but are on a limited budget, I'd recommend one of the following: 1) look at the British Parker-Hale; 2) buy a military Mauser and have a good but reasonable gunsmith turn it into a sporter; 3) haunt the gun shows for an old J.C. Higgins, Marlin, or some such turnbolt built on an F.N. action; 4) buy a used pre-1964 Model 70 Winchester, which is the best of the Mauser derivatives. If you are well heeled, or don't mind saving for a year or two, take a look at one of the current pre-'64 M70 clones, some of which feature the best of both the Model 70 and the Mauser '98, and at prices that require but one second mortgage.

This is the Interarms Mauser Mark X, a 7mm Magnum Whitworth Express.

In 1988, Interarms picked up the line of Japanese-built turnbolts formerly by Smith & Wesson, then Mossberg. The guns are made by Howa, the Japanese firm that produces Weatherby's Vanguard series. In fact, except for stock configurations and bolt shrouds, the two rifles are twins. And they are both quite good.

The action is modern, boasting an adjustable (to some extent) trigger, hinged floorplate, plunger ejector, short-claw extractor, pivoting safety button just aft of the bolt handle, typical two-lug bolt head and comes in two action lengths. The Interarms permutation is produced in heavy varmint-barreled rendition, and a servicable but homely and cumbersome sporter.

I've fired a couple of the Smith & Wesson versions, which were identical to the current Interarms offerings; they shot acceptably and functioned perfectly. I have also had experience with two or three of the Weatherby items: ditto for those. Groups ranged from around 1.20 inches for the best one (a .30-06), to 1.85 inches for the least impressive (a .308 Weatherby Vanguard).

The Interarms turnbolts and the Weatherby Vanguards are perfectly adequate rifles, with the latter having superior walnut and wood-to-metal fit in the samples I've examined. I certainly wouldn't feel handicapped if I had to hunt with one from now on, at least so far as utility is concerned. I would want to look at several to pick one with a decent trigger, but that goes for most of the other rifles on today's market. The Interarms/Weatherby Vanguard duo should do well.

KDF. KDF is a smallish outfit out of Seguin, Texas, that produces what some claim to be the most accurate sporting rifle in the world. (Whether they are remains to be seen.) KDF rifles are built on the German Voere turnbolt action, which carries three locking lugs at the head of the bolt, those locking into a Stellite insert that is secured at the front of the receiver. The action has a two-piece firing pin and ample gas venting, but the bolt shroud does *not* seal off the rear of the bolt. Should gas enter the bolt via the firing pin orifice, I'm not certain where it would end up. The ejector is of the modern plunger type, and the ubiquitous short claw extractor is in evidence. The magazine is a detachable box, built of heavy-gauge steel. It's a big, sturdy, tough-looking, Germanic action.

The stock styling ranges from fairly classic to outlandish California, depending on exactly which model you choose. The stock detailing is excellent, the checkering nigh flawless, the wood-to-metal fit gapish in the extreme. I'm not sure why, but all KDF (and Kleinguenther, which was their former moniker) rifles I have examined have exhibited this haphazard fit. Perhaps the maker feels the need for unusually spacy clearances for some secret reason.

All KDF rifles I've tested have worn sling swivel studs for QD units, nifty red rubber recoil pads, oil-finished stocks and well done cheekpieces. Some have worn Monte Carlo combs and angled forend tips of exotic wood, others schnabel forend tips and simple styling. I liked these last ones best.

KDF has one unusual aspect to their persona; they guarantee each rifle's accuracy. The guarantee used to be three shots in one-half inch with proper loads; I understand that now the claim is for five shots in one inch. Or maybe it's one minute-of-angle, which is 1.05 inches. Bear in mind that the company does not state that their guns will *average* such groups, simply that before they leave the factory, all KDF rifles must shoot at least *one* group that meets their accuracy guarantee. Not too tough, is it? But still, it *is* a guarantee.

And every KDF I've tried except one would easily meet the factory claims. That one was a .411 KDF, a hell-for-leather wildcat fabricated on necked-down .458 Winchester Magnum brass. For all I know, no one even makes .411-diameter bullets that will *group* into one MOA, so I can't blame my failure to

Author with one of several ground-hogs taken on a morning's hunt with a fine-shooting KDF .25-06.

produce such tiny clusters on the rifle. Besides, I have fired only factory ammo in the test gun and one bullet weight averaged right at 1½ inches, which I think is just fine for such heavy-recoiling ordnance.

My most accurate K-15 (the KDF model designation) is a .25-06. It is one of only three sporters I have ever tested in a big-game caliber that would group under three-quarters of an inch for five-shot strings at 100 yards. The .25-06 averaged .697 inch with the 120 Nosler Solid Base bullet and a modicum of IMR 4831 powder. Pretty good!

Kimber. Kimber is the Oregon-based gun manufacturer that turns out those super-neat little high-grade .22 rimfires. They're not cheap, but they sure are nice.

In 1984 Greg Warne, president of Kimber, announced the availability of a bitty centerfire rifle reamed to such short cartridges as the .223 Remington and the .222. A year or two later, the wildcats 6 X 45, 6 X 47 and .17 Mach IV were added, as well as the .222 Remington Mag., .221 Fireball and .17 Remington. Although these cartridges are not big-game rounds—not even the

Author and this beautiful Kimber Super-America teamed up to deck this magnificent sika deer. Horns were measured, and if entered, would have taken the SCI Number Seven slot.

6mms, except under limited conditions—hunters everywhere proclaimed the Kimber Model 84 to be a delight.

The M84 is sort of a miniature Mauser, featuring a side-spring extractor and pivoting ejector at the left rear of the receiver. From the Mauser-type staggered-row magazine the cartridges feed up under the extractor claw as they rise, in true controlled-feed fashion. The safety button lives behind the bolt handle, is nearly silent and is serrated for positive operation. The two-lug action is slick to manipulate, even bereft as it is of a guide rib on the bolt body in true Mauser fashion.

Of single-stage design, as are most modern units, Kimber's trigger snaps crisp as an icicle, with most examples breaking at about four pounds. The finger piece is smooth-faced but wide, yielding a good feel and ample control during firing.

Kimber does classic rifles better than almost anyone. Wood-to-metal fit is precise, accoutrements artfully conjoined, and everything generally works well. I have had a Model 84 with an ill-fitting extractor, and another that needed a minor adjustment to its feed rails, but such can happen to any maker. Usually does, in fact. Kimber fixed my guns promptly, at no cost to me. Not even shipping.

Accuracy of Model 84 rifles I've owned has been beyond reproach. My .223 averaged .818 inch for three five-shot strings with a pet handload, and factory Federal Blitz ammo went just over an inch. Good? Darn right, especially for a 6¼-pound sporter. My 6 X 47 printed .975 inch with Hodgdon's H-4895 pushing the 85-grain Nosler Solid Base, a load good enough for several clean kills on deer-sized animals. Good? And then there's my favorite, a 6 X 45 wildcat; groups ran just under an inch at 100 yards with the 80-grain Speer spitzer. Everything I've aimed that Kimber at has dropped with one shot, and one of those was a sika buck estimated at 250 pounds live weight. Good? Remember, none of the foregoing trio exceeds six pounds by much, and all were gifted with sporter-weight barrels. This level of precision is almost unprecedented in such light rifles. I can think of nothing in their weight and price class that is even in their league. Good? No. Superb!

Kimber plans to introduce the BGR (for Big Game Rifle), a turnbolt featuring design aspects from both the vaunted pre-1964 Model 70 Winchester and the respected Model '98 Mauser. When and if this gun comes to life, I predict it will be a runaway success. My order's in.

Parker-Hale. The British firm of Parker-Hale plies the American market with a neatly done, "modernized" Model '98 Mauser. The action is the well-known Spanish Santa Barbara; the rest of the gun is likely turned out in England. The gun features all the vaunted Mauser amenities, is offered in a variety of stock styles and chamberings, wears a fully adjustable trigger, good walnut in most models and has a hinged floorplate with release in the guard bow. Most come with iron sights, probably a waste of money these scope-conscious days. That goes for every other firm that does the same, not just Parker-Hale.

I've tested Parker-Hale rifles in a variety of chamberings, from the good old 6.5 X 55mm Swedish Mauser to the excellent but ignored 8 X 57 Mauser. Most precise was a Model 1100 lightweight reamed to 7 X 57 Mauser; it would group into well under 1¼ inches at 100 yards, and that's five-shot groups, of course. Most accurate 7 X 57 I ever tested. The 8mm printed well under two inches, thus went to Wyoming with me one fall to slay antelope, not to mention taking a whitetail buck at about 250 yards or a bit more. One shot. Through the heart. Dead deer.

All four P-H rifles I've fooled with have worked without a hitch, something that I can't say about their arch competitor. Nice guns.

Remington. Remington's series of turnbolt sporters is the current bolt-action standard, make no mistake about it. The Models 700 and Seven are direct descendants of the 721-722 rifles introduced in 1948, which were the first to utilize Remington's flat C-shaped clip extractor that has been so thoroughly maligned all these years, erroneously. It is as good an extraction system as is currently offered.

The Model 700 was one of the first commercial turnbolts to offer a plunger ejector, maybe *the* first. By using such an extractor/ejector arrangement, a completely enclosed bolt head was made possible, with no weakening cuts necessary to break its continuity. For additional security and strength, the bolt nose protrudes past the locking lugs out front, and the breech end of the barrel is machined to receive it. With the barrel thus securely surrounded by the receiver ring—into which it is screwed, of course—the much-advertised and very strong "three rings of steel" result. All things considered, it is doubtful that any shoulder arm ever had a stronger action than the Remington 700, or ever will.

Although there are no overlarge gas ports to direct errant gasses away from the shooter, there is a hole in the right side of the receiver ring to enable bleed-off should gas escape around the bolt/barrel joint, which is extremely unlikely. In the event of a pierced primer or severely expanded primer pocket, any gas that enters the action through the firing pin hole would be routed into the left lug raceway by a hole drilled into the left side of the bolt. I have experienced blown primers with the 700 action, and no gas made it back to my rugged and handsome face. Were I a hotrod wildcatter, I'd build all my brainstorms on Remington actions. And buy a lot of good insurance.

Then there's the highly-praised Remington trigger which is screw-adjustable for everything but treble and bass. Naturally, such tuning should be undertaken by a competent gunsmith only, unless you really know what you're doing. Although Model 700 triggers don't come out of the box much better than similar units from other makers (because of the spectre of litigation), it takes but

The fine British-built Parker-Hale Model 81 Classic.

Anson Byrd dropped this fat North Carolina whitetail with the Remington Model 700 BDL he is holding. The 700 is the modern standard of bolt action rifles.

a gifted hand and a few moments to remedy the situation. Not so with many other brands.

Remington's hammer-forged barrels are as good as any gun maker's and better than most. Thus, accuracy is usually first-rate. I have fired a Model 700 or two that exhibited accuracy a bit on the plebeian side, and one .243 was pretty awful. But by and large, Remington Model 700 sporters are at the top of the accuracy heap. The heavy-barreled varmint versions in particular warrant special notice. To date I have experimented with a .223, a 6mm Remington, a 7mm-08 and a .308 Winchester—and briefly a .222. All of these guns would print under .70 inch except for the .308, which suffered from a split stock, and *it* would go under three-quarters of an inch! If I wanted a very accurate rifle of moderately heavy persuasion, and had less than a grand to spend, it is doubtful that I could improve on the Model 700-V.

The Model 700, as well as the very similar Model Seven, wears a reasonably quiet rocking type safety just aft of the bolt handle. Alas, it does not lock the bolt handle down. The bolt release—one of the things I like least about Remingtons—is located just in front of the trigger, deep within the trigger mortise. It works, is unobtrusive, and unfortunately sticks sometimes when it shouldn't. Upon activating the release on any 700, I make certain to pull the tab back downward with a finger nail; otherwise when I replace the bolt, the stop just might not pop up under its own impetus.

Quality control on the Model 700 series is a whimsical thing. Metal work and wood finishing range immoderately from excellent to sad indeed. Aside from somewhat schizoid stock styling (superb on the Mountain Rifle, Model Seven, and Classic, acceptable on the ADL and miserable on the BDL), the Model 700 is pretty tough to beat. Many custom rifles are built on 700 actions—despite their lack of a Mauser extractor and ejector—and that says a lot for these guns. I've been working with Chub Eastman's Gentry-modified .280 Remington, and it's a dandy rifle. Smooth, accurate, reliable, light and handsome. Not cheap, either.

The Model Seven, incidentally, is perhaps the quintessential brush-country whitetail rig. It is perfectly stocked for scope usage, light in weight (6¼ pounds, unscoped), short of barrel, more than adequately accurate, possessed of the superb trigger required of a snap-shooting gun and comes in several proper deer chamberings- —not the least of which is the wonderful 7mm-08 Remington. The Model Seven is likely the most precise of the true lightweight rifles, at least among the popular-priced brands.

In years to come I firmly believe that the Remington 700 will become the rifle by which all other designs are judged. Shucks, it might be already.

Ruger. Ruger's turnbolt Model 77 came out, if memory serves, in 1968. It was hailed as a breakthrough by conservative rifle nuts everywhere. Why? I'm uncertain; it certainly broke very little new ground, although it combined specific design elements in a way no sporting rifle had before.

Example? Well, it boasted a Garand-style plunger ejector in conjunction with a traditional Mauser-type long sidespring extractor. (For the record, I have no idea why we writers refer to the plunger ejector as a "Garand-style" device; my Remington Model 81 semi-automatic wears a similar unit, and it preceeded the Garand by a year or two. Its forebearer, the Model 8, predated the Garand by a decade or two.) Now, I'm admittedly a fan of the long Mauser extractor, assuming its bearing surface is ground in such a manner as to take a healthy bite on a cartridge rim. Unfortunately, the Ruger 77's extractor doesn't always exhibit the proper purchase. Some examples I've seen had less engagement surface than many short-claw extractors! No matter; the Ruger 77 usually manages to withdraw a case from its resting place in the chamber, although I have seen one .22-250 that wasn't as reliable as it might have been in that regard.

Further annoying some reloaders is the fact that the plunger

This young hunter proves the Remington Model 7 is deadly on groundhogs. The author believes that in 7mm-08 chambering, this rifle makes the base for the quintessential whitetail rig.

ejector pushes the withdrawing cartridge case hard against the right inside surface of the receiver ring, where there happens to be a sharp corner. This corner etches a mark into the case right at the body/shoulder junction. Doesn't hurt anything, nor does it weaken the case, but it is unsightly.

The M77 has an angled front action screw, which is touted as pulling the barreled action backward snug against the rear of the recoil-lug mortise as it is simultaneously drawn down tightly into the stock. Maybe. Maybe not. Most shooters simply look upon such kinks as mild aberrations and forget them.

The action has three screws securing it in the stock, as does the Model 70 Winchester. If anyone has ever proved this to be a significant advantage, I'm unaware of it. It does provide an easy way to stress the action unduly; simply turn the middle screw in extra tight. Proper form—on both the M77 and the Model 70—is to tighten the center screw just snug, and leave it alone.

Perhaps there *is* one worthwhile aspect to the three-screw system. Should the floorplate be loose and rattly, sometimes a bit of judicious adjustment to the trigger guard/floorplate juncture can eliminate the irksome situation. It's time consuming, but worth it to some folks.

The Ruger carries its safety on the tang; it is positive but not silent. Not even quiet. Additionally, since the safety button is connected to the safety mechanism by a long bent wire—which will fall out quite readily if extreme care is not taken when removing the barreled action from the stock—it has been known to ''jump'' the wire and jam in one position or the other. Admittedly a rare phenomenon, it has been known to occur.

Ruger uses an integral scope-mounting system on the Model 77, similar to the one seen on the single-shot Number One rifles. It is handsome, strong, inexpensive and allows a scope to be removed and replaced without affecting the rifle's zero. Some gunners deride the Ruger system; a pox on them. I've tested it, removing a scope time and time again, even in the middle of a five-shot string. In my experience, the Ruger method provides near-perfect return to zero.

Ruger offers one of the best factory trigger pulls in the business, especially among popular-priced boltguns. However, they are difficult to adjust if they don't please you. The ballyhooed set screw installed in the trigger's face is all show, no go. You can turn it all you want and get no discernible difference in pull weight. But what can we expect these lawsuit-happy days? A competent

Author and Ruger 77 and defunct fallow buck.

gunsmith can regulate a Ruger's trigger into a thing of joy.

Most of the hoopla that surrounds the Ruger 77 centers on its stock. To the company's credit, when most other gun manufacturers were leaning toward shiny woodwork bedecked with white-line spacers, angled forend caps, Monte Carlo combs and oddly-shaped cheekpieces, Ruger hired the late Len Brownell to whittle out a classic-style handle. He did a fine job of it, too. Today, most every company has followed Ruger's lead in offering a functional, attractive stock design. Ruger offers the original style on the 77R and RS, and a similar but much slimmer, handsomer version on the Model 77 Ultra Light. Also catalogued at present is the M77 International, a full-stocked beauty in the Mannlicher tradition.

Over the years I have shot numerous Ruger 77 rifles, in all persuasions. About half were adequately accurate, with a goodly percentage exceptionally so. Unfortunately, a larger than normal number were unsatisfactory when compared to other brands of similar price and configuration.

I owned a .22-250 varmint rig in the late '60s that would group under three-quarters of an inch with factory Remington ammunition. My buddy Ed White used to stable a factory-issue M77-V in the same chambering that would print under a half-inch all day. A .243 sporter that once lived in the Harvey domicile was an honest sub-minute-of-angle gun. (That's under one inch at 100 yards.)

Conversely, I worked with a .308 varmint-weight M77 that wouldn't go under an inch, try as I might. So I bought another; it was worse. A 7 X 57 came along; wouldn't group like it should; went away. And so forth.

I don't let the above worry me much. I still test Model 77 Rugers on a regular basis, and they seldom shoot poorly. As hunting rifles, they generally manage to please. It is only as braggin' guns that they don't always make the grade so far as accuracy is concerned. Nonetheless, no factory-produced hunting rifles feed smoother or are more reliable. That's why they sell in record numbers. They *work*.

Sako. The Finnish-built Sako rifles have been imported into the United States since the mid-1950s, and superbly crafted articles they are. Available in three action lengths to handle cartridges from the .222 Remington up through the massive .375 Holland & Holland, not to mention several stock styles and weights, Sakos have always been a steady seller despite their somewhat hefty price. The action is a two-lug design with a full-length guide rail on the right side of the bolt, which appears at first glance to be a

Mauser-type extractor. Not so. The Sako extractor is of the short-claw style, and has been copied by several outfits such as the prestigious Ultra Light Arms Company. As a rule, this extraction system is functionally reliable, although maybe not quite as foolproof as the Remington C-shaped spring.

The ejector is of the Mauser type, pivoting at the inside rear of the receiver bridge to enter a slot in the left locking lug, whereupon it kicks the empty case clear of the action. An advantage to this design is that the shooter can control the force with which the cartridge case is ejected; he can jack the bolt rapidly and propel the brass with vigor, or manipulate it slowly and drop the case on the bench top. (Not so a plunger ejector; at least not so easily.)

The Sako's bolt release button is at the outside rear of the bridge, opposite the bolt handle, as it is on the Mauser design and such modern rifles as Browning's A-Bolt although the operation is a bit different on all of them. The Sako's is perhaps easiest to use.

Fully adjustable, the Sako trigger may well be the best out-of-the-box unit in current mass production. Nearly every one I've encountered has been reasonably light, very crisp and completely reliable, varying little from squeeze to squeeze. There are screw adjustments if you want to tune your own, but be certain you know what you're doing. Or let a gunsmith do it; it would not be very expensive.

Accuracy of the Sakos I have fired has ranged from normal to mediocre, although I know of several that are real bell-ringers. A .270 I owned years ago would print five shots around an inch as I recall; I have long since misplaced the targets. A beautiful Classic in .30-06 averaged 1.20 inches for eight five-shot strings at 100 yards, which is just about as good as any .30-06 I've tried. At the other extreme is a pair of little .222 Magnums; one wasn't too bad, going into 1.33 inches with its favored ammo. The other would barely stay under two inches, and that with but one load.

My only other complaint with Sako is that most examples are pretty heavy. Too much wood, too much steel in the barrels, too long of barrel in most models. But then they offer such amenities as sling swivel studs, hinged steel floorplate, recoil pad and wood-to-metal fit on par with the best. So who am I to gripe? If you don't mind a heavy gun, Sakos are just fine.

By the way, the guns reamed to big, belted magnums hold *four* cartridges in the magazine, not the customary three, or even *two* in some models. If I were planning a hunt for dangerous game, such

Sako .222 Magnum. A light, neat varmint outfit.

as Alaskan brown bear, I'd give the subject of magazine capacity more than passing consideration.

Savage 110. The Savage Model 110 series, and its derivatives such as the fancy Model 111 and the 112 varmint iterations, are serviceable if not fancy hunting arms. I have tested many, many of them over the past decade and most were exceptionally accurate, capably if not artistically crafted, not unattractive to look upon. Alas, many were as unwieldy as a two-by-four.

The action, designed by Nick Brewer of Savage and introduced in 1958, is a Mauser-type, two-lug number fabricated from more component parts than the average turnbolt. For example, the bolt is comprised of a separate bolt head that carries the locking lugs and is pinned to the bolt body. Between the bolt head and the body is fitted a gas baffle that resembles a second set of lugs. (The Browning A-Bolt features a similar arrangement, likely copied from the Model 110.)

While originally the 110 boasted a C-shaped extractor fitted within the counterbored bolt face, and an ejector consisting of a rod that functioned through a slot cut in the boltface wall, since 1966 a more conventional short-claw extractor and plunger ejector have been utilized.

Bolt handle is of the collar style, and there is a bolt cap screw in lieu of a traditional bolt sleeve. The bolt release is on the right side of the receiver just in front of the bolt handle; it requires a bit more than the usual in manual dexterity to operate, but it's not impossible. The trigger is adjustable by means of various screws; it is relatively easy to obtain a good pull if the adjuster knows what he's about.

The barrel is threaded into the receiver in normal fashion, but a barrel-locking nut is affixed ahead of the receiver to facilitate headspacing. This makes life easy for the manufacturer, but when a Savage 110 is rebarreled, this nut is normally tossed out by the 'smith. A sandwich-style recoil lug is installed between the barrel nut and the receiver.

With its safety button on the tang, the Model 110 is relatively convenient to ready for a fast shot. However, the button is set deep within the hollowed tang, thus isn't so quick and easy to snap off as the units on, for instance, the Ruger 77 or Browning A-Bolt.

Functionally, the Savage 110/111 is not quite so laudable as many of the other current turnbolt offerings. Feeding is generally reliable; extraction much less so. In fact, I have had more extraction troubles from the Savage 110 series than all other actions *combined*. Still, if you can locate a good one, things just might work out between you.

As mentioned earlier, the Savage boltguns are often quite remarkable in the accuracy department. A 112-V I once tested—reamed to .223 Remington—would group five shots under a dime, time after time, firing at 100 yards. A model 111 prototype chambered to .250-300 Savage was one of the few sporters I have ever had that would group an honest inch at 100 yards, five-shot strings, of course. Another 111, this one a .243, would print 1.1 inches like clockwork. Nope, accuracy was never a problem with Savage turnbolts.

Ultra Light Arms. The tiny West Virginia-based firm of Ultra Lights Arms can lay claim to several "firsts" and "mosts". They produced the first successful production-line rifles featuring Kevlar and graphite stocks. They were the first (and only, at least at this time) factory-produced rifles to weigh under six pounds with scope mounts in place. In fact, most Ultra Light guns go around *five* pounds. They were the first, and so far, the only, company to produce a turnbolt action capable of handling deer-sized cartridges while weighing but 20 ounces. They offer the tightest tolerances in the firearms business, at least to my knowledge. They offer a unique three-position safety that locks the bolt handle in place when the action is closed, enables working cartridges through the

Though considered less than attractive by some, the Savage 110-C has a great reputation for superb accuracy.

magazine while on "safe," and what's more is readily adaptable to the Remington series of turnbolts.

The Ultra Light Arms rifles (which I shall abbreviate henceforth, using the acronym ULA) are offered in four sizes. The .223-length cartridges are handled by the smallest version, with .308-sized loads made up on the Model 20 action. The Model 24, for 24 ounces, is the .270/.30-06-sized permutation, with the Model 28 housing such short magnums as the .300 Winchester and the .338.

Resembling a slim, trim Model 700 action, the ULA differs significantly from the Remington. First, it utilizes a Sako-type short claw extractor. Second, its bolt release is on the left side of the tang, aft of the receiver bridge, as on the Winchester Model 70. Third, the trigger (which is the only part of the action not designed and built by Melvin Forbes, president and founder of Ultra Light) is a fully-adjustable Timney unit. On all but the magnum actions, the ULA's bolt diameter is .600, as opposed to Remington's (and nearly everyone else's) .700. Naturally, bolt/receiver tolerance,

Cheery Melvin Forbes, president of Ultra Light Arms, with a ULA Model 20 used to take this tom.

locking lug bearing, bolt face alignment and other such items are a tight step in the right direction from the products of other rifle makers, as they should be. After all, an Ultra Light retails for about three times the tariff of a Model 700 or Model 70; more care and attention *should* be paid to such matters. And it is.

Quite frankly, in my experience the ULA rifles are unequivocally the most accurate true lightweight rigs ever produced. Heck, they are the most accurate sporting rifles (not varmint weight) I have ever tested, gun to gun. How accurate are they? Well, my .22-250—which weighs in at five pounds even—grouped five five-shot strings into .544 inch with handloads the first time out, and with the first handload tried. One string went under one-quarter inch! Accurate? Even with factory ammo, the little gun is a wonder. Six five-shot groups with Federal's zippy 40-grain Blitz hollow point showed a .696 aggregate. Accurate?

My 7mm-08 grouped .789 inch with careful handloads featuring a 168-grain match bullet. The .284 over in the corner shoots .95 to 1.00 inch with Speer's excellent varmint-weight hollow point. My bear gun, affectionately dubbed the Green Bean (for its color), prints 1¼ inches with no sweat, for five strings with the 160 Hornady round nose, not exactly a prime candidate for an accuracy load. Its caliber? The ancient 6.5 X 55 Swedish Mauser. Most recently, I acquired a .358 Winchester Model 20. With very limited shooting it has averaged 1.225 inches with factory ammo. Note: not one of these five rifles has failed to print under 1¼ inches at 100 yards; three have gone well under an inch; one will nearly group in ½ inch, for the *average*, and has stayed under the 0.5 mark for 15 percent of its total groups, below three-quarters of an inch fully 35 percent of the time with factory and handloads, poor loads and good. Are Ultra Light rifles accurate?

But accuracy isn't everything. Stock fit is important. ULA's fit me as if they were tailored with Harvey in mind. The factory will provide you with whatever length of pull you want on your stock, from 12 inches up to something along Big Foot's lines. No extra charge. Comb height is perfect for scope use, and the ULA rings (provided with the guns, no extra charge) place the scope exactly where it should be in relation to your shooting eye. DuPont Imron paint, really tough stuff, is used in your choice of color, including camo. The finish is rough-textured to provide purchase under wet conditions. No extra charge. There are sling-swivel studs, a recoil pad and stock-to-metal fit that is unparalled by anyone, anywhere, for any price.

Oh, the guarantee: If you don't like your Ultra Light, for *any* reason, just ship it back. They'll refund your money. Simple enough, right? So why doesn't anyone else do it?

Weatherby. Despite the fact that the .300 Holland & Holland Magnum and the burly .375 H & H have been available since the early 1900s, Roy Weatherby was really the guy who put the ''M'' in Magnum. Starting with the .270 Weatherby Magnum during the World War II wind-up, Roy built a rifle company based solely on his view of ballistics and rifle style. What were those views? Bullets should go fast, hit hard and all cartridges should wear a belt; rifles should be fancy, shiny, glitter like new money. And Roy practiced what he preached.

Weatherby's popular Mark V in all its splendor.

With the exception of the .224 Weatherby Magnum and the 7mm Weatherby Magnum, all Weatherby Magnum cartridges offer more punch (read, *speed*) than either standard cartridges of the same bore diameters or other companies' magnum loads. Originally, Roy Weatherby used whatever rifle actions he could get, including the 1917 Enfield, F.N. Mauser and Model 70 Winchester. Then, in 1958, he brought forth his own design, the now famous Mark V.

Built in Germany by J.P. Sauer and Sohn, the Mark V sported nine artillery-style (interrupted-thread) locking lugs at the head of the bolt, a counterbored bolt face, a short-claw extractor and plunger ejector. The barrel was machined to accept the bolt nose as on the Remington 721-722 series, now the Model 700.

The receiver is made from one chrome-moly steel forging, the bolt likewise. There are three gas ports in the right bolt wall, opening onto the ejection port when the bolt is in battery. The one-piece bolt sleeve is fully enclosed at the rear; any gas escaping into the bolt due to a pierced primer is precluded from impinging on the shooter. Thus the Mark V and the Remington Model 700 are

Hunter slings his Weatherby Vanguard while glassing for deer.

probably the strongest, safest bolt actions ever built. Incidentally, the rifle is now made in Japan by Howa.

The Mark V is also pretty heavy, well suited to the big, potent Weatherby cartridges. The little .224 Weatherby is housed in a short-action version of the Mark V. If I were interested in a lightweight hunting gun, the full-sized Weatherby is not what I would choose. However, were I building a custom rifle reamed to a belted magnum, I would seriously consider buying a Mark V action to use as a foundation. Or I could simply buy a Mark V rifle to begin with.

Aside from its looks, which admittedly some people really dote on, the Weatherby is hard to fault. All the samples I have worked with were accurate, most printing under 1½ inches for an average with their best ammo. They all worked well, with no feeding or ejection difficulties. The much-copied Weatherby stock design does indeed seem to cope with recoil quite well, and is comfortable to snuggle up to. Aside from a sometimes spongy trigger letoff, necessitated by Weatherby's double use of the trigger (it activates the bolt stop), the Weatherby Mark V is pretty hard to fault. If the company would offer a true classic-style stock, I'd be hard put *not* to recommend the Weatherby series if an expensive magnum-weight sporter was on the agenda.

Winchester. Beginning in 1937, the Winchester Model 70

established itself as the premier bolt action arm. In fact, it became known as "The Rifleman's Rifle." For the better part of three decades, its supremacy was unchallenged. Then, Olin (the Winchester parent corporation at the time) did a Bad Thing. In 1964, under the guise of "product improvement," the Model 70 was changed. It metamorphosed from a moderately homely rifle to a truly ugly one, boasting impressed checkering (stamped into the wood by pressure and heat), had a free-floated barrel so afflicted with "gaposis" that a snake could have crawled in to hibernate, and in general caused dedicated Winchester enthusiasts to wail and rend their garments. Even today, conservative former-Winchester disciples grit their teeth when confronted with the Big Red "W".

Since 1964, Olin's engineers have visited upon the Model 70 many detailed improvements. Cut checkering was reinstated; the floated barrel and its hog trough of a forend was abandoned; the stock styling grew more tasteful and understated. No use. The boys continued to turn their backs on Winchester products, which was a real shame.

The good old pre-'64 Model 70 was a nice gun. It was built around one of the finest turnbolt actions ever devised, especially those of the controlled-feed school of rifle engineering. There was an indescribable *feel* to the old gun when you worked its stout bolt back and forth. There still is. And the old-style M70 trigger is considered by some to be the finest ever affixed to the bottom of a rifle receiver.

But that sums it up, folks. The pre-'64 had going for it those three things: controlled-round feeding, a super trigger design and "feel." That's all. Sure, it was accurate, but no more so than any other rifle. Sure, it was reliable, but no more so than a commercial Mauser. Sure, it was strong, but less so than several of its contemporaries, particularly the Weatherby and the Remington 721-722-700 series. Its quality of fabrication was mundane, no better than many of its competitors and not up to such as the F.N. Mausers in their best examples, or the Mannlicher-Schoenauer. The wood-to-metal fit was above average, but the quality of the metalwork was not. Sorry. I hate to take pokes at an icon, but let's view things as they are, not as folks tell us they were. Go to any large, well-stocked gun store and look at a few pre-'64 Model 70s for yourself, then decide.

Now, about these current M-70s. In 1980, Olin introduced the handsomest factory-built rifle ever to grace a gunshop, the Model 70 Featherweight. It was well made, wore cut checkering, a

Author with a sika buck he slew at long, long range with this Winchester Model 70 Carbine in .250-3000 Savage.

jeweled bolt, a steel floorplate (hinged of course), the good old reliable Model 70 trigger, had satin-finished wood and a nice blue job, boasted a checkered bolt knob, stainless steel magazine follower, sling swivels of the detachable variety and a red rubber recoil pad. Nice. Very nice. It weighed about 6¾ pounds, depending on wood density, so you could carry it all by yourself. Every example I ever fired but one—a .257 Roberts, which might explain why it wouldn't group—was quite accurate, despite a very light barrel contour. The post-'64 action is stronger than the older one, or at least safer; it did away with the coned breech featured on the elder rifles. The extractor is not so reliable as the long side spring unit of the old M70, but most of my M70s have worked out okay. Since more than one African hunter uses the current-issue guns to back up their clients, I suspect that the short-claw design has withstood tough field duty. And no one I know claims that the plunger ejector used on the new Model 70s fails to toss out empties with glee.

Currently, the Model 70 comes in several walnut-stocked versions, a laminated camo number and a light synthetic-stocked

Browning's modern version of the famed Winchester Model 71.

iteration dubbed the Winlite. I have recently been testing two Winlites, one a .300 Winchester Mag. and the other a .338. Aside from beating me to death from recoil (they weigh but seven pounds, naked), they are doing right by me. The .300 has been my most accurate rifle so-chambered, grouping 1.18 inches with factory 180-grain Norma soft points. My .338 isn't quite so precise, but it functions as well, has a superb trigger, and'll be all that's standing between me and the next big bad bruin I take.

If you gather that I like the Model 70, you're right. The new models have been taking it on the chin for far too long; they're as good as anything else you can buy for anywhere near the money.

That about wraps it up for the bolt guns that are readily available to North American hunters. If there's one thing to remember it is this: if you shoot well with any of these guns, then the one you've got is right for you!

Lever Actions

Browning. The Browning Arms Company catalogues a bevy of leverguns. Foremost is the BLR, a modern multiple-lug, front-locking, rack-and-pinion operated carbine chambered for such potent loads as the .243 Winchester, .257 Roberts, 7mm-08 Remington, .308 Winchester and the elk-bustin' .358 Winchester, not to mention such vermin loads as the .223 Remington and the .22-250. Whew! The little gun features a detachable box magazine that allows the use of spitzer bullets, something not featured on most competitors' lever actions.

An exposed hammer gives the BLR a Western look, as does a barrel band, a straight-grip, two-piece stock and what resembles a magazine tube but ain't. There is cut checkering on the walnut stock, a recoil pad and a very high-gloss finish. No sling swivels;

a mistake. The trigger is gold plated in typical Browning glitz, and rides down with the lever when it's articulated, so as not to pinch a digit. Iron sights are provided, and fairly good ones at that.

The BLR is a very accurate rifle, perhaps as precise as any levergun ever offered. My crony Ed White once housed a .22-250 that would print five shots into 1½ inches all week. My .358 will group under two inches at 100 yards with 200-grain Silvertips, easily. Around 2½ inches is the best my .257 Roberts BLR can provide, but I didn't expect much better from a Roberts. The only levers I have shot that would shade the foregoing .358 on a regular basis were one Winchester Model 88 in .308 Winchester and a pair of Savage 99s in .250-3000. The BLR will shoot.

Caveats? Well, ignoring that ugly gold trigger, only three; two of them readily correctable. The length of pull is too long; I cut mine off. The trigger pull is not anything to write home about; not much can be done about it. Sling swivel studs should be added. That's all. Nice gun, the BLR.

Also in the Browning stable is the B-92, a modern copy of John Browning's immortal Winchester-built Model 92. Offered in .357 Magnum, the B-92 is pretty much limited in purpose. For close-range varminting, predator calling or hunting javelina, I suppose it would work well. Better would be a .44 Magnum, which was once catalogued. The B-92 is not really a serious hunting tool, at least in .357 chambering, unless one of the above mentioned persuits is your bag.

Finally, from year to year Browning offers various revivals of bygone John Browning lever-action designs. So far there have been two Model 1895 chamberings (the .30-06 and the .30-40 Krag), the Winchester 1886 in .45-70 and most recently the Model 71, reamed to .348 Winchester. All of these rifles are viable hunting arms for ranges up to 200 yards or so, on most any North American big game. None of them adapts to a scope sight gracefully, but all will accept a receiver sight if drilled and tapped. (The Model 71 came that way from the factory.) All of them exhibit exceptional workmanship, typical of Brownings.

If you're into levers, Browning likely has one for you.

Marlin. The Marlin Firearms Company has been around for about a century, turning out quality leverguns at affordable prices. They have two basic centerfires, the 336 (and its variants, such as the Model 444) and the Model 1894. The former is catalogued in .30-30, .35 Remington (the only mass-market firearm still chambered for the venerable round), .444 Marlin and .45-70

Browning 1895, a copy of Winchester's original 1895.

The Marlin 336-C accounted for a sika doe. Caliber was the time-tested .35 Remington.

Government. Barrel lengths run from 18½ inches on the 336-TS, 20 inches on the 336-CS and bargain-basement 336-AS, through 22 inches on the .444 and .45-70. The TS version wears a straight-grip stock; the others sport a pistol grip. All feature a tubular magazine slung underneath the barrel and an exposed hammer.

The 1894 is sort of a short-action permutation, reamed to .25-20, .32-20, .357 Magnum, .41 Magnum, .45 Colt and of course the .44 Magnum, at least at the time of this writing. The little carbines weigh from six to 6¼ pounds according to factory literature, with their more powerful brethren going from 6½ pounds (for the 336-TS) up to 7½ pounds (the .45-70). Several of the 336s boast a rubber recoil pad, most notably the .45-70 and the .444. (The best chambering Marlin ever offered—the .356 Winchester—also wore a rubber pad; it was recently discontinued. If you like the Marlin 336 rifle, I strongly suggest that you avail yourself of a .356 while some dealers still have one.)

The Marlin levers are adaptable to scope mounting since they eject their empties out to the starboard side, not straight up as do older Winchester levers and some of the current Browning and Italian copies of same. There is a problem, however, though it is certainly not exclusive to Marlin. If a rifle is stocked properly for iron-sight usage, as the Marlins are, then its comb is sure to be too low for proper scope sighting. This feature doesn't bother me much, as I feel that the Marlin levers don't need a scope. Selling point to the traditional levers—aside from nostalgia—is their *handiness*. A scope sight goes a long way to nullify this virtue. Therefore, none of my Marlins, Winchesters, nor copies from other countries, wears a telescope sight. When I want optical assistance, I choose another rifle. When I'm after handiness, I usually reach for a traditional *unscoped* levergun.

Marlin levers not only offer the conventional half-cock safety notch so long indigenous to the exposed-hammer lever-action genre, but an ancillary cross-bolt safety located just below and forward of the hammer, at the side of the receiver. It works fine, is silent if manipulated correctly and is not particularly obtrusive. It unfortunately can be forgotten, left in the on-safe mode and yield a *click* instead of a *boom* when a buck suddenly quits its bed. I recommend much familiarization firing with a Marlin of current manufacture to prevent such a happening.

Good things abound. Most Marlins have an adequate trigger pull; sometimes an excellent one. Further, a good gunsmith can make one shine like a new penny—crisp, clean, light.

And Marlins work. If I have ever had a miscue of any kind with any Marlin centerfire, I don't recall it. And I've tested a *lot* of Marlin carbines over the past two decades!

Marlins are accurate. My files show that not one Marlin 336 series has ever failed to group five-shot averages under three inches at 100 yards with one load or another, and I have tested them in six chamberings. (Alas, the 1894s that I've test fired haven't been so precise.)

I'll ease out on a limb: My current Marlin 336ER, reamed to .356 Winchester and sighted via a Lyman peep, may well be the single best deep-woods big-game rifle I have ever used. Maybe the best ever made. It is light to tote, quick to shoulder, fires five shots as fast as I can recover from recoil, groups where I want it to and disrupts a bunch of tissue when its big 220-grain slug strikes home. If there's anything better, I haven't run across it. Probably never will.

Savage. The famed Savage 99, weaned in the late nineteenth century, has fallen on hard times. Why? For one thing, one of its most heralded features since its inception—its rotary magazine—is no more. In its stead is a humdrum, if efficient, removable box magazine. But even worse, no longer does the company catalogue the .250-3000 nor yet the .300 Savage, both of which collaborated in making the Model 99 a household word, at least in hunting households.

The only two chamberings available today, in new guns, are both Winchester foals, the .243 and the .308, which are fine for their purposes, though scarcely better than the above mentioned pair. Nonetheless, the more recent cartridges are infinitely more popular, so I don't blame Savage for turning their backs on their own spawn, but I refuse to *applaud* the choice!

There are several viable reasons to choose a Savage 99 if lever actions set your heart to racing. They are readily scoped, and in their current versions have a proper buttstock for scope use. Further, spitzer bullets are acceptable to any Model 99, rotary magazine or box, which gives it a distinct practical advantage over tube-magazine rifles. Icing the cake is the ability of the strong 99 action to handle high-intensity cartridges such as the .243 and .308, not to mention the .250-3000, .22-250, 7mm-08 Remington, .300 Savage, .358 Winchester and .375 Winchester, all of which have been housed in the M99 during the past decade.

The Savage is not so short and light as some of its competitors, such as the Winchester 94 and Marlin 336, but takes loads that will outreach anything offered in those guns. The 99 is also heavier, wears a longer (22-inch) barrel, and its action is not so slick to operate. On the other hand, the Savage action will contain escaping gas better than a M94 or Marlin, is more convenient to load and unload, comes standard with sling swivel studs and *good* fully-adjustable iron sights and wears a rubber recoil pad. The stock, as on the more expensive versions out of New Haven and North Haven, is crafted of walnut. It is also checkered on the 99C, the only model produced at this time.

Accuracy with the 99 is just fine, thanks. In fact, the two most precise leverguns I ever fired were both Savages, and were identically chambered: .250-3000 Savage. Each printed exactly the same average for several five-shot strings with selected handloads: 1.32 inches. Friends, if I had a dollar for every turnbolt I ever fired that wouldn't equal that performance, I could buy 478 goldfish. And an aquarium.

Feeding of any Savage 99 is picture-perfect, in my experience. Extraction less so. I have had one or two failures to extract in the

Savage's venerable Model 99 levergun has been much loved by hunters through the years, but today it is in danger of passing from the scene.

past two dozen years. Not many, is it? I fret not about M99 reliability.

Model 99 triggers run from dismal to moderately decent. I suppose tuning one would not be beyond the ken of a good gunsmith. If I were planning to purchase one, that's likely the first thing I'd do to it. And I will buy another 99. I like 'em.

Winchester. The Winchester Model 94 is, quite simply, the most successful sporting rifle ever produced. Unless my brain is scrambled, somewhat more than six million of them have been sold, most to the public although not a few have gone south of the border and elsewhere to fight a battle or two. Calibers for which the old 94 has been chambered go like so: .25-35 Winchester Centerfire (WCF), .30-30, .32 Special, .32-40 WCF, .38-55 WCF, .375 Winchester, .307 Winchester, .356 Winchester, .44 Magnum and the hoary .45 Colt revolver round. The 7-30 Waters, maybe the most accurate cartridge ever put in the 94, has gained some degree of acceptance. I've owned a couple, and one of them shot like blazes.

For many, many years the M94 featured top ejection, its empty cartridge cases being ejected straight up, like toast. A centrally-mounted scope sight was naturally precluded by such an arrangement, so folks wanting a glass sight simply used a side mount or stuck a long-eye-relief job up on the barrel. Worked okay, but made the little carbines a tad unwieldy. Current issue 94s feature what Winchester calls "Angle Eject"; empties are booted out to the side. Thus, a scope can be mounted atop the receiver. Comb height on most M94s is not conducive to scope use, although a version called the Model 94 Big Bore was available for a few years. It wore a Monte Carlo comb, putting the shooter's eye in the right plane for telescope viewing.

Some Model 94s wear 24-inch barrels; some boast a rubber recoil pad; some come hand-checkered. By and large, the typical 94 sports a steel or plastic buttplate, a 20-inch barrel with full under-barrel magazine, open sights, and a plain walnut stock unadorned with checkering, pistol grip or any other furbelows. Just a working gun.

And Model 94s *work.* Oh, I've run across a few that had problems, but not in their basic design. More on the order of quality-control *faux pas.* Stick cartridges in the magazine; jack the lever; one will feed up and into the chamber, *click* like that. Work the action again and the chambered round will come out, fly away and another of its fellows will fill the breech. Every time.

Author with spike buck he managed to down, (author in hat). The old Model 94 Winchester is as efficient as ever at close range.

Accuracy of the Winchester lever is not what made it famous, although it is normally adequate. In fact, the best three-group aggregate I ever received from any traditional lever action (meaning one with a tubular magazine), came from an iron-sighted Model 94 rifle reamed to 7-30 Waters, and with factory ammo. The average? A tight 1¾ inches. Unfortunately, such precision is not the norm with most 94s. Although I have fired others that printed under 2½ inches, most were in the three- to 3½-inch neighborhood. Typical are these groups, fired recently in my .32 Special pre-'64 M94: 1.58, 2.25, 3.19, 2.31, 5.27 (one wild flyer), 2.31 and 6.25 (another flyer) inches. The average is 3.31 inches, and all were fired with 170-grain Winchester Silvertips. The flyers, of course, killed the average. That's why I shoot so many groups, to get a representative sampling instead of flukes. Note: with 170 Federal soft points, the same gun posted the following: 4.02, 4.69, 4.84, 2.28 and 2.75 inches, for a larger 3.72-inch average but a smaller variation in group size. For consistency, I'd likely pick the Federal load despite its inferior mean.

No, the Model 94 is not the most accurate hunting rifle in the woods, nor the most modern. It isn't at its best when wearing a scope sight. But it's inexpensive to purchase, reliable, powerful

Remington's medium-priced pump is the Model 7600.

enough for deer and similar-sized critters and portable. Besides, it has put more venison on the table than any other gun. Long may it live.

Pump-Action Rifles

And now on to the pump—or trombone—action, which won't take long. There's only one, Remington's Gamemaster Model 760 a.k.a. the Model Six, or 7600, or Sportsman 76. Lot of names, huh?

Remington's well-known Gamemaster pump (the name began life in 1936 or thereabouts with the Model 141-A pump, an entirely different gun than the current item) comes in three flavors: top of the line is the Model Six, complete with cut checkering, walnut woodwork, a Monte Carlo comb for scope use and a few other niceties. The Model 7600 wears impressed checkering, a straight comb stock (thus is inferior to the Model Six for scope use), a less hand-filling forend and retails for quite a bit less than the high ticket M-Six. Aside from the fact that it boasts no checkering nor a fancy walnut stock, the bargain basement Model 76 is likely the best choice of the bunch. Its strength, accuracy, trigger pull and smoothness is equal to its more expensive stablemates, as is its fit and finish. Actually, the M76 is finished up more to the liking of many than the 7600 or Six; it is dull and nonreflective. Only the low-combed stock goes against the grain of today's deer stalker, since Remington trombones are so readily scope sighted.

Featuring the same basic extraction and ejection system as the vaunted Model 700 series of boltguns, the Gamemaster is a reliable gun indeed. Feeding is accomplished from a detachable-box magazine of heavy-duty steel. I've never known one to bobble while chambering a round.

Functioning is generally 100 percent. One caveat: do *not* pull back on the forend when you fire the gun—as one is taught in basic marksmanship training—unless you're absolutely *certain* you'll remember to release that tight grip when it comes time to pump the handle. If you do *not* remember to do so (or even better, to push slightly *forward* on the forend), you'll not be able to manipulate the mechanism. More than one buck has escaped because the gunner was unaware of this mild idiosyncrasy.

Accuracy is often astounding, always acceptable. My experience has been that the Remington pump rifles virtually always outshoot Remington's semi-automatic rifles. For example, my Model Six in 6mm Remington will group into 1⅝ inches with Remington 80-grain Power-Lokt factory ammo, for several five-shot strings. A handload featuring the 75-grain Speer hollow point and a dose of Hodgdon H-380 does almost as well.

A Model 760 (forerunner of the current triumverate) I once owned, reamed to .35 Remington, would stay in 2½ inches with handloads. An M-76 in .30-06 I tested last year printed 2.30 inches for three five-shot strings with the 150 Federal soft point factory stuff. Next up was Hornady's 180-grain factory soft point at 2.38 inches. Moral: Remington's pumps shoot pretty good! And so on to the semi-automatic hunting rifles, which isn't going to be quite so cut-and-dried as I thought when I began this lengthy chapter. Why not? Well, I've decided to eliminate paramilitary rifles for several reasons, the most pressing being that many hunters (and landowners!) view such arms in a negative light. I don't necessarily agree with such a viewpoint, but there isn't much I can do about it here. Already I'm on the horns of a dilemma; what about the Ruger Mini-14? Since it resembles somewhat the ancient and venerated G.I. M-1 Carbine, it isn't tainted quite so thoroughly as such truly lethal-looking ordnance as Colt's excellent AR-15 or the F.N.-LAR. However, it would hardly be fair to Colt or F.N. to discuss the Ruger Mini while ignoring those manufacturer's products. So I won't. Springfield Armory offers a wood-stocked civilian iteration of the Army's M-14, and Valmet peddles a cut-checkered, wooden-handled version of their Model 78, dubbed the Valmet Hunter. Are these too military oriented for the traditional minded? Alas, I judge it to be so.

Ruger's little M-1 lookalike .44 Carbine has been deep-sixed by the Connecticut firm, so unless you haunt the used-gun section of your local gunshop or frequent gun shows, you're not likely to stumble onto one. So I'll disregard that one also, at least in this section of the book.

What's left, you ask? Browning's superb BAR, Marlin's little

Browning's fine BAR tames the recoil enough for even distaff hunters to handle relatively large calibers.

Camp Gun (admittedly of limited hunting utility) and the ubiquitous Remington 742/7400/M-74/Model Four series. Now let's have at it.

Semi-Autos

Browning. Aside possibly for Remington's zoot-suit Model Six auto-loader, the Browning BAR (pronounced *bee-aye-are,* not *"bar"*) is the only big-game self-feeder that is correctly stocked for a telescope sight. It is also properly stocked to reduce felt recoil, to provide a secure and comfortable bond between itself and its user and to look handsome in the bargain. It offers cut checkering, a hand-filling forearm and pistol grip and wears sling swivel studs. Unfortunately, it comes only in high gloss at present; but with the rising popularity of camo laminates and synthetic stocks, I suspect that we'll soon be able to purchase a shineless BAR. Hurry the day!

The BAR is the only auto to come in magnum chamberings; you can buy a 7mm Remington Mag. or a .300 Winchester, and the .338 is again available. The non-magnum version has to live with a lighter, shorter barrel and a plastic buttplate (the magnums boast a recoil pad), but is otherwise pretty much like its larger sibling. Chamberings run the gamut from varmint/deer (the .243 Winchester) up through the potent and popular .30-06, with several others in between.

Aside from its super fit, feel and finery, the BAR has one other quickly-noted aspect unusual to semi-autos: an excellent trigger pull. In fact, among current rifles, the average BAR usually has a pull superior to the average turnbolt. To the bolt guns' credit, most have at least some means of adjustment; the BAR has naught.

And then there is accuracy; the BAR really has it. I've tested BARs reamed to 7mm Remington Magnum, .308 Winchester and .300 Winchester Mag.; all averaged under two inches from the bench at 100 yards, with factory ammo. The 7mm went 1.20 inches with careful handloads, better than any 7mm Mag. I ever shot except one turnbolt, and I've tested 16 at last count. The Browning will shoot, period.

And function. In all the hundreds of rounds I've put through various BARs, I've experienced one malfunction. That came from a neck-resized handload; everyone knows that semi-automatics require full-length-sized brass. My fault. And to the Browning's credit, it digested every other neck-sized case fed it.

The BAR isn't cheap. It's just good.

Marlin. Marlin's nifty little Camp Gun comes in two persuasions: 9mm Parabellum (the Model 9) and .45 ACP (the model 45). Neither is much of a deer gun, but either will kill coyotes or javelina if a bullet is stuck in a tender spot from a moderate distance. If full-jacketed ammo is utilized, the Camp Gun will take small game for table fare. For jack rabbit gunning, I suspect the Marlin might be about as good as you can get, especially the 9mm version.

These carbines feed from detachable magazines. The 9mm comes with 12- or 20-shot specimens; the .45 holds seven rounds. I've shot one example of each caliber and functioning was perfect.

Accuracy was, shall we say, *adequate* at close range. For small game up to 35 or 40 yards, predators out to maybe 60 or so, the Camp Gun will handle the chore. Past those yardages, look to something more potent and more precise.

Trigger pull quality on both my samples was loathsome.

Marlin's camp gun isn't available in any big game rifle calibers, but it sure might come in handy for small game and vermin around the hunting shack.

Heavy. Very heavy. Gritty as well. Not conducive to expert shooting, particularly from offhand.

The guns are light in weight (catalogued at 6½ pounds), short and handy, feature a very positive Garand-type safety and wear a slim rubber recoil pad. Sights are similar to those found on Marlin lever action rifles, and are fully, if somewhat crudely, adjustable. There is a manual bolt hold-open device, a magazine disconnect safety and a loaded chamber indicator. The receiver is drilled and tapped for easy scope mounting.

For home defense or campsite protection, the Marlin is in its element. For hunting it is less so, but there's a limited niche there somewhere.

Remington. The immensely popular Remington series of self-feeders is basically similar in style, stock configuration and lock-up to the Remington pump rifle. The older 742 featured a multiple-lug front lock-up, which has been revised in the current version. The extractor is no longer pinned in place, and the locking lugs (four in number now) are fewer, but sturdier. Some gunsmiths laud the "new" gun as being safer and more reliable and less prone to parts breakage than the 742; other equally erudite 'smiths applaud the older models as superior, pointing primarily to the extraction system. Actually, both models are quite good, being basically reliable and trustworthy.

The Achilles heel of the Remington autos is the absolute necessity of keeping their chambers spotless, which is why the factory provides the purchaser with a chamber brush. (The BAR, incidentally, while not so sensitive to miscues due to a dirty

Remington's popular autoloading Model 7400.

chamber, is susceptible to gas-port rusting to a degree not present with the Remington.) So, keep that chamber squeaky clean.

As mentioned above, the Remington autos come in a high-gloss, cut-checkered, beaver-tailed-forend permutation, catalogued as the Model Four. The cheaper M7400 is a clone of the M7600 pump, with impressed checkering, straight-comb stock, etc. The least pricey is the Model 74; once again I find this one preferable as a hunting piece due to its less ostentatious profile. All are equal in the dependability, fabrication and accuracy departments.

And speaking of accuracy, that's the main reason the Remington autos have never appealed to me particularly. For all their weight and bulk, there is scant return in precision. Some 742s a.k.a. 7400s *et al* will group under three inches at 100 yards, but darned few will go into two inches. I'd place the norm at from 2¼ inches to three and let it go at that.

One of the most precise of my Remington autos is a .30-06 Model 74; it groups five shots on average into 2.44 inches when fed a diet of 150-grain Remington Bronze Point ammo. The next best load—including handloads!—is the 180 Norma Protected Power Cavity at 3.44 inches. Not great, but still better than most Remington self-loaders I've had dealings with.

One 6mm version belonging to my crony Dick White gave me a two-group average of 2.05 inches. But that same gun wouldn't go much under 3¼ inches with any other load, including another lot of the above mentioned super accurate number.

Most recently, I purchased from Chris Latta (owner of The Base Camp, a fixture for local hunters in Washington, North Carolina) a Model 7400 reamed to .270 Winchester. Chris, who is one of the 7400's staunch supporters, had not performed any of his gunsmithing magic on this particular Remington; it was box-stock and factory fresh. With a near-max prescription of Hodgdon's

H-4831 under the superb Nosler 150-grain Ballistic Tip bullet, three five-shot groups averaged 2.44 inches, with the largest at 3.19 and the smallest a tight 1.53 inches. Runner-up load was the 150 Norma soft point at 2.55 inches, with the 150 Federal Premium Partition next at 2.81. Obviously, that particular M7400 is a pretty good one! But then most .270s group well, regardless of the rifle. If all Remington autos shot so well, I'd be a bit more charitable in their regard. Still, for hunting out to 275-300 yards, they can cut the mustard.

One final point about the Model Four/7400/M-74: the guns have a smooth-working, reasonably *silent* crossbolt safety, as does the Remington pump. A lot of hunters dote on silent safety devices; they spook less game. A point to remember.

And that takes care of the semi-autos, leaving only the single shots to cover. Aside from a few modernized versions of 19th-century buffalo rifles—which are of limited value except to history buffs—there are only three: Browning's Japanese-built rendition of the old Winchester High-Wall, dubbed the 1885; Ruger's famed Number One; Thompson/Center's TCR '87. Here we go.

Single Shots

Browning. The big beautiful Browning single shot is a sleeper among hunting rifles, and not just among the one-shooters but repeaters as well. How so, you query? Well, for sitting on a stand watching a vast open space, an 1885 reamed to 7mm Remington Magnum is one of the most ballistically advantageous guns you could lay across your lap.

Consider: the 1885 sports a 28-inch barrel, and does so with the same overall length and heft as the average 24-inch-barreled turnbolt sporter. Stoke your chamber with a top-loaded 140-grain spitzer boattail and said 7mm Magnum will shoot plumb flat for half a mile then raise up a mite. Well, almost. Plus, it is as easy to tote as any other magnum hunting gun. Interesting?

And suppose you like the .22-250 for vermin. That heavy, octagonal 28-inch tube will squeeze about as much juice and precision from the old cartridge as any gun anywhere near its price range and weight class. Sound good? You bet it does.

The 1885 stock styling is classic, straight of comb and schnabel of forearm tip. There's enough meat to cling to both at the front and the rear, and a rubber buttplate is provided to keep the stock at your shoulder when you're prone in the weeds. Sling swivels provided on my sample 1885 are Pachmayr, the best you can buy, and the least obtrusive. The wood finish is matte; the metalwork is brightly blued, more's the pity. The trigger is typically Browning: gold plated. Shines like a miser's tooth!

Workmanship, as with all Browning arms, is hard to fault. Quite hard indeed. Wood to metal fit is excellent; the hardware is conjoined properly, the sling swivel receptacles deep and splinter-free. Nice. The trigger pull on my .45-70 test rifle is heavy but crisp; a trigger job would be in the works if I intended serious hunting with the 1885. But then the same goes for almost all guns made today; what else is new?

My test .45-70 acquitted itself satisfactorily, grouping 1.96 inches for four five-shot strings with Winchester's 300-grain factory hollow points. That's the best performance I've ever received from any .45-70, including the 1885's progenitor, the Browning B-78.

Two nice points about the 1885. First, the empties are tossed well clear of the gun when you work the lever, something not many single-shots can boast. If you're a handloader who worries about where his brass ends up even as yonder buck departs, you can set a little rotating cartridge stop (located atop the tang) to snag the case rim as it pops out of the chamber, thus keeping your precious brass aboard. I don't recommend it while hunting, but it's handy when you are testing the gun from the bench.

Second item: the exposed hammer design lets you know at a glance whether the gun is cocked, plus offers quiet operation if done properly.

If you feel that a single-shot rifle meets your needs, the Browning 1885 warrants serious consideration.

Ruger Number One. Ruger's elegant Number One has been around for 20 years as this is written, and just might make it for 20 more. It's an excellent design, lending itself to graceful good looks, acceptable hunting accuracy and a reasonably moderate heft. It's as strong as any turnbolt, and isolates the shooter from errant gasses in the event of a case failure or pierced primer. Like the Browning 1885, the stock design is classic and of two-piece construction as on a typical lever-action carbine. There are advantages and disadvantages to such an arrangement, and they pretty much cancel each other out. The Number One can be had in several barrel configurations, with lengths running from 20 up to 26 inches. Forend designs are semi-beavertail, Alexander Henry (sort of schnabel) and Mannlicher-style (running clear out to the muzzle and tipped with a metal cap). Extremely lightweight barrels are offered, as well as standard sporter weight and a heavy-varmint number. Most any chambering can be purchased, or has been made available at one time or another.

The falling-block action is similar in looks and manipulation to the British Farquharson, being activated by an underlever. There is no exposed hammer, but a safety button on the upper tang. The forend is attached to the barrel with a tenon. Upward pressure can thus be tuned somewhat to obtain variations in accuracy.

Sling swivels and studs are provided. Scope mounts, supplied by Ruger with most models, attach directly to a quarter-rib affixed to the barrel, obviating any problems that might be caused if one scope ring were tied to the receiver and the other to the barrel. On some versions, iron sights are provided, with the rear element dovetailed into the quarter-rib. The stock finish is dull; the metal semi-gloss. Cut checkering is provided on all models.

I've tested numerous Number Ones, in chamberings ranging from .22-250 up through the .458 Winchester Magnum. Only one, a .220 Swift, would group under an inch at 100 yards, and it barely made it. A .22-250 owned by woodchucking buddy Jimmy Michael groups right at an inch. It will often go a bit under, but not for an average. Years ago I tended to a .270 that would stay not much over an inch, but wouldn't quite sneak under it.

By and large, the Number One seems to be a 1½-inch rifle in most calibers. That is not damning with faint praise; such precision is more than adequate for any big game gunning I can envision. And since the varmint chamberings generally come close to one-MOA accuracy in most Number One rifles, groundhogs out to 300 yards are in mortal danger, assuming a good shot behind the plate.

Trigger quality is only average on most Ruger single shots, sometimes a bit worse. Assembly quality is good, and some Number Ones exhibit nice wood grain. Others are plain as a stump. Chosen carefully, a Number One will do yeoman work in the game fields. Examine several before you pick the one you'll take home to Mom.

Thompson/Center. In 1983, the well-known New Hampshire firm of Thompson/Center—maker of high quality single-shot hunting pistols, not to mention a complete line of blackpowder guns—introduced a break-open single shot to the gun scene. Reamed to such popular calibers as the .22-250, 7mm Magnum and .30-06, it made immediate inroads into what had theretofore been mostly Ruger territory. The new gun offered several singular features including readily interchangeable barrels, European-type set triggers and an unusual crossbolt safety that required two separate but simultaneous movements to disengage. This safety arrangement has garnered more than its share of unfavorable press. Disregard it. It is a good system that requires minimal familiarization, even for a gun writer.

The two-piece stock, generally a very good grade of walnut, is basically classic in shape. The pistol grip is a bit open for my taste, necessitating a long reach to the trigger, but individuals with large hands will likely have little difficulty. While the buttstock is checkered, the forend is grooved longitudinally, and left untouched by the checkerer's tool. Sling swivels studs are in evidence, and a solid rubber recoil pad is affixed in all chamberings.

And speaking of chamberings, T/C catalogues quite an eclectic array. At present you can buy a TCR '87 reamed to .308 Winchester, 7mm-08 Remington, the .32-40 Winchester Center-fire, even a 10 or 12 gauge version. Of course such standards as the .22 Hornet, .223 Remington, .270 Winchester and a few others are available.

A couple of years after the TCR made its debut, a less expensive iteration called the Hunter Model insinuated itself into gunshops around the nation. Differences between it and its higher-dollar brother were minor, and in one particular aspect, an improvement: the Hunter wore but one trigger. It was single-stage, adjustable and could be tuned to yield the best pull of any single-shot hunting rifle on the market. In fact, it was better than the triggers found on many target guns. Crisp, light, eminently controllable. Nice job, T/C; makes one wonder why other companies can't do it right.

The current TCR '87 is sort of an amalgam of features found on both the TCR '83 and the Hunter version. No longer are iron sights offered. Redundant; scoping is easy. Both sporter and heavy-barreled options are rendered, to suit the individual.

Extremely well thought-out, the T/C has a large trigger guard to accept a gloved digit. The opening lever, pivoting on the upper tang, can be manipulated either left or right at the user's whim. The gun actually opens itself when the lever is rotated, slick as gun grease. When you snap it shut, it's like locking home a Fox Sterlingworth—absolute solidity. Bank vault tight.

Wood finish is matte. The metal is semi-gloss. Everything fits properly; the woodwork is finished with an adept hand; the machining is first rate. The gun is handsome, lightweight (6¾ pounds in the sporter persuasion), and sells for nearly $200 less than the offerings out of Utah and Connecticut. Good deal? Danged right!

And will it shoot? My TCR '83 did right well with either its .22 Hornet barrel or an identical one reamed to .223. First the Hornet. Using Norma's 45-grain hollow point factory ammo, six five-shot strings at 100 yards averaged 1.16 inches, which is the second best accuracy I've ever received from a Hornet. The scope was a 3-9X T/C, set at six power.

With the same scope sight riding the .223 barrel, I managed a five-group aggregate of 1.30 inches with Federal 40-grain Blitz hollow point. Bridesmaid was a 53-grain match hollow point over 25.5 grains of H-4895, with groups averaging 1.72 inches.

My sample TCR '87, a silhouette-barreled .308 Winchester, printed 1.80 with Federal's 168-grain match factory ammunition. Hornady's match-grade 168-grain load went 2.06 inches. The TCR is accurate, reliable to a fault, easy carrying and can be purchased in calibers that other single-shot makers ignore. To say the least, I'm enthusiastic about the Thompson/Center. The fact that it also undersells its competitors *considerably* is frosting on the cake. Delicious frosting, at that!

Tying Up Loose Ends

The foregoing should cover most of the salient points relative to today's centerfire hunting rifle market. We've discussed nearly 30 specific rifles in some detail. It's time to go on, talk about matching the gun and the cartridge to the intended game animal. But first let's tie up some loose ends.

The question will be asked whether a hunter should strive to strike a balance between rapid firepower and the superior accuracy inherent in a turnbolt design.

As we've discussed, I feel that the boltgun's vaunted precision is marginal. Even if it weren't, most hunters can not really take advantage of it in the field. On the other hand, the first shot is—*with rare exceptions*—the best one you'll get. Super quick follow-ups are nice to have on tap, but any significant real-life advantage to the hunter is more abstract than demonstrable.

And is there such a thing as the preferred action type for the one-gun hunter? Sure. Whatever that particular hunter likes, what feels good to him or her, and what he shoots well. Other considerations are of no significance. Sure, a gunner will do better with a rifle having an excellent trigger; most actions can be modified by a good gunsmith to provide such. Some hunters might do better work with a rifle they know to be extremely accurate; others rationalize, quite correctly, that searching for a rifle that groups into an inch is fruitless and unnecessary, since they, meaning the hunter, can't group like that in the field.

My advice: choose quality; choose what you feel proud to own and shoot; choose what you can afford.

Which brings up one last point. Do the more expensive brands—or specific models within a brand—shoot more accurately than the less expensive ones? Nope.

Wait, qualify that nope—unless you get into a price bracket far exceeding $1,000. In that rarified atmosphere, true intrinsic precision is superior in many cases. But again, it is of interest only to a select few super marksmen, or those who view themselves as such.

Perhaps the most accurate factory production rifle ever produced was a low-dollar item: Remington's late, lamented Model 788. Marlin's fine little 366 carbine will nearly always outgroup the more expensive Remington semi-auto, at least in my experience. Within a given marque, my files tell me that I've had as good results from Remington's Sportsmen's series as I have with the much more expensive models Remington offers. Savage's budget 110-K is remarkably accurate. And so on.

The added cost of most "deluxe" guns is due to such furbelows as cut checkering, fancy finish, recoil pads, sling swivels and other such desirable but expense-adding features. None of them aids accuracy or reliability. And that's the truth.

4

Cartridges For
White-tailed Deer

Whitetail deer are unique. Not only are they found in most of the lower 48 states, but usually in huntable numbers within easy driving distance. No other big-game animal can boast such proliferation. Adding to the mystique is the fact that a record-book white-tailed buck is perhaps the most difficult to bag of all North American game. Many nimrods seek such a heavy-antlered specimen all their lives, to no avail.

Whitetails are hunted in more varied terrain and with more widely varying methodology than any other animal. The following styles of hunting are used annually to take whitetails: stand hunting in the forest; stand hunting overlooking open terrain, such as cultivated fields; stand hunting in varying terrain, such as watching a bedding area in the morning and a soybean field in late afternoon; hunting from a canoe or other small boat; drive hunting, in front of human pushers; drive hunting in front of dogs; stillhunting; stalking (these two are *not* the same, despite what you may read to the contrary); tracking; "jump" shooting (in a bedding area, for example); vehicular road hunting; ambush at a watering hole or stock tank; horn rattling, "grunting," or any other means of attracting deer to the hunter. I probably have neglected a few!

It should be obvious that not one type of rifle will serve ideally for such a broad range of hunting modi. I own several rifles which I use only for whitetail gunning, or for the persuit of critters of similar size, such as sika deer. The bulk of my whitetailing can be handled by a medium-heft, 22-inch barreled gun taking a cartridge capable of 300-yard shooting. The rest of my whitetail battery is specialized. An example... .

For still hunting in forested country, I like a rifle to be as short, light and well-balanced as I can find. The chambering is secondary, since I am careful of my shots. A real first-string still-hunting firearm is the Ultra Light Arms Model 20, reamed to .358 Winchester. It tips the beam at four and three-quarter pounds unscoped, wears a 20-inch barrel and fits me like an old pair of tennis shoes. Using a low-powered variable scope that rides the bridge, I can get off an aimed first shot with my ULA as quickly as with almost any rifle I have, assuming good weather conditions.

Hunting with gun writer and NAHC member Rick Jamison last fall, I spent most of a chilly, wind-swept day deep in the Missouri woods with an impressive whitetail herd. I passed up more than a dozen deer that day, including four bucks that were larger than any I had taken previously. Stupid? Maybe. But I was seeking a specific buck, the shed antlers of which I had been admiring for two days back at the lodge.

As we had planned, Rick and I met back at the Texas-style shooting tower to spend the last hour of daylight scrutinizing an area where the deer frequently enjoyed their evening repast. From the top of the 30-foot edifice we glassed seven or eight deer as the light waned, a few of them bucks. But not the big guy.

I tip-toed to the east side of the tower to examine an open area adjacent to a creek, some 250 yards northeast of the tower. One doe fed placidly near the bank.

Rick hissed, ''Quick! Two bucks. One of em's big. *Both* of them are big! One is *real* big!''

During this fervent appraisal, I had rushed back to the west-facing window, poked my muzzle out the opening, thumbed off the safety, and was now peering intently through my scope. The big buck whose horns I had been drooling over was standing majestically on the horizon, limned by the dying light. His head was up, questioning. All was not right in his world.

His partner, nigh as magnificent as the giant, seemed unconcerned; he shouldered a smaller buck out of his way and began to sup. The big fellow moved not a muscle, just stared straight at us. I squeezed the trigger... .

The strident *boom* of my rifle; the insistent nudge of recoil; a 200-grain Silvertip bullet sent on its way. The sodden *whap* of

The whitetail buck is sought by more hunters under more varied conditions than any other North American big game animal. That makes matching the cartridge/rifle combination to the situation more than confusing.

impact came to us; the buck spun to his right, dug in his heels. Death run. He collided with a sapling, entangled his horns, and died.

"Helluva shot," shouted Rick.

I danced around a bit, kicked up my boots, then pounded down the ladder to have a look. Rick stayed in the tower in case the buck should get back up. It didn't.

One of the reasons I had chosen the .358 for that hunt is because it isn't restricted to close range. While my 175-yard shot wasn't really a barrel stretcher, it would have been at the far edge of a .30-30's neighborhood. My still-hunting rig had performed a task that I had not intended it for, but that was not beyond its capabilities. That's a good reason to avoid true close-range cartridges when you're considering a load for woods hunting. One day a buck might catch you *out* of the woods.

My bullet had centered his heart, expanding perfectly, then traversed his body lengthwise. The butcher found the mushroomed slug in a ham. Nothing else would have put that buck on the ground any quicker, and a whole bevy of cartridges wouldn't have done as well. My choice was a good one.

I think it wise to avoid limiting myself significantly by my pick of whitetail armament for various occasions. Another example. Let's suppose that I plan to spend a lengthy portion of my hunting day in a stand overlooking a large expanse of unforested real estate. For such work, I lean toward a 24-inch-barreled 7mm Remington Magnum. Let's further postulate that a buck slips out of yonder thicket and I nail him. But not quite right. Instead of giving up the ghost, he sails back into the treeline.

Now I have to go after him. If my bullet was really off, he may travel quite a ways, perhaps lying up until he detects me on his backtrail, then skulking off to another hidey hole. Depending on just how much damage he has sustained, we could play this game all day. Should I be offered a chance at all, it will likely be a snapshot in heavy cover. Is a moderately heavy, long-barreled turnbolt the gun for the task? I think not. But unless I were near enough to my vehicle to fetch a more suitable rifle, I'd have to tote what I had along. The moral of all this is: *Avoid extremes!*

Now, before we delve any deeper into rifle choice, let's discuss cartridges. Virtually every cartridge in existence has been turned against a whitetail deer at some time or another. Some are fine choices; some are less so. I have slain whitetails with the following rifle cartridges: .223 Remington, 6 X 47, 6mm Remington,

Author and the majestic whitetail he took at Pamlico Manor's Western Division in Missouri. Rifle is Ultra Light Arms Model 20 in .358 Win.

.250-3000 Savage, .257 Roberts, 6.5 X 55 Swede, 7mm-08 Remington, .284 Winchester, .280 Ackley Improved, 7mm Remington Magnum, .270 Winchester, .30-06 Springfield, .300 Holland & Holland Magnum, .32 Winchester Special, 8 X 57 Mauser, .358 Winchester and .35 Whelen. With some of these, I slew but one or two deer; with others somewhat more. Two points here: 1) I have tried *a lot* of different loads; 2) anything will work if you stick your bullet in a precise spot.

Most rifle cartridges can be broken up into groups based on usage. These classifications run like so: close-to-moderate-range varmint and predator cartridges, such as the .22 Hornet, .222 Remington and the .223; long-range varmint cartridges, including such high-velocity numbers as the .22-250 and the .220 Swift (both of these first classifications are not even legal for deer in some states); combination varmint/deer loads like the .243 Winchester and .257 Roberts; long-range loads for medium-sized game, the .25-06 and .264 Winchester Magnum for examples; brush-country cartridges for game up to 300 pounds or so, including old timers like the .30-30 and .35 Remington; brush-country cartridges for heavy, non-dangerous animals, with the .30-06 as a classic example; long-range loads for game heavier than deer and pronghorns but excluding trophy elk, which would consist of such magnum cartridges as the .270 Weatherby at the low end and the .300 magnums at the top; bone-breaking magnum loads for dangerous North American critters like brown bear, beginning with the .300 Winchester Mag and going all the way up to the .375 Holland & Holland; cartridges for big, mean, nasty African fauna such as elephants and cape buff.

Of this formidable list, only certain cartridges have proper application for whitetail deer. We'll look at one or two from the first category, a couple from the second and some from the next three classifications at least cursorily. We'll begin with the ...

.223 Remington

The little .223 Remington is basically identical to the military 5.56 mm NATO. It is, of course, offered in hunting-bullet guise, not limited to military full-jacketed ammo. Factory stuff is supposed to yield around 3,240 feet per second (fps) from a 55-grain bullet. Sometimes, in some guns, such is the case. However, since many .223 rifles are short of barrel, I'd peg the average muzzle speed of factory ammunition in the 3,025 to 3,200 fps range. Federal offers a speedy 40-grain hollow point that runs

Rattling and calling of whitetails presents a whole new set of circumstances. Ranges will be short, but the buck is liable to be pumped full of adrenalin. He's coming, looking for a fight.

Author tested this rifle for guide Anson Byrd, then borrowed it to try on whitetails. One shot, one buck. Anson duplicated the feat a week later. For one who knows a deer's anatomy and can shoot (and only shoots at stationary deer) the .223 will kill cleanly at moderate ranges. Be sure to check if any of the .22 calibers are legal for deer in your hunting area before you uncase one.

close to 3,500, but it is *not* a deer load. Good handloads will squeeze but a few extra fps out of the average .223; the factory stuff is good indeed.

Most writers admonish against using the .223 on whitetails, and rightly so. Unfortunately, a lot of hunters don't listen. Further, many budding hunters (such as adolescents and ladies) want a cartridge exhibiting almost nonexistent recoil. So fathers and husbands and boy friends cater to these neophytes with such cartridges as the .223. I don't often advise it, but I can't ignore it.

To see what the .223 would do on a whitetail, I borrowed from famed North Carolina guide Anson Byrd a Remington 700-Varmint so reamed. Anson bought it for crow gunning, hence the heavy-barreled version. It is extremely accurate with Federal's 55-grain hollow point boattail, so that's what I used.

I was tooling along in my pick-up late one evening, intending to fetch Mike Holloway—my hunting partner—from his stand. I spotted a little buck watching me from a windrow. Stopped the truck. He didn't spook, just stood there peering at me curiously. I snaked the heavy Remington 700-V from its perch, eased out of the truck, chambered a round, folded up into a solid position, and scoped the buck. He hadn't moved. The crosswires rested at the base of his neck as I touched off. He dropped as if a barn had fallen on him!

My bullet wrecked the left lung, clipped the spine about halfway to the rear, was lost in the paunch. Pretty good penetration! That deer never knew what hit him.

The following week, Anson shot a nice seven-pointer. Same

gun. Same load. Same result. He hit the sizable buck in the center of the chest as it faced him from about 75 yards. Pole axed.

Do not deduce from the foregoing that the .223 is a real gee-whiz deer load. If one isn't a good shot, or shoots at an excited, adrenalized deer, or tries to angle a slug into the boiler room through too much muscle or bone, or any of a dozen other scenarios, the .223 hasn't enough juice to get the job done reliably. But ...

If a hunter is not readily excitable, can place his or her shot with precision, chooses a good bullet, and limits the range to 100 yards or less, a load of limited power can do a clean, quick job. The stress is on *skill*, not power.

Two other mild-mannered cartridges should be mentioned here, although in my view neither deserves much attention as a deer load. The moribund .222 Magnum is ballistically identical to the .223. Which is good, right? Well, kind of. But there's a problem: except for the smaller outfits, who build guns one at a time, hardly anyone offers the .222 Mag. any more. No loss; anything the .222 Mag. will do, the .223 will handle at least as well, and the latter is available in an infinite array of firearms. Forget that the .222 Magnum ever existed, if indeed you were aware of it before I brought it up.

The .222 Remington, progenitor of the two cartridges we've been discussing, began life in 1950. It boasted a new head size, pretty impressive ballistics, superb accuracy and was available in an inexpensive rifle of good repute, Remington's vaunted Model 722. The cartridge took off like gangbusters.

It's still good, better in fact than ever. It offers similar muzzle speeds to the .223, albeit with a bullet 10 percent lighter. With bullets of the same heft, it yields a couple of hundred fps to its younger sibling. No big deal on vermin, but since we need all the juice we can get out of such small capacity cases when they are applied to deer, I'll take the slightly more potent .223 every time.

There are several middle-of-the-road .22 centerfires such as the .22 PPC of benchrest fame, the .224 Weatherby Magnum and the obscure .225 Winchester, but I can scarcely imagine anyone buying one of those for deer. We'll skip them here, not because they are inferior to the foregoing cartridges, but simply because they are too esoteric for most *varmint gunners*, let alone deer hunters. Which leaves us with the two prime large-capacity .22-bores.

.22-250 Remington

Although I have never shot a whitetail with a .22-250, I carried an Ultra Light Model 20 so chambered to West Virginia this past season. I had it stuffed with handloads featuring the 60-grain Nosler Solid Base and a stiff dose of IMR 4350 powder. Muzzle speed out of my 22-inch barrel was about 3,400 fps, plus or minus a foot-second depending on the temperature. That was sufficient for sub-minute accuracy, 1,540 foot-pounds of energy at the nozzle, and very mild recoil. Had I managed to sock a whitetail in the lungs, heart, spine or brain with that concoction, I have little doubt it would have reduced it to venison. Expeditiously.

The factories claim 3,680 fps from a 55-grain bullet in the .22-250. In my tests, one ancient lot of Remington 55-grain soft points managed a sizzling 3,840 fps in a 24-inch-barreled Remington 788; a newer lot hit 3,730. Pretty impressive! That same old lot of Remington stuff clocked 3,718 in a 24-inch BBR, still well ahead of notices. Recently, a batch of Federal's Premium 55-grain boattail hollow points showed but 3,560 fps in my 22-inch Ultra Light. In a Weatherby Vanguard I got 3,576 fps from a sampling of Remington 55-grain Power-Lokt, and 3,434 from an uncommonly laggard lot of Federal's Premium HPBT.

For you hotrod fans, Federal offers a zippy 40-grain Blitz hollow point at a listed 4,000 fps. And will it get it? Well, it managed 3,940 in my Vanguard, 3,820 in my Weatherby Mark V, and 3,782 in my Ultra Light. (Six five-shot strings in this last rifle averaged .696 with the Blitz factory load. Good?) Admittedly, the foregoing numbers don't equal 4,000, but they are certainly not pokey.

Despite the fact that the .22-250 is more powerful than the .223 and its ilk, I do not recommend the larger cartridge for deer in factory-loaded form. Simply too much speed for those fragile little bullets. Handloaded, the .22-250 becomes an acceptable cartridge for modest ranges in the hands of a good shot, assuming good *game* bullets are utilized. The 60-grain Nosler and 70-grain Speer soft point come to mind, or one of the fine Barnes custom soft points. Without such bullets poking out of my brass, I'll pass on the .22-250 as a deer cartridge.

.220 Swift

The Swift is more than five decades old, and it has been rubbing out deer since its inception. So what? As I have said, lots of cartridges will take deer. The .220 is offered in factory form by

Although the .22-250 is better suited for varmint shooting, as it is being used here, it can serve in deer country if handloads are used and it is shot accurately.

Norma and Hornady. Norma's version features a 50-grain soft point at a listed 4,110 fps muzzle speed, for 1,875 foot-pounds. At 200 yards, retained energy is well over 1,000 foot-pounds, with about the same remaining velocity as the .222 Remington has at the muzzle! Obviously, the Swift has sufficient *energy* to down a deer, although like all the hot .22s, it is a bit light of bullet in its most common iteration.

Hornady proffers a 55-grain soft point at a listed 3,650 fps, and a 60-grain number at 3,600. Muzzle energies are 1,627 and 1,727 respectively. At 200 yards, the light-bullet load carries 939 foot-pounds, with the heavier slug hanging on to 1,063. I would not hesitate to use the 60-grain Hornady factory load on a normal-sized whitetail should the occasion arise, but I would be very picky about my shot, and would never make an attempt at a running animal.

In my chronograph testing, one lot of the hot 50-grain Norma

The .220 Swift is like the .22-250, only a bit more so. It does have an advantage, besides its extra speed. Hornady makes a factory heavy-bullet rendition (60 grains), which would likely work better on deer than the faster and more frangible 55-grain.

ammo hit 3,971 fps, a second managed 4,013, both in a Ruger Number One-B with 26-inch barrel. In a 26-inch Number One Varmint, the slow batch hit but 3,885, with the quicker lot getting 4,048. As you can see, one sample was considerably shy of press notices, while the other was within 100 fps.

In the same heavy-barreled Ruger, Hornady's 55-grain load hit 3,490 fps—not too close to published data. The 60-grain fared better, clocking 3,538.

Using stout but safe handloads, I've reached 3,567 fps with a 63-grain soft point, and driven Speer's semi-pointed 70-grain bullet to about 3,300 fps. Ammunition so loaded would bode a deer-sized animal no good. Still, I prefer heavier bullets for deer if given my druthers, because I don't *always* manage to stick my slug in exactly the right niche. The small-bore centerfires offer scant margin for undistinguished shooting.

In closing on the hotshot .22 centerfires, a final precaution. The aforesaid have two primary applications: 1) as very low-recoiling calibers for the physically impaired, distaff or younger shooter, with these last two hunting only under careful supervision; 2) use by an expert shot who is knowledgeable of game anatomy, does not get excited easily, and who never shoots at running game.

And now we'll look at the varmint/deer class, beginning with the most popular member of the group, the ...

.243 Winchester

When it began life in 1955, the .243 Winchester had a distinct advantage on many other cartridges. It was chambered in one of history's most beloved rifles—the Model 70 Winchester—and one of the country's best-read gun columnists was firmly in its corner. Warren Page, of *Field & Stream*, ballyhooed the nascent load at every opportunity. (He did likewise for the .244 Remington, which took two decades to take hold. Such are the vagaries of success.)

Of course the cartridge was and is a good one. Initially offered with an 80-grain pointed soft point for vermin, and a dandy 100-grain missile for deer and pronghorn, the .243 was simply an idea whose time had come. Never mind that its ballistics were pretty wildly inflated, especially those of the 80-grain load. In those days, chronographs were scarce as Martian women; even few gun scribes had them. The giddy ballistics published in the ammo companies' catalogues were accepted as gospel.

And what were those numbers? The 100-grain load was quoted at 3,070 fps, and the lighter bullet was said to yield 3,500 fps at the muzzle. Ha! Today, those figures are toned down a bit, with the 100-weight slug billed at 2,960 and the varmint bullet at 3,350. In some rifles, such speeds are at least approached.

For example, I received the following results from a Ruger 77-R with 22-inch barrel: 100 Norma FMJ, 2,929 fps; 100 Remington PSPCL, 2,833; 100 Winchester SP, 2,768; 80-grain Federal SP, 3,127; 80-grain Winchester SP, 3,162. The Norma factory stuff came close, but the others were far arrears. And this from a 22-inch Browning A-Bolt: 100 Winchester SP, 2854; 100 Hornady SP, 2804; 100 Remington PSPCL, 2861; 80 Winchester SP, 3114. Of the newer bullet weights factory loaded, the 85 Federal HPBT gave 3109 fps in my A-Bolt, with Hornady's 75-grain varmint number showing 3139.

Thus, if I had to pick a norm for .243 speeds, it would be around 3,150 fps with the 80-grain stuff, and 2,850 or so with the deer-weight bullets, all in 22-inch tubes, of course. Add two inches of barrel and you'll pick up from 50 to 75 fps; delete a couple of inches and you lose a similar amount.

Handloads are another matter. Given at least 22 inches of

As gun scribe Layne Simpson illustrates here, the .243 Winchester is a good open-country whitetail round so long as the range is limited to 250 yards, maybe a tad more with good handloads. South Carolina guide Mike Scearce shows Layne the way back to camp.

barrel, I have pet handloads that yield the following: from 3,340 fps to 3,425 with 75-grain hollow point varmint bullets; 3,350 fps with the 80-grain numbers; from 3,300 to 3,330 with 85 and 87-grain bullets; and from 2,975 to as much as 3,075 with 100-grain big-game bullets, depending on the gun. As you can see, it is possible to achieve factory-quoted speeds without rupturing anything, at least in strong actions and with barrels showing only a moderate level of throat errosion. One caveat: the .243 is notoriously prone to barrel wear, which is why the factories have throttled back on their ammunition. If you have a much-used .243, be very careful about your reloading procedures and charge levels.

The .243 is a fine deer load for moderate to medium-long ranges, say 250 to 300 yards maximum. A busload of game has fallen to its throaty bark over the past 30-odd years, and much more will in the future. If a suitable bullet is chosen, and said projectile placed in the heart/lung area of a whitetail, a humane kill will be the result. There is less margin for error with this class of cartridge than, say, with the .270 Winchester or .308, but never let it be said that the .243 is not adequate if properly directed.

6mm Remington

The .244 Remington, now known officially as the 6mm Remington, began life in 1955 (as did the .243, remember). The .244 was regarded, it is said, as primarily a long-range vermin duster, not a dual varmint/deer cartridge. Remington erred. The .243, loaded by Olin with two distinctly different bullets—for two distinctly different jobs—gained quick prominence in the game fields. The .244 languished in a quagmire of public apathy. Half a dozen years later, Remington redubbed the .244 as the 6mm, ballyhooed a change in barrel twist rate, and offered the cartridge in their upgraded and soon-to-be-renowned Model 700 turnbolt. The little .24-bore finally acquired a following.

Although to this day the 6mm isn't as popular as the .243, it is by a slight margin the better cartridge. The factories claim 3,470 fps for the 80-grain varmint load, and 3,100 fps for the deer/pronghorn version. In a Remington Model 742 auto, I clocked the 100 Remington PSPCL at 2,917 fps, the 100 Federal soft point at 2,920, the 80 Federal soft point at 3,309, and the 80 Remington Power-Lokt at 3,306. Not up to press notices, but a bit better than the .243 with similar bullet weights. In a 22-inch Remington 788, the 100 Federal factory load showed 2,956 fps, and the 80-grain Federal soft points managed 3,366.

Some years ago I chronographed in a Remington Model 700-V (24-inch barrel) these: 80-grain Remington PLHP, 3,346; 90 Remington soft point, 3,189 fps (quoted at 3200 fps in the catalog); and a whopping 3,207 fps with the 100-grain Remington Core-Lokt! Pretty fast gun. Even in the abbreviated 18½-inch tube of my Remington Model Seven, I clocked the 80 Winchester soft point at 3,340 and the 80 Remington varmint load at 3,320 fps. It takes 22 inches of barrel and hot handloads to get that in a .243! Even with factory ammo, the 6mm Remington is ahead of the .243 at its handloaded best.

When you reload your 6mm, the gap widens. In my 788 Remington, it takes a stiff but safe charge of IMR 7828 to yield 2,980 fps from a 100-grain soft point boattail. Hodgdon's H-4831 will boost the 100 Nosler Solid Base to 2,964 fps with ease in my Remington pump. For groundhogs, I like a 60-grain hollow point and enough H-414 to show 3,665 fps in my 788. None of the

This gunner shows good form practicing with this Remington M700 Classic in 6mm Remington. The 6mm is a good choice on whitetails out to 250-300 yards if a good bullet is chosen.

foregoing are especially hot loads, and I could kick the speeds up a bit if I were so inclined. However, the above recipes do all I desire to the critters I hunt, and offer superb accuracy. So why mess with success?

Last season, I popped a spike buck in the ribcage at perhaps 100 yards. He went into a blind run for 20-25 yards and fell over. Dead when I reached him. The 100-grain soft point boattail had tagged his left lung, coursed on into the paunch, exited the right flank.

Later that day, I put another of those lethal soft points into a doe's lungs as she stood broadside at 225 yards or so. She galloped perhaps 50 yards, slid sideways into a heap. Never got up again.

The 6mm will do as good a job on whitetails as any cartridge in its class, and better its trio of competitors when varmints are on the list. It's a great all-around load for big game up to 200 pounds or so, or little creatures as far away as you can hit them. I like it.

.250-3000 Savage

Savage's diminutive .250-3000 began its career in 1912, supposedly instigated by Charles Newton. Actually, it is at least as likely that experimenter Harvey Donaldson fathered the round in collusion with Savage's ballistic engineer, John Pierce. No matter who gets the credit, it is a fine cartridge.

Originally, it was introduced with an 87-grain bullet ostensibly loaded to 3,000 fps at the muzzle. Why the odd bullet weight? Because Savage wanted the advertising advantages of the magic "three-oh-oh-oh", and such a speed could not be obtained with a bullet heavier than 87 grains, at least not with the powders available at that time. Later, a 100-grain bullet was added in response to those who thought the 87-grain missile more in tune to vermin than deer-sized animals. The 100-grain load was listed at 2,810 fps for years; today it is shown as getting 2,820. The .250's one of the few cartridges that has actually shown an *improvement* in published data!

Until the advent of the .243 and .244 in the mid-'fifties, the .250 Savage and the .257 Roberts were the loads most often recommended for use by youngsters, ladies, and those gents who couldn't take much shoulder abuse. The 6mm twins clearly supplanted the older .25's in less than a decade. Even with the assistance of famed writer Larry Koller, who espoused it at every turn, the .250-3000 languished. For several years, it wasn't even available in a factory production rifle. Then, in the early 'seventies, Ruger dusted off the ancient and honorable load, stuck it into their Model 77 line-up. The interest thus generated revived the chambering at Savage; the .250 was returned to grace. Church bells pealed; quarter-inch fans danced in the streets.

The .250 Savage should never have gone away. With Remington factory 100-grain soft points, the .250-3000 will usually clock in the 2,770 to 2,810 velocity range—assuming at least 22 inches of barrel—which is pretty close to notices. As we've seen, the average .243 100-grain factory load manages but 2,850 or so, less than 70 fps faster than the .250.

Handloads mimic the factory-loads' performance. With 100-grain big-game loads, the norm for the .250 runs from about 2,910 to 3,030 fps with top handloads in 22-inch barrels. That's within 50 fps or less of the better .243 recipes I have tested. A similar gap occurs with the 75-grain varmint loadings; the .250-3000 will reach from 3,340 to around 3,400 fps, depending on the gun. Even in a 20-inch tube, incantations are not required to achieve 2,900 fps with 100-grain loads, and to better significantly 3,200 fps with the lightweight projectiles. Not far off the .243's pace.

And will the little .250 perform in the game field? You bet!

I've taken both whitetail and sika deer with a Winchester Model 70 Carbine. No complaints. My hunting partner Mike Holloway uses a decrepit Ruger 77-R as his primary deer rifle. No problems.

David Rushing was hunting a hot scrape a while back. He betook himself to the woods with a sleeping bag, thermos, and waited all day in a tree lounge. The buck showed up at 4:30 in the evening. Stopped. Looked around. His mistake. A 100-grain Hornady soft point slammed into his shoulder, removed half of a vertebra, dumped the buck so fast Dave thought he'd disappeared. The range was short, maybe 60 yards, but that is typical .250-3000 performance. Dave estimated the deer's live weight at 190 pounds; it was a seven-pointer, aged by a biologist at eight to ten years. A big, old, gray buck, and a dandy trophy. David used a Ruger Ultra-Light Model 77.

Mary Hill chose a Ruger 77 International, the full-stocked model, to take her first buck. One shot, 40 yards, in the heart. Her deer jogged a few steps to its right, then a few to the left, then went into its death run. Twenty yards or so and it was all over. Reckon she likes the .250?

So do I. It has hardly any recoil, is incredibly tractable—both in accuracy and loading tastes—and its bark is scarcely noticeable. Nice cartridge, the .250-3000.

.257 Roberts

The .257 Roberts was the brainchild of Major Ned Roberts, and was intended as a long-range groundhog cartridge. Instead, it found favor as a combination deer/vermin load. Remington legitimized it in 1934, dubbing it the .257 Remington Roberts, though it was basically the same cartridge the good major had nurtured so lovingly. The Ilion firm fiddled with the shoulder angle a bit, loaded it for some unknown reason to mild pressures and burdened it with deep-seated round-nose bullets ... maybe it wasn't quite Major Roberts' version after all.

The .257 has been fraught with problems. It is very difficult to get to shoot accurately in many rifles. Its ballistics—a 117-grain round-nose soft point at 2,650 fps—are mundane. Even the new Plus-P (higher pressure) loadings are not earth-shaking in that regard: 100-grain pointed soft point at 2,960 fps, 117-grain soft point at 2,780, 120-grain Nosler at 2,780. Potent, sure. In the .243 and 6mm class, certainly. But nothing singular.

Rifles reamed to .257 Roberts do not grow on every tree. Browning makes their A-Bolt, and catalogues the BLR lever

As loaded by Federal, the .257 Roberts is pretty good on deer. The 120 Nosler Partition is listed at 2,780 feet per second, and would do a buck no good if one were stuck in his heart.

action. Ruger offers the Model 77 and the single-shot Number One. Ultra Light Arms will sell you a Model 20 short action, or a longer Model 24. Aside from a few small shops, that's about it.

So why buy one? I probably wouldn't. Too much trouble getting one to group. However, it must be admitted that a 100-grain .25-caliber soft point starting out at about 3,100 fps will do all that needs doing to a deer. And when you shove a 120-grain Nosler along at 2,800 fps or so, it will drive deeply into whatever it runs into, at least more so than most any slug fired from a 6mm. Thus, if I intended to take on a caribou or black bear with a .257—which I do not—I would likely stuff my magazine with handloads featuring the Nosler bullet. (Or maybe Federal's Premium loading of the same bullet.)

If all I used my .257 for was deer hunting, I suppose I might find bliss in its arms. But since the raison d'etre of this class is a suitability to both vermin and bigger game, I require my rifles so-chambered to provide exactly that. Most of my .257 rifles have come up a bit short in the precision department for long-distance varminting.

But this chapter is dedicated to the whitetail deer. And for that purpose alone, the .257 Roberts is a mighty fine load.

.25-06 Remington

Remington's big, booming quarter-incher is the .25-06. Less than two decades old as a factory load, this lengthy cartridge is thus the youngest of the .25s. Originally designed by a gent named Niedner, back in the late teens or early '20s, the .25-06 is—as its name implies—simply the .30-06 case necked to .25 caliber. Until the advent of really slow-burning propellant powders, the .25-06 was a bit large in the bottle to be efficient; it held too much. Then IMR 4350 and Hodgdon's surplus H-4831 hit the market, and the .25-06 could really show its stuff. It did.

When Remington added it to their queue in 1969, its ballistics sheet went thus: 87-grain bullet at 3,500 fps; 120-grain big-game bullet at 3,120. Fast, indeed! A 100-grain load was added a few years later, and quoted at 3,240 fps. Today, the 87 is shown at 3,440 fps, the 100 at 3,230, and the 120-grain at but 2,990. Federal offers a 90-grain hollow point at 3,440, and a 117 at 2,990; ditto for Winchester.

Recently I spent some range time with a Browning A-Bolt in .25-06, which is a bit unusual among turnbolts of the caliber—it wore a 22-inch barrel. Most .25-06s are provided with a 24-inch tube to enable its lofty ballistics. In my A-Bolt, the following: 87 Remington Power-Lokt, 3,259 fps; 90 Winchester hollow point, 3,290; 117 Hornady soft point, 2,792; 117 Federal soft point, 2,754; 120 Remington PSPCL, 2,842; 120 Winchester hollow point, 2,836. With a 22-inch barrel, the .25-06 spits its heaviest slugs out at about the same speeds that the .243 kicks along its deer-weight projectiles, but a bit slower than the 6mm with the same bullets. Further, the 87 and 90-grain .25-06 varmint loads are a bit faster than their 80-grain .243 counterparts, but a little slower than similar slugs in the average 6mm Remington.

Look at it this way: in barrels of the same length, the .243 as factory loaded is equal in trajectory to the .25-06 with deer bullets, and only a slight margin behind with the vermin numbers. The 6mm will equal the .25-06 in trajectory across the board, and the .257 Roberts will push handloaded 117-grain bullets nearly as fast as similar-weight factory loads from a .25-06. The upshot is that if you intend to stick to factory ammo, the 6mm Remington is likely a better choice than the .25-06 unless you plan to seek game larger than deer.

Handloaded properly, the .25-06 does indeed impress. In a 22-inch KDF turnbolt, I can achieve 3,308 fps using the 100 Speer hollow point in conjunction with IMR 4831, about the same from

This .25-06 KDF is the most accurate sporter the author has tested in a true big game chambering. With its pet recipe—featuring the 120 Nosler solid base and IMR 4831—this moderate-heft rifle prints .7-inch for five-shot groups at 100 yards.

the 100 Hornady soft point paired with the same propellant. The 120 Nosler Solid Base can be booted along in excess of 3,070 fps in my KDF, with groups averaging an incredible .70 inch for five shots while so doing. Additionally, one exceptional lot of Remington's 120-grain pointed Core-Lokt clocked an astounding 2,988 fps in the KDF, despite its short tube. That same batch showed 3,003 fps in a 24-inch Ruger Number One Varmint, with the 90-grain Federal hollow point getting 3,375. Obviously, *some* lots of factory ammo (and good handloads) are notable in the .25-06.

For the hunter of groundhogs and whitetails, the .25-06 is a viable choice, although it is tough on barrels, louder than it needs to be and recoils a tad more painfully than the foregoing quartet. Nonetheless, if only a couple of hundred shots are fired in a year, a good .25-06 will serve its owner long and well.

It also requires a long action when housed in a boltgun, adding to both length and heft. Further compounding the difficulty, most .25-06s come with 24-inch barrels. Since most .243, 6mm, .250 Savage and .257 Roberts turnbolts come with short actions and

22-inch barrels, they are much handier to tote than most .25-06 rifles.

Thus, while the .25-06 offers plenty of power and a trajectory sufficiently flat for any kind of whitetail gunning, its advantages over such as the 6mm Remington and the .257 Roberts are insignificant on game in this class. I'll pass.

Aside from such cartridges as the .257 Weatherby Magnum, the .264 Winchester and a few others of similar singleness of purpose, that covers the varmint/deer class. It's time to look at the so-called "brush country" deer loads.

7-30 Waters

This modern cartridge was designed by gun writer Ken Waters, and has been offered only by Winchester—at least in repeating rifles. It is basically a necked-down .30-30, taking a 120-grain Nosler soft-pointed bullet as loaded by Federal. Muzzle speed is said to be 2,700 fps in a 24-inch barrel, which happens to be the length provided on the Model 94 AE. Believe it or not, my two sample rifles would exceed the factory-quoted numbers significantly. The average for two different lots of ammo tested in both rifles was 2,748 fps instrumental velocity at 12.5 feet. Wow! Retained energy at 200 yards is a little over 1,000 foot-pounds. When sighted 1.3 inches high at 100 yards, with zero at 150 yards, the 200-yard drop is but a hair over three inches. (A scope sight mounted 1.5 inches over the bore is required to achieve these numbers.) If there is a true 200-yard factory cartridge among the brushy-terrain members, the 7-30 Waters is it.

But it takes good accuracy to hit a whitetail's vitals at 200 yards, right? And the M94 has it when reamed to 7-30. One of my test rifles averaged 1.76 inches for three five-shot strings with the Federal factory stuff. Bingo! Either rifle will print inside 2½ inches all day, with any lot tested to date. I'd say that's plenty good for 200-yard shooting.

Two problems with the Model 94 AE 7-30 Waters. First, the stock has quite a bit of drop, so recoil is not exactly a caress. It isn't painful, mind you, but the neophyte will find it formidable. Second, 24 inches of barrel in a brush rifle are four inches too many. I suspect that the velocity loss would not be traumatic if barrel length were reduced by 17 percent, and the benefit in portability would be marked.

Given the adequate ballistics, unusually fine accuracy and proven reliability of the Model 94 design, I suspect that a whitetail

The physical size of the whitetail you're after may also play a part in cartridge/rifle selection. Big deer can be tougher to bring down.

What's your definition of "brush country"? It's liable to vary depending on what part of North America you live in.

hunter could do much worse than the 7-30 Waters.

.30-30 Winchester & .32 Winchester Special

I'm going to discuss these two as a duo simply because they are as alike as two peas in a pod. The 30 caliber has a .308-inch bore; the .32 takes .321-inch bullets. Each fires a 170-grain slug in its most common form, with the .32 Special getting perhaps 50 fps more speed than the .30-30. From a 20-inch barrel, both run in the 2100 to 2150 foot-second range, although the catalogues credit each with another 100 fps or so. Some shooters feel that the slightly higher velocity of the .32 makes it a better killer than the .30-bore. Nonsense. Others tout the superior bullet length in relation to diameter (sectional density) of the smaller caliber as being significant. Horse radish. The two are ballistic twins; what one will do, so will the other. Period.

The .30-30 does have a couple of important advantages. It's

available in a wider variety of factory ammo, in bullet weights from 55 grains (Remington's sabot-encased varmint iteration) through 125 and 150, ending with the heavy 170-grain numbers. The .32 Special is offered in but one weight and configuration. Further, the .30-30 is available in a wide array of rifles and carbines that has at one time or another included pumps, single-shots and turnbolts. The .32 Special has for the past several decades been found only in lever actions.

For those of you who are interested, the 55-grain Remington "Accelerator" is listed at 3,400 fps, about as fast as some .22-250 factory loads. I chronographed a batch at 3,270 fps in a 20-inch Model 94 Winchester. Federal's 125-grain hollow point (designed for vermin and predators, not deer) is listed at 2,570 fps. In my 18½-inch Marlin 336-T, my test sampling managed but 2,460. In a 24-inch rifle, both of these loads should come close to quoted statistics.

The 150-grain jobs—often chosen by deer hunters who think they might expand a bit more reliably than the 170-grain ammo, or shoot a little flatter—are listed as getting 2,390 fps. In my Model 94, one lot of Norma soft points shaded that by five foot-seconds! Remington's round-nose Core-Lokt clocked 2,269 in the M94, with Federal's 150-grain soft points showing 2,293. In the Marlin 336-T, the 150 Remington managed 2,356 fps in one lot, 2,360 in another. Pretty good!

In that same Marlin, this: 170 Norma soft point, 2,184 fps; 170 Federal Premium (using a Nosler Partition bullet), 2,228; 170 Federal soft point, 2,130; 170 Remington round nose Core-Lokt, 2,188. In my Winchester M94: 170 Remington hollow point, 2,024 fps; 170 Federal Premium, 2,163; Winchester 170-grain soft point, 2,042; 170 Hornady flat point, 2,055.

From my pre-1964 Model 94 .32 Special, the following: 170 Federal soft point, 2,101 fps; 170 Winchester Silvertip, 2,109 for one lot, 2,110 from another, and 2,114 from a third; 170 Remington hollow point, 2,135; and one elderly batch of 170 Winchester Power Points gave 2,197. All from a 20-inch barrel.

Like I said: the two cartridges are Siamese twins. But will they kill deer? You betcha.

A typical example is the spike buck I decked with my .32 last season. I socked him in the left shoulder as he quartered toward me at 45 paces. The 170-grain Silvertip smashed the shoulder joint, demolished his heart, exited after pulping his right lung. Two large pieces of bone were blown up into his neck! At the hit, he galloped 50 yards or so and piled up.

I don't consider the .30-30 or .32 Special to be much count past 150 yards, perhaps 175 at best. Several reasons. Most rifles so chambered are only moderately accurate, although there are exceptions. Also, retained energy, at less than 1,000 foot-pounds with most factory fodder, is getting down on the low side. Finally, but most importantly, I expect bullet expansion would become erratic at the velocity levels we are dealing with here, say 1,600 fps or thereabouts at impact. Taking all these things into consideration, I personally limit myself to 150 yards if at all possible when carrying my .32 Special.

The foregoing is not damning with faint praise. Far more whitetail deer are taken under 150 yards than over. *Far* more! So the .30-30 and .32 Special are not as handicapped as some would have us believe. And neither is the ...

7.62 X 39 Russian

This little cartridge began life in the 1940s, as a military round. It has been chambered mostly in military arms such as the Russian SKS and AK-47 for decades, and has been noticed only in passing (if at all) by American sportsmen. The introduction of Ruger's Mini-Thirty combined with the recent influx of surplus arms so-chambered has given the 7.62 X 39 a shot in the arm. Which is fine by me; it's a good little round.

PMC factory ammo shows a 125-grain soft point at a listed 2,320 fps, for nearly 1,500 foot-pounds at the muzzle. At 100 yards, retained punch is 1,161 foot-pounds, and the pointed bullet hangs on to around 900 foot-pounds clear out to 200 yards. Thus, the 7.62 is ballistically equal to the .30-30 and its ilk out to about 175 yards, at which distance I would draw the line on deer.

I have run chronograph tests of the PMC ammo in both a Ruger and an SKS semi-automatic. The Ruger clocked 2,283 fps in its 18½-inch barrel; the 20-inch SKS showed 2,297. Considering the abbreviated barrels, I was pleased with that showing. My favorite handload gets 2,268 fps from a 125-grain soft point, and groups 2½ inches in my Mini-Thirty for five shots at 100 yards. Runner-up handload pairs the new 123-grain Hornady soft point with H-335 ball powder, for three-inch grouping at a 2,328 muzzle speed.

In the SKS surplus rifle, BL-C(2) works best with the Hornady soft point. Groups average four inches at 100 yards. Fastest load in

Hornady was the first American company to make a soft point bullet specifically for the short Russian 7.62 x 39mm. In a good autoloader, this bullet/cartridge combo will group around 2½ at 100 yards and bop a deer with gusto.

the old gun uses Hercules Reloder 7, and yields well over 2,400 fps!

Should anyone tell you that such ballistics are inadequate for whitetail deer at close to moderate ranges, don't buy a used car from them!

.35 Remington

The old .35 Remington is one of my favorite loads for close-in deer hunting. I like its relatively moderate recoil, its performance, its easy accuracy in rifles of brush-country persuasion; heck, I even like its looks. Aside from Remington's custom shop, it is available only in the Marlin 336 lever action among popular-priced arms. That's fine by me; the Marlin lever is nigh perfect as an iron-sighted whitetail rig.

Said to push 200-grain round-nose bullets out its muzzle at 2,080 fps in factory form, I have found that in typical .35 hunting guns, such is often the case. Two-hundred-yard retained energy is only 840 foot-pounds—which ain't many foot-pounds. But out to 150 yards or so, the factory-loaded .35 has enough to get the job done. Besides, it gets a large percentage of its power from bullet weight, not speed, and that weight doesn't change with range.

Remington offers a 150-grain pointed number. I hunt occasionally with a North Carolina whitetail guide named Tommy Midgette; he has taken many, many deer with a pair of elderly .35 Marlins and the strange little pointed Remington round. He swears by it. For the rest of us, the 200-grain factory stuff is better.

From left to right, the .35 Remington is shown with some of its competitors in the whitetail arena. The .375 is almost as good as the .35 Rem., but is dying of public apathy. The .44 Magnum is doing okay in the Marlin 1894, but it's setting no sales records as a rifle round, and is inferior to the .35 as a deer slayer when ranges lengthen. The .444 Marlin and the .45-70 Government are more potent than the .35, at least on paper and at moderate ranges. Once the 150-yard mark is reached, things shift back in the .35's favor. When handloaded, the .444 and particularly the .45-70 make the smaller .35 eat their dust at any range.

When handloaded, the .35 really shows its stuff. The excellent 180 Speer flat point can be driven to speeds approaching 2,400 fps in a 20-inch Marlin. Under such impetus, the 200-yard punch is close to 1,200 foot-pounds, a nearly 50-percent improvement on factory-load specs. It's no trick to reach 2,150 fps with a 200-grain round nose in my Marlin, with two different propellants. Such numbers make the .35 into a genuine 200-yard cartridge if its rifle, sighting system and shooter are up to the task.

While I have never taken a whitetail with the .35 Remington, I have slain a couple of sika deer. One took a 200-grain Hornady round-nose soft point in the center of its chest. No bones were struck, and the bullet exited a ham! The other animal, a doe, absorbed a similar bullet just aft of its right shoulder. The slug, perfectly expanded, lodged inside the ribcage on the off side. Not much penetration there! Why the disparity in performance? I dunno. But it shows why one shouldn't base too much on an isolated incident when it comes to game-killing performance.

There is little else to say about the antediluvian .35. It has always been a workhorse cartridge. It's not flamboyant, wears no belt, isn't loaded to case-stretching pressures, doesn't come in high-buck, flossy-glossy rifles, won't shoot flat as a taut wire and doesn't belt you out from under your toupee. But pointed right and fed proper ammunition, it will kill whitetail deer *stone* dead at reasonable ranges, with little fuss, bother or bark. Pleasant load, the .35 Remington.

.375 Winchester

I missed one of the finest bucks I have ever seen in the woods while carrying a Winchester Model 94 Big Bore reamed to the then-new .375 Winchester. Since that depressing afternoon, I have been uninfatuated with the cartridge. Dumb, but there it is.

It isn't the cartridge's fault. So far as my intellect can discern, there are few flies on the .375. Accuracy, while not on par with such similar loads as the .30-30, .32 Special, or .35 Remington, is at least adequate for whitetail hunting at normal ranges. Of the three .375s I have tested, the first grouped five shots into 3.11 inches on average, and that with a handload. Second best averaged 3¼ inches, again using a handload. In that first Big Bore 94, factory ammo printed like so: 200 Winchester flat point, 4.53 inches; 250 Winchester flat point, 3.77. A second carbine managed 4.28 inches with the light-bullet load, 5.07 with the heavy item. Not very good.

Most recently, I tested a Model 94 Angle Eject. It grouped wonderfully with a new lot of the 200-grain Winchester Power-Points, 2.40 for three five-shot strings. I thought I'd *finally* acquired an accurate .375 Winchester! Alas, my hopes were dashed. The little carbine was so wildly imprecise with the 250-grain factory load that I didn't bother to measure the groups. (In the neighborhood of eight inches at 100 yards!) Maybe I'll give up.

Ballistically, the .375 has all that's required to take a whitetail buck. Quoted at 2,200 fps, the 200-grain Power-Point is the better choice for game of this size. In my 20-inch rifles, two different lots of ammo gave 2,110 and 2,126 fps. The 250-grain is allegedly intended for game larger than deer, but it is pretty slow at 1,900 fps quoted. In my chronograph testing, 1,855 fps is all the portly bullet could provide. If I were after such sturdy critters as black bear, I'd still opt for the 200-grain loading, despite the longer bullet's theoretical advantage in penetration.

This is the only handloader bullet available at popular prices for the .375 Winchester. The author had some input on this bullet's design.

Actually, I wouldn't use factory ammo at all in a .375 Winchester. Hornady's excellent 220-grain soft point is so superior to either of the factory loads, I could scarcely pass it up. Coupled with Hercules Reloder 7, a top reload will push the Hornady bullet nearly as fast as the 200-grain Winchester factory load! Considering the 10 percent increase in bullet heft, and a similar boost in energy, handloading is the path to take with this cartridge.

One distinct convenience offered by the .375 that its bottle-necked competitors lack: case trimming is seldom, if ever, necessary, regardless of how many times the cases are used. The brass simply doesn't stretch much. That makes for a more uniform crimp than is the case with a whole bevy of similar cartridges unless they are trimmed meticulously and often. Score one point for the .375 Winchester.

The Revolver Cartridges

There have long been fans of the big, bellowing .44 Magnum revolver cartridge who wanted to pair their sixguns with a carbine similarly chambered. Ruger was the first manufacturer to cater to this demand way back in the early '60s with their Deerstalker .44 carbine. Marlin climbed aboard the bandwagon a few years later with the 336, then dropped the load in that gun to revive their Model 1894. Other companies—notably Winchester, Browning and Rossi—followed suit at their own pace.

The .357 Magnum devotees clamored loud and long for equal treatment. Marlin, Browning, Rossi and maybe one or two other firms complied. Then Marlin added the .41 Magnum. Even the .45

Colt is now offered by at least three purveyors of lever action carbines. So what have we wrought?

Frankly, while the .41 and .44 Magnums are acceptable deer loads out to 100-125 yards, I can see but limited use for the .357 and .45 Colt. When this latter cartridge is handloaded to higher than industry-standard pressures, it becomes quite formidable indeed. But as stoked by the factories, it is best kept out of the deer woods. Certainly the .357 will kill a deer if the bullet is placed *just so*, but the margin for error is quite small. Almost nonexistant, in fact.

It's another story with the .44. The factories claim 1,760 fps for the 240-grain jacketed soft and hollow-point ammo, which is good for 1,650 foot-pounds. At 100 yards, retained smash is still in excess of 1,000 foot-pounds. An even better choice for deer in my opinion is the 180-grain hollow point offered by Federal. In my Ruger carbine (18½-inch barrel), the zippy Federal number clocked 2,148 fps. That, friends, is *fast!* (Remember that a .30-30 usually shows only 2,100 fps or so from a bullet ten grains lighter.) Out at the 100-yard marker, the 180-grain load hangs on to about 1,000 foot-pounds, and has plenty of expansion potential.

Incidentally, the .44 factory ammunition comes pretty close to factory listings when actually chronographed, and in some instances exceeds it. To wit, all in my Ruger carbine: 240 Winchester JHP, 1,737; 240 Federal JHP, 1,709; 240 Speer JSP, 1,866; 240 Hornady JHP, 1,624. The 180-grain Hornady hollow point clocked 2,031. Not as fast as the Federal, but still quick.

I suspect that the factory-loaded .41 Magnum ammo will about match the .44 stuff, since such is the case in handguns. Thus, I'd look for about 1,700 to 1,750 fps from the 210-grain hollow points, maybe a bit more. Such speeds would carry in the vicinity of 1,350 foot-pounds or better at the nozzle, maybe 800 out at 100 yards. I like more energy than that if possible, but I can't overlook the large frontal area and lumbering heft of that .41-caliber bullet. That equates to killing power a bit beyond "paper" ballistics.

The .357 Magnum matches its larger brothers in speed, but trails significantly in energy. If you can shoot your buck at 20 or 25 yards, the .357 will likely hold up its end. At longer ranges, more clout is requisite. Ditto in spades for the low-pressure, low-energy .45 Colt in factory form.

Unless you just happen to *like* the .44 Magnum (or maybe the .41), I can think of few reasons to buy a rifle chambered for it. Except for the Ruger carbine—which is no longer produced—a

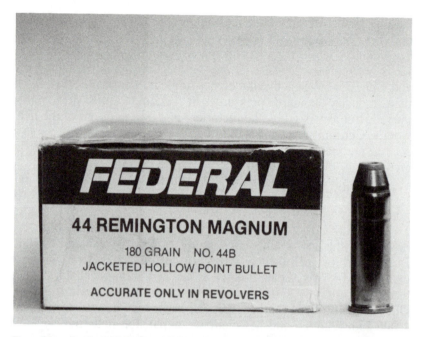

For whitetail, the 180 Federal factory load is a good bet. It is fast, and it will expand. Bullets heavier than 200 grains generally will not, with one or two notable exceptions. One point: when shot from a rifle, this factory load retains as much velocity at 100 yards as when the same load exits a revolver's muzzle. And it will kill deer!

.44-chambered long gun offers but marginal handling improvements over such similar ordnance as Marlin's 336-C in .35 Remington. And the .35 is a *much* more serious deer load than is the .44 Mag. The bottom line is that the .44 Magnum makes eminent good sense when stuffed into a burly handgun, much less so in a rifle.

The Mild .30s

There are four mild-mannered .30-caliber cartridges that should be covered in any discussion of deer loads, if only for the sake of completeness. Three border on obsolescence, and are no longer offered in new sporting rifles. The fourth virtually duplicates the ballistics of the other three, and though you can purchase a new gun so-chambered as I write this, I doubt that will continue to be the case. The cartridges are the .300 Savage, .30-40 Krag, .307 Winchester, and the .303 British. (This last is not a true

The author used the 240-grain Federal factory hollow point on this monster Ohio buck. The bullet made the same sized hole on exit as on entrance, and the deer ran 85 yards before he fell. For that reason, the author prefers an expanding bullet in the .44 Magnum.

.30-caliber, but takes .311 bullets. Don't nitpick.) Although these cartridges are shown to provide somewhat differing speeds in the factory literature, in the real world they are much alike.

The .300 Savage claims 2,650 fps from its 150-grain bullet, 2,350 from its 180-grain loading. The .30-40 Krag is offered only in the 180-grain rendition, said to provide 2,430 fps. The .307 Winchester is shown at 2,760 fps with the 150-grain soft point, and 2,510 with the 180. The ancient .303 British is listed as getting 2,460 fps from its 180-grain ball in domestic versions, with Norma's 150-grain soft point claiming 2760. The truth?

This from my 24-inch Savage M99 take-down: 150 Remington pointed Core-Lokt, 2,539 fps. In my 22-inch Model 99E: 150

357 MAGNUM
145 GR. SILVERTIP® H. P.
X357SHP

Although some hunters tout the .357 Magnum, the author is less than enthralled with it as a rifle round. For quite modest ranges, when placed carefully, it will do an acceptable job. But don't stretch it.

Remington pointed Core-Lokt, 2,581; 150 Remington round-nose Core-Lokt, 2,585; 180 Remington round nose, 2,343 fps.

In a .30-40 Krag carbine, the 180 Winchester Power Points clocked but 2,224 fps. From a Browning 1895 lever action's 24-inch barrel, I got 2,397 fps from the same load, with Remington's 180-grain pointed Core-Lokt showing 2,399. Winchester's 180 Silvertip hit but 2,295 in the Browning, and an elderly lot of the discontinued 220-grain Remington round nose crossed the screens at 2,210 fps. (That last data goes under the heading of trivia.)

In one of my test Model 94 carbines, the 150-grain .307 Winchester load clocked 2,597 fps; in another, 2,622. The 180-grain Power-Point hit 2,375 fps in the first gun, 2,423 in the latter. Barrel length was 20 inches.

Tested in an 18½-inch-barreled British SMLE jungle carbine, the .303 provided the following: 180 Norma round nose (now discontinued), 2,585 fps; 180 Winchester Power-Point, 2,167; second lot of same, 2,211.

Now to compare. I've never tested any of the 150 Norma .303 ammo, but in the .300 Savage, that bullet weight averaged 2,568 fps. The .307 averaged 2,610 from the 150-grain Winchester Power-Points. That's only a 42-foot-second spread between the two cartridges, albeit from differing barrel lengths.

With 180-grain factory ammo, fired in guns of varying barrel lengths, the velocity averages went like so for the quartet: .303 British, 2,321 fps; .30-40 Krag, 2,329; .300 Savage, 2,343; and the .307 Winchester, 2,399. That's only a 78-foot-second spread among all four. Not much difference, right? I told you so.

So what will they do? Well, if limited to their round or flat-nose iterations, most are about 225-yard deer loads at best. Energies run in the 1,100 to 1,200 range at the 200-yard mark, and bullet drop is close to a foot at 250 yards, assuming a 150-yard zero. However, several are offered with pointed bullets. That moves them out into the 275-300 yard bracket. The pointed 180-grain bullets yield from 1,200 to 1,300 foot-pounds clear out to 300 yards, and the Norma 150-grain .303 loading claims 1,240 at that distance. Plenty for deer. Further, the Norma data shows less than 10 inches of drop at 300 yards when the gun is zeroed dead-on at 200. Plenty *flat* for deer.

Thus, if you are in the used-gun market, or have recently inherited a well-used smokepole from your Uncle Harry, be not dismayed if you espy the legend ''.300 Savage'' or ''.303 British'' on a barrel. If you choose your ammo wisely, sight the old gun in carefully and shoot it well, it will bring home the jerky. Remember also that the .307 Winchester is a quite modern cartridge intended to breathe new life into a venerable rifle. And it does. Even hampered by the use of flat-pointed bullets, the .307 will handle any deer or black bear-sized chore clear out to 250 yards or so. Only one other load ever offered in the Model 94 can equal that claim.

Don't look down your nose at any of these cartridges. They'll reach farther and group tighter than most of their owners. We'll begin with the ...

The Creme De La Creme

And that brings us to the creme de la creme of whitetail cartridges. Those loads that will do it all: reach out across a soybean field to hammer a buck to the ground; group in the right rifle at 1½ inches or better, often *much* better; provide all this at a recoil level anyone can learn to tolerate. Additionally, a couple of them are available in a multiplicity of action types and weight ranges, from 6¼-pound flea weights to 10-pound sniping rigs.

6.5 X 55 Swedish Mauser

The 6.5 X 55mm debuted in 1894, which makes it older than my aunt Lucille, but not by much. It was used by the Swedish

This hunter didn't spend all kinds of money to gain a serviceable rifle. That's a cut-down 6.5 X 55 Swedish Mauser he's holding, which happens to be a super deer load in an acceptable hunting rifle. The mouflon is the size of a small whitetail, and it was slain quite cleanly.

armed forces until only recently, when the 7.62 NATO was adopted to provide standardization between Sweden and its allies. Swedish moose hunters don't give a whit about standardization; they still take many thousands each annum with the ancient cartridge.

Original military specs showed a 156-grain full-jacketed round nose at roughly 2,400 fps in the protracted 29.1-inch Model 96 Mauser. The short-barreled (17.7 inch) Model 94 Swedish carbine produced more like 2,150 than the above mentioned number. Still, in the mid-1890s, such were pretty flashy speeds.

Norma of Sweden imports through its American marketing arm—Federal Cartridge Corp.—the 156-grain load, now shown as getting 2,650 fps in soft-point form. I have no idea how long the Norma 6.5 test barrels are, but 30 inches wouldn't surprise me. I clocked a batch of the heavy, blunt loading in an original Model 96; it showed 2,584, to my surprise. In the handier 22-inch length common to such rifles as the Ultra Light Models 20 and 24, the

Sako AIII in all its permutations and the special-run Winchester Model 70 rifles, the following: 2,387 fps in my Model 70 Featherweight; 2,392 fps in the M70 Sporter.

Better for whitetails is Norma's other 6.5 X 55 offering. Featuring a 139-grain hollow point (called a Protected Power Cavity by the ammo maker) at a claimed 2,850 fps, the light bullet carries 2,515 foot-pounds at the muzzle, 1,270 out at 300 yards. In my tests, this: M70 Sporter, 2,742 fps; Model 70 Featherweight, from a second lot of ammo, 2,590; ULA Model 20, 2,805 fps from yet another lot; 2,831 fps from my 96 Mauser with its elongated barrel. This stuff makes good deer medicine.

The 6.5 X 55's strengths are deep penetration (due to the sectional density of that 156-grain soft point), accuracy (it has long been used in world-class rifle competition by the Scandinavian countries) and mild recoil (it kicks only slightly more than the 6mm Remington, but offers a significant increase in killing power).

I shot a 468-pound black bear with the 160-grain Hornady roundnose last year. One of my bullets hit him just behind the neck, plowed all the way through the body lengthwise, exited his rump. Good penetration?

Recoil is subjective, but I've never known anyone to complain about the kick dished out by a properly-stocked 6.5. I once hunted boar with a slightly-built 12-year-old who carried a much-modified Model 96. He got his pig! Obviously, recoil was not excessive.

When it comes to accuracy, there is little that needs to be said. The Swedes wouldn't have used the cartridge in competition if it weren't up to snuff in the precision department. Even my iron-sighted military surplus job will average five-shot groups well under two inches, easily. My ULA goes inside 1¼ inches with factory hollow points, and both Model 70s group just a tenth or so off that pace.

Component bullets are available and offer a sufficiently broad selection to cover all hunting bases. Hornady's 100-grain soft point can be driven to 2,900 without pressure pains, maybe faster. For small deer, that one just might work. Better I think is the 120 Nosler Solid Base; in my Model 70 Sporter, I get just under 2,800 fps with that bullet, and superb accuracy.

Perhaps my favorite all-purpose 6.5 X 55 recipe is a goodly portion of IMR 4831 pushing the 125 Nosler Partition to 2,824 fps in my Ultra Light M20. I used that load on a big nine-point whitetail season before last. When my slug hit his chest, it blew a chunk of his heart *out on the ground*. He ran in a tight circle. I served him up another, whereupon he bit the dust as if he were sliding into home plate. Later that day I axed a five-point; one shot to the ribs, instant dead. The Nosler had sliced through both shoulder joints, taking out the tops of the lungs. It may still be going as far as I know.

The 6.5 Swede is one of the finest whitetail loads extant. If an American ammo manufacturer would add it to the line, I'd be real happy. Regardless, you'll have to look far to find a demonstrably superior deer cartridge.

7mm-08 Remington

If there is a quintessential whitetail round, the 7mm-08 Remington is it. Introduced in 1980 via the Remington 788 and Model 700 Varmint Special, the cartridge had been in use for years by metallic silhouette competitors. The nascent .28-bore didn't take off at first, primarily because it was housed in the wrong rifles. The 788, while strong and accurate, was Remington's bargain-basement offering. Buyers of inexpensive arms generally don't choose leading-edge cartridges. The heavy-barreled M700 was fine for silhouette gunners, but not so great for anyone else.

And then came the Model Seven. Remington finally got it right; the M7 is perhaps the finest all-around whitetail rifle ever produced at a popular price. Although available in several other whitetail calibers, the 7-08 is the prime choice. It is a better deer load than either the .243 or the 6mm Remington in virtually every way, and it massages one's shoulder with much less vigor than the .308. The perfect compromise.

The Remington catalog claims 2,860 fps for its 140-grain deer buster, which yields 2,542 foot-pounds as the bullet leaves the barrel. Retained at 300 yards is a 1,490 foot-pound blow, and 1,228 way out at 400. Those are serious figures.

There is a 120-grain varmint number, listed at 3,000 fps from a 24-inch pressure barrel. Although I wouldn't advise its use on deer, I figure a sizable hunk of hunters will give it a try. The hollow point slug still totes 1,316 foot-pounds at 300 yards; I suspect a deer socked in the bellows with that load will join its ancestors with commendable alacrity.

Now, just why am I so enthusiastic about the 7mm-08 Remington, you query? Not just because of its more-than-adequate deer-downing ability, its tendency to shoot very flat at all reasonable ranges, its excellent factory bullet. Nope, several other

Guide Anson Byrd borrowed the author's Ultra Light Model 20 in 7mm-08 and slew this fine eight-point buck, in the rain, which is what synthetic stocks are all about.

cartridges offer equal or greater facility along those lines. What I love about the little 7-08 is its eagerness to please. (Which is the same reason I treasure the .250-3000.) Let me explain.

In order to meet my criteria for a high "eagerness to please" quotient, a cartridge must exhibit several virtues. First, it must be uncommonly accurate. Second, it must offer a mild report and temperate recoil for its power level. Also, it should be efficient with powder, yielding ballistics out of proportion to its modest capacity. Why this last item? Because it not only makes reloading less expensive, it is much, much easier on barrel steel. Fourth, I require that a cartridge be flexible in loading, not inordinately particular about which powder is crammed down its maw. That way, should I run low of a specific propellant right before an expensive hunt, I can switch to something else without spending hour after hour at both the loading bench and the range. Finally, I look with considerable favor upon a cartridge that comes close to its factory-quoted ballistics in barrels of hunting length. Let's see how the 7mm-08 fares on all these points.

Accuracy first. The *least* accurate 7-08 I can recall was a Browning BBR that I tested for *Shooting Times* magazine in 1984; it printed 1.63 inches with its pet handload. My first two Remington 788s were in the same league; my third would print five shots under an inch regularly. A Remington Model Seven I have here will group just over an inch-and-a-half, and it is fitted with one of the slimmest barrels known to man. My Browning A-Bolt Hunter averaged .989 when fed 46.0 grains of IMR 4064 and the 115 Speer hollow point. (That is my all-time favorite 7-08 accuracy recipe.) Using 43.5 grains of Hodgdon H-380 under the 145 Speer match boattail, the *largest* group I ever shot from my Savage 110-S silhouette rifle was .80 inch. The Model 700 Varmint Special that Remington's Dick Dietz lent me grouped .69 inches for six five-shot strings with 35.9 grains of IMR 4895 and a 168-grain target bullet. My Ultra Light Arms Model 20 will stay inside ⅞ inch with its favored fodder. That's five out of nine rifles that would print sub-MOA. I can make that statement about no other big-game cartridge.

You'll have to hear the bark of a 7-08 and decide for yourself whether it is sufficiently hushed, but we can reduce the recoil to numbers. When loaded as the factory does it, with a 140-grain bullet at about 2,800 fps, an eight-pound 7-08 stirs up 15.1 foot-pounds at its aft end. Kick a 130-grain bullet to 3,000 fps from a .270 Winchester of the same weight, and you'll get tagged with 18.2 foot-pounds of thrust. That's a 20 percent increase, and its observable when you're behind the buttplate.

The 7-08 scores high in efficiency. It burns powder in less than 50-grain doses as a rule, but still gets as much speed as it needs to do its job properly. Since it has a relatively short case, it burns its propellant charge cleanly, and its abbreviated powder column is easy to ignite.

And tractability. I have utilized powders as fast as Reloder 7, as slow as IMR 4350. Medium-slow numbers like IMR 4064, IMR and Hodgdon 4895, and Hodgdon H380 all work well, giving good speed and excellent accuracy. No one-powder cartridge, the 7mm-08. Bullets from 100 grains in weight up to 175 are available from the major bullet producers, and such premium bullets as the Barnes 195-grainer are found in large, well-stocked gun shops.

And will the 7-08 reach its factory figures? Here are my chronograph results, all with the 140-grain factory big-game load: 24-inch Remington M700-V, 2,895 fps from one lot, 2,937 from a second; 22-inch Savage 110-S, 2,801 fps; 22-inch Browning BBR, 2,807 fps; 22-inch Browning A-Bolt, 2,817; 18½-inch Remington 788,2,683; 18½-inch Remington Model Seven, 2,741 fps. Thus: the 24-inch average *exceeded* the factory data (140-grain soft point at 2860 fps) by 35 fps in one lot, 77 fps with a second. The 22-inch average was 2,808, only 52 fps behind factory claims, which are taken in a 24-inch barrel. Even in 18½ inches, the actual velocities averaged just 148 fps below the factory numbers. Very few cartridges can equal that record. *Very* few.

And, naturally, with handloads the cartridge is even better. The load I used on whitetails two years ago featured the 130 Speer soft point boattail driven to 3,019 in my Ultra Light Model 20. I decked a fat four-point with it, then lent it to Anson Byrd who promptly dropped two bucks, a four and an eight-point. None required a second shot.

When coupled with Hodgdon H414 ball powder, it is possible to get 2,825 fps at the muzzle with a 150-grain Nosler Ballistic Tip, and with fine accuracy. My favorite pronghorn load matches the 139 Hornady soft point boattail with sufficient IMR 4064 to achieve 2,932 fps and 1½-inch clusters at 100 yards. My pet turkey taker combines Hornady's long 175-grain spire point and just enough Hercules 7 to get around 2,000 fps. That load will dump a gobbler without expanding and tearing up too much succulent turkey breast. The 7mm-08 is nothing if not versatile.

Should you faunch for a 7-08 of your own, Browning makes

the A-Bolt for boltgun fans and the BLR for lever lovers. Sako catalogues the cartridge in the Hunter, Deluxe, Super-Deluxe, mannlicher-stocked carbine, Handy and Fiberclass (synthetic) Handy. Remington still turns out the little Model Seven, as well as a short-actioned Mountain Rifle, the synthetic FS, the M700 BDL, the Varmint Special and several versions from the custom shop, including the super-accurate 40-XB. Ultra Light Arms will happily sell you a 7-08 made up to your specs, on either the short Model 20 or the longer M24 if you want to seat your bullets way out. As you can see, there is no dearth of 7mm-08 rifles.

Which is good. It's one whale of a cartridge.

7 X 57 Mauser

The 7 X 57 Spanish Mauser was nearly expunged from the American scene during the mid-'50s, and remained dormant through the early '70s when Ruger revived it in their Model 77 and Number One. Savage picked it up in the Model 111; Winchester and Remington turned out a few thousand; and various importers stressed the efficacy of the cartridge. Its comeback began.

The famous African hunter W.D.M. "Karamojo" Bell used a 7 X 57 (called the .275 Rigby by the British) to kill the bulk of his thousand or so elephants. When this is mentioned to a layman, it makes the ancient load sound like one hell of a game slayer. It is, but it's not magic.

There were two major reasons why Bell selected the 7mm. First, it had moderate recoil and blast, and thus could be shot very accurately. Second, it fired a long, bluff-prowed bullet of great sectional density, which enabled it to bore through a pachyderm's skull to its brain. Most any other cartridge offering such attributes—like the 6.5 X 55 or the 6.5 Mannlicher—would have worked just as well. Indeed, both were used on elephant, but misfires were common with ammo used at that time. Hence Bell's reliance on his 7 X 57.

Jack O'Connor, Townsend Whelen, Harvey Donaldson and Robert Chatfield-Taylor wrote admiringly of the 7 X 57. Few diatribes were seen. And no wonder; it works. African game still falls to the old round every day, and will undoubtedly do so for decades to come for the same reasons Bell espoused: it is easy to hit with, and with good bullets will do a businesslike job on whatever it runs into.

American factory ammo for years featured just one load, a 175-grain round nose at a listed 2,440 to 2,490 fps. Because of its

This hunter used a Ruger M77 reamed to 7 X 57 Mauser to take this fine Missouri whitetail.

unstreamlined profile, it would not retain its relatively modest muzzle speed very long. By the time it had traversed 300 yards, velocity was down to only 1,600 fps, which is worth but 1,000 foot-pounds. That's no love tap, but it's no powerhouse either.

The Europeans have long loaded the 7 X 57 up to its potential. An example is Norma's 154-grain soft point. Catalogued at 2,690 fps at the muzzle, the slug holds on to 2,120 of those foot-seconds at 300 yards, for 1,530 foot-pounds. That's a 53 percent improvement on domestic ammo!

In recent years, our ammo makers have emulated the Europeans. Virtually all of them now offer a 140-grain pointed soft point at a claimed 2,660, which still carries 1,266 foot-pounds at 300 yards by Remington's reckoning, 1,330 according to Federal. Federal, incidentally, is the only company to offer the legendary Nosler Partition bullet in the 7 X 57, at least so far as I know.

It is easy to see that as factory loaded, the 7 X 57 is an excellent whitetail cartridge, though not the equal of the 7mm-08 Remington. In my chronographing sessions, these figures came to light: 140 Federal soft point, 2,555 fps; 140 Remington soft point, 2,595; 175 Remington round nose, 2,206; 175 Winchester round nose, 2,331; 175 Federal round nose, 2,360. The foregoing were taken in a 22-inch Parker-Hale Model 1100. In a similar-length Winchester Model 70 Featherweight: 140 Remington soft point, 2,595; 140 Federal soft point, 2,613; 150 Norma soft point boattail, 2,720; 175 Federal round nose, 2,390. The average 140-grain loading thus gets around 2,590, way off the pace of the 7-08 rendition of similar heft.

As usual, handloading shifts the picture a mite. Using IMR 4320 in my Model 70, I can drive the 139 Hornady soft point boattail to better than 2,900 fps with adequate hunting accuracy. A 160-grain soft point boattail can be pushed to 2,610 in my Model 70, with seemingly mild pressures.

So far as accuracy is concerned, the 7mm Mauser will hold its own with most other cartridges. The most notable exceptions in this class are the 7-08 Remington and .270 Winchester, both of which are more accurate than the 7 X 57. My Ruger 77 averages around 1½ inches with its pet loads, and my Model 70 Featherweight prints 1.38 inches with its top recipe. The best of my 7 X 57s is the Parker-Hale Lightweight M1100. With the super-accurate 115 Speer hollow point, it printed a 1.18 aggregate.

My pal Dick White has perhaps the least tempermental 7 X 57 I have tried. I spent time at the range with his gun recently, testing the 150 Norma soft point and Federal's 175 round nose. The average for both loads, including all groups fired, was only 1.38 inches. With factory ammo! One should never worry about a 7 X 57's precision. Nor, from what Dick tells me, about its effectiveness on whitetail deer!

.308 Winchester

A cartridge I've always been soft on is the .308 Winchester. It was the load chambered in my first new centerfire rifle, a Remington Model 600 given to me by Herman Atkins, my "shooting uncle." I slew my first and best elk with a .308, my second best mule deer. The second most accurate rifle I've ever owned was a .308. The first sporting-weight big-game rifle from which I managed to extract a genuine sub-one-inch group average was reamed to .308. Lots of memories there.

Olin managed to attach its name to the 7.62 X 51 NATO cartridge—for which our Armed Forces chambered the ill-fated but excellent M-14 in 1952. Good move. Since that day it has felled a mountain of big game, set a covey of world records in all types of centerfire rifle competition (including bench rest), gained a following among the paramilitary sect second only to the .223 Remington, sold many a sporting rifle of every action type, been accepted by the police for special assignments and spawned a family tree that includes such popular loads as the .243. Not bad for an unassuming little cartridge that's impeccably mannered in every way.

Original military specs for the .30-06 mentioned a 152-grain ball at a nominal 2,700 fps. The .308 was hailed as equaling those numbers, despite being one-half inch shorter. It did so by using a new spherical propellant, plus being loaded to a bit higher pressures than was the 'ought-six. Fans of the older .30-bore shouted long and loud, derided the .308 at every turn, in general raised quite a ruckus. I never figured out why.

There has been a multitude of factory loads for the .308, in bullet weights running from 55 grains up to 200. In the middle are the 110, 125, 130, 147, 150, 165, 168 and 180s. (The 110- and 125-grain loads, I believe, have been dropped recently.) Even the .30-06 can't boast such an array of choices. There isn't space here to cover all those loadings, but I'll hit the most popular ones.

The 150-grain version is listed at 2,820 fps; the 165 is shown as reaching 2,700; the 180-grain soft points are said to achieve 2,620. But will they? I recently pulled out all my chrono records

Leupold's Chub Eastman is shown with author's Heckler & Koch SL-7 chambered to .308 Win. Author had to beg and plead to get Chub to reliquish the handy carbine.

for the past few years. Then I averaged all the different brands fired in several rifles, then averaged the barrel lengths. Here's what I found: the 150-grain stuff showed a 2,706 mean, in barrels averaging 20.4 inches in length; the 180-grain ammunition managed 2,538 fps, in barrels averaging 21 inches in length. Federal's 165-grain Premium ammo clocked 2,579 fps in a 19½-inch Heckler & Koch Model 770, 2,656 from a 22-inch Savage Model 111, 2,715 in a Savage 99 with 22-inch tube.

Handloaded, the 125-grain varmint bullets reach 3,100 fps or a bit better when launched from at least 22 inches of barrel. The 150s can be driven easily to 2,850-2,900 fps from similar rifles, and the 180s will march along in excess of 2,630 with the right wattage. Good solid ballistics, not only for whitetails, but heavier game as well.

Since the .308's competition record is well known, there is little point in dwelling on accuracy. The cartridge itself is a superbly accurate one; obviously it will do well in any properly-bedded rifle. In my experience, even some *semi-autos* will print five-shot groups of 1½ inches for an average, with Savage and Browning leverguns just off that pace. Most turnbolts will stay under 1¼ inches or less with very little load development; heavy-barreled models often group inside three-quarters of an inch.

Considering all the above, plus the relatively benign recoil levels, the availability of inexpensive surplus ammo and the plethora of firearms in all price ranges and action types, you'll probably agree that you can't go wrong with a .308 Winchester.

8 X 57 Mauser

The oldest of all the cartridges discussed in this chapter is the 1888-vintage 8mm Mauser, also known as the 8 X 57mm, the 8 X 57JS and the 7.92mm. It was originally blessed with a .318-inch bore diameter, but in 1905 it was enlarged to .323. That creates considerable confusion, even to this day. If you run across a surplus Mauser rifle chambered to the 8 X 57, be certain to have a gunsmith check the bore specs *before* firing it.

Like the 7 X 57, the 8mm has been ignored for years, with no company offering pristine new sporting rifles for it in this country. Also like the 7 X 57, American factory loads are watered-down specimens designed to be fired safely in questionable rifles, not to be ballistically effective. Again like the 7 X 57, European factory ballistics are far ahead of their Yankee counterparts.

Domestically, the 8mm is offered in one guise, a 170-grain

Author took this good nine-pointer in Missouri, with a Parker-Hale 8 X 57 Mauser and 200-grain Nosler handloads. Range: about 250 yards. Number of shots: one. Good load, the 8mm Mauser. Good rifle, the Parker-Hale.

round-nosed soft point at a nominal 2,360 fps. So flaccid is this loading that it offers .30-30-equivalent energy levels at 200 yards. Norma, on the other hand, catalogues a couple of loads that make the old warhorse really prance. Foremost is a 165-grain hollow point at a listed muzzle speed of 2,850 fps, which is 150 fps faster than the *quoted* velocity for the potent .308 Winchester with the same bullet weight! Retained energy of that loading is a whopping 1,795 foot-pounds at 200 yards, 1,015 way out at 400. Thus, the light-bullet Norma loading hits harder after sailing 400 yards than the domestic 8mm versions do at half that distance. Impressed?

For heavier game, there is the 196-grain Norma soft point at a listed 2,530 fps, good for 2,775 foot-pounds at the muzzle. That's in .30-06 country, fellows, which ain't bad company! If zeroed for 200 yards, the 165-grain Norma load is said to be just 3.7 inches down at 250, 9.4 at 300. That's plenty flat for normal whitetail gunning, and virtually identical to the 150- and 180-grain .308 Winchester factory figures.

I chronographed a sampling of each of the Norma bullet weights in my Parker-Hale Model 1200 Super, which wears a 22-inch barrel. The 165-grain version hit 2,700 fps, with the 196-grain round nose getting 2,513. Not quite up to par, were they? Nonetheless, the Norma 8 X 57 ammo is good stuff. Winchester 170-grain soft points hit but 2,197, which is as far off quoted data as the Norma ammo, but Remington's 170-grain Core-Lokt came close at 2,321 fps.

None of the factory ammunition was particularly accurate either, at least in my Parker-Hale. The 196 Norma round nose was best by a slim margin, averaging 2.20 inches for eight five-shot strings. The Remington was next at 2.31.

As always, handloads tell the tale. With a stout portion of IMR 4064 under the 200 Speer Spitzer, I managed 2,488 fps and a 1.41-inch group average. Switching to the 200 Nosler Partition Spitzer, groups increased only slightly to 1.44 inches, with the muzzle speed at 2,515. That was my best effort in the Parker-Hale. So I took it hunting.

I was sitting in an elevated stand in Missouri, overlooking a creek bottom. A doe or two and a smallish whitetail buck had been feeding since daybreak, but nothing I wanted to shoot. I had been told that the distance from my aerie to the creek bank was around 175 yards. I perched in my stand and pondered. Didn't look like 175 yards to me. More like 250 or so. But what did I know?

After a half hour of fidgeting, out walked a fat nine-pointer. He dropped his head to munch some weeds while I looked his shoulder over through my scope. I held low due to the steep downhill angle and turned loose a 200-grain Nosler soft point. I heard the wet *plop* of impact as I slammed back my bolt, belted in a fresh round, peered through my scope just in time to see the buck take one convulsive leap out of sight. It didn't take me long to get down the hill!

There he lay, dead as a fire hydrant. My slug had broken his near leg just below the shoulder joint, bulled its way through the top of the heart, pulped the off leg on exit. His frantic leap had propelled him 25 feet, where he landed in a heap with both front legs folded crisscross beneath him.

I had nearly missed his chest. Holding for 175 yards (it was nearer 250, as I'd suspected) my bullet had dropped lower on his body than I'd intended. I relearned a valuable lesson: range estimation is critical, especially at the outer limits of effectiveness of one's rifle and cartridge combination.

In Wyoming, I took a young pronghorn buck with that same gun and load, at perhaps 325 yards. I had to hold a bit high, of course, since the Nosler strikes from 12 to 14 inches low at that range as I had it zeroed. Took several shots, despite the fact that the first one took out a portion of one lung. I was stretching the gun and load, which is imprudent and almost never completely successful. Another lesson: a 2,500 foot-second cartridge is not a true long-range load.

Of course I *could* have been shooting a 150-grain soft point, at about 400 fps faster. And *should* have been. Had that been the case, I'd have zeroed the rifle for a bit longer distance, and had only six or seven inches of drop to contend with. Better all around, for me *and* the antelope.

I fully intend to hunt deer and sundries with the 8 X 57 again. Next time I'll use a lighter, flatter-shooting bullet, but that's the only change I'd make. It's a good, dependable, adaptable cartridge that is seldom appreciated in the United States. It should be.

That covers the whitetail cartridges. There are plenty of other good loads, of course, but I consider them to be combination cartridges for both deer *and* bigger game, or to offer no advantages over the ones we've discussed. Either that, or they are simply too esoteric for inclusion here. We will discuss other loads in appropriate places further on.

Confused?

Now that we've looked at what I consider to be prime whitetail cartridges, perhaps you are a bit confused. Sure, we've covered plenty of ground, canvassed a multitude of loads and looked at all kinds of ballistics, but maybe that has muddied the waters for some of you. What you want is a list of the *best* cartridges for whitetail gunning, not *all* the cartridges for said persuit. Okay. Let's narrow it down. But remember, what follows are *my* views, not necessarily those of other hunters, writers or readers. So let's take the bull by the headgear.

The "Best" Whitetail Cartridges

First we'll cover the specialty items, those guns and loads of limited and specific intent. They have virtually no reason for existing in the whitetail battery other than one, but for that singular purpose they are the best there is.

For still-hunting in dense brush, nothing is quite as good—all things considered—as a Ruger .44 Magnum semi-automatic

Author opines that the defunct Ruger .44 Carbine was the finest rig ever for rainy-day still hunting. Although this young fellow prefers a scope, Harvey likes his to wear a peep sight to alleviate any worry of condensation on the scope's lenses.

carbine mounted with a large-aperture receiver sight and a big white or gold front bead. I've tested it, and *nothing* is quicker to shoulder and fire accurately than the little Ruger. Some, like the Remington Model 7, the Ultra Light Arms Model 20 and the Marlin and Winchester leverguns, are close. But the first two are best used with a scope, and the second pair are heavier than the Ruger, slower for quick follow-up shots and kick a bit more in their more potent chamberings. Admittedly, the difference is slight and might never cost a hunter his deer, but it *is* there.

The reason I would eschew a scope on my ideal still-hunting

Although the cartridge isn't discussed in detail in this chapter, the 7mm Remington Magnum is the author's pick of long-range whitetail loads. This is a typical Big Seven, the Model 70 Winchester.

rig is that often the most productive time for such a method is in a drizzling rain. Aside from using scope caps, I have never found a satisfactory and successful method of keeping scope lenses drip-free when the humidity is 110 percent. So why not use scope caps? Because they slow you down when you need to snap off a shot.

One problem with the Ruger: it is no longer made. However, I see them frequently at gun shows and on the used-gun rack in gun shops. If I had to recommend a currently-available rifle for still hunting, I'd have to go with the Marlin 336. I would choose either the .35 Remington or the newer .356 Winchester (discussed in detail in Chapter Six) and not be unhappy.

For my long-range deer sniping, I would lean to a 7mm Remington Magnum. I have no trouble handling its recoil in a normal-weight rifle; it is plenty accurate for long-range work; it has worlds of power. Most importantly, it shoots very, very flat if loaded correctly. When a 140-grain Nosler Ballistic Tip is started on its way at 3,300 fps, it drops only 14.9 inches at 400 yards, assuming a 200-yard zero. If the rifle is sighted in four inches high at 200 yards, the 400-yard drop will be less than nine inches. For reaching out to touch something on the far side of 40-acre field, such a load works best.

But, you say, I haven't even *mentioned* the 7mm Magnum as a whitetail cartridge. You're right. It *isn't* a whitetail load. Nonetheless, if one needed a true long-range deer rifle/cartridge combo, it's what I would pick.

Here's why. Once upon a time I spotted a pair of deer 250 yards away, standing in the shadows at the edge of a soybean field.

They also spotted me, and stood side by side to look me over. At the time, I figured they were both facing me. Unfortunately, such was not the case. They were standing broadside to each other, but one was facing the treeline. Feeding. I couldn't see its head. The other watched me.

I settled into a comfortable position, looked through my riflescope. The gun was reamed to the .280 Ackley Improved, a wildcat cartridge beloved by ace gunsmith Kenny Jarrett who had built the rifle. It was stoked with 140-grain Nosler handloads that were good for around 3,100 fps, not far behind the speeds achievable when fired from a 7mm Magnum.

I aimed at what I believed to be the chest of the larger deer, and tossed a bullet across that field. I heard the hit, like an ax into soft wood. One deer humped up, stood spraddle-legged; the other ran off. Then another! What? Three deer?

The wounded deer stood still, all hunched up, for as long as it took me to work my bolt. I broke its neck with the next shot. Its pals left the arena.

A gut shot! I was crestfallen. It was simple to reconstruct the scene. What I had thought was *one* deer had been *two*, standing so close as to blend together in those deep shadows. The rump of the nearer animal had been even with the chest of the other. When I took aim at what I thought was the buck's chest, I was actually shooting at the paunch of the rearward-facing deer on the left. And that's right where my bullet went.

The point? Well, I have hit more than one deer a bit too far back, much to my chagrin. Never before had an animal so stricken failed to run off immediately. In this instance, the deer was too badly hurt to gallop off, thus enabling a quick follow-up. That's why I like a little bit more punch than necessary for long-distance work. If I hit a deer on the edges, that extra pizzazz just *might* anchor it long enough for a finisher.

It is not something to rely on. Precise bullet placement is the only way to go. I simply look on it as a bit of inexpensive insurance.

There are too many good 7mm Magnum rifles available to pick just one. I demand at least 24 inches of barrel. The 28-inch length of the Browning 1885 single-shot would not be remiss, although I'd be concerned about the single shooter's sluggish second-shot capability.

My final single-purpose item would be strictly limited to hunting before coursing hounds. I seldom do that any more, but when I do I have a Browning BAR .300 Winchester Magnum in my mitts. When a deer is being hounded (beg your pardon) by dogs, it becomes aggitated and is almost always running when the hunter spies it. Under such circumstances, it is sometimes tough to drop quickly, even with a perfect lung or heart shot. I want all the power I can muster in a quick-firing package. Hence the Browning auto. A side benefit is the BAR's gas operation, which assuages the recoil to a marked degree.

Now, for the average deer hunter at normal ranges under usual conditions, I would choose either the 6.5 X 55 Mauser or the 7mm-08 Remington. Both have sufficient power to make clean kills as far out as the average gunner should be shooting, say 300 to 350 yards *maximum*. Recoil, as we've seen, is manageable to grown-up shoulder muscles, barring injury of course. More bullets are available to the handloader in 7mm caliber than 6.5, which is to the 7-08's favor. Twice the factory big-game loads are offered in the 6.5 than for the 7-08—two to one. Remember, the 120-grain Remington hollow point is *not* a deer load. Actually, I'd toss a coin for the difference except for one thing: the 7mm-08 is turned out in more rifle models and action types than the 6.5 X 55. Unless the rifle of choice is an Ultra Light Arms, which is made in both calibers, I suppose the little Remington 7mm is the winner in the all-purpose whitetail cartridge sweepstakes.

For the young, recoil-sensitive novice who will restrict his or her shots to 100 yards, and most commonly be under close supervision, I would lean reluctantly toward the .223 Remington if my charge were mature enough to handle a semi-auto. For the expert who likes to wait near a watering hole or sit on a stump deep in the woods, and who will pick his aiming spot very carefully and shoot only at unexcited deer, a turnbolt .223 or 6 X 45 wildcat would work very well. (I've taken eight head of big game with either the 6 X 45 wildcat or the similar 6 X 47, at ranges past 200 yards in some instances, and on animals up to an estimated 290 pounds in live weight. If the bullet is placed right, such mild loads will kill quick and clean. The emphasis here is on shot placement and anatomical knowledge, which is why I said these loads were for the expert.)

The .22-250 will work as well as the above, certainly, with the right loads. But it isn't necessary under the conditions described; it's louder than either of the foregoing duo; it belts you harder; practice shooting is more expensive; wear on barrel steel is much more pronounced. Besides, the noise and recoil of the .22-250 is

The Remington Model Seven chambered to 7mm-08 is a leader in the pack of ultimate whitetail hunting rigs.

edging up into .243 territory, so why not choose that worthy.

For the youngster who can stand a bit more of a bash in the chops, the Ruger Mini-Thirty—or one of the military-style rifles—in 7.62 X 39 would be a first-rate choice. Ranges should still be held to 100 yards if possible, 125 at the outside. As with the .223, practice ammo is cheap if military surplus is acceptable to you; it should be. The bark of the 7.62 is scarcely distinguishable from that of the high-pitched voice of the .223, and most folks can't tell much difference in back-end bite. And the 7.62 X 39 might be a little more sure on deer than the .223. Barring the extremely recoil-sensitive shooter, I'd go with the bitty Russian immigrant.

For the middle teen-ager or female gunner, the ubiquitous 6mm Remington is a first-rate choice. Such shooters can take game out to perhaps 200 yards if they practice regularly, and the reliable 6mm will handle its end nicely. If said hunter is also of a varmint bent, the same gun and load will work fine to 400 yards if a good frangible bullet is selected.

Of course, the .243, .250 Savage and .257 Roberts can serve the same functions about as well for all practical purposes, but handloading is required for best results. Not so the 6mm Remington.

Let's outfit a typical family of whitetail hunters. Ten-year- old Teddy totes a Ruger Mini-Thirty; he's small, but mature enough to handle a semi-automatic responsibly. His twin brother Bernie, not quite as grown-up as Teddy, uses a factory-loaded Ruger M77 International bolt action reamed to the .250-3000. Sister Sally,

The distaff hunter is best served by a moderate-recoil cartridge like the old .250-3000, the .243 Win. or the 6mm Remington.

robust and athletic at 16, shoots her bucks with a Remington M700 ADL chambered to 6mm Remington. Mom likes her Sako Fiberclass 6.5 X 55, handling it like a virtuoso violinist. Pop takes to the woods with an Ultra Light Arms (after all, he's earned such a deluxe item) Model 20 in 7mm-08 Remington. No such a disparate group of hunters was ever more suitably armed for their task—the humane harvesting of whitetail deer.

5

Cartridges For
Long Range Game

The taking of large animals at long range is perhaps the most difficult aspect of big game hunting. Several factors conspire against the hunter to make life difficult. Range estimation is risky, often virtually impossible to ascertain within acceptable limits of the rifle/cartridge combination. Wind drift is almost always a problem, sometimes the most pressing of all. Mirage becomes a factor during those rare times when the breezes are quiet.

Light conditions can be nettlesome as well, especially if the animal is in the shade while the hunter is subjected to bright sunlight or, nearly as bad, when the animal is bathed in alternating light/shadow patterns. Shooting position is equally important, and often determined by terrain.

Recoil is a significant factor. Although many of us can control a hard-kicking rifle sufficiently to hit a whitetail's vitals at, say, 140 yards, even while jerking the trigger or flinching mildly, such is not the case when our bullet must traverse three football fields or more. The gunner's skill level must be honed to a much finer degree in order to connect on a soccer-ball-sized target at 350 yards than a similar mark at 100.

Any impedimenta between you and the animal become much harder to see as the range increases, particularly if said object (such as a rock, branch or even coarse grass) is much closer to the animal than to you. Obvious but seldom considered is the fact that the

Though the selection of the right cartridge for long rang shooting is crucial, there's even more to connecting for a clean kill. Here Rick Jamison uses a rest and steadys his shot with a sling. A spotter is also helpful to aid in correction for follow-up shots.

animal can move before your bullet arrives; enough, perhaps, to move the point of impact from lungs to paunch. Finally, retained energy is crucial in making a clean kill. Let's discuss each of these encumbrances singly and briefly.

Range Estimation

Range estimation should be practiced regularly by every hunter who plans to attempt a shot past 200 yards, unless he carries an exceptionally flat-shooting rifle. Unfortunately, few of us actually do practice.

Many factors hinder correct range estimation, a few being: the size of the animal being hunted, which can vary tremendously even within a given species; the topography, not only in relation to the lay of the land, but to the presence of trees, large rocks or anything else that can assist the nimrod in guessing the size of the animal; the light conditions—things appear quite different on a cloudy day than they do when brightly sunlit; the depth perception of the individual trying to judge range.

There are range finders available on the market, some at a reasonable cost. In my experience, those I can afford are insufficiently accurate beyond 200 yards or so, which is when I need them most. The precise military range finders are too expensive for anyone but an oil-soaked sheik, so provide no service for most of us.

Some rifle scopes have range-finding reticles or other geegaws in their interiors; some of these are a real assistance. When coupled with the user's experience at judging distances, such aids can narrow the estimate from maybe a 20-percent error to 10 or 15 percent, which under certain circumstances could spell the difference between a killing hit and a wound.

However, range-finding devices have problems of their own; they are not only clumsy to use, but time-consuming as well. Ofttimes, an animal can lie down and take a nap while you fiddle with your ranging device; more likely, it will depart the premises.

Range-finding reticles are a little better, but still require: 1) a variable scope, which introduces its own set of bugaboos; 2) the use of at least one hand to operate, when the best place for said appendage is on the rifle.

In my opinion, there are two ways to put the odds in your favor when it comes to long-range hitting. First, you should choose the flattest-shooting rifle/cartridge combination possible, and load it with the correct ammunition. Second, practice range estimation as much as possible in the area you will be hunting. Oh, I also advise cheating whenever possible. How can you cheat? Here's an example.

Where I hunt in eastern North Carolina, I often frequent farm-access roads that are long and straight. Deer commonly cross these roads, even use them as we do, for unencumbered travel. (Once you step three feet off these byways, the foliage swallows you up.) Deer can be spotted with optical assistance as far as two miles away, let alone 400 yards, and they generally look much closer than they actually are. So I cheat.

Power lines flank some of these roads, marching alongside mile after mile, each pole 100 yards from its fellows. I have made more than one successful shot while sitting at the edge of such an access road, on a whitetail whose proximity I had correctly estimated—within 20 yards or so—by counting the poles that separated us. If, for example, the deer in my sights is standing about halfway between the third and fourth pole from me, I can figure him for 350 yards, plus or minus, and be about on the money. It works, and it illustrates how to cheat when you can. Anything that reduces the risk of a wounded animal should be embraced like manna.

Although it may smack of heresy, I prefer a fixed-power scope to a variable for long-range work. Why? Because it is easier to get to know exactly how a specific critter looks at varying ranges. If one uses a variable scope and keeps changing the power when viewing distant objects, said viewer can't get a "feel" for how his quarry should look at a specific distance. For example, if you look at enough mule deer at 200 yards through your 4X scope, you'll soon memorize just how big they are supposed to appear. Then, if they look noticeably larger, you'll know they are closer. And vice versa.

On the other hand, if you spot a buck at 4X, then turn the dial to 9X to scrutinize him more carefully, then switch down to 6X to take the shot so that your body's tremors won't be so obvious, you'll never learn how a mule deer buck is supposed to look at a given range when your scope is at a set power. Moral: Use your binoculars for scrutiny, your rifle scope for shooting.

Actually, as we'll discuss later, I feel that the big game hunter should concern himself with only one range: the distance past which he should never shoot at an unwounded animal. Such a range is determined by factors we will now address.

Wind Drift & Mirage

Wind drift, and to a lesser extent, mirage, is nearly always present to one degree or another, and the long-distance rifleman must learn to contend with them. If he or she doesn't practice "doping" the conditions, then shots past 200 yards or so should not be attempted except under moderate wind or mirage conditions. The heavier the winds, the more our hunter should resist any temptation to shoot.

The competitive rifleman learns to deal with wind and mirage as part of his training, but the target panner is a *shooter*. The antelope hunter is not always (or, alas, even *often*) a conditioned, practiced shooter, so isn't likely to have acquired much in the way of wind-doping skills. Sad, but true. And the worst part of it is that the competition gunner will only drop a point or two, at worst lose a match, if he reads conditions incorrectly. Should the long-range hunter flub his shot, he can cause undue pain and suffering to a fine game animal.

Wind-drift tables provided in ammomakers' catalogues and the reloading manuals are helpful to be sure, but do you know what 8.9 inches looks like on a big-game animal at 350 yards? Or 14.2 inches? I don't. And what if the wind isn't blowing from a 90-degree angle, or how about if it's shifting every few seconds, or blowing in different directions between you and your target? Not only can all these things happen, they are likely to happen.

The bottom line on wind and mirage is this: If there is much of either present, and you are not accomplished at reading prevailing conditions, *do not attempt a long shot*. Period. And, you ask, how long is "long?" It depends entirely on... you guessed it... prevailinq conditions. All you need to know is whether the wind is too strong for you to be certain of a telling hit at whatever range you are considering. If that certainty is not present, try to close the distance by stalking carefully or waiting patiently if the game is moving toward you, or simply pass up the shot altogether.

Light Conditions

Light conditions are something you can do little about. You might try to change your position, placing the sun at a more advantageous angle. You could wear a wide-brimmed hat to keep the sun out of your eyes, and sun glasses. All these things can help, but if you're already in the field with no hat or glasses, or if the animal you are watching is also watching you, then the foregoing advice isn't worth much. The moral is to plan ahead, trying to use the light to your advantage, realizing that the game is going to do likewise. Oh, and wear a hat that'll keep your orbs in the shade.

A factor that actually has little to do with lighting conditions but which is dependent on visual acuity is the color of the animal. A grey mule deer will stand out less sharply against his habitat than will a glossy black bear. A white mountain goat will be more difficult to spot amidst deep snow than against a rocky mountainside, both of which complicate range estimation. Generally, the better defined the animal, the closer it will appear.

Shooting Position

One's shooting position is, naturally, very important in determining where the bullet will go. Some type of solid but

When it comes to long-range hunting shots, the author encourages cheating any way you can to improve bullet placement. Here the author's friend and fellow NAHC member Rick Jamison uses a bipod to steady his aim. Use any method available to help you put your bullet precisely where you want it!

resilient rest is best, with prone next. A bipod or some other artificial support can be a big help. Unfortunately, sometimes the terrain will prevent any of the foregoing, forcing the gunner to adopt a sitting position, hopefully with a tight sling. If the grass is high, or short shrubs block the view, or if the animal is about to depart, an offhand shot might prove necessary.

The above positions are listed in order of precision, with the solid rest being most accurate and offhand the least. Concomitantly, the range at which our attempt will be made should decrease proportionally to the increased difficulty of the shot. Whereas a good, experienced shootist might well connect under ideal conditions on a 400-yard animal when firing prone with his rifle rested on a daypack, the same gent could have difficulty placing a telling shot at 150 yards if compelled to fire offhand. Such considerations must always be taken into account when sizing up an attempt. If things don't add up in the animal's favor, a closing of the distance is in order.

Recoil

Recoil is a factor that can't be ignored. As we will soon see, a cartridge that retains a significant portion of its initial energy is needed for long-range success on mule deer or caribou, and such a cartridge must possess creditable ballistics to begin with. In addition, our long-distance load must shoot flat, *the flatter the better*. High residual energy and a taut-string trajectory go hand in hand with increased recoil. Increased kick makes precise shooting more difficult, for everyone. Now, some folks' recoil tolerances are higher than others, for various reasons, but all of us do better with firearms that don't hurt us. Engrave that in stone.

It is easily seen, then, that the hunter must balance the need for high retained energy and scant bullet drop with his own ability to withstand the abuse of recoil. Otherwise, we could all tote rifles chambered to the .50 caliber machine gun cartridge, and worry not about energy or trajectory, just our hitting ability. Obviously, such is not the case. (Lest you think I jest, there is a cabal of hunters who think the Big Fifty just right for long-range gunning of plains and mountain game. A quick look through the catalog section of *Gun Digest* will provide the name of a manufacturer or two.)

Shooter Skill

It should go without saying that the skill of the shooter is the single most important aspect of the long-range shooting equation. In order to become a skilled tennis player, one is expected to spend

In some calibers, recoil can be a bugaboo of long-range shooting. Bob Nosler is shown here with his pet mule deer rifle. Note the muzzle brake designed and built by his dad, John, who started Nosler Bullet Company.

hours on the court, dollars on proper coaching, not to mention having an aptitude to begin with. The Olympic diver does not emerge from the womb able to perform a flawless half-gainer. But we hunters, it appears, are all descended from Natty Bumpo. Not only can we glide silently through the glen, spot unerringly any animal within three-quarters of a mile, hear the slightest scraping of a squirrel's claw high in a sweetgum, but we can all shoot the eyes out of a gadfly at 90 paces. It's our birthright as Americans!

Horse excrement. If you want to be a fine shot, you'll have to practice. A lot. As in any other sport, if you possess the right combination of attributes, it will be easier for you to become a crack shot than for someone less blessed with genetics. Still, you will have to stay tuned up or your less fortunate crony will surpass you by dint of practice, not good fortune.

One way to get in the requisite practice is to purchase a .22 rimfire rifle similar in weight and handling characteristics to your big-game gun. That works pretty well at first, but does naught to inure you to recoil. Better in my view is to choose a caliber for which inexpensive ammo is readily available, like the .308 Winchester, or to take up handloading.

What's Between You And Your Target

The problem of bullet impediments, such as twigs and the like, is not so insoluble as many other hindrances to your bullet's travel. The key is to watch out for them as best you can, because that's about all you can do, except maybe have your partner watch out for you.

Let me spin an anecdote to illustrate my point. Although it didn't involve big game shooting, it's a perfect illustration of the care that must be taken when gunning for game at long range.

My woodchuck hunting partner, Bob O'Connor, was zeroing in on a fat whistlepig that was feeding unaware perhaps 350 yards away on a pastured slope opposite the one upon which we were perched. I was watching through the binoculars. Bob, as is his habit, was busy fidgeting and complaining and fussing with his gear and querying me as to what the chuck was up to now. I advised him that said rodent was munching and rambling, bent for a segment of pasture blocked from Bob's view by the uppermost foliage of a huge oak tree that sprouted from the valley floor about halfway between us and the groundhog. From my vantage point, some 20 yards to Bob's left, I could see all of the pig; O'Connor, however, had a problem. The left edge of the treetop obscured

This is what most western hunting is all about: glassing for game. The hunter not only needs to locate game, but determine what kind of obstructions lie between the bullet and the critter's vitals.

about half of the chuck. Bob was intent on hurrying off his shot, so he did.

At the ear-splitting crack of his .220 Jay Bird (a wildcat cartridge) a branch broke off near the crest of the oak and tumbled slowly to the ground. As a result of this unscheduled deflection, Bob's bullet hit nowhere near the pig, which fed on out of sight unalarmed.

So what should Bob have done? Either fired before the chuck became screened by the branches or moved his position to a point offering a clear, unobstructed view.

Animal Movement

One factor that is seldom considered when shooting at long range is animal movement. Believe it or not, an animal can move sufficiently *during the time it takes your bullet to reach it* for a good killing hit to become a slow, painful death. For example, let's suppose our hunter is toting a .30-06 Springfield loaded with a 165-grain spitzer leaving the barrel at 2,800 fps. That speedy, pointed slug will use up more than one-half second in flying from the muzzle to an animal 400 yards distant. Thus, if the critter is about to take a step just as the trigger is pulled, it can shift its moorings amply to cause a poor hit. There's nothing the hunter can do about it, since it is pure happenstance.

Other Long-range Gremlins

Retained energy is extremely important, and the amount required is dependent on the size and tenacity of the game. We'll examine that subject when we begin our cartridge discussion in detail. Trajectory considerations hinge on cartridge/bullet choice, so I'll demure on that subject as well. But before we leave the matter altogether, let me toss in a few more gremlins that the long-range shooter must allow into his life, though it's beyond the scope of this chapter to delve into them deeply. To wit: the excitement level of the hunter; the difficulty in identifying at long range whether an animal is of trophy size or simply mediocre, in fact whether it is even legal; whether the shot is uphill or down, and at how steep an angle; the hunter's level of exertion at the time of the shot; the density of the air where the hunting is taking place (Is it the same as when the rifle was sighted in?); whether proper zeroing procedures were carried out to begin with.

Final thoughts on this long-distance business: Do your homework; practice; memorize the ballistics of your load as delivered from your rifle; study game anatomy; monitor the conditions—wind, mirage, lighting—and learn to read them; choose a flat-shooting cartridge that hits hard way out there. Most importantly, *know when not to shoot.*

On to game and guns.

Pronghorn Antelope

Jack O'Connor once wrote, in a little tome entitled *The Hunter's Shooting Guide,* this:

"Pronghorn antelope are shot at the longest average range of any North American game animal. After reviewing my own experience I would say that most antelope are taken at 250 to 275 yards. Others are shot—and shot at—at much greater ranges. Because the antelope is an open-country animal it is seen at a distance and many hunters are tempted to blast away out of range."

As usual, Jack was right. I've just averaged the ranges at which my last half-dozen pronghorn were slain. The mean came to 280 yards. Since most of those shots were taken at estimated distances,

I could be off a yard or three on the long side, which would put me right in the middle of Jack's yardage claim.

There's a legion of good antelope cartridges out there, beginning with the little wildcat 6 X 45 and ending with whatever the shooter happens to own. I'd place the upper limit for a pure pronghorn rifle at the .270 Weatherby, but such a potent—and *loud*—load is certainly not requisite.

The .22-250 and .220 Swift will work on pronghorn at modest ranges, but neither has a surfeit of energy as the distances lengthen, and both are more wind-sensitive than is ideal for the Western plains. If the hunter is an experienced and successful varmint gunner who has the judgement to pass up risky shots, either of this duo will harvest the game. But there are much better loads.

The .243 Winchester, 6mm Remington, .250-3000 and .257 Roberts work great on pronghorn. My pal Gary Sutherland and his sons Dan and John like the .257 Roberts. They use varmint-weight projectiles to flatten trajectories a bit. Penetration on broadside and facing shots is generally adequate with such bullets, so long as major bones are not encountered. I would not recommend raking shots (from the rear forward, usually through a section of paunch) with true varmint bullets; there simply isn't enough sectional density.

Were I to unleash one of the 6mm twins on a pronghorn, I'd likely choose the 85 Speer spitzer boattail or the similar Nosler Solid Base, and stoke them as hot as accuracy and pressure would permit. In factory form, I'd lean to the 80-grain Federal soft point in both.

With the .25-bores, I'd handload 100-grain Nosler Ballistic Tips. I would not hunt long-range game with .250-3000 factory ammo except under rare circumstances. The 100-grain fodder from Federal, Hornady or Remington should serve nicely in the Roberts.

The .25-06 may well be the ultimate non-proprietary cartridge for antelope slaying. With good 100-grain factory ammo it shows only about 20 inches of drop at 400 yards from a 200-yard zero. Prudent handloaders can better this figure by four inches or so, and zeroing the rifle for 300 yards instead of 200 will give a 400-yard drop of but 9.1 inches and a mid-range rise of only 3.7. That's flat!

Considering as well the .25-06's fabled accuracy, modest recoil, plethora of affordable rifles and array of factory ammunition, it's no wonder that the venerable round is so often chosen by stalkers of the little prairie goat.

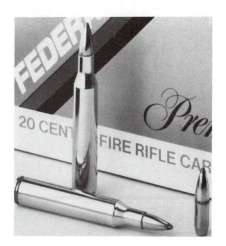

The .25-06 is one of the best mule deer cartridges, and is also near the top for antelope. A good load, especially for muleys, is the 117 Federal boattail.

However, if I were planning the ultimate antelope rifle, it would be reamed for none of the foregoing. Instead, I'd opt for one of the following two cartridges, beginning with the...

.240 Weatherby Magnum. Roy Weatherby's hot 6mm came to life officially in 1968, 13 years after its more plebeian predecessors, the .243 and the 6mm Remington. And wow, was it fast! Quoted by Weatherby were the following speeds: 70-grain bullet (now defunct), 3,850 fps; an 87-grain soft point at 3,500; 100-grain spitzer at a claimed 3,395. Even with the 26-inch barrels often provided on Weatherby Mark V rifles, such velocities are not reached, but some lots of ammo come close. The *Nosler Reloading Handbook* lists 3,332 fps from their 24-inch test barrel, with the 100-grain soft point. In the July-August 1979 issue of *Handloader* magazine, Bob Hagel shows the 87-grain factory load at 3,318 fps and the 100-grain number getting 3,198 fps, all from a 24-inch Mark V.

Averaging various loads in several guns, and considering only factory 100-grain stuff since the smaller 6mms don't offer 87-grain factory permutations, the above listed speeds shade the .243 by about 12 percent. Federal's 85-grain hollow-point boattail, for instance, trails the .240's 87-grain load by as much as 200 fps. The 6mm Remington runs closer to the .240 Weatherby, but still falls short, especially with 100-grain ammo.

Handloaded, the .240 Weatherby will exceed 3,300 fps in a 24-inch rifle if the proper propellants are chosen. The .243 will shade 3,000 in most rifles with the right powders, and can run to 3,050 or so in some. Just ahead is the 6mm, which is capable of about 3,100 if you hold your mouth right. Thus, I'd say that when all are correctly nourished, the .240 will outdistance the lesser duo by 200 fps on average.

So what does that mean in trajectory and retained energy? Well, according to the *Nosler Reloading Manual, Number Two,* the difference in 400-yard drop from a 200-yard zero is on the order of three to four inches, depending on the exact speeds attained in each of the three cartridges and assuming the use of the 100 Nosler Solid Base. The difference in 400-yard energy runs from about 160 to more than 200 foot-pounds.

None of the .240 Weatherby's advantages are earth shattering, but neither can they be ignored when the supreme cartridge for such a specific purpose is being sought. And of course the .240 has its own set of negatives.

First, it is available only in the Weatherby Mark V, an expensive rifle. Second, since it uses more powder than either of the competing 6mms, it is not only louder, but more corrosive to barrel steel. Third, ammunition is much more expensive to purchase, and the .240 costs a bit more to reload than the .243 or 6mm. Finally, ammo, dies and rifles are more difficult to come by, although by no means impossible.

If I were planning a rifle to be used specifically on antelope, for shots come-what-may, and I wanted a .24-caliber, I'd look long and hard at the .240 Weatherby, weighing carefully its advantages and its drawbacks. But then I'd also consider the...

.257 Weatherby Magnum. One of the earliest of Roy Weatherby's cartridges was the quick, brassy .257 Magnum. It was gestated around 1944, about a year before Roy went into the gun business commercially. For years it was the *bona fide* gee-whiz speedster in the American family of big-game cartridges. It still is. The .257 was based on a shortened .300 Holland & Holland belted case, blown out to reduce the body taper. It of course features the trademark Weatherby double-radius shoulder, and will work in standard actions such as those intended for the .30-06 or 7mm Remington Magnum.

Weatherby quotes thus: 87-grain soft point, 3,825 fps; 100-grain soft point, 3,555; 117-grain round-nosed soft point, 3,300 fps. All these loads give energy levels in the 2,800 foot-pound range or a bit higher. But will they do so on an

Tad Hall, son of famed Tom Hall of Weatherby, popped this nice antelope buck at 313 long paces with the .257 Weatherby Mark V shown. The .257 Mag. is likely the ultimate long-range antelope cartridge.

impartial chronograph? My Oehler says not quite. They will, however, manage 3,730 fps with the 87-grain load, 3,550 from the 100 grain and 3,277 fps from the 117 round nose—all in a 26-inch Mark V. Wow! Pretty close. Much closer than most magnum cartridges, that's for sure.

Handloads are good, but in this particular cartridge not as quick as factory stuff, at least not in my experience. My top 75-grain varmint load reaches but 3,713 fps, which is slower than the factory 87-grain version. I can squeeze but 3,373 out of a 100-grain Hornady soft point, while Weatherby manages 3,550 in the same gun! A bit over 3,230 is possible with the 120 Hornady hollow point, which I suppose about equals the slightly faster but also lighter factory 117-grain iteration. The only instance in which I could exceed the factory stuff's delivered energy levels was when I compared my 120-grain handload to the 117 factory round nose: 2,785 foot-pounds to 2,783. The highest energy of all came from the 100-grain Weatherby load, at 2,794.

Thus, if I were planning a pronghorn foray and wanted as much in my favor as possible, I would tote a rifle reamed to .257 Weatherby Magnum, and stoke it with 100-grain factory ammunition. Someday, I might happen upon a handload that equals the factory 100-grain load, but I doubt it. Until then, I will plug happily along with Weatherby ammo, at least for long-range plains game.)

Interested in the down-range ballistics of the above load? Here they are, assuming a 300-yard zero: rise at 100 yards, 2.6 inches; rise at 200 yards, 3.4 inches; drop at 400 yards, 8.3 inches. Retained punch out at 400 is a healthy 1,260 foot-pounds, plenty for the toughest pronghorn if he's hit right.

Imagine, you could hold one-third of the way up the body of a broadside pronghorn without worrying about drop unless you figured the range longer than 350 yards. You could then hold a couple of inches below the hairline and be on the money clear out to 400 yards. Is that a flat trajectory?

Accuracy in my test .257 was just fine, thanks, with the 100-grain hotshot going around 1¼ inch at 100 yards, for an average of five-shot strings. Top handload bested that only slightly, going 1.23 inches.

One caveat: the .257 Weatherby is loud. *Real* loud! When shooting one at the range, I wear both ear plugs and muff-type protectors. Further, I would never fire a .257 Mag. in the field without at least using ear plugs, unless the situation was an emergency. Although the .257 Magnum shares with all its siblings in the Weatherby family the problems of ammo and firearms expense, in this case I feel it may well be worth it for the serious trophy hunter of pronghorn antelope.

To put it succintly, the .257 Weatherby Magnum is the premier pronghorn cartridge.

Other Antelope Loads. There are, of course, other cartridges well suited to antelope gunning at normal ranges—say to 300-350 yards—but most of them (not all) recoil a bit too much for the average gunner to hit with reliably at long range. Such loads as the 6.5 X 55 Swede, the 7 X 57 Mauser and the .308 Winchester all offer a sufficiently flat trajectory for 90 percent of all pronghorn taking, when fed proper loads. The .264 Winchester Magnum, the .270 Winchester and Weatherby, the .284 Winchester, the .280 Remington and the Big Seven magnums all shoot plenty flat for true long-range shooting, but again, they all slam back at the butt end with more exuberance than necessary for game of this size. After all, most of us don't drive carpet tacks with an eight-pound sledge.

Much of the time, when you find one of the foregoing calibers on an antelope hunt it's because its wielder uses the same gun for other game. For example, I spent a few days in Wyoming with Wilson Patzer, seeking antelope with a Parker-Hale 8 X 57 Mauser slung over my deltoid. I zapped a young buck at somewhere between 300 and 325 yards, clipping his left lung. He didn't go down at the hit, but ran toward me a few yards and stopped. My second shot took him low in the ribcage at maybe 285 yards or so.

I was using the 200-grain Nosler Partition, loaded to a bit more than 2,500 fps muzzle speed. The 300-yard drop was a little over 10 inches as I had the rifle zeroed, so I had to hold just over the buck's back to slide the big bullet home. Not an insurmountable problem at the distance mentioned. However, had the range been much farther, I likely would have passed up the shot.

The longest one-shot kill I ever made on a pronghorn—or any other animal, for that matter—was with my Ultra Light Arms 7mm-08. I flung a 139-grain Hornady soft-point boattail across 325 yards (estimated carefully) of turf, at a steep uphill angle. My bullet entered the animal's left front leg just above the elbow, chopped off the top half of the heart, perforated both lungs, broke the off shoulder. Needless to say, it was an instant drop.

The longest kill I ever made came with the same rifle and load,

Assisted on a Wyoming antelope hunt by Wilson Patzer, the author slew this buck at more than 400 yards, although he had not intended to take it so far away and does not advise it under any circumstances. Rifle is an Ultra Light Arms Model 20 in 7mm-08.

also on a pronghorn, but more by accident than design. I was backing up a fellow hunter at my guide's request. When he fired, I thought I saw the animal react to a hit. (It was probably reacting to the sound of the bullet's passage, as it was not hit by my partner.) Since the buck didn't drop immediately, I fired my "back-up" shot. I connected, but not well. We had to follow him up, finally closing to within 200 yards or so. The buck was quartering uphill, hoofing it along at a good clip, when I poked him in the left side. My slug sawed off a half-dozen ribs as if they were slats in a fence, then dug on forward, wrecked the left lung and lodged in the chest muscles. Dropped like a stone.

Two points: one, I never should have fired at such a range (estimated at 450 yards), and wouldn't have had I not thought the buck wounded; two, *long shots are lousy, no matter what load you are shooting.*

Mule Deer

The big difference between mule deer and pronghorn hunting is the vast disparity in size and structure of the two animals. An antelope is small, light, lean and thin of bone compared to a robust

This small buck fell to the author's Kimber 6 X 47 wildcat. It's based on the .222 Remington Magnum case necked up to take .24 caliber bullets. The 6 X 47 is adequate in the hands of a careful hunter.

mule deer buck, which can go to 300 pounds on the hoof in rare instances. Thus, a bullet/cartridge combination that is just the ticket for a 75-100 pound prairie goat is often too light and poorly constructed for use on a big muley.

Mule deer are often found in wooded canyons, where short-range opportunities are offered, not unlike whitetail hunting. When Rick Jamison, Bob Nosler (of Nosler bullet company), Chub Eastman (of Leupold scopes) and I hunted Colorado muleys last fall, we spent much of our time prodding scrub-oak thickets in the hope of spooking a buck toward one of our brethren. Sometimes it worked, too.

I was perched at the edge of an uncommonly precipitous rim, trying to keep from going to sleep or falling off or both, while Chub Eastman worked his way around the slope. Not long after I'd begun to warm a rock with my backside, along came a pair of nice bucks, wasting no time. I was caught unaware; by the time I'd assumed the vertical and shouldered my rifle, the duo had put sufficient distance between them and me to make the shot decidedly risky. I passed. If I had been as quick on the draw as, for example, Rick Jamison, I'd have surely bagged one of those big

As Rick Jamison proves with this beautiful trophy, the .308 shoots plenty flat for pronghorn.

fellows. (The worst part is that they were the biggest bucks by far that I saw on that trip!) Naturally, I felt a bit vapid when Chub rejoined me, asking if I'd seen the bucks he'd shooed right under my nose. Confessing that I had indeed espied the pair, but alas hadn't managed to jerk off a hasty shot, I toed the ground and tried to look sheepish. Chub, ever a gentleman, didn't rub it in. Much.

Of course, not all mule deer are found amid the junipers. Hunting one year with Hody Ewing, I sat in one Indian ruin or another, smack in the middle of a huge alfalfa field, and glassed as many as 50 deer a day. Sometimes the range was at least 1,000 yards, with no viable way to close the gap. Occasionally, an animal or two would feed ever closer to me, finally offering a 150-yard shot. My limited experience with muleys indicates that they are more often taken at fairly long range than at pitching distance.

This is the kind of country pronghorns haunt. These two hunters are putting the stalk on a small band of the prairie goats.

The year Hody and I hunted together, he tried his best to put me on a good buck, even a legal one since the weather was conspiring against us. That was a season when forked-horn bucks were not legal in Colorado; we needed to find at least a three-by-two. After many arduous days, I finally had one waltz out with a herd of does and a half-dozen small two-pointers. The bucks

This mule deer, taken at about 275 yards with a Savage 99 in .358 Winchester, illustrates two things; 1) muleys do not always require true long-range cartridges; 2) a lever action works fine out West.

Another beauty for Rick Jamison. This one taken in Arizona with a .300 Winchester Magnum and 180-grain slugs. Most folks consider that overgunned for antelope, but you can't argue with results like these.

jousted with each other, obviously in hormonal homage to the coming rut. I crawled through some high sage brush to the edge of my ruin, where an annulus of rocks was still in place after all the centuries since the Anasazi tribe ruled this area. The feeding herd milled around restively while I gathered myself into some sort of viable shooting position and centered my crosswires on the only legal buck in the crowd.

I was carrying a Heckler & Koch SL-7 semi-auto that day, chambered to .308 Winchester. While it was not exactly the epitome of long range rifles, it was very accurate and had a superb trigger. I had it loaded with enough Hodgdon H-380 to boost a 150-grain Nosler Ballistic Tip to better than 2,600 fps at the muzzle. I held on the buck's ribcage, held my breath, and let fly. The buck ran off at the strike, stopped, changed directions. I tagged him again. Too far back, but it stopped him. A third ended the ball game.

The range was just a few paces short of 200 yards; the deer was walking when I fired my initial shot; the Nosler impacted too far back. As I fired my second shot, the buck was running, and once again I failed to allow sufficient lead. My fault, not the gun's nor the cartridge's nor the bullet's. Mine.

I have shot mule deer with but three cartridges, the .308, the .270 Winchester and the .358 Winchester. Only one was killed under 200 yards, the buck I just discussed. Conversely, I have never taken one past 300 steps, although I did try once. I'll hazard a guess that my average distance on mule deer has been about 225 yards.

All this proves only one thing: if you are content to pass up long shots (past 225 yards or so), then such loads as the .243, 6mm Remington, .250-3000 (handloaded), .257 Roberts, .307 Winchester, .30-40 Krag (handloaded), .300 Savage, .303 British and 8mm Mauser are acceptable for use on mule deer. Some of these, most notably the last four, are perfectly capable of making clean kills much farther out than 225 yards, but only with top handloads utilizing the most streamlined of projectiles in modern firearms.

Although the .30-30 class of cartridges has taken a pile of mule deer, they were used mostly by experienced hunters who could get closer to their quarry than many of us. Anyone who chooses such a load today is needlessly handicapping himself.

For the average hunter, to whom 300 yards is very long range, even under ideal conditions, I would recommend the following cartridges among those we have discussed in detail elsewhere in

The author again displays his contrary nature by taking to the Western plains with a "brush" rifle chambered for a "close range" cartridge. The gun is a Heckler & Koch SL-7 reamed to .308 Winchester. It let the sand out of this muley buck quite adequately, and not at arm's length either!

this book: the .240 Weatherby, preferably with 100-grain bullets, particularly the Speer 100-grain soft-point boattail or the Nosler Partition; .25-06 Remington with bullets 117 grains or heavier; the 6.5 X 55mm Swedish Mauser, especially with bullets ranging from 120 to 140 grains, with the 125 Nosler Partition perhaps the best choice; the 7 X 57 Mauser with bullets from 130 grains up to 145 in heft; the excellent 7mm-08 Remington with the same weight bullets, and also the superb 150 Nosler Ballistic Tip; the .308 Winchester with 150-grain bullets or the 165-grain boattails, such as Federal offers in their Premium factory load; the 8 X 57 Mauser, but only when handloaded with bullets in the 150- to 170-grain range.

All the foregoing, when paired with the right ammunition, will show nine inches of drop or less at 300 yards if zeroed for 200, and administer adequate energy out there to kill cleanly with a solid hit in the thorax. Few nimrods need more than that. For some hunters, the mere fact that they are carrying a true long-range rig is sufficient inducement for them to make a risky attempt, one that surpasses *their* skill, even if not that of their equipment. Thus, the honest-to-goodness long-distance numbers should be relegated to the expert, not the average hunter, and especially not the novice.

One point about this group of cartridges: Some of them are capable of true 400-yard shooting—provided they are in proper hands, strong modern rifles having at least 22 inches of barrel and with exactly the right handloads. Most notable are the .25-06, the 7 X 57 Mauser, the 7mm-08, the .308 Winchester and perhaps the 8 X 57 Mauser if loaded with 150-grain spitzers.

And now let's look at some top-flight mule deer cartridges, beginning with what may be the most popular of all time for said fauna, and certainly deserving of the title "classic" if any round ever was.

.270 Winchester. The .270 Winchester, often known as "Jack O'Connor's cartridge" since he aggrandized it single-handedly, began its career in 1925. Today it's more popular than ever, which is no wonder considering its attributes.

Aside from the fact that the .270 was the original flat-shooting plains cartridge, it boasts these virtues: uncommonly good accuracy; moderate recoil, especially for a round that is generally considered adequate for elk-sized game; widespread availability of both ammunition and guns, in almost all action types, price ranges and countries of origin; plenteous energy levels for animals up through 500 pounds in body weight, and adequate power for even

This Montana hunter poses with a big mule deer rack. His rifle is one of the long-discontinued Swedish Husqvarnas in .270 Winchester.

heavier game, provided a good, premium bullet is meticulously applied.

When it debuted, the .270 was quoted as giving 3,140 fps to a 130-grain missile. Pretty speedy for the 1920s, when the .30-06 was considered a zippy number with its 180-grain bullet at 2,700! Later a 100-grain varmint bullet was added—said to deliver 3,540 fps—and a 150-grain soft point at a listed 2,770. This latter version was supposedly designed to allay the complaints of hunters who thought the .270 too destructive on eatin' meat. I've also heard that it was intended for deeper penetration on heavy game than that provided by the 130-grain. Other folks adduced that it was intended specifically for the woods hunter of whitetail deer and the like, since it was of round-nosed design. Your guess is as good as mine.

Most writers of the era, being a somewhat fusty lot, denigrated the upstart .270 at every opportunity. Or simply ignored it altogether. Finally, Monroe Goode descanted a few kind syllables, and the eminent Colonel Townsend Whelen climbed into the .270's corner. The new load began to gather fans instead of cobwebs.

Today, all the original ballistic bases are still covered, albeit a bit differently. The 100-grain varmint number is still with us, now shown at 3,430 muzzle speed. Of course the 130-grain soft point is the .270 mainstay, and can be had from the ammo companies in spitzer-boattail iterations as well as the original pointed flat-base configuration, all quoting 3,060 fps except for Norma, which still claims 3,140. There is now a 140-grain soft point boattail factory load from Hornady; I suspect other outfits to follow. It is catalogued at 2,940 fps. Federal offers three bullet styles at 150 grains, a flat-based round-nosed soft point, a boattail soft-point spitzer, and the Nosler Partition premium game bullet. The other companies carry the same weight, but not in such an array of choices. Norma shows their 150-grain semi-pointed soft point at 2,800 fps, with the other firms claiming 2,850. No shortage of .270 alternatives!

And what doth my chronograph say? Given 22 inches of barrel, the following speeds are about the norm for a factory-loaded .270, and were taken recently with current lots of ammunition in a Browning A-Bolt: 130 Remington Bronze Point, 2,827 fps; 130 Federal Premium boattail, 2,989; 130 Federal soft point, 2,973 fps; 130 Norma soft point, 2,977; 150 Federal Premium boattail, 2,800 fps from one lot, 2,815 with a second; 150 Federal Premium

Partition, 2,800; 150 Federal round-nose soft point, 2,805; 150 Norma soft point, 2,724. A while back, I received from a 22-inch Remington Model 700 Classic: 100 Remington soft point, 3,055 fps; 100 Winchester soft point, 3,380; 130 Winchester soft point, 2,930; 130 Federal Premium soft point boattail, 2,960.

As can be seen, Federal ammo comes pretty close to published figures with some loads. Remington's ammo is generally a bit dilatory compared to the competition. Winchester and Norma 130-grain ammo is acceptably speedy, with the Olin 100-grain rendition but 50 fps off its claimed velocity. The Norma 150-grain load fared poorly, 76 fps in arrears of factory predictions.

Proper handloads give both good speed and excellent accuracy. Ninety-grain hollow points can be driven to 3,450 fps without pressure pains, and the 100 Hornady spire point will reach 3,460 fps in my Model 700 Classic when paired with IMR 4320 powder. Top 130-grain loads run between 3,050 and 3,125 fps, depending on an individual rifle's appetite. I use IMR 4831 exclusively with that weight, although H-4831 and IMR 4350 work nicely as well. My A-Bolt likes 57.3 grains of Hodgdon's H-4831 under the 150 Nosler Ballistic Tip, for 2,844 fps. The largest five-shot string fired with that recipe measured .90 inch!

Which brings up accuracy. The .270 Winchester, in my experience, provides the finest accuracy with factory ammunition of any big-game cartridge extant. That includes such highly praised items as the .243 Winchester, the .25-06 and the .308 Winchester. My Browning A-Bolt averaged .96 inch for three five-shot groups with the 130 Federal Premium load. The worst average it has shown with any load, of 10 tried, was 1.82 inches with the Federal 150-grain boattail. That, folks, is uncommon precision.

My hunting buddy Mike Holloway owns a Remington Model 700 ADL, which he bought from a gent sorely in need of cash. Mike's rifle will routinely group five shots into three-quarters of an inch from a rest at 100 yards. It won't *average* quite so tightly, but those quarter-sized clusters are by no means rare. His pet load features IMR 4831 and the 130 Nosler Ballistic Tip; with it he decked a fat six-point South Carolina whitetail. One shot.

Two years ago, I tested a Stevens 110-K, the new (at that time) laminated-stock version of the old Savage M110. With 140 Hornady soft-point boattail factory stuff, it printed a four-group aggregate of 1.03 inches. Trying Mike's favored load, I received an average of 1.10 inches.

Now, a .243 or 6mm Remington turnbolt will do as well, but not as often as the average .270 unless said .243 or 6mm is a varmint model. The 7mm-08 Remington and .284 Winchester will match the average .270, maybe even shade it a mite, but only with handloaded ammunition. The .270 user need not reload his own ammo—nor seek someone to do it for him—in order to find a super-accurate load for his rifle.

Currently offered by domestic ammo producers are 16 different factory .270 loads. Norma and PMC list a couple as well. Virtually every boltgun maker, whether indigenous or foreign, catalogues a .270; Browning and Remington offer autoloaders; Remington makes their pump in several price brackets; Ruger and Thompson/Center offer single shot rifles. There is no paucity of .270 firearms or ammunition.

The .270 offers muzzle energies in the 2,700 foot-pound neighborhood, which is akin to that of such worthies as the .308 and .30-06. Out where the game is, a streamlined .270 bullet retains: about 2,300 foot pounds at 100 yards, around 2,000 at 200, roughly 1,700 at 300 yards and is still hanging on to nearly 1,500 out at 400. These figures are for 150-grain factory-loaded boattails. Handloads look better yet.

Kick a 150 Nosler Ballistic Tip along at 2,900 fps (which takes just the right powder, and at maximum working pressures) and you get the following retained energies: 2,457 at 100 yards, 2,147 at 200, 1,869 at 300 and 1,624 foot pounds clear out at 400. Potent, right? You bet. Three of the four Hornady 7mm Remington Magnum factory loads shade the .270's 400-yard energy by a mere 53 foot-pounds or less, and that's going strictly by *claimed* ballistics, not those actually delivered. Yes, the .270 when properly handloaded will equal or exceed many *factory-loaded* 7mm Remington Mag. offerings!

And the good ole .270 will do all this without requiring its shooter to gulp down an anodyne after an extended range session. The recoil generated by the average .270, while perhaps a bit harsh for the young or distaff gunner, is usually no problem for a healthy adult male. Muzzle blast, while not really obstreperous, is not exactly balm for the ear drums. Still, a .270 can be fired in the field a time or two without reminding its owner of the incident for hours afterward. All things considered, the .270 Winchester is never a mistake. It will reach out farther than most of us should ever attempt, is sufficiently accurate and flat-shooting and mild of backpoke to enable its use on vermin and provides enough energy for the humane harvesting of game up to elk in size. A bonus is that handloading isn't required to squeeze out most of its vitamins.

.264 Winchester Magnum. Winchester's hot .264 Magnum stepped onto the stage ostensibly in 1958, accompanied by much hoopla, although it's unlikely that rifles so-chambered graced many dealers' shelves until late 1959. I suspect that Olin was taking aim at two cartridges at once with the nascent 6.5, Weatherby's .257 and .270 Magnums. If that is indeed true, their aim wasn't too far off the mark. However, while the .264 is a potent load, it doesn't shoot quite so flat as the .257 Weatherby, nor hit as hard as the .270 Magnum. Further, it fails to live up to its ballistic claims by a goodly margin, even in 26-inch barrels. Handloading helps, but not enough to enable it to match completely its California rivals. Finally, in my experience the .264 isn't nearly as tractable in the accuracy department as most other big, belted mags.

Original published ballistics showed a 100-grain spitzer at 3,700 fps, and a 140-grain soft point at 3,200. Today, the numbers read 3,320 and 3,030 respectively, but neither of those is reached either. I checked two lots of 100-grain Winchester ammo in a pre-'64 Model 70 Winchester: one clocked 3,181; the second accomplished but 3,027, which is about what a handloaded .243 will achieve. The 140-grain Winchester ammunition gave similar dismal results: 3,012 fps with the first lot, 2,924 from the second. Remington's 140-grain Core-Lokt embarrassed itself by easing along at a paltry 2,761 fps, slower than Hornady's factory .270 Winchester loading of the same weight, even when fired from a 22-inch barrel! My point is this: If you intend to stick to factory ammo in your .264, buy Winchester 140-grain stuff. And cross your fingers.

My top handloads went thus: 100-grain hollow point, 3,206 fps with only fair accuracy. If I pushed any faster, groups suffered. The 120 Nosler Solid Base could be jacked up to 3,370 fps, while providing 1¾-inch grouping. That gains it my nomination as the top long-range deer/antelope recipe, since it's a bit faster than the .257 Weatherby will provide from a bullet of identical heft, albeit at a marked decrease in precision. Top speed with a 140-grain spitzer handload was 3,226 fps; obviously no slug. Alas, groups were so erratic I didn't measure them, and the velocity variation for five shots was an unacceptable 134 fps. Dropping to 3,026 fps—provided by 74.0 grains of AAC 8700 powder and the 140 Speer spitzer—gained a group average of 1.43 inches. Fine for game up through caribou as far away as they should be shot.

Most accurate load in my Model 70 was 59.0 grains of Accurate Arms Company's AAC 3100 under a 100-grain varmint bullet. Group average worked out to 1.33 inches. Not exactly lachrymose, but not especially laudable either. The tightest factory average came from the slow lot of 140-grain Winchester Power Points, at 1.49 inches. Tempermental, that's the best word to describe the .264 in both the velocity and precision arenas.

When it comes to killing game, the .264 has the same Jekyll-and-Hyde personality as do most of the high-speed big-game loads.

The problem is that in order to retain a raft of killing power way out yonder, there must be lots of speed to begin with. That's fine if all your game is shot from one mountain peak to another. The flip side of the coin is that if you blunder onto a critter up close, you'll reduce it to a red mist if you smack it with one of those heat-seeking missiles. Examples are in order.

Once upon a time, my pal Chub Eastman was seeking mule deer near Winett, Montana. He watched with acid stomach as five hunters zoomed up a mesa on their dirt bikes, setting the local deer herd all aboil. Presently, a much-agitated doe crossed the hogback ridge upon which rested our hero. Then a half-dozen more. Then a buck. A large buck! Chub, lulled into a torpid state by all the females, was not quite as percipient as he might have been. Nonetheless, he snapped out of his reverie, tossed up his Browning Safari grade .264, slapped the 28-inch four-pointer with one of Steve Hornady's 129-grain soft points, right through the lungs, in and out, at maybe 300 yards. The big fellow dashed 50 or 60 yards and fell dead. Eastman says the lungs poured out of that deer!

Good job, right? Right. The cartridge performed the task for which it was intended, and to perfection. Time to view Janus' other face.

A little doe stood looking at me, perhaps 100 yards away. I needed the meat; she looked tender, fryin' pan size. Off to the truck; fetch the Model 70 .264; hoof back over to the spot from which I'd seen the deer. Still there. I slipped a 140-grain Winchester factory round up the spout (the fast lot of ammo), scoped her chest, whacked her one offhand. Just a bit too far back, nicking one lung and smoking the liver. She kicked up her heels, all 75 pounds of her, and took off. I sent another Power-Point after her as she raced away, demolishing a ham. A postmortem revealed that the first shot had exited the left ribcage, leaving in its wake a shoulder entirely bloodshot.

Moral: When you hunt with the hotrod small-bore (under 7mm diameter) magnums, choose your shots carefully. Regardless of the range.

Please bear in mind that the above admonishment is not intended as a slight on the .264 Mag. I've seen similar damage inflicted by many other cartridges, including such non-magnums as the .270 Winchester. Such extreme tissue destruction is one of the primary reasons many experienced hunters use heavy bullets in cartridges capable of Mach-3 velocities with the lighter ones. The .264 is such a cartridge, so choose your bullets accordingly.

.270 Weatherby Magnum. Weatherby's .270 Magnum was, contrary to the belief of many, the first of that company's line of belted cartridges. It and the .270 Winchester are the only factory cartridges available in this country taking .277-inch bullets, as opposed to the .284 diameter of the 7mm bunch.

Based—as was the .257 Weatherby—on a shortened, blown-out, shoulder-modified .300 H & H Magnum case, the .270 has plenty of boiler room to get as much speed as pressure limitations allow.

Weatherby literature boasts of these velocities, all taken in a 26-inch barrel: 100-grain soft point, 3,760 fps; 130-grain soft point (which Weatherby refers to as "pointed expanding"), 3,375; 150-grain soft point, 3,245 fps. Those are pretty big digits! In my 26-inch Mark V, I got 3,670 fps from the 100-grain varmint load, 3,307 with the 130 grain soft point; the 150-grain version clocked 3,183, good for 3,375 foot-pounds at the muzzle. Heady figures, indeed. Average for all three factory loads fell short of the published mark by only 73 foot seconds.

Using a heavy charge of Norma's MRP, I managed to belt a 130-grain Hornady spire point out the muzzle of my Mark V at 3,353 fps, which is good for 3,246 foot-pounds and shoots flat as a Nebraska interstate. Better for larger game than mule deer, such as big bull caribou or elk, might be the 150-grain Nosler Partition. If started at 3,200 fps, the Nosler retains nearly 2,000 foot pounds at 400-hundred yards! Talk about being a death ray! Switch to the 150 Nosler Ballistic Tip, and there are still 2,021 foot pounds out at 400, and the bullet drop is only 16 inches from a 200-yard zero.

But if you desire the best combination of high residual energy and a string-taut trajectory, consider a handloaded 130-grain pointed boattail at 3,350 fps zeroed for 300 yards. At the 100 yard mark, your bullet will strike 2.8 inches high; at 200, the impact will be 3.7 inches up; at 400 yards, bullet dip will come to only 8.4 inches, and there are 2,049 foot-pounds still on tap. If you aren't impressed by such numbers, go back and peruse those for the .257 Weatherby. Wait, I'll save you the trouble. The 130-grain .270 Weatherby boasts a virtually identical trajectory but hits 63 percent harder! So, for game the size of mule deer and caribou, I'll take the .270 Weatherby and run.

Accuracy is no problem, either. My test Mark V is the second most accurate belted magnum I ever shot, going into 1.10 inches with its favorite handload. Second place recipe went 1.24 inches, and the 130-grain factory load showed a 1.22-inch mean. Two other reloads printed 1.27 and 1.28 inches, and the 100-grain factory stuff averaged 1.37. That's six out of 11 loads tried, both factory and handloads, printing inside 1⅜ inches for the *average*. Cause for jubilation, believe me.

Of course, like all magnums, the .270 Weatherby stomps a bit harder at its rear end than standard cartridges. Naught is ever gained for naught. Barrel wear is accelerated, boom exacerbated and the cost of ammo augmented considerably over that of the more plebeian chamberings.

But if you use your rifle primarily for hunting, practicing with it only once a month or so, you shouldn't wind up in the poor house. Besides, it will reach out and touch something like few other cartridges can, assuming you are up to it.

Not only Weatherby offers the chambering, either. Ruger sticks it in their Number One single shot; KDF will build you one, but not cheaply; ditto for Ultra Light Arms. Best bet if you're on a budget is a Winchester Model 70 Sporter. As for me, color me loyal. If I want a Weatherby cartridge, I'll buy it out of South Gate. Roy gets the credit for his cartridges' prowess; it's only fitting his firm should get the money as well.

.284 Winchester. The most powerful non-belted medium-sized (.308 Winchester length) rimless cartridges ever developed by a large ammo company in the United States is the .284 Winchester. Since 1963 it has been the victim of unprecedented public apathy, with only the most erudite of shooters cognizant of its existence. Builders of expensive semi-custom rifles—such as Alpha Arms—have done a land-office business peddling .284 rifles to well-heeled sportsmen who can't buy such guns from major arms producers, since none offers the load today. (Actually, Ruger made a special run of Model 77 turnbolts so-chambered in 1987. They

were scarce then, scarcer now.) Ultra Light Arms Company turns out .284s regularly; the cartridge is their number-one seller, despite the fact that the West Virginia-based outfit produces four action lengths, and will provide you with virtually any chambering extant, factory or wildcat. Someone must like the .284.

I do. So does Pennsylvania gun scribe Bob Bell, who told me that no other cartridge has provided him with such a long string of one-shot whitetail kills, 15 at the time he wrote to me, as the .284, including such belted behemoths as the 7 X 61 Sharpe & Hart Magnum. My Alaskan pen pal, E.J. Hiett, has used the .284 off and on for years, as have many members of his family. E.J. wrote: "Have been using 54.4/(IMR)4350 and the 140 Nosler Partition with good results (2,890 fps). Pretty accurate and minimal bloodshot...they don't take more than a few steps." In this instance, he is speaking of deer, but that's not all he hunts with the .284. To wit:

"I also took a little sheep trip for myself in British Columbia and took a decent bighorn with the .284...shot him at about 45 yards, a little above center of the cape line, twice. (He) turned and went about 15 yards, then stopped and rolled down the hill." E.J. enclosed a color snapshot of his ram; it went just shy of 40 inches around the curl.

The quickest I ever decked a buck was with my Alpha Arms .284. He was a sassy six-point, caught stuffing his face around 9:30 one morning in the middle of a field. I watched him from about 185 yards away, with him quartering toward me, until he lifted his head for a look around. Then I slipped a 145 Speer soft-point boattail into his chest. He dropped out of sight so fast I thought Scotty must have beamed him up! He'd died so suddenly all four of his legs were folded up beneath him as he lay on his stomach!

Since my book *Popular Sporting Rifle Cartridges* hit the stands, I have gotten more mail from readers relative to the .284 Winchester and the .250-3000 than all other cartridges combined. Obviously, the .284 has more fans than Bob, E.J., and me.

Although only one iteration is factory loaded by Winchester, there used to be two. Currently available is a 150-grain pointed Power Point at a quoted 2,860 fps. For comparison, note that the .270 Winchester is listed at 2,850 fps with the same bullet weight, the .280 Remington is shown as getting 2,890, the .308 Winchester claims 2,820 fps and the 150-grain .30-06 version is said to achieve 2,910. As can readily be seen, there is no significant difference amongst this puissant little assemblage.

I have clocked the 150-grain number in a 24-inch Shilen DGA at 2,964 fps; in my 22-inch Alpha Arms, another lot gave 2,812. One of my favored handloads features a heavy dose of IMR 4350 pushing the 140 Nosler Ballistic Tip to 3,000 fps at the nozzle of my 22-inch Ultra Light Arms Model 20. Most accurate in that gun is 58.0 grains of Hodgdon's H-4350 under the 115 Speer hollow point, with groups averaging .95 inches.

In addition to its competent ballistics, the .284 has always proven to be an accurate cartridge for me. A Ruger 77 I owned years ago showed an aggregate for four five-shot strings of 1.19 inches with no handload development at all. My Shilen DGA grouped under 1⅛ inches with more than one handload, and my Alpha Arms easily manages 1.48 with my deer-killing load, with almost no development time involved.

Any warts? Three. The first I have never experienced, but since John Wootters stressed its existence, and since I have the utmost respect for his expertise I'll give it credence here. The .284 boasts a very sharp shoulder; such an abrupt angle does not always provide evenly distributed circumferential resistance to the pressure of bullet seating. The result can be a slightly buckled shoulder and a mildly canted bullet, which does nothing good for accuracy.

Blemish number two is simply that factory ammo is, er...unimpressive in the accuracy department, not to mention sometimes hard to find. The .284 is—like the 7mm-08—mostly a handloader's cartridge unless you confine your shots to 200 yards or so. But then why choose the .284 in the first place?

Finally, a fat-bodied, minimum-tapered, sharp-shouldered, small-headed cartridge case is not the epitome of smooth-feeding configurations. Many a gunsmith has found this out the hard way.

But none of the foregoing flaws have afflicted me. All four of my .284s have worked fine, thanks, and provided me with uncommon precision as mentioned earlier. The fact that it's primarily a handloader's cartridge bugs me not, since I do reload. For the average hunter, I'd suggest passing up the .284; its liabilities outweigh its assets. But for the serious hobbiest shooter, it has much to recommend.

.280 Remington. Remington's .280, also known as the 7mm Express Remington, virtually duplicates the ballistics of the .284 Winchester, but requires a long (.30-06 length) action to do so. The .284 is short and squat, the .280 long and lean. Based on the .30-06 case necked down and slightly modified, the .280 has a

coterie of devoted and fervent followers. I'm not sure why.

Ballistically, it will do anything the .270 Winchester, .284 Winchester and .308 Winchester can do, and in most instances will manage any chore for which the .30-06 is suited. It is amply accurate for a big-game cartridge, sufficiently flat-shooting for the taking of mule deer and similar critters clear out to 400 yards with the right load, and it won't pop out your dentures under recoil. Adequate, that's the .280. It displays no verjuice whatever, simply bland competence.

Such knowledgeable gunners as Jim Carmichel espouse the .280; the esteemed Colonel Townsend Whelen doted on it (he called it the 7mm-06); Bob Nosler, the indefatigable honcho of Nosler Bullet Company, carries one regularly; Chub Eastman, Leupold's resident hunting swami, thinks the .280 is the best development since sliced beer (or is it canned bread?); Remington's Dick Dietz, a very savvy hombre and big-game slayer of uncommon experience, is the head of the ".280 Bund," or something like that. And so forth. Among the elite of Huntdom, the .280 is regarded as something of an icon.

As loaded by Remington, the .280 offers a 140-grain pointed soft point at a listed 3,000 fps, a 150-grain pointed Core-Lokt at a quoted 2,890 and a 165-grain round nose at an alleged 2,820 fps. Norma lists a 154-grain semi-pointed soft point at 2,870, and a 170-grain PPC (hollow point) at 2,710. Federal makes a Premium .280 rendition, topping the case with a 150-grain Nosler Partition at a claimed 2,890 fps. The best of the above loadings still totes 1,435 foot-pounds at 400 yards, assuming of course that the factory numbers are actually achieved. Well, are they? Nope.

In my Remington Model 700 Mountain Rifle, this: 140 Remington soft point, 2,792 fps; 150 (the 154-grain current version is obviously new) Norma semi-pointed, 2,761; 150 Remington Core-Lokt, 2,855; 170 Norma PPC, 2,595. Hmmm. Not so close, huh? Then there was my Browning A-Bolt: 140 Remington soft point (different lot from above), 2,780 fps; 150 Norma, 2,736; 165 Remington round nose, 2,593; 170 Norma PPC, 2,583. Perhaps there was an energy shortage when all this ammo was loaded? So I dug out my pristine and very rare Winchester M70 Featherweight and plied it against the Oehler: 140 Remington, 2,748 fps; 150 Norma, lot 1—2,835 fps, lot 2—2,741; 150 Remington, lot 1—2,792 fps, lot 2—2,667, lot 3—2,783; 165 Remington, 2,733; 170 Norma, 2,573. Unimpressed? Me, too.

I repaired to my file cabinets, researching the deep dark past in hopes of unearthing some .280 data that might support the factory hype. In 1983, a Remington 7400 autoloader yielded 2,673 fps from a lot of 150-grain Remington stuff, and 2,631 with a batch of the 165 round nose. No help there. So I dug even deeper. In the late '70s I tested a Remington M700 BDL, and received: 2,835 fps from a lot of 150-grain Remington ammo marked "7mm Express Remington"; 2,768 fps from a sampling of then-current 150-grain ".280 Remington" ammo in green boxes; 2,715 fps from the Remington 165 blunt nose.

Now, all the foregoing rifles were blessed with 22-inch barrels, as most factory-produced .280s are. The averages for all guns and loads look like this: 140 Remington soft point, 2,773 fps; 150 Remington soft point, 2,768 fps; 150 Norma semi-point, 2,768 fps; 165 Remington RN, 2,668 fps; 170 Norma PPC, 2,584 fps. Respectively, those numbers fall short of factory expectations by 227 fps, 122 fps, 102 fps, 152 fps and 126 fps. (Note please that I have not tried the Federal loading.)

As we have seen, it is far from unusual for factory data to be exaggerated, with velocities reached in the real world only vaguely related to press notices. However, remember if you will that the 7mm-08 Remington showed 2,808 fps with 140-grain factory ammo, in 22-inch barrels, whereas the larger .280 gets but 2,773. Bear in mind that the 150-grain Norma 7 X 57 iteration clocked 2,720 fps, only 48 foot-seconds shy of the bigger-cased .280. Look to the .270 data earlier in this chapter and you'll see that the average 130-grain factory load outraces the 140-grain .280 by 170 fps. (Those two bullet weights offer directly comparable sectional densities.) Note also that the 150-grain .270 ammo usually exceeds 2,800 fps, whereas the .280 averages but 2,768, regardless of brand. Lastly, don't ignore the fact that the short-coupled .284 averaged 2,888 fps for two lots of 150-grain factory stuff, in a mean barrel length of 23 inches. Deduct 30 or 40 foot-seconds for the added one inch of tube length and the .284 still trounces the .280 by around 85 fps.

OK, you demure, the .280 ain't so tough in factory guise, but it's a real go-getter when handloaded, right? Agreed, it's pretty good. Stuffed to the gills with just the right propellants, it will reach 3,000 fps with a 140-grain bullet. (Although some reloaders claim 3,100, the loading manuals do not bear them out. Most, in fact, hint that 3,000 fps is pushing it.) According to Speer data, a bit better than 3,100 can be achieved with their 130-grain spitzer and IMR 4350 powder. In my Remington 700 BDL, I used a maximum charge of IMR 4350 to get 2,943 fps from the 150 Nosler Partition, which is pretty speedy indeed. There's no need to quote numbers for heavier bullets here, as those of 150-grains or less are all that are needed for plains game and caribou, and some folks would include elk in that assessment if a good stout slug is chosen.

The bottom line is that the .280 Remington, when handloaded, is equal to the .270 Winchester and .284. Equal, not one whit better. The .280 does have a slight advantage on the .270 in that more 7mm bullets are available than .277-diameter ones. Big deal. How many different slugs does a hunter need? So long as there are good varmint bullets around (and there are, in both .270 and 7mm), suitable deer/antelope projectiles (there are, in both calibers) and a controlled-expansion heavy-game bullet (ditto), there is little need for more unless target shooting is on the agenda, and that doesn't affect the hunter.

Well, if the .280 is no ballistic wonder, how about its precision? Only fair, folks. Sorry. I've tested a half dozen .280s and none of them printed much under 1.5 inches at 100 yards, for an average with their *best* load. Even a much-modified (and expensive) .280 belonging to a friend grouped 1.46 inches for four five-shot strings with his carefully fabricated reloads. Only one .280 that I have fired was a stinker, but it was a self-loader. The most accurate .280 I ever tested is a Browning A-Bolt Medallion Grade, which prints 1.34 with its favorite reload, the 115 Speer hollow point over 59.0 grains of IMR 4350. Instrumental speed with that varmint concoction is 3,189 fps, incidentally. Bridesmaid in my Browning is the 140 Remington factory load, which goes 1.70 inches. Nothing else has gone under two inches in that rifle.

If the .280 isn't a true powerhouse, and if it's not especially accurate, what does it have to recommend it?

I already mentioned its virtues, way back at the beginning. It's sort of an amalgam of the so-called all-around cartridges, offering most of the features indigenous to the group. While it's not so accurate on the average (in my experience) as the .270, and isn't as proficient with factory ammunition, it is at least in the same league. And with handloads, it offers .270 power if not its precision. Gun and ammo availability favor the .27-bore as well, but the .280 can be had with heavier bullets for those who equate weight with power and penetration.

The .280 is no better on deer than the 7mm-08, but is at least as good and is available in a wider array of factory (albeit it underloaded) ammo. Plus, many .280 loads are more accurate than Remington's 140-grain 7-08 version. Handloaded, of course, the 7mm-08 leaves the .280 for dead in the precision market.

The 7 X 57 is less potent than the .280, not so flat shooting, but is at least as accurate and kicks less. The .308 clusters its bullets tighter than the .280, but won't always reach the longer cartridge's energy levels, and exhibits more bullet drop at long range. The .30-06 shoots about as flat as the .280, groups tighter on the average, but boots its user more forcefully since it's a more powerful load. The .284 is at least as good as the .280 in every practical way except rifle and ammo attainability, and comes in lightweight, short-action rifles. And so it goes, from cartridge to cartridge.

It takes no genius to discern that the .280 is indeed a distillation of all the cartridges in its class. For many hunters, such a common denominator is just their ticket: a jack-of-all-trades and master of none. That doesn't make it undesirable, by any means. Quite the contrary, in fact. But it doesn't instill it with charisma, either. Quietly competent, the .280. Like I said, adequate.

7mm Remington Magnum. When Remington announced its new Model 700 boltgun in 1962, it was offered in an equally fresh chambering bedubbed the 7mm Remington Magnum. The offspring of a combined developmental program between Remington engineers and gun writer Les Bowman, the burly belted cartridge laid the boys in the aisles. It has continued to do so to this day.

And it's no wonder. Remington's Big Seven had it all; plenty of romp and stomp and bark, all the accuracy anyone could ever use in the hunting fields and big-bore target ranges, and it was soon available from every major rifle builder in the civilized world. The .280 Remington, for which the folks at Ilion had high hopes, was left at the starting gate. Winchester's hot .264 Magnum, itself only a few years old, also took it on the chin. Yep, the day of the belted sevens had arrived.

It had been long in coming. The .275 Holland & Holland, an early British development, had fared poorly, as had such wildcats as the .276 and .280 Dubiels. In the '50s gun pundit Phil Sharpe collaborated with a Swedish ammo maker, bringing to our shores the 7 X 61 Sharpe and Hart. It enjoyed but modest success. Nonetheless, Remington remained convinced that a big-cased 7mm was just what the public needed. *Field & Stream* Shooting Editor Warren Page obviously agreed, since he published report after report of his accomplishments with the 7mm Mashburn Magnum. The stage was set.

The Remington version was in reality a member of the Winchester family of so-called "short" magnum cartridges, all based in one way or another on the .458 Winchester Magnum. Designed to work through what was then known as a medium-length action (long enough to accommodate the .30-06), the 7mm Mag. was listed like so in 1962: 150-grain pointed soft point at 3,260; 175-grain round-nose soft point at 3,020 fps. Muzzle energy for both versions was 3,540. A few years later, this latter speed was adjusted upward to 3,070 fps; I dunno why, since the original figure was more than a little optimistic. In the late '60s a 125-grain load was added, at a supposed 3,430 fps. And that, it was thought, covered all the bases.

Current thought runs differently. You can buy at your local gun emporium, the following renderings. From Federal: 140 Premium Partition at a claimed 3,150 fps; 150-grain Hi-Shok at 3,110 fps; 150 Premium soft-point boattail at the same speed; 160 Premium Partition at 2,950; 165 Premium boattail at 2,950 fps; 175 Hi-Shok soft point at 2,860. Federal also distributes Norma ammo, from whom is available a 154 soft point at a listed 3,180 fps, and a 170-grain PPC hollow point at 3,020. Remington offers a 150-grain pointed soft-point Core-Lokt at 3,110 and a 175-grain loading at 2,860. Winchester makes the same weights at identical published speeds in their Power-Point design. Hornady offers a 139-grain boattail at 3,150, a 154 soft point at 3,035, a 162-grain soft point boattail at 2,940, and the old standard 175 soft point at 2,860. (Note that no one makes a varmint load anymore, although the 139- and 140-grain numbers might work pretty well for that task.) The 7mm Remington Magnum is produced by the leading domestic makers in 14 iterations, with Norma and PMC offering five more between them, for a total of 19. That's a bunch of choices. Winchester's new Silvertip boattail should be out soon, to make it an even 20!

In a Browning Stainless Stalker, I clocked these: 140 Federal Partition, 3,071 fps; 150 Remington PSPCL, 2,940; 150 Federal Hi-Shok, 2,902; 150 Winchester Power-Point, 2,950; 175 Remington PSPCL, 2,817. In a similar 24-inch standard Browning A-Bolt, my Oehler read: 150 Norma semi-pointed (now a 154-grain), 3,124 fps; 139 Hornady boattail, 3,002; 150 Federal soft point boattail Premium, 3,100; 175 Federal soft point, 2,821; 162 Hornady soft-point boattail, 2,943. In a Browning BBR, also with 24-inch barrel: 139 Hornady, 2,895; 150 Remington, 2,992; 150 Federal Hi-Shok, 2,936; 150 Norma, 3,063; 150 Federal soft-point boattail, 3,080; 175 Federal soft point, 2,751; 160 Federal Partition, 2,833; 165 Federal soft-point boattail, 2,895. I've chronographed lots of ammo in scads of Big Sevens, but these are representative.

Averaged, the 139- and 140-grain loads show around 2,990 fps; the domestic 150-grain stuff goes just a hair under 3,000 fps instrumental speed, with the Norma ammo clocking about 100 foot-seconds faster. The 160-, 162- and 165-grain loads show a mean of 2,890 fps, with the heavy 175s averaging about 2,800. As you can see, the 139-140 loads run 160 fps below what the makers claim; the American-built 150-grain stuff averages about 110 foot-seconds off the published pace, with Norma's offering a bit less to the rear, but still not quite up to quoted snuff. The 160- to 165-grain class comes within 50 or 60 fps of notices, which is one reason this bullet weight is often considered the ultimate for a Big Seven. Averaging just 60 fps or so short of the claimed 2,860, the 175-grain bullets certainly do not embarrass their producers, either. All things considered, the 7mm Magnum is an impressive ballistic package, especially with bullets of 150 grains or heavier.

Please note that in factory guise the Big Seven gets about the same speeds from 150-grain bullets as the .270 Winchester achieves with 130-grain missiles, and extracts from the 175-grain elk busters velocities similar to those of its 150-grain .270 counterpart. Famed gun writer Ken Waters once wrote that the 7mm Magnum "...mates the striking power of a 180-grain .30-06 with the velocity and flat trajectory of a 130-grain .270." Right on, Ken.

Handloading, as you might expect, makes a good thing better. It's no trick to achieve in excess of 3,000 fps with a good 175-grain soft point over 78.0 grains of Hodgdon's H-870, a maximum load. Accuracy is generally excellent. Pairing the same propellant with the fine 160 Nosler Partition showed 3,200 fps in my Stainless Stalker, with no pressure signs. For vermin, I load the 115 Speer hollow point over 72.2 grains of IMR 4831, getting 3,451 fps in my rustless Browning, and superb grouping. Additionally, that load averages under an inch in my A-Bolt Medallion while clocking 3,324, and does nearly as well in a Browning BAR semi-auto, providing 3,360 fps and under 1¼-inch five-shot groups! When I'm asked to recommend a precise target load for any Big Seven, that's the load I sanction.

My school chum, Fred Ritter, took a Remington 700 Classic with him to Colorado last year. He filled its larder with 150-grain Federal Premium boattail soft points, then began to negotiate a mountain. Taking a breather, he spotted a pair of hunters way off in the distance. So did three buck mule deer, who hurriedly vacated the hunters' proximity. The trio hoofed it along a ridgetop; then one splintered off from the group, ran a bit, stopped in a saddle.

Fred looked him over real good; decided to take a try. The range was long; perhaps too long. Holding an estimated 12 to 14 inches over the buck's backline, Mr. Ritter touched off. His slug seemed to take forever getting there, but get there it did. The buck appeared to flinch, but didn't run off. Fred fired again. Too hot for the buck; he disappeared over the hump.

Thinking his quarry might reappear, Fred dipped into his pockets for more ammo. Must have been pretty excited; he pulled out a tube of Chap-Stick and tried to stuff it in the magazine. Didn't work out well. Eventually, he got his ammo resupply sorted out and his adrenaline rush abated. Now he could check on the buck.

One of his bullets had entered the rear of the deer's ribcage, angled forward into a lung, lodged under the off armpit. The buck, a big five-by-five with a 22½-inch spread, had run only a few yards before cashing in its chips.

That isn't the only mule deer Ritter has taken with his Big Seven. I've heard him voice no complaints.

My own bag of game grounded with the 7mm Remington Mag. is not especially extensive, but has run the gamut from groundhogs through coyotes and fallow deer, on up to whitetails. (Although I've carried one into elk country, the wapiti failed to cooperate. Cowardly lot.) Not only has all my game been killed with one shot, none took even a single step after being swatted, not one! I can make that statement about no other cartridge, even those with which I have slain but a couple of animals.

Accuracy is never a problem, either, at least in a properly set up rifle. Most 7mm Magnums will group under 1½ inches, and with full-bore hunting loads, not match ammo. Many will print in the 1.3-inch range, with an occasional singular specimen going under an inch for five-shot averages fired at 100 yards. My experience indicates that the average 7mm Remington Mag. is a tiny bit more precise than the average .30-06, although in the field the difference would be indiscernible.

The Big Seven will shoot as flat over all game ranges as will such hot items as the .270 Weatherby Magnum. It recoils about the same as the Weatherby cartridge, is as accurate and has an equal beller. (Loud!) The belted 7mm has the same advantage over the .270 Weatherby that the .280 Remington has over the .270—a wider array of component bullets. And of course there is the availability of the heavy 175 Nosler Partition for use on big, tough game. All in all, the 7mm Rem. Mag. is a little more versatile than the .270 Weatherby.

7mm Weatherby Magnum. We might as well include the 7mm Weatherby Magnum in this discussion. Though it's a bit longer in the neck, has the odd Weatherby double-radius shoulder and is offered in fewer factory permutations, when handloaded it's a ballistic clone to the Remington version. Factory loads are another story, with the Weatherby cartridge getting the performance nod. In a 24-inch Weatherby Fibermark, I clocked the 154-grain factory load at 3,180 fps; the 175-grain version hit 2,954. That's about a 150-fps advantage for the proprietary cartridge. If I shot only factory ammunition and could afford a Weatherby Mark V rifle, I would go with the Weatherby Seven in lieu of Bridgeport's offering. Since I handload, and due to the virtually unlimited number of rifle options—not to mention action types—I'll cast my lot with Remington.

The Big Sevens are magnificent cartridges. Although they will shoot as flat (for all practical purposes) as the best of loads, they are by no means limited to medium-sized plains game. While they dish out plenty of power, they are not especially punishing at the aft end. Very few big-game cartridges are more intrinsically accurate; even fewer are so easy to feed. There is nothing on this continent I would not tackle when armed with a good, reliable 7mm Magnum and my own handloads.

.30-06 Springfield. The .30-06 is the grand old man of the cartridge world. It's the standard by which most other big game rifle cartridges are judged, and will remain so until the sphinx learns to cha-cha.

Longevity has a lot to do with it, but since such luminaries as the 8mm Mauser, 7 X 57, .30-30 Winchester, and .30-40 Krag pre-date it by a decade or more, advanced age cannot be the sole explanation for its popularity. Veterans of World Wars I and II feel an uncommon propinquity for the venerable round, since it saved

Oregon gun scribe Steve Timm took this fine buck with a Browning BBR .30-06, using 150-grain Speer spitzer handloads.

their bacon on numerous occasions, but many of those same soldiers have gone to their rewards and the .30-06 trundles steadfastly along, more popular among the current crop of nimrods than ever. The fact that it is a fine target cartridge has certainly not hurt its eclat, though most hunters could care less about its prowess over the target course, only its effectiveness in the game fields.

The heart of the matter is that the .30-06 has a fine reputation as a slayer of large game, is readily attainable in a tremendous variety of armament, is owned and used by a veritable army of hunters, and is available in an absolutely astonishing array of factory ammunition. At last count, there were 35 distinct versions of domestic ammo, with Norma and PMC offering eight more between them. Bullet weights range from 55 grains up to 220, with 125, 130, 150, 165, 168, 180 and 200 in between. Hollow points are produced, full-jacketed stuff, pointed soft points, protected points, spitzer boattails, semi-pointed slugs, round-nosed projectiles, Nosler Partitions and maybe one or two I forgot.

A quick look at quoted muzzle speeds goes like so: 55-grain soft point (the Remington Accelerator) at 4,080 fps; 125 soft point at 3,140; 130 semi-pointed (Norma) at 3,210; 150-grain bullet in pointed, semi-pointed, and boattail configurations, at about 2,910 (Norma data claims 2,990, while PMC says but 2,773); 165 pointed and boattail spitzers, 2,800 fps; 168 match hollow-point boattail at 2,790; 180 grain in virtually any shape you want, at a nominal 2,700 fps (Norma says 2790 and PMC a conservative 2,550); 200 PPC (Norma) at 2,640; and finally the hulking 220-grain bowling balls at a listed 2,410.

Time for the lie-detector test. In my Churchill Highlander's 22-inch tube: 125 Federal soft point, 2,953; 150 Norma semi-pointed, 2,853; 150 Federal soft point, 2,776; 150 Federal Premium boattail soft point, 2,712; 165 Federal Premium boattail soft point, 2,753; 180 Remington pointed Core-Lokt, 2,633 fps. Not any of 'em too enthusiastic, were they? In a 22-inch Butch Searcy-modified Model 70, the same lots went thus: 150 Norma, 2,919; 150 Federal soft point, 2,851; 180 Remington, 2,677. A little better. In the same Model 70, these: second lot of 150 Federal soft points, 2,923 (now we're cooking!); 180 Federal round nose, 2,559 (oops, slipped again); 180 Norma round nose, 2,693 (that's better). Lest this become unwieldy, I'll simply list the averages for several bullet weights in my Model 700 Remington (22-inch): 125 (Winchester) soft point, 2,879 fps; 150 soft point (Federal Premium, Norma and Remington), 2,726 fps; 180-grain spitzers (Remington and Norma), 2,614.

It appears that the venerable ought-six runs no closer to published numbers than many of its brethren, despite the ammo companies having had more than 80 years to refine their products. Rounding everything off, I'd expect to achieve close to 4,000 fps from the 55-grain Accelerator, which I did in a Model 700 ADL and a 22-inch Ruger Number One; somewhere around 2,950 from most anyone's 125-grain factory load; about 2,800 in the run-of-the-mill 150-grain weight; 2,770 from the average 165-grain load (which ain't far from catalog claims); from 2,600 to maybe 2,640 with most 180-grain stuff; and around 2,330 or so from the 220-grain loads. Incidentally, Hornady's superb 168-

grain match hollow-point boattail averaged 2,814 fps in my two 24-inch barreled .30-06s, and the same firm's 165-grain hunting load showed a mean of 2,780 in nine different rifles, with barrel lengths ranging from 22 to 24 inches. Good stuff.

Handloaded, the .30-06 will reach from 3,300 to 3,400 fps with a good 110-grain hollow point over 57.5 grains of IMR 4064. This has long been my favored accuracy load when testing any .30-06, and is death on vermin. Speeds of 3,200 fps are not unattainable with 125-grain spitzers, and Speer's 130 hollow point is nigh as fast and frequently more accurate. The 150-grain bullets can be goosed to 3,000 fps with just the right propellants, and 2,900 is easily reached with most any of them. The norm for 165-grain projectiles is 2,800 fps, though some rifles will manage close to 2,900 in concert with a good slow burner and a knowing hand at the powder scale. The loading manuals claim 2,800 is feasible with the 180-grain slugs, although I have never had much luck driving bullets that fast. Most of my top loads—such as 54.0 grains of IMR 4350 and a good 180-grain spitzer—show between 2,700 and 2,750, depending on the gun. I prefer the 200-grain pointed bullets to the 180s, and have no problem driving them in excess of 2,600; some powders will manage 2,650 or so with no excessive pressures in evidence, and provide fine hunting accuracy while doing so.

When choosing hunting loads for the .30-06, I stick to three bullet weights. For groundhogs and similar fauna, I like the aforementioned llO-grain hollow point handloads. The speed is sufficient for a flat trajectory, accuracy generally superb, bullet expansion on impact something to behold.

For plains game like pronghorn and mule deer, I like a good 150-grain spitzer boattail. Loaded to 3,000 fps, the 150 Nosler Ballistic Tip, for example, is but 6.8 inches down at 300 yards, assuming a 200-yard zero. Switch to a 250-yard zero and you won't even have to consider drop clear out to 325 yards or so; just hold center and let fly. Retained punch at 400 yards is a healthy 1,577 foot-pounds according to Nosler data.

For anything bigger or meaner than deer, I lean toward the 200 Nosler Partition. It shows less than an inch more 400-yard bullet drop when started at 2,650 than the streamlined 180-grain Nosler Solid Base (a boattail design) when boosted from the muzzle at 2,750. Further, the 200 Nosler carries nearly 1,900 foot-pounds of energy way out there at 400 yards; the lighter 180 Solid Base retains but 1,707. In addition, the Partition bullet is a better

Another big buck which fell to the crack of a .30-06. Many, many have.

performer on heavy game than the Solid Base, giving deeper penetration and superior bone-breaking crunch.

So why not choose the 180-grain Partition? Because it retains only 1,595 foot-pounds at 400 yards, and exhibits no trajectory advantage over the heavier Partition. Why give up the 300 foot-pounds and deep-digging qualities of the 200-grain Partition to gain nothing except a miniscule decrease in recoil sensation?

There is one exception to the above. Were a caribou hunt in the planning stages, and if I intended to use a .30-06, I would opt for a stout 165-grain spitzer loaded as hot as pressures and accuracy would allow. I feel that a big bull caribou needs more sectional density than is provided by a 150-grain .30-caliber bullet, and I'd also desire as flat a trajectory as possible. Hence the compromise 165-grain weight.

If limited to factory ammo, I would choose the 55-grain Remington Accelerator if my .30-06 would handle it accurately. Alas, many won't, at least not with acceptable varmint precision. For game up through mule deer, I would choose a good 150-grain load, likely the 150 Federal Premium boattail for its ballistic properties. For non-trophy elk or caribou, I would buy the Hornady 165-grain soft point boattail. For anything heavier, or a combination mule deer/elk hunt, I'd fill my magazine with the Federal Premium 180-grain Nosler loading.

We haven't looked at accuracy yet, for there isn't much need to. The .30-06 will in a good bolt-action or single-shot rifle group between 1.10 inches and 1.50 inches, almost without fail. I know of some .30-06 owners who swear their sporters will print sub-minute, and I've run across a few rifles that wouldn't quite cut the 1½-inch criterion, but guns in either group are quite rare. Suffice to opine that the typical .30-06 turnbolt offers precision aplenty for any big-game task, and many varminting chores as well. (The other action types are often another matter, but the limiting factor is the *rifle*, not the .30-06 cartridge.)

I shot my first groundhog with a .30-06, and my first whitetail. Toted one in a saddle scabbard over half of Idaho in search of trophy elk. One of the most accurate rifles I ever shot was a Winchester Target Model 70 which would group around .6 inch with the regularity of a dowager on prune juice. If I had to spend the rest of my days hunting big game with one rifle, I would not feel unduly handicapped if it were chambered to .30-06. Nor should you.

Rick Jamison likes the .300 Win. for everything he hunts, including long-range game like mule deer and pronghorn.

The .30-06 Springfield conforms to the upper limit I would place on loads to be used specifically for mule deer. While the .300 Magnums are literally hell-on-wheels, and will knock the burliest of mule deer bucks flat on his keister at any reasonable range, there is no justification I can conjure up for coping with the Big Thirties' prodigious recoil. Besides, if a hunter zaps a mule deer properly with a good bullet fired from any cartridge we've been discussing, he will not travel far. And if the bullet strays too far afield, the buck likely will, too, no matter what he's socked with.

So now let's close the mule deer colloquium with my personal preferences in armament. Away we go.

The "Best" Mule Deer Cartridges

For mule deer hunting at all "normal" ranges, say to 300 yards maximum, I could find bliss in the arms of any of the following: .25-06 with 117 to 120-grain spitzers; .257 Weatherby Magnum with same; the 6.5 X 55 Swede with 120- to 140-grain handloads, or the 139 Norma factory load; the 7 X 57, using 139- or 140-grain factory stuff, or better yet with top handloads; the 7mm-08 Remington, especially with handloaded ammo; the .270 Winchester; the .280 Remington; the .284 Winchester with handloads; the

.308 Winchester; the .30-06. Now to separate the starting team from the bench warmers.

The .25-06 is a bit weak in the knees with factory ammo, unless unerringly directed by a calm head. With handloaded 120-grain Nosler boattails, it would likely be all anyone would need. It's accurate, available and doesn't slap its shooter too strenuously.

The .257 Weatherby is as good as the .25-06. Negatives: it comes mostly in expensive rifles; factory ammo depletes one's bank account rapidly; it is very, very loud; it is tough on barrel steel; it isn't needed for 300-yard shooting. I'll relegate this one to the bench.

The 6.5 X 55 is great for the recoil-sensitive shooter. When handloaded, it shoots plenty flat and hits hard, even way out there. New guns for it are relatively scarce and not inexpensive, although surplus arms are pretty cheap. The Norma light-bullet load is potent and generally quite accurate. For 300-yard shooting, it'll do.

The 7mm-08 kicks a tad more than the 6.5 X 55, a bit less than the .270 Winchester. It shoots a bit flatter than the 6.5 X 55, not quite so taut as the .270. Factory 7mm-08 ammo is often insipid when it comes to grouping, but handloading brings a bloom to its cheeks. A plethora of rifles can be found. Brass is easy to form from .308 cases, so it will never be hard to build ammo for. Against it is a lack of options in factory ammunition.

The 7 X 57 is just fine when handloaded, lackluster as groomed by the factories. Not many domestic arms are reamed to it, although there are plenty of factory loads to choose from. It can be accurate in the right rifle, and recoil is barely noticeable to anyone but the occasional shooter. As with the 6.5 X 55 and 7mm-08, muzzle blast is less than deafening should an occasion arise for the hunter to get off a shot without ear protection. Nonetheless, it requires a long action, is not quite as powerful or flat-shooting as the 7mm-08 and most factory loads are low on zip. Good, but not quite first-rate; it's in the shadow of the 7mm-08. Second squad.

The .270 Winchester is, as we've discussed, the classic mule deer cartridge. When ranges to 300 yards are on the agenda, nothing outclasses it. The 7mm-08 will nearly equal it ballistically, kicks a bit less, may be a hair more accurate and needs only a short action to house it. Big hairy deal. Most .270s will shoot rings around most 7mm-08s with *factory ammo*; the .270 is made in all action types except the lever; dealers' shelves bulge with good, fast, accurate ammunition; inexpensive turnbolts can be had. The .270 is a star player.

The .280 Remington has long been talked down to by the loading companies; it requires a knowledgeable handloader at the helm to get it off its knees. Even then it is less potentially accurate than the 7-08 or .270, and recoils a bit more than either when its flames are fanned. On the plus side is a goodly assortment of factory ammo, even if most of it is loaded to three-quarters throttle. Lots of guns around, although none of them is a bargain-basement special. Good, but no cigar. I'll ignore the .280 for mule deer; there are better loads.

The .284 is another fine cartridge handicapped by one-legged factory ammo. With this load, speed is not often the problem; accuracy is. Handloading helps, but I'm uncertain how long into the future Olin will keep on turning out ammo. Since it is easily formed from no other case, that's a distinct disadvantage. For the reloader who is willing and financially able to stockpile his brass, the .284 is great. But since it is found in few guns, is only 100 fps or so ahead of the 7mm-08 when both are loaded to max, and since its future is in jeopardy, why bother with it? Second string.

The .308 Winchester is another story. With handloads or factory fodder, it groups like a champ, shoots flat enough for 300-yard feasibility on most anything, is produced in all action types. Factory ammo is not only common, but correctly loaded to yield good speed and is available in a multiplicity of alternatives. On the down side is its recoil, heavier than such loads as the 6.5 X 55, 7 X 57, and its offspring, the 7-08. But that's the .308's only wart; it makes the starting line-up.

Finally, there's the good old .30-06. Fed good ammo, the ought-six will reach out with the best of 'em, hit as hard or harder, group as tight or tighter than most and both guns and ammo can be had in bewildering profusion. Alas, the old vet stomps one's shoulder a bit less tenderly than its competition, and its power is not needed on mule deer. The .30-06 gets tossed when a deer-only load is sought.

So who makes the team? The .25-06, 6.5 X 55, .270 Winchester, 7mm-08, and the .308 Winchester. (Remember now, we're looking at 300-yard cartridges here.) Let's narrow the field further, although I'd about as soon toss a coin as try to make a decision based on merit.

More results of the .300 Win. used on long-range game. Rick is not recoil sensitive.

Since the .25-06 needs to be handloaded to acheive stardom, is limited to one bullet weight and since most guns reamed to it wear long, weighty 24-inch barrels, I'll give it the heave-ho. But that's only because I'm trying to come up with a winner here, so I'll have to be real picky.

The 6.5 X 55 is limited in both guns and ammunition, although what's out there is good. It too wants handloading to look its best, since no spitzer bullet is offered by Norma. Only if a non-reloader were especially recoil-sensitive would I suggest choosing the 6.5 over all others. It offers the most punch out front with the least punishment out back. But for normal gunners, I'll turn my back on the good little Swede.

The 7-08, much as I love it, is a handloader's cartridge. That alone puts it in the ditch as a load for all people. Good-bye, little feller.

The .308 is a logical candidate for Mule-deer Load of the Year. However, it kicks a bit much, isn't so flat as it might be and no factory makes a light-bullet boattail to assist in retaining its head of steam. Handloaded, it is exemplary, but lots of hunters don't know powder from porridge, and furthermore don't care that they don't. The .308 is designated runner-up.

Which means the .270 wins! By virtually any criteria, the ancient .27-bore has what it takes for mule deer at 300 yards. And beyond. In fact, were I to stretch the range to 400 yards (only for experts), the .270 would be one of only a half-dozen loads I'd consider. What are the others?

For true long-distance mule deer slaying, the .257 Weatherby, .270 Winchester, .270 Weatherby, .284 Winchester, .280 Remington and the 7mm Magnum(s) are in a class by themselves. Among those listed, I would delete the .284 and .280 Remington for reasons abovementioned. The other loads can stay, and I refuse to choose among them. They all have virtue.

Now, for you combination hunters, those who like to hunt two types of game on your annual Western sojourn, there are other factors to consider. If you lean toward mule deer and antelope, then I suggest opting for such flat-shooting loads as the .257 Weatherby or .270 Winchester. Why those two? Because they have all the juice necessary without an attendant proclivity for knocking you out from under your hat.

If on the other hand I were casting about for an elk to balance my mule deer tag, I would lean toward the top end of the cartridge power ladder. Such as? Well, the .270 Weatherby, one of the Big

On the light end, the .243 can do the job, too.

Sevens or maybe the .30-06. My own choice would be the 7mm Remington Magnum unless I planned to carry a Weatherby rifle, at which time I would toss and turn all night choosing between the .270 Weatherby and the 7mm Weatherby Magnum. And if I had a trusty .30-06 with which I had slain my whitetail buck every year since Watergate, with maybe a couple black bear thrown in, I'd simply top its tank with 200-grain Nosler handloads or the Federal 180-grain Premium Partition and truck Old Betsy out West.

Them's *my* druthers. If you disagree, that's fine. You may be right, for *you. Hunt with what you like, what you handle well, assuming you have the experience to back up your choice.*

Caribou

Although some species of caribou are found in wooded country, most are shot on treeless tundra or high mountain passes where they often feed above treeline, amongst the wild sheep. Thus, caribou gunning is often at long, undetermined range.

Caribou are larger than mule deer, with some big bulls as heavy as an average elk. They have stouter bone structures than deer. When your bullet runs into one of them, it will need to be stiffer than if it had collided with a piddlin' deer-sized critter. Thus, caribou should be shot with bullets either heavier or sturdier or both than those one might choose for deer.

Magnum cartridges are not requisite. Although caribou are sometimes nigh as big as elk, they are nowhere near so tough, so

The same guns that take mule deer will work fine on caribou, just stuff them with stouter bullets. This bull fell to a .30-06.

hard to put down, so incredibly vital! Any load suitable for a big muley at long range will work equally well on caribou, just so long as a robust bullet is used.

For example, if I were to take to the caribou trails with a .270 Winchester, I'd stuff its pantry with ammo tipped by 150-grain Nosler Partition bullets. If I carried a 7 X 57 or 7mm-08, I would want the same Noslers, and would restrict myself to 300 yards. In the .284 or .280, I'd load either 150 or 160 Nosler Partitions, perhaps the 150 Remington pointed Core-Lokt in the .280. For the large-cased 7mm Magnums, the 160 Nosler should work well, and my .30-06 would likely be crammed full of 165-grain spitzers. And so forth.

Get the drift? Whatever rifle you like for mule deer hunting will work as well on caribou, given a prudent selection of projectiles.

My personal pick? Well, if I were leaving for a hunt up north next week, I'd spend the interim developing a handload for either my Winchester Model 70 Winlite or my Browning A-Bolt Stainless Stalker, both 7mm Remington Magnums. If I hadn't the time, I would stock up on Federal Premium 160-grain Partitions. Those rifles have in common synthetic stocks that are impervious to the caprice of foul weather, and both are fairly portable. Either will carry the freight when the moment of truth stares me in the face.

6

Cartridges For
Black Bear & Boar

*H*e plods along ponderously, swinging his huge head to and fro;
belly-full and sleepy. His rolling gait, always the sign of a
really big bear, carries him slowly across the plundered soybean
field. Pungent early-morning smells waft to him on the breeze; his
weak eyes probe the dimness for any sign of the slightly smaller
bruin that has been dogging his steps of late. He stops...
sniffs...peers dolefully around...funnels his ears. Nothing. The
steady drizzle mutes the normal wood's noises, veils his vision to a
marked degree, reduces his sense of smell to a fraction of its
normal facility. He trundles along, growling softly, bent on
shelter, slumber, solitude. And the rains fall.

I've been sitting soaked and cold since before sunrise, back to
a brush pile, feeling sorry for myself. The rain is relentless;
chilling rivulets snake down my spine. A sky the color of zinc,
laden with thick, heavy clouds; my rifle glistening in the
dampness, its scope clouded with condensation. Miserable.

I want to heel it back to the truck to get warm, dry. Swill a
steaming cup of coffee. Take my boots off. Instead, I sit waiting
for a bear. A big bear. Like the one that outfoxed me just
yesterday, right here.

I'd spotted him way across the soybean field, easing along
unconcerned, heading for the thick forest to my left. I had jumped
down into the field from the access road, run hunched over, like

Quasimodo, forgetting that at this distance (more than half a mile) the bear likely wouldn't have been able to see me had I been eight feet tall and dressed in chartreuse knickers.

By the time I'd closed the distance to 400 yards or so, the bear had dropped into the canal that separates the woods from the field. If he ever came out again, I didn't see him.

I was not happy. And I dwelled on my discomfiture. Sulked. Which I believe is understandable; this was really a large bear!

It seemed to me that if that sofa-sized bruin followed this same route tomorrow, I'd better plan to close the gap beforehand. A change of venue was in order.

Along the western edge of that giant bean field marched a phalanx of brushpiles, pushed up for incineration by a farm employee astride some giant earth-moving apparatus. They sat, about 100 yards apart, like huge anthills.

A plan began to form....

Obviously the bear was accustomed to these silent sentinels, comfortable in their presence, oblivious to any danger they might represent. Perhaps I should shift my ambush site to one of those piles of rotting wood, dead center in that mile-wide soybean patch.

And thus did I come to my damp and surly and self-pitying state.

A puff of man-smell, vague and uncertain on the shifting tides of air, assaults his nostrils. He wrinkles his brow, tests the currents, twisting his nose this way and that, apprehensive but unafraid. The unceasing tumult makes it tough to get a fix. Impossible. He hesitates, uncertain of the best route. Sniffs. Again the noisome odor. One of those spindly, hairless, bear-like predators lurks nearby. His nose tells him so. But where?

No further clues. His attenuated vision helps not a whit as he attempts to pierce the gloom, his giant head swinging back and forth like a great hairy metronome, porcine eyes squinting against the dampness. No use. He plods on; the sanctuary of the forest looms near.

A wave of irresolution has just swept over me like a weighted cloak when I spy the bear. My wandering attention zeroes in as if programmed, as indeed I suppose it is. Nothing else exists but that distant bear and me, actors on a setless stage.

I shift my rifle without letting my eyes leave the bear. As I watch, he stops, tests the wind, peers uneasily around like a second-story man who's just heard a sound in an empty house. He hesitates....

How far, I wonder? Maybe a bit more than 100 yards, I answer. Gosh, he's big, I think. Keep your mind on what you're doing, I remind myself. Never mind how big he is.

Check the scope. The lenses are opaque with moisture. I lift the rifle, peek through the glass at the bear. Two items register: he has not moved; I can but barely make out the crosswires. Abruptly, he lumbers on. A few more paces and he will disappear behind the brushpile just to my front.

Looking frantically through the edges of my lens—most of the accretion is centered on the glass—I plaster the reticle against the bear's shoulder as best I can. Snick off the safety. Swing with him as he walks, faster now.

My chest feels enclasped, constricted by tight metal bands. Breathing is difficult. The crosswires are swinging all over the bear. Pulse is racing, heart pounding.

The stock is wet, slippery. My finger is cold against the trigger, little feeling in the tip. Bet the trigger is slick too, I think. Forget it, I admonish, just squeeze off. Now!

So I do.

A forepaw lifts suckingly free of the mud, reaches forward, the bear's center of gravity shifting along with it, when a great shattering weight smashes in from nowhere. In an instant, the bear loses control, falls heavily on his side, rolls over on his back, all four feet waving. Nonplussed, he tries to regain his equilibrium, right himself, like an oversized turtle. The difficulty of such a normally simple task momentarily overwhelms him.

At my shot, the bear falls instantly, into an unseen depression. All I can see are four feet flailing the air, as if peddling a bicycle. Obviously hit hard, he may not be down for the count. I jack the bolt, hop to my feet, try desperately to see what is going on. Through my scope, a dull grey blur.

And then he heaves himself to his feet.

Despite a broken shoulder, the bear rights himself, regains his footing and bolts upright. Instantly, he is off and running, aiming for the sheltering forest, great glops of mud flying from his feet as he pounds on, staggering when his weight comes down on the injured leg.

A sodden boom *splinters the dampness; the supersonic crack of the bullet as it passes. The woods are closer. Another* boom; *mud sprays the glossy pelt. Then another blow, disorienting, to the wind. And he stops. The canal is there; right there. Close. So close.*

The author's North Carolina coastal black bear weighed 468 pounds and was taken with the Ultra Light Arms Model 20 shown, in 6.5 x 55 Swede.

He stands head down, punchdrunk. Out on his feet.

I'm out of ammo. The bear has been hit again at least once, maybe twice. He has stopped at the edge of the canal. Too weak to cross it? I hope so, fervently, as I dig frantically through my pockets for more cartridges. I find some, pull two out, load them by feel as I watch the bear.

Once more, a crushing punch jerks his feet from beneath him. Falling disjointedly to the ground, he rolls over and over, over and over, until a final bullet douses the flame of life.

All is still.

And the rains fall....

I walk over to my first bear, pacing slowly, not because of fear, but because I am played out emotionally. Rubber-legged. The adrenaline surge has deserted me, leaving fatigue in its wake. The aftermath of intense excitement.

Then I am there. At his side. My bear. *My* bear. Mine in a way no non-hunter can ever understand. Part of me. As long as I have a memory, that bear will live.

And so it is with bears, at least for me. No other animal on this continent engenders the level of intensity, the feeling of camaraderie, of kinship, as does the family *ursus*. I hope it will always be so.

It appears that many hunters harbor a similar notion; interest in bear rifles and cartridges abounds. So let's take a look at what the well-prepared bear hunter might tote when pursuing his quarry.

What Makes A Bear Load?

For years I have heard the opinion that if a gent has a good deer rifle, he also owns plenty of bear medicine. Not in my book! Sure, a .243 or .250-3000 will do in an average-sized black bear, maybe even quickly enough so's he won't waltz over and rearrange your toupee. But then, maybe not.

I want a minimum bullet diameter of .264, and as much bullet weight as I think necessary to penetrate heavy bear bones without bullet break-up. That's no small order!

In the .26-bores, for example, black-bear slugs begin with the 140 Nosler Partition, although the 125-grain Nosler might do okay on economy-sized bruins. (Say 200 pounds or less.) Perhaps even better is the 160 Hornady round-nosed soft point I used on the aforementioned bear, which incidentally weighed 468 pounds. My final bullet tunneled completely through that bear, from neck bone to hip meat; the first bulldozed a path through both lungs, then reduced the off shoulder to shrapnel. Good enough? I think so, especially from the modest 6.5 X 55 Swede.

From .270 on up, there are a goodly number of bear-killing bullets on the market, in both factory persuasion and as components for handloading. As a general guideline, a hunter should choose one of the heavier bullets in any given bore size. Examples would be 150-grain slugs in the .270 Winchester, 150 up through 175-grain soft points in the various 7mm cartridges, from 165 to 200 in the .30 calibers, with 180 grains perhaps ideal. In 8mm diameter, I'd go with the 200-grain Speer or Nosler Partition, choose the 210 Nosler or heavier in the .33-bores, opt for 220 grains and up in the various .35s, 240 or better in the .44 Magnum or .444 Marlin, and 350-grain soft points in the .45-70. And, for you .375 Winchester fans, I guess I'd recommend the 220 Hornady in handloads, maybe the 250 Winchester Power Point in factory ammo. But I'd not be real happy with a .375 in the first place.

I realize that the average black bear is *said* to be only a little heavier than the typical deer. Not where I do most of *my* hunting! Of the 20 or so black bear I've seen killed during the past two one-week seasons in coastal North Carolina, more than one-third exceeded 390 pounds in body weight, and I'm speaking of bear actually weighed, not estimated. The new North Carolina state record hefted 601 pounds, and the group I hunted with took three that surpassed 450, including my own. This year: I downed a 300-pounder; hunted with Doug Solomon of Blacksburg, Virginia, who slew a 413-pounder; photographed a bear killed by a

Nine-year-old Brock Eakes took his first black bear with a single shot to the head from his Marlin 336 in .30-30. The old .30 will do the job, but there are much better cartridges for bear.

This bear fell to a .338-06 wildcat. The bear was feeding on the fawn kill (background) when the hunter took him. Ready to butcher, the bear hefted 378 pounds; it squared six feet nine inches. Would you want to tangle with a bruin like that if you were carrying a .30-30 or .243?

nine-year-old boy that tipped the scale at 390 even. Further, I saw two mounts in preparation at Pelletier's Taxidermy, of Stantonsburg, North Carolina. The *smaller* of the pair had weighed 560 pounds; the larger had never been weighed! Eastern North Carolina is *the* spot for really big black bear, but you face every chance of meeting a behemoth bruin every time you enter the woods in bear country anywhere; why not be prepared?

My boar is currently in the care of taxidermist Larry Strader. He has measured the skull carefully, and tells me it just misses Boone and Crockett by a fraction of a point. He had to order a medium-sized *grizzly* form in order to handle my mount; no black bear form was large enough!

So...if you are willing to shoot undersized bear, then most any .30-30-class cartridge will do, assuming—as mentioned above—a long, heavy (for the caliber) bullet. If you intend to hunt *grown* bear, look for more gun.

Just how, you query, did so many hunters come to take so many black bear with so many deer cartridges if such arms aren't adequate? Good question. Because most bear not taken ahead of dogs or over bait are killed purely by chance by nimrods who *are seeking deer.* Folks who set out after bear, not deer, have long toted stouter armament if they had a choice.

Black bear are furtive, and blessed with auditory and olfactory equipment a cut above many other animals. They are normally too elusive to take without canine help. (Or the assistance of a pile of ripe goo, the odor of which will permeate sheet metal. The bear, of course, find the smell irresistible, which is their Achilles heel.) Thus, the practice of coursing bruins with hounds is an ancient and honorable sport. Productive, too.

For such pursuit, the .30-30 class—not to mention other mild loads like the .44 Magnum, .35 Remington, even the .30 Carbine—of cartridges is all that is needed. These bear are often shot out of the tree in which they sought refuge from a howling pack. The range is close; there is usually plenty of time for the shot. Under such conditions, a .357 Magnum revolver might well suffice, let alone a deer cartridge!

When a cornered, angry, slobbering, vindictive bear is on the menu, things shift a mite. The .44 Mag. and its ilk will work, and work well if the hunter knows bruin anatomy like the contents of his wallet, doesn't get nervous, and if said bear will cooperate and stand still enough for a telling shot. Alas, this is not always the case. The bear gets tagged in a painful but not incapacitating area, runs amuck among the hounds, and things generally get kinda sporty for a spell. Upshot: The bear suffers; the dogs often suffer; and the hunter, usually unscathed, should feel ashamed of himself.

Another consideration rears its head: over-penetration. Many dog men feel that a powerful cartridge taking a heavy, deep-penetrating bullet, might well zing right on through Br'er Bear to poke a hole in one of their pet pooches. That makes no one happy. However, if a judicious choice of bullet is made, such excessive penetration can be avoided.

I will close now on the bear-chasing hunter. Let him pick what he—and his dogs—can live with. For the baiter of bear, the stand hunter, still hunter, or bear glasser, there are plenty of good loads. We'll look at 'em now.

Although I have used the 6.5 X 55 Swede on black bear, I don't think I would recommend it for the average hunter unless shots are restricted to 200 yards or less, and then only with heavy bullets as discussed above. The 6.5 Remington Magnum is better ballistically, but the chances of finding one for sale are about the same as winning a state lottery. Besides, ammo is scarce and the cartridge mediocre; I can think of few reasons to purchase one. The

.264 Magnum has plenty of punch for black bear, especially with 140-grain handloads, but again the guns are uncommon, not to mention being as unweieldy for brush hunting as a snow shovel.

The .270 Winchester makes fine bear medicine with 150-grain slugs or heavier. The 130 Nosler Partion or Barnes copper-tubed bullets might work all right on smaller bears at normal ranges, but I personally would want more heft. The same goes for the .270 Weatherby Magnum, and in that number I might use the 180 Barnes round nose if it would group in my rifle. Still, I prefer to stay away from long, unwieldy magnum rifles for black bear hunting.

Any 7mm cartridge larger than the 7-30 Waters will handle a bruin. For brush-country use I would opt for the 7mm-08 Remington or the .284 Winchester, both in short, light rifles. For hunting over bait or glassing yon mountain slope, the .280 Remington would get my nod. The 7mm Remington Mag. is fine for the latter if you're willing to tote the avoirdupois.

Any of the medium-mild .30s—like the .300 Savage, .307 Winchester, .30-40 Krag, or .303 British—have all the punch required at modest ranges. Use 180-grain bullets, though. The .308 Winchester is better, the .30-06 a bit better yet; I'd choose the former for forested terrain, the latter for stump sitting. The Big Thirty Magnums are not needed on black bear, although they work nicely in the hands of someone who can shoot them accurately. In particular, the .300 H&H is a good choice—reasonable of recoil, relatively mild of voice. Tough to find, though, and lengthy as a cane pole.

The little 7.62 X 39 is outclassed on black bear, as is the .30-30, .32 Special and others of this power level. I *know* that many, many bear have been killed with them, and some of them cleanly. So what? With perfect shot placement, they'll kill a hippopotamas, but they still aren't the ideal loads for the job.

The 8mm Mauser is fine. Use Norma 196-grain factory ammo, maybe the 165 Protected Power Cavity if you anticipate long ranges. Handloads should feature the 200 Nosler Partition, maybe the Barnes 200 or 225 if you don't plan to shoot one in the next county. The 8mm Remington Magnum is simply not needed on animals of 600 pounds or less, so that and the .338 are best left to the masochists.

The .35 Remington and .375 Winchester will do a workmanlike job on black bear *if* a proper bullet is chosen. I would not be happy with less than the 220 Speer flat point in the .35 and the 220

Hornady flat point in the .375. But at moderate distances, this duo can cut the mustard.

And that brings us to the first team, the loads I would pick for normal black bear hunting, at ranges up to 200 yards, maybe 250. When hunting the vast bean fields of Eastern North Carolina, or the wide canyons of the Mountain West, I suggest a longer-ranging cartridge, which we will cover directly. But the starting players for the bulk of my bruin seeking begin with the...

.348 Winchester

First introduced in 1936, in an improved version of the famed Winchester 1886, the .348 Winchester was hailed as a bull-elk, moose, and grizzly buster par excellence. T'weren't bad, neither. Featuring a 200-grain soft point at an alleged 2,520 fps, and a 250-grainer at 200 foot-seconds less, the big-cased load provided energy levels quite close to 3,000 foot-pounds. Impressive.

For distances out to perhaps 150 yards, the .348 may indeed do a satisfactory job on a bull elk, and more than one big bear has fallen to its roar. But I'd prefer closer ranges on elk or moose, and more retained energy on really large bruins if I had to stand behind the plate. But for black-bear sized critters, the .348 is just about right.

Although Olin is said to have dropped the load recently, the revival by Browning of the former Winchester-built Model 71 has elicited a special run of ammunition. My 1985 Olin catalogue shows the 200-grain Silvertip as the only offering, still listed at 2,520 fps. Retained energy at 200 yards is 1,656 foot-pounds, assuming current factory fodder to be capable of attaining its press notices.

I chronographed a batch of factory stuff nearly 15 years ago in an original Winchester Model 71 (discontinued in 1957). At that time Remington listed a 150-grain loading; it clocked 2,796 fps in my 24-inch rifle, against an advertised speed of 2,880 fps. The 200-grain Winchester Silvertip hit 2,449 fps; a lot of Remington 200-grain Core-Lokt managed but 2,421. Thus, the old cartridge failed to live up to its claims by around 80-100 fps with the lighter bullets. I've never tried any of the 250s.

Hornady offers a 200-grain flat-pointed soft nose, and has for years. Barnes Bullets lists a 250-grain of similar shape. In my 24-inch Model 71, the lighter slug could be boosted safely to 2,546 fps with a now-defunct ball powder; its replacement may or may not equal that performance.

The Browning Model 71 is a fine woods rifle for black bear. The kind of terrain shown here is typical .348 Winchester country. It's one heck of a good black bear cartridge.

My favorite combo paired the 200 Hornady with a dab of Hodgdon's H-4895, for 2,532 fps and just over two-inch groups at 100 yards, with iron sights. In my Browning carbine, I intend to duplicate that recipe.

Best results with the 250 Barnes came via H-4831, with speeds in the 2,210 range. Not a barn burner, but not laggard, either. Remember, the average .30-30 won't reach such speeds with a bullet 80 grains lighter!

I would not for one second hesitate to poke a black bear—of any size or temperment—where he lives with a suitably-loaded .348. And I might just do it next season. Good cartridge, the .348 Winchester, housed in a fine modern levergun, the Browning 71.

.358 Winchester

The .358 Winchester was birthed concurrent with the .243 Winchester, in 1955. The little 6mm took off like the Concorde; the pedestrian .35-bore trudged along, never quite sufficiently moribund to die off altogether. Which delights me, since it works so well.

It is said that the .358 was intended as a replacement for the dying .348 Winchester, with similar ballistics from the newer, smaller cartridge. Quoted as giving 2,530 fps to a 200-grain soft point, getting 2,250 from a 250-grain bullet, the .358 fell right alongside the elder .348 ballistically. So far, so good.

But Winchester goofed. Badly. They introduced the short, stubby cartridge in a long, heavy *bolt-action* rifle, the Winchester Model 70. Big mistake. Not long afterward, the Model 88 levergun appeared, which was more like it. Alas, the 88 was too long of barrel, lousy of trigger pull, heavy and non-traditional in appearance to have much impact on the woods-hunting crowd. The long-range bunch—particularly the southpaws—took the gun to their collective bosoms due to the availability of such reach-out cartridges as the .243, .284 Winchester and the .308. But the close-range boys took a look at the Model 88 and yawned. The snapping shut of their coin purses shook the land.

Mannlicher-Schoenauer of Austria tried to make a buck peddling .358 boltguns over here. Their accountants shrieked and rent their garments. Savage made two separate attempts to breathe life into the load; both failed. Ruger even offered their Model 77 reamed to the .35 caliber; maybe five people bought one. Such small outfits as Alpha Arms Company and Shilen have catalogued the .358, and others like KDF and DuBiel will build you anything you want within reason; still the .358 languishes. But it doesn't die.

It so happens that the two best .358 hunting rifles—with one possible exception—are available today; not on special order, but right out of their makers' literature. (The single exception is the Savage 99, the passing of which I lament very much.)

What are these two rifles? The excellent, accurate and fairly traditional Browning BLR lever action and the Ultra Light Arms Model 20, perhaps the finest hunting turnbolt one can buy.

For woods hunting, either of this duo will perform to perfection. Both can be had short of barrel; the BLR comes only with a 20-inch tube, the ULA with just about whatever you want. One is moderately priced, the other expensive; both are at home in the woods.

One common mistake is to assume that the blunt .358 is limited to short range. It is at its *best* at 250 yards or less, but when handloaded carefully using Hornady's spire-pointed 200 grainer, it will show but 8.3 inches of drop at 300 yards, from a 200-yard zero. Choose the pointed 250 Speer soft point and you'll have a 300-yard dip of less than 12 inches and about 1900 foot-pounds of energy remaining. Sound like a short-range cartridge to you?

I have killed only whitetail and mule deer with the .358. Oddly, the closest shot I've made was about 175 yards or so, the longest just shy of 300 yards.

Rick Jamison conked a charging black bear on the bean with his Savage 99, at tobacco-spittin' distance. He had been calling alone (which he *knows* is a no-no), his attention riveted on a game trail to his front. A huge black bear—one of the heaviest ever taken in Arizona—zeroed in on him from the rear and came a'runnin'. When Jamison's mental radar finally pinpointed the direction from which the bruin was closing the attack, he barely had time to turn, center the crosswires on the bear's noggin, and let one go. Fortunately, Rick has extraordinary reflexes, is a superb big-game shot and was firing a bullet of sufficient drive to punch through a brawny skull at close range. He survived the encounter intact, if somewhat shaky. And wiser.

Mr. Jamison used a 250 Speer spitzer on his bear. Linda Jamison used the same gun and load on a magnificent six-point bull elk that year. She whacked the old boy in the center of his chest at maybe 80 yards as he stood watching her. He spun around, attempted to extricate himself from the battlefield. She shot him again, and again. He gave up and expired.

This bear came to Rick Jamison's predator call. The bear was within spittin' distance when Rick conked him on the bean with a 250-grain bullet from his .358 Win. Savage 99.

Neither I nor Rick nor Linda have ever shot anything that weighed under 200 pounds on the hoof with our .358 Winchester rifles. Only Linda's elk required a second shot to bring it to ground. For game up through bull elk in heft, the little .358 works fine, thanks. That, of course, includes black bear.

.356 Winchester

The .356 Winchester cartridge looks like the .358 Winchester wearing overshoes. Aside from a difference in operating pressures (the .358 is loaded hotter), the newer .356 is but a rimmed version of its elder brother. So why do we need it?

In order to bolster the sagging sales of the still-popular but under-powered Model 94 Carbine, Winchester introduced the .375 Winchester in the late 1970s. Although the .375 was a little more potent than the .30-30—due primarily to a higher chamber pressure threshold—the .375 was still not as powerful as the .444 Marlin, which was available in a comparably-sized package. The boys at Winchester marshalled their forces.

The Marlin 336-ER in .356 is one of the author's favorite rifles for bear to 200 yards.

The result was a duo of new brush loads housed in the Model 94 Big Bore (a beefed-up iteration of the venerable carbine). The smaller cartridge was dubbed the .307 Winchester and was basically a rimmed .308 Winchester, toned down a bit in juice. The larger bore was the .356. *Now* Winchester had a pair of real he-man cartridges for the seeker of deer, bear and even bigger game at close quarters.

Nobody rushed out to buy them. Too bad. The .307 fails to stir my blood, for several mostly esoteric reasons, but the .356 is a damned good cartridge. In the Marlin 336 lever action, it is likely the best deer and black bear outfit for ranges up to 200 yards ever introduced.

Quoted ballistics are mouth watering for a cartridge in this class. Olin says their 200-grain flat point will reach 2,460 fps; the 250-grain of similar construction is listed at 2,160. Not bad, right? Unfortunately, in a 20-inch carbine barrel, things are not as they seem. One lot of the 200-grain stuff exited my 20-inch Marlin at 2,283 fps; another virtually matched it. The 250-grain load ran from 2000 fps up to 2,043, depending on the lot and the temperature. Not disgusting, but not palpitation-inducing, either.

As with so many cartridges, handloading tells the tale. Slip the 220 Speer flat point into your brass; stoke it up to 2,300 fps at the muzzle. Retained 200-yard energy is a whopping 1,600 foot-pounds, give or take a couple. The powerhouse .444 carries but 1,150 or so at the same range, the .45-70 Government around 1,000 in its best Remington factory version, and the .30-30 class of loads runs 10 percent less than that. Even the .307 Winchester shows but 1,400 foot-pounds or so at 200 yards, and that's according to factory figures, which are not realized in the real world.

Nope, nothing ever stuffed into a Marlin 336 or Winchester 94 equals the .356 when it comes to toting lots of energy clear out to the limit of its trajectory. The only cartridge in its league is the .348 Winchester, and that only with handloaded 200-grain Hornady bullets and a barrel at least 24 inches long. (Remember, all .356s boast a 20-inch tube.)

The .356 is fading fast. Winchester deserted it a few years ago, and Marlin has recently dropped it as well. If you're a woods hunter, I suggest you grab one quick, assuming you can locate it. They aren't plentiful, but they're good.

.444 Marlin

Marlin's big, crushing .444 came along in 1964, stuffed into a modified 336 lever action, complete with 24-inch barrel and a Monte Carlo buttstock. This was a brush rifle? Well, the new round was certainly a brush *cartridge*, anyway.

Early write-ups of the load harped on several points. To wit: 1) the rifle itself was too long, too heavy, too awkward for a woods gun; 2) the rifle/cartridge combination was unusually accurate; 3) the muzzle energy (over 3,000 foot-pounds) made it a real earth-mover of a load; 4) very frangible pistol bullets were loaded by the factory (Remington), and were subsequently certain to get some hapless bear hunter et or moose hunter stomped on.

Item number one was indeed correct, and has been attended to quite satisfactorily by Marlin. The current-issue Model 444 (a variation of the 336, incidentally) boasts a traditional buttstock and but 22 inches of barrel. (Still a couple inches more than I like for rooting around in the bushes, but any decent gunsmith can fix that pronto.)

In my experience, the .444 Marlin *is* uncommonly accurate. The only traditional lever-action cartridge from which I have received superior accuracy is the little 7-30 Waters. Though the .356 Winchester is in there pitching. Several shooters whose word I'll accept have told me of .444s that will group good ammo (sometimes even factory ammunition) under two inches at 100 yards, with some claiming 1½-inch capability. My own testing has not achieved such remarkable clusters, but my Marlin will easily slip under 2¼ inches without undue labor at the loading bench, and with iron sights at that.

In factory-loaded form, the .444 won't make 3,000 foot-pounds, at least not in my gun. However, one lot managed 2,240 fps at the muzzle, another 2,241. Consistent? Such speeds are good for nearly 2,700 foot-pounds. (Factory claim for the 240-grain

.444 is 2,350 fps, for 2,942 foot-pounds.) Remington also offers a heavier 265-grain rendition, in answer to Item Four above, at a quoted 2,120 fps and 2,644 foot-pounds. My Marlin kicked that one out at 2,042 fps, giving 2,453 foot-pounds.

Make no mistake; such are serious numbers. At modest distances—say to 150 yards—they will reduce the burliest of black bear to a rug if bullet placement is up to snuff. Nonetheless, the .444 is no long-distance number. It will do to a bruin at 150 yards what a .44 Mag. carbine will at about 50, so take that into consideration. Handloading, of course, improves the look of things.

Achieving 2,360 fps with a 240-grain soft-point bullet is a piece of cake if you select your components wisely and have at least 22 inches of barrel to launch from. My favored recipe moves the Speer 240 Magnum soft point at such a speed, and I have fired it into flesh and bone. Not only will it expand, it will hang together nicely. For a bit deeper penetration, one can go to the 265 Hornady flat point, one of the Barnes pure-copper-tubing soft points of up to 300 grains in weight, or use the new Freedom Arms .429-inch pistol bullets. I have fired the 300-grain version from this latter company into a boar hog at an estimated impact speed of about 1,200 fps. It penetrated from breast to buttocks and expanded to .58 caliber. For a long-range .444 load, that's a whale of a slug!

There is something to be said for the sheer volume of tissue that the .444 displaces as it bores through game. Add to the equation the hefty energy at reasonable ranges and the heavy, expanding bullets; it's easy to see that the .444 is an unpalatable dose of lead when properly applied.

.45-70 Government

A real oldy, the .45-70 Government. Since 1873 its fortunes have waxed and waned as numerous generations were beguiled by its thumb-sized bullet, only later to fall victim to younger, faster cartridges. Or sometimes the reverse. Having started off with flat-shooting loads, somewhere along the line a light, fragile bullet failed to negotiate thick bones, tough sinews, and a disillusioned hunter sought more bullet, less speed. No matter the route, sooner or later most gun enthusiasts arrive at the .45-70's doorstep.

For many, many years a 405-grain soft point at roughly 1,330 fps was standard fare. The big, bluff slug held onto about 1,000 foot-pounds clear out to 200 yards, but its trajectory resembled that of a softball tossed underhanded by a geriatric patient. In days of yore (*really* yore), a 500-grain load was common and well thought of. Aside from an ability to penetrate 97 cinder blocks, I can't imagine it had much practical usefulness.

Today, only Remington continues to offer the old 405-grain bullet. *De rigueur* today is a 300-grain jacketed hollow point at a quoted 1,810 muzzle speed in the Remington catalogue, 1,880 fps according to Federal and Winchester. This is one of the few discrepancies found in current factory-load data sheets. Not only does the Remington fodder yield 70 fps to its competitors at the muzzle, it gives up 173 foot-pounds. The difference becomes more pronounced as the range lengthens. By the time the Remington bullet has sailed the length of two football fields, it carries but 1,031 foot-pounds. The Federal and Winchester entries retain 1,355 at the 200 yard mark. Curious.

In trajectory, the Remington load relinquishes two full inches of drop at 200 yards to its opposite numbers. Not significant, but not really trifling either, especially for a cartridge that needs all the help it can get in the flatness department. Curiouser and curiouser.

In my view, the factory-loaded .45-70 is a 150-yard load at best. Handloads are the key, even more so than with most other cartridges. Such modern rifles as the Marlin Model 1895-SS and Browning's copy of the 1886 Winchester are strong enough to handle pressures exceeding those of the ancient relics for which the factories must load their ammunition. Even stronger are the Ruger Number One and Browning 1885 single shots, which are chambered for magnum cartridges routinely loaded to 54,000 c.u.p. Naturally, the owners of these stout firearms need not feed their rifles such milquetoast as the ammunition companies provide.

When loaded judiciously, the .45-70 easily provides energy levels in the 3,200-3,400 foot-pound neighborhood, which unfortunately is a pretty painful district, both for the shootee and the shooter! Thus, most .45-70 velocity levels are limited by their owners' resistance to discomfort, not any arbitrary pressure limitations placed on their armament.

For game of black bear bulk and strength, I'd stoke the furnace as hot as I could stand without losing control of my accuracy, i.e. developing an uncontrollable flinch. Slinging a 350 Hornady round nose to about 1,900-2,000 fps at the muzzle seems to be my point of diminishing returns, at least in most .45-70 rifles. We're talking well over 3,000 foot-pounds here, and plenty of it left out at 150 yards, where trajectory limitations take over.

Accuracy is no problem. I've never fired a .45-70 I can recall that failed to group inside three inches at 100 yards, which would correspond to five inches or so at 150. That's good enough. For those of you who are still inquisitive about the .45-70's precision, I'll relate two items: 1) it was used in long-range rifle competition for decades, and did right well; 2) my Browning 1885 goes under two inches at 100 yards with factory stuff. Fret not about the .45-70's ability to keep bullet holes close together, on paper *or* game.

The .45-70, like the .44 Magnum, .375 Winchester and .444 Marlin, has a straight-sided case. That makes for minimal case stretching, thus minimal case *trimming*, one of handloading's most Sisyphean tasks. Most slab-sided cases respond best to the quicker rifle powders, which are easy to ignite. The quicker powders are also used in smaller quantities than their slower-burning counterparts, which is good for economy, both of propellant usage and of recoil effects.

As you can see, the .45-70 has several strong suits, few warts. If I had to do all my black-bear gunning amidst crowded vegetation, I would likely toss a coin between the .444 Marlin and the .45-70. And if I were limited to the use of non-premium bullets instead of the Barnes line or the Freedom Arms, I would pick the .45-70 solely on the basis of the Hornady 350-grain round nose. On the other foot, were I restricted to factory ammunition, I'd eschew the .45-70 altogether and go with the 265-grain/.444 combo.

Special-Situation Black Bear Cartridges

That brings us all the way through my first-team choices of black-bear loads. The bulk of my hunting could probably be handled amply by any of the foregoing. However, sometimes I find myself overlooking one of those extensive Pamlico Manor bean fields, glassing a bear some 350 or more yards away. Such times will find me most often with a magnum rifle in my lap. The 7mms (Remington or Weatherby), the .300s, the 8mm Remington, even the .338 and .340 Weatherby Mags are not too much gun for a really big black bear at long range. Sometimes not even at *close* range.

My buddy Doug Solomon shot his 413-pound black at virtually point-blank with a .338 Browning BAR. He was sitting in ambush, watching a beehive, when old *ursus* came in to the sound of honey. Lighting conditions were poor, and Doug's bullets didn't go exactly where they were supposed to. The bear roared a bit and ran

Doug Solomon took this big 413-pound black bear in coastal North Carolina, with a Browning BAR in .338 Winchester Magnum and the help of trail dog Molly. The bruin was hit hard, but took off. A night-time follow-up led to an exciting climax.

off. Three guides followed him up late into the night, with the assistance of a dog named Molly. Several times Molly found the bear, flushed it, whereupon its pursuers let off a round or two. Blood everywhere. But never a carcass.

Finally, the bear decided he'd had enough. The last time Molly dug him out of the reeds, he carried the fight to the hunters. One emptied his shotgun, a second his rifle, the third fired all six shots from his Ruger Redhawk .44 Magnum into the bruin, all at arm's length. The bear gave up his spirit grudgingly even then.

Further argument for sufficient power at long range: Think back to this chapter's opening story. My first bullet—all 160 grains of it—had traversed the bear's lungs, smashed the off shoulder, exited. The estimated impact energy was about 1,550 foot-pounds, which is nearly identical to that retained by a .300 Holland & Holland Magnum factory load at 400 yards, and superior to some .300 Winchester Magnum loadings. Do you still wonder why I like a magnum round for long-range work?

The .35s work well on both bear and boar. Here are three of the better ones.

There are areas I hunt where a 250- to 300-yard shot might occasionally be offered, but normally ranges are less than that. Under such conditions, I carry a rifle like the Browning A-Bolt .280 I used to take my bear last season. Any cartridge in the same league—the 7mm-08 Remington, 7 X 57, .284 Winchester, .308 Winchester or .30-06 as examples—will work fine, as we discussed earlier. I can make no fine distinction among them although, as when whitetail hunting, if I plan to spend much time in the woods, I lean toward a short, light gun such as the Remington Model 7. For more open terrain, give me a 22-inch moderate-heft outfit in any of the above chamberings and I'll be perfectly happy.

But to set it in stone, let's reiterate my choices. For shots out to no more than 150 yards, with 100 or less most likely, I like the .444 Marlin or the .45-70 in a repeater like the Marlin 1895-SS. For shots to a maximum of 200 yards in mixed terrain, I'd tote a Marlin .356 and never look back. For come-what-may gunning, from ranges hard off the muzzle to 300 yards maximum, I'd purchase a Remington Model 700 Mountain Rifle in 7mm-08 Remington or .308 Winchester if money were tight. If the old bank account were flush, I'd carry an Ultra Light Arms Model 20 reamed to .284 Winchester, .308 Winchester or .358 Winchester. And for stand-hunting over a considerable expanse of real estate, I would want my A-Square .340 Weatherby Magnum, although any good 7mm Magnum (especially my Winchester Model 70 Winlite) would serve about as well. Equally good—and preferable if I have to walk far—would be an Ultra Light Arms Model 28 .338

Magnum, with muzzle brake. Them's my picks, friends.

About Hogs

This chapter also concerns the proper armament for taking wild hogs, whether feral, part-Russian, European, or Bolshevik. Makes not one whit of difference in the killing; they are all *tough*.

Although I do know of a few hogs that were *killed* with only one shot, I know of only one that was stopped in his tracks unless: 1) the spine was hit solidly; 2) the brain was hit; 3) both shoulders were broken, at the joint. So long as a good, deep-penetrating bullet is used and at least 700 or 800 foot-pounds of energy are on tap at impact, it doesn't seem to make much difference what you slap a hog with, assuming the lungs, spine, brain or heart are damaged. Regardless of what load you use he will generally run away, often as if he were not even touched assuming the bullet does not connect with items 1, 2 or 3 (from above!)

An example. A few years ago I popped a 350-pound pig (estimated weight) at about 100 yards with a 240-grain bullet from a Marlin .444. My slug sliced through both lungs and lodged in the offside ribcage. I could scarcely see the hog; he was behind some trees, milling around with several of his cronies. At my shot, the little herd vanished. A moment later, here they came, chuffing down the game trail beside which sat Mrs. Harvey's little boy.

The lead hog was a big red brute; his three cabooses were smaller and darker. The big guy spotted me, stopped, peered myopically at my handsome visage. Figuring that none of these porkers was the one I had ventilated, I stepped out from behind my tree, figuring the movement would spook them. The rearmost trio turned, pointed their curly tails at me and vamoosed. Big Red stood his ground. I didn't like that much.

I shook my gun at him, holding it well away from my body to be certain he could distinguish me from a mountain laurel. He could, all right. He dipped his head, shifted his weight forward, and charged. I deterred him by blowing a .44-caliber hole in his ribs. When the heavy soft point collided with his chest, he sank back on his haunches from the thrust, stared me straight in the eye, and gave up the ghost. That hog *wanted* me!

Turned out that Big Red was the pig I'd shot some distance up the mountain. The bullet wounds crisscrossed his barrel-like rib box. And yet he had shown no evidence of being hit. Typical.

Dave Petzal, of *Field & Stream*, zapped a big sow once, from a treestand. Using a 100-grain soft point in his .257 Roberts, he

The .444 Marlin is another good choice on both bear and hogs.

gassed her right between the shoulder blades. Dave suspects his bullet must have touched her spine, since at the hit she sank to her knees. Not for long, though. In an instant she was up and running. She fell dead before making many more porcine tracks, but if Dave had been on the ground and in her path, things could have gotten right lively!

Mr. Petzal slew two more hogs, both with a hot-loaded .270 using Nosler Partition bullets. Though each was well hit—in the lungs—more than one shot was required. As I said, pigs are tough.

I've been on hunts where boars were shot with .30-30s, .308s, and .30-06s, with .223 carbines, .357 Magnum revolvers, .45 Autos, .41 and .44 Magnums. The result was usually predictable; hit in the heart or lungs, all of them ran a spell, often as not

You really can't be overgunned for hogs. They'll absorb a lot of lead before they figure out they're dead. In the meantime, those tusks could do some nasty carving on your calves.

straight at the hunter. When major bones were struck, they hit the turf. Even then, they were reluctant to die.

An example is the pan-sized black pig I dropped last month, the first boar I ever decked on the spot, with one shot. He was running full-tilt, bent on Ridgewood, New Jersey, or some such distant place, when I waylaid him by pulping both shoulders with a 300-grain bullet fired from 15 steps. He took a dive into a pile of forest litter, all 150 pounds of him, lay there with both shoulder joints burst beyond repair and tried to rock himself up with his hind legs! I ran over and heaved another 300-grain soft point into him; it impacted just to the right of his sternum, negotiated the gristle plate, disintegrated his heart, and wound up in the tenderloin on the opposite side, near his pelvis. Still took him a minute or so to quit breathing. A whitetail hit thus would be rendered into venison nigh instantly, especially if both shoulders had previously been softened by absorbing 1,000 foot-pounds of energy!

The thing to remember, again, about hogs is to use a good, stout bullet for deep penetration, and to aim for big bones. If the pig is close, and you have no designs on his head for mounting, a brain shot will work well. However, a pig's brain is both small and well-protected; if you have to *angle* that slug into his cranium, bullet deflection is a very real possibility. For that reason, I feel the shoulder is better. But remember most of all that a hog almost *never* drops at the shot unless his brain or spine is disconnected.

So, what gun and load is best at keeping a big boar hog from chewing up some of your favorite parts? Most anything, although the smaller calibers often provide insufficient penetration regardless of bullet selection. A good .44 carbine like the Marlin is fine, as is a .30-30 or .35 Remington. More power doesn't seem to kill them any quicker.

Marginal power, on the other hand, *definitely* kills them slower! I've assisted in slaying hogs with a .357 revolver, and watched them take hit after hit in the chest and keep going. The .357 *revolver* (and the .223 Remington rifle load) is *not* a hog load. But let's look at the other side of the cartridge.

I hunted last fall with Fannie Flint and her husband, of West Unity, Ohio. Mrs. Flint used a Savage over/under rifle/shotgun combination. Her rifle barrel was reamed to the .357 Magnum cartridge.

Fannie had a 180-grain Federal hollow point up the spout when her pig came along. She shot the 100-pounder (estimated) in the heart, whereupon he galloped a spell and fell dead. Impact energy

Good bullets are essential in a pig load. There is a lot of cartilage and gristle to grind through before the projectile hits vital organs.

was perhaps 900 foot-pounds, which was sufficient as fired from a *rifle*. I doubt that hog would have reacted differently had she bopped him with a .338 Winchester Magnum. His pump was wrecked, so he was not long for this world. But pigs take their own time expiring.

Short, light, easy to handle, mild of recoil—that adds up to a boar rifle. I prefer iron sights, since in most areas shots are often measured in *feet* rather than yards, and sometimes the action comes fast and furious. But whatever else you retain about them, be certain to file this: *pigs are tough.*

7

Cartridges For
Mountain Game

When North American hunters refer to mountain game, the two creatures commonly alluded to are the various species of sheep and the Rocky Mountain goat. Other animals, like grizzlies and caribou, haunt the wind-swept peaks, but "mountain hunting" involves sheep and goats in the average hunter's mind.

Sheep

Actually, most any cartridge is an OK sheep cartridge, excepting of course the .22 centerfires and the close-range whitetail busters. Dedicated sheep seekers choose their *rifles* first, then decide which cartridge will fit into it. That's the proper course of action, at least in my view.

Wild sheep are not especially large animals, about the size and heft of the average mule deer, with only rare specimens going as heavy as 300 pounds. Nor are they especially tenacious of life; some experienced sheep hunters opine that a big whitetail buck will absorb more misplaced lead than any sheep, and travel farther while doing so. A mean, wooly-headed cartridge is out of its element here. Further, such ordnance could be a decided hindrance. How so?

For one thing, hard-hitting cartridges do so at both ends. As I keep saying, because it has been proven time and again, the harder you get whacked when you squeeze the trigger, the more likely you are to shoot something in its umbilical area. Not good.

Almost as bad is the fact that rifles chambered to the more muscular cartridges, especially the magnum clan above 7mm, come mostly in one size—long, heavy, awkward. Toting such a monstrosity over hill and shale is not only obtrusive, not only fatiguing, not only threatening to your ticker, it's just plain dumb. And unnecessary. If you're hunting correctly, no sheep is so tough, no shot so long, that a belted bellerin' magnum is requisite. But there you'd be, wheezing from the burden of a cumbersome, oversized load, trying to stick a bullet into an area the size of a cantaloupe way out there at 190 yards, from a rickety sitting position, with the wind tugging at your toupee and a guide in your ear whispering stridently, "What're you waitin' for?"

And then there is the danger factor. The danger factor? Absolutely. Scaling cliffs is hazardous enough without having a rifle as long as a punting pole slung over one shoulder, stabbing rocks and brush, unsettling your tenuous balance at exactly the wrong moment. Equally unnerving is to be perched precariously atop a knife-edged rim pointing Old Boomer at yon ridge, then to touch off a shot and be catapulted into the void. This is *not* farfetched; deer hunters have been booted out of tree stands by hard-kicking firearms. And somersaulting 10 feet out of a sweetgum is not correspondent to losing your perch atop a Yukon peak.

An additional consideration is the vertical geography in which sheep conduct their business. A steep uphill or downslope angle can threaten your shooting orb if your scope is short on eye relief. Take my word for it, with some of the nastier magnums, you need as much eye relief as you can get when shooting level, let alone at a 45-degree angle. Besides, as mentioned above there is no demonstrable need for one of the big-bore magnum loads. So which cartridges do I suggest? Let's prescribe some parameters.

Although more wild sheep are taken at under 200 yards than over, let's assume that if your luck runs true to form, the biggest ram you'll ever see will be bedded in the lee of a boulder 297 paces away. To be prepared for such an occasion, I recommend that a sheep hunter choose a cartridge capable of pushing a bullet of 6.5mm diameter or larger, weighing at least 120 grains, at a muzzle speed of 2,660 fps or better. With such a load, 300-yard drop from a 200-yard zero would be nine inches or less. Retained energy with a good streamlined bullet would run to at least 1,150 foot-pounds. Such cartridges as the 6.5 X 55 Swedish

Big hairy-chested magnums are not prerequisite for sheep hunting. Young Scott Hiett did a fine one-shot job on this Dall ram with his .270 Winchester.

Bob Nosler, of Nosler Bullet Company, illustrates how steep some shooting for mountain game can be. Careful caliber/rifle choice will make such awkward opportunities more comfortable and safer.

Mauser, the 6.5 Remington Magnum, the .270 Winchester, 7mm-08 Remington, 7 X 57 Mauser, .280 Remington, .284 Winchester, .308 Winchester, .30-06 and the 8 X 57 Mauser all have what it takes, and without heavy recoil. The 7mm Magnums do too, of course, and a lot of hunters cling to them. I do not intend to fulminate their choice, only note that I don't endorse the Big Seven for this application.

You may have noticed that I cited a cartridge in the above list you might not be familiar with, one I haven't brought up before: the 6.5 Remington Magnum. I've avoided its mention simply because it is nearly dead, was in fact virtually stillborn except in one iteration, now also defunct.

When originally issued in the mid-'60s, the 6.5 Magnum was housed in the ugly little Remington Model 600 carbine, which bore a laminated stock (before its time), one of the homeliest bolt handles ever to grace a turnbolt, a stubby 18½-inch barrel (also before its time), a bolt release that required a prestidigitator to manipulate, a synthetic (again, before its time) floorplate/trigger guard assembly, a ridiculous ventilated rib made of the same material and burdened at its forward end by a shark's-fin front sight that had everyone laughing and pointing. However... the rifle weighed only 6½ pounds (again demonstrating its precociousness), gave roughly .270-class ballistics from its abbreviated tube, shot like the blazes, kicked moderately due to an excellent stock design and didn't set a potential buyer on his ear from sticker shock. Alas, the outfit wouldn't wash.

Remington tried to allay the dismayed reactions the strange little rifle evoked by lengthening its barrel a smidgen, tossing that horrible, warp-prone vent rib into the waste can, and otherwise cleaning up its act. Didn't work. In a last-ditch effort to salvage something from all those developmental dollars, Remington stuck the squat, belted 6.5 cartridge into the Model 700 queue, fitted it with a 24-inch medium-heavy barrel and Monte Carlo stock, then sat back to watch the public's reaction. Said response was narcoleptic. Even Ruger couldn't help out, although they tried with a short run of Model 77 turnbolts, even a Number One or two.

The cartridge, now orphaned among the major producers, is remembered vaguely, if at all. Should you run across one of the original Model 600 carbines, it might make a dandy sheep getter. I'd consider snatching it up if its price didn't reflect collector status. So much for esoterica.

I suppose it's tough for you to accept the premise that one doesn't require a *bona fide* flat-shooting terror for use on wild sheep, especially if you've never hunted them. Don't take my word for it. Let me quote an excerpt from Jack O'Connor's excellent work, *Sheep and Sheep Hunting*, published by Winchester in 1974:

"The little 7 X 57 cartridge is still an excellent all-around cartridge, one with light recoil, excellent accuracy, and with lighter bullets a trajectory adequately flat for 95 percent of all sheep hunting. The light recoil of the little 7-mm is of great importance because except for some hairy-chested outdoor writers most of us shoot rifles of light recoil better than we do rifles of heavy recoil and also because the sheep hunter must often shoot from odd and uncomfortable positions from which he may be hurt by heavy recoil. He might even be kicked off a rock ledge.

"That first ram of mine, as I now remember it, was shot at around 30 yards (good quail range), certainly not over 50 yards. This short range was by no means exceptional, but the fact that the sheep was running was. Actually most sheep are taken when they are standing or perhaps more often lying in their beds. This short-range business may take some non-sheep hunters by surprise .... The last desert ram I shot was not over 30 yards away, and the best Dall I have ever taken was maybe 40 yards from the muzzle when it went down. The reason for the close shots is that sheep are often but not always found in rough country where they can be approached from behind ridges. On occasion longer shots must be taken, but the rule by which the sheep hunter should abide is never to take a shot that he is not absolutely certain he can make, be it 30 or 300 yards.'' Amen!

In the Outdoor Life book, *The Art of Hunting Big Game in North America*, also by Jack O'Connor, he mentions an old-time sheep-hunting acquaintance of his named Charlie Ren. Described by O'Connor as a skinny, tough little character, Ren was a mining engineer who spent much of his time in the desert, prospecting and hunting sheep. Jack claims to have been astonished when he discovered what Charlie used on most of his bighorns: a haggard old iron-sighted Model 94 Winchester levergun reamed to .25-35 WCF, an outdated number even in the '30s. No external finish remained on the carbine, either on wood or metal, but its bore shown like a freshly-minted gold dollar.

When Jack pumped him about sheep rifles, he reported Ren's response thus: ''Hell's bells, the trick of sheep hunting is to find the damned things. Once you've done that you can knock them over with just about anything.''

O'Connor noticed that Charlie carried fine binoculars, a large, much-used pair of European Hensoldt roof-prism jobs that he suspected were 10 X 50s. ''Give me a good glass,'' Ren stated, ''and I'll hunt sheep with a .22. I don't care so much about the caliber of the rifle just so long as it's light.''

Which is as good a way as any to lead into the crux of any discussion of sheep armament: the rifle. You just read Charlie Ren's opinion, stressing light weight above all else. So how about O'Connor? What did he deduce after all his years seeking sheep in numerous countries on several continents? Let me quote him from the aforementioned Outdoor Life tome: ''Above all a sheep rifle should be reasonably light and handy.''

O'Connor once wrote that he left a Sonora sheep camp at four o'clock in the morning, climbed around in jumbled-up country all day and returned to camp after midnight. He has also stated that the day he shot his largest Stone ram, a real monster, he and his guide left camp as soon as they could see, killed his ram somewhere between seven and 10 miles from the campsite and about 3,000 feet above it. It was well after dark when they got the meat and cape back to camp.

Need any more convincing?

For sheep hunting, lighter is better. But then that's my philosophy for all hunting on-the-move. So let's talk about rifles.

If I were after the ultimate sheep tool, and had to pick from affordable rifles found on dealers' shelves, I would lean toward as short and light as possible. Prime examples would be: Ruger Ultra Light Bolt-Action Rifle (the 20-inch RL) in .308 Winchester (because it doesn't come in 7mm-08) or .270 Winchester; Remington Model 7 (especially the synthetic FS version) in 7mm-08 Remington; Browning's A-Bolt Micro-Medallion in 7mm-08; Winchester Model 70 Lightweight (particularly the Win-tuff laminated permutation) in .270, .280 Remington or .308; and finally, the synthetic Weatherby Fiberguard in .308 Winchester. I would hesitate to narrow my choice further except to say that due to several reasons, especially the vagaries of sheep-country weather, I lean toward synthetic stocks as first choice, with a good wood laminate as runner-up.

Now, about my caliber selections. I discount all calibers below 7mm for two reasons: 1) no popular-priced lightweight rigs are available in 6.5 X 55 as of this writing; 2) sheep country, as mentioned earlier, is also grizzly country. While I would not choose to pursue a grizzly with any cartridge mentioned above, I believe I could prevent a truculent one from chewing on me if armed with any of them, assuming I'd selected my bullets carefully.

I would go about that selection thus: for the 7mm-08, I'd handload a good 140-grain spitzer for sheep, and try to develop a load that would print close to the same point of impact with the 175 Nosler Partition in regards to the unpleasant prospect of having to fend off a feisty bruin. If unsuccessful at matchinq said impact points, I'd switch to the lighter 160-grain Partition and try again. Should my rifle remain obdurate, I would abandon the two-bullet concept and center my loading experiments around the 150 Nosler Partition, using that bullet for anything I had to shoot. For the hunter who does not handload, and who doesn't know someone who is a competent reloader, I would not recommend the 7mm-08.

In the .270 Winchester, I would simply handload to maximum the Nosler 150-grain Partition and be done with it. That bullet would handle any chore asked of it, including scrambling a grizzly's innards if required. If I thought the possibility of encountering a grizzly extremely remote, and was certain I wouldn't want to add a moose to my bag, I'd choose a good

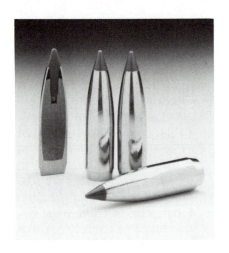

Nosler Ballistic Tip bullets are some of the best made for long-range gunning of thin-skinned game.

pointed boattail like the Speer or Nosler Ballistic Tip for sheep. I would still stick a few of the 150 Partition handloads in my pocket in case I ran into bear trouble, however unlikely. The non-handloader can have his cake and eat it too, since Federal has seen fit to offer the superb Nosler 150-grain Partition bullet in factory guise.

For the .280 Remington, I would duplicate my .270 strategy, although I might go to the 160 or 175 Nosler Partitions for bear medicine if I could coincide the point of impact of the sheep load with my bear recipe. The factory-load user has the same option available as does the .270 shooter; he can just ante up for a few boxes of Federal's Premium 150-grain Partition rendition and head north.

Any good 150-grain pointed soft-point boattail will do nicely for sheep out of a .308 Winchester. Once again I'd try to match its point of impact with a 180- or 200-grain Nosler Partition, should a grizzly express intent on repositioning my gizzard. If I ran into difficulty doing so, I'd go to a 165-grain boattail for the horned game, and use a 180 Partition as my bear repellent. If my rifle still refused to cooperate in grouping both bullet weights close together, I would either wrap it around a tree or shoot 180-grain bullets at everything.

Actually, this latter course isn't such a bad idea; a good boattail like the Speer or Nosler Ballistic tip can be driven to 2,600 fps out of a 20-inch .308. Zeroed for 200 yards, the dip at 300 is only 8.9 and 8.8 inches respectively. Moving the zero range out to 240

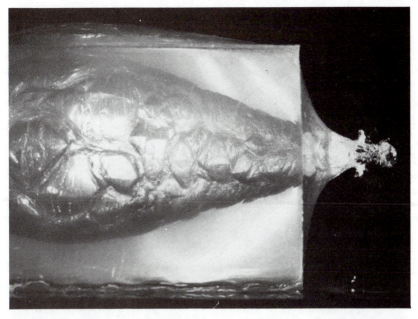

In ballistics gelatin, the results of Winchester's Supreme Silvertip boattail are impressive. Likely it will be likewise in game.

yards wouldn't put mid-range rise too high, and would subjugate the long-range drop tellingly. A handful of 180-grain Partition handloads could then handle the self-defense situation.

Factory ammo presents more of a problem because of the absence of Nosler bullets in this chambering. So here'd be my plan for the .308: I would shoot the 165 Federal soft-point boattail Premium at sheep, and tote a quantity of either the 180 Remington pointed soft-point Core-Lokt or the new 180 Winchester Supreme boattail Silvertip as a bear foil.

Them's my thoughts on the subject. Are you wondering what Jack O'Connor, the old master, had to say about his preference in sheep loads? Here he is, quoted from the aforementioned Outdoor Life book: "For my money the standouts in the field are the .280 Remington and the .284 and .270 Winchesters. With their 125- and 130-grain bullets they are all flat-shooting, deadly and generally very accurate in a tuned-up rifle of light weight. Recoil is light, even in well-stocked 7½- and 8-pound rifles, and yet they are powerful enough for the moose and grizzlies one is apt to run into in sheep country.''

Winchester's new Supreme Silvertip boattail is available in several sheep and goat getting calibers, like 180-grain .30-06.

One final admonishment about this business of bear-prevention ammunition. In the first place, a grizzly generally won't bother you if you leave it alone. In the second place, if one does decide to pick a fight, you may be able to steal away unscathed. This is preferable for several reasons, not the least of which is the dim view taken by game-department officials of hunters shooting bears without having valid bear tags regardless of provocation. Thirdly, for a bear to do much damage, it has to be close, right? If Bre'r Bear is at arm's length, the exact point of impact of your load is not too important, at least within reason. The moral is not to put too much effort into getting your bruin-stopper to hit right on the button; much better to zero precisely your sheep load, since that's far and away the one you're most likely to use.

If a sheep hunter could afford any outfit he desired, which is likely given the cost of hunting wild rams today, here's what I would recommend: an Ultra-Light Arms Model 20 in .284 Winchester. I would tote handloaded 130 Speer soft-point boattails for sheep, with a few 175 Noslers readily accessible so I could sleep soundly. I'd zero for 250 yards, then would be only 3.5 inches low at 300, 8.5 down at 350. The maximum ordinate would be 2.9 at 145 yards, which wouldn't present a problem in close-range shooting. Retained energy at 350 yards is 1,531 foot pounds, plenty for sheep-sized game.

There are likely to be some hunters who will worry more about the possibility of a grizzly attack than how best to harvest a sheep. If I leaned that way, I'd choose a ULA M20 in .358 Winchester. It would wear a 20-inch barrel, sport a muzzle brake that tames the recoil to that of a .243 and kick 250-grain soft points from its snoot at nearly 2,400 fps. So boosted, a 250 Speer spitzer drops just over 11 inches at 300 yards when zeroed at 200, and hangs onto 1,900 foot pounds at that extended range. More importantly for the bear-wary nimrod, that hulking Speer soft point would slap Mr. Bruin with a 2700-foot-pound punch at 50 yards, which I doubt he'd be able to shrug off easily.

My pal Ken Warner, ramrod of *Gun Digest* and one of the most erudite gentlemen I know, told me that if he were hieing off to Alaska in pursuit of an elusive Dall ram, he would take along a Custom Gun Guild-modified Remington Model Seven takedown carbine in 7-08. Ken says he'd break it down (takes maybe five seconds for him, two or three for anybody else), stick it in his rucksack, choose a sturdy man-sized staff (Ken is, if nothing else, *man-sized*) and take to the hills. Should he run across a shootable ram (mostly a matter of luck, I suspect), he'd off with the pack, out with the rifle halves, a quick flick of thick wrists, and *presto* ... dead sheep. That approach is typical of Mister Warner: logical, workable, good common sense. So why didn't I think of it?

That takes care of the sheep situation. Remember, go light, carry a moderately powerful round that shoots flat enough for 300-yard gunning (or a bit more if you're up to it) and look with a jaundiced eye on barrels longer than 22 inches.

One final thought from Jack O'Connor, out of his tome *Sheep and Sheep Hunting*: "I have heard some tales by sheep authorities whose hunting experience is very limited about how difficult sheep are to kill. All stuff and nonsense! Sheep are wounded and missed for two reasons. For one, hunters often get wildly excited and miss rams at 50 yards or less. For another, they blast away at long and

In sheep hunting, the terrain dictates the rifle and caliber. That means short, light and low recoil.

doubtful range, sometimes wounding but more often missing and scaring the rams out of the country.''

Excellent advice, from a man who has been there. More than once.

Exotic Sheep

During the past decade, the importation of exotic (non-native) sheep for hunting purposes has been gaining momentum. Game ranches have sprung up all over the country. Many of these offer the paying hunter one species of ram or another, some of them several. Nothing wrong with that, either; it gives an enthusiast something to hunt when most game seasons are closed. Since sheep don't shed their horns like antlered game, they can be sought year-round.

Perhaps the most popular of the exotics is the little mouflon, the smallest of wild sheep. It takes a whopper to go 100 pounds, but not only do they grow impressive headgear, their distinctive coloration makes them extraordinarily handsome. Originally a native of Corsica and Sardinia, the mouflon thrives best in the Southern tier of the United States, although I have hunted them in climes as cold as that of Missouri.

Most of my mouflons have been slain with various handguns, since the country in which I've hunted them lent itself well to covert stalking. The longest distance I ever nabbed one was about 70 yards at the first shot—which hit just a wee bit too far back. He scampered off a ways, quite sick, and stopped at 110 yards. I waxed him from there, clean through both lungs; he took a few steps and crumbled.

I was hunting whitetails in Missouri with Bobby Rupert some years ago, on Pamlico Manor's western properties. Gerald Ryals, manager and resident game biologist, told us that two extremely fine mouflon were living on the half-section of land amongst the deer. He'd tried on several occasions to get close enough to tranquilize them, but no dice. They were too wary. He gave me permission to dump one if I ran across him, but said the chances were pretty slim.

I sequestered myself near a creek bed that was littered with whitetail tracks, fewmet and other signs of recent and frequent use. I'm biased toward sitting in the woods when I can, so I disappeared—I hoped—into the treeline within sight of the main trail leading to water.

A doe and a small buck came by. I let 'em pass. Made the mistake of moving once, to squash an especially persistent mosquito, and heard a buck snort derisively behind me. I swiveled the old bean as much as my vertebrae would allow, but couldn't get a fix on him. Dusk arrives more quickly when a canopy of leaves deflects such light as there is; when it became too dim for shooting in deep where I was perched on the elevated trunk of a fallen tree, I slipped down and pussyfooted out to the edge of the woods.

Two critters were doing their own brand of four-legged pussyfooting, caught in an open area between one copse of trees and another. Up came the Bausch & Lomb 7 X 24s, which I've carried around my neck so many miles they seem to sprout there. Sheep! I estimated the range at 60 yards (later paced at 52) as I

Mouflon rams are popular game for hunters carrying handguns chambered for rifle cartridges. This one fell to Bill Miller's Thompson/Center Contender in .30-30 Win.

dropped to a kneeling position. The rams noticed the movement, stopped, peered intently at me. Gulp!

Through the four-power scope mounted atop my Kimber 6 X 47 wildcat, I sought a shoulder. The bigger ram stood his ground, but I noticed he'd dropped his hips low for a good launch should flight suit his fancy. Without conscious thought, I took up the required trigger pressure and the little rifle nudged me gently in recoil. The sheep's legs went out from under him as suddenly as if he'd been trying to polka on ice. He lifted his head once. Tried to rise. Nothing left. Dead when I reached him.

The speedy 85-grain Nosler Solid Base had devastated the left lung, cut a groove in the right. Quick and clean. His horns were magnificent, although I doubt he'd have weighed 110 pounds with overshoes on all four feet. Gerald measured the curl, consulted a record book, said that if I chose to enter my ram, it would likely slip into the 28th slot. Not bad!

I took another ram another time, a white wooly thing the guides called a "Barbarossa," whatever that may be. He was nice and fat, had outward-curling horns argali style, was estimated by my guide at perhaps 200 pounds on the hoof, and was—so far as I know—the first large animal ever taken with a Kimber Model 84 6 X 45.

I used an 85-grain Speer soft-point boattail on that one. He was at the top of a steep rise when I shot him, looking down at me. Although the range was only slightly in excess of 100 yards, I forgot to hold as low as I should to allow for the angle. My bullet hit the lower edge of his right horn, went bulling on through, dug deep into his neck to break a vertebra, and wound up in his offside. Pretty good penetration for what is not touted as a game bullet.

And that's enough of sheep. We need to cover, cursorily at least, the ...

Rocky Mountain Goat

Two things you need to know about goats: 1) being incredibly phlegmatic, they often exhibit absolutely no immediate reaction to having a bullet poked into their vitals; 2) they display a penchant for kicking themselves from high places, which does nothing at all good for their tiny, fragile horns. Bear those two items in mind, and you'll be well informed about goat *shooting*.

Goat *hunting*, we'll not spend much time on. Basically, they live in country that would give a bighorn ram vertigo. Since they're as sure-footed as Mikhail Baryshnikov, and nearly as graceful, they seldom suffer mishaps due to their choice of bailiwick. Hunters, on the other hand, sometimes do. Thus, the same rule of thumb holds true in the selection of a rifle for mountain goats as in selecting one for mountain sheep. The magic words are: short, light, unobtrusive.

Caliber is unimportant. Goats have been taken humanely with everything, and the .243 or 6mm Remington will certainly knock one over if a good bullet is well directed. Goats are built funny, with long hair hanging down all over, and even a beard. Neck shots are not recommended due to the difficulty of locating the spine. For goats I'd pick the same rifles and loads used for sheep; there's no need to tote an unusually mild number, nor yet a strapping magnum. Just something middle-of-the-road that won't kick you out from under your beanie when you touch it off, but that carries enough energy and bullet weight to tunnel through some pretty tough muscle and hair.

Further advice: If your goat even twitches after you plug him, shoot him again. And again if need be. Don't let him take a header off a mountain if you can possibly prevent it, meat loss be damned.

And that's what you need to know about goats.

8

Cartridges For
Elk, Moose and Big Bear

The surest way I know to get an elk hunter—*any* elk hunter—riled is to tell him his choice of armament is not especially savvy. If he doesn't immediately introduce your nose to his knuckles, he'll assault your eardrums with such a barrage of invective that you might wish he'd simply knocked you on your keister and been done with it.

Now you must understand something: It doesn't make any difference *at all* what kind of rifle he shoots at elk, nor yet its chambering. He will defend it as staunchly as if it were his wife, or his mother's cooking. I know a gent who totes to the Rockies a .243 sporter that would be too heavy if it were a .30-06, let alone a combination varmint/deer number. Yet he dotes on it, can kill groundhogs so far away I usually can't even see them, and doesn't seem to mind its excessive avoirdupois. A writing buddy of mine corresponds with a Montana resident who mows everything down with a .22-250, *including* elk.

In Idaho some years back, there were four hunters in my elk camp, counting your 'bedient serv'nt. Represented were the 7mm Rem. Mag. (owned by a doctor who had taken about everything there is to take on this continent with that very rifle, since he owned no other), the .308 Winchester, the .30-06 (carried by a Pennsylvania convenience-store magnate, who had used the gun on whitetails for years and thought it should be the berries on wapiti as well) and a .338 Magnum. All were bolt actions. All but one of us got his elk. None with one shot, I might add.

Now the foregoing cabal included some pretty experienced big game hunters, myself excluded, of course, for modesty's sake. All my pals had hunted elk before except our representative from Pennsylvania, and three of us had shot a critter or two other than whitetail deer. In other words, few pilgrims here. Yet no cartridge got so many as two votes, let alone a quorum. (Discounting the .30-06 that I carried as my second rifle, which was never aimed at anything alive on that trip.) That's the way of it with those who spend time in the mountains seeking elk; each thinks he has the inside track on what constitutes a real gee-whiz elk whacker.

Me, too. But I won't bore you with my recondite convictions until we've examined all the options. Before we do, a word about elk.

The American elk, also called wapiti, is a relatively recent immigrant from Asia. There is said to be a pocket of its first cousins still prospering in the Tian Shan mountains of China. Back when the Pilgrims were busy establishing a beachhead, elk ranged as far east as what was to become New York and Pennsylvania, as far toward the setting sun as Vancouver Island. They traveled in vast herds all over the Great Plains, dwelled amid the high Arizona and New Mexican peaks.

Very important to the hunter are several of the elk's physical characteristics, all of which add up to a very formidable opponent. First, a full-grown bull is big. *Real* big. Not so large as a moose, maybe, but from three to five times as heavy as an average mature mule deer. Some hunters swear they're harder to kill by the same ratio!

Second, an elk—not unlike a mountain goat, though not to the same extreme—often fails to react noticeably to a bullet strike, even if it's to a fatal area. Consequently, they're frequently wounded without their assailant's being aware of the hit, then go off to lie down and feed the buzzards.

Third, an elk possesses as part of his genetic fabric the same annoying trait that a whitetail buck exhibits: When you hurt him, he often runs off. Moose and billies, being more considerate, usually just stand around and think about things for a spell after you shoot them. Then they kind of come unhinged and topple over. Not so for elk. Poke a bull with a bullet and he generally seeks quieter pastures; he can travel a long way even when mortally stricken. This lack of solicitude for the hunter has given him the reputation of being very, very hard to drop. Yes, elk display an amazing tenacity of life.

An elk's sheer bulk is a formidable obstacle to any rifle bullet. The mass and strength of their bone structure presents another. It takes a long (for its caliber), toughly-constructed projectile to punch through the massive rib cage, perforate both lungs and continue on through the offside hide to leave a blood trail. Alas, many bullets lose their ambition before managing such a feat.

There are hunters who advocate shooting at a retreating elk's hindquarters, which is *bad* advice. There are few if any soft-point slugs on the market that can be *depended on* to trek forward into the boiler room. In my opinion, the fanny shot on elk should be avoided like your brother-in-law. If you insist on going in through the back door—regardless of what I or anyone else says to dissuade you—then for Pete's sake use a solid bullet in a large-caliber rifle, say the .375 Holland & Holland Magnum as a good example. Art Alfin's A-Square company offers such ammunition in factory persuasion and a variety of chamberings. But I want to stress that I don't now and never will recommend taking potshots at an elk's caboose, unless, of course, the hapless critter has been wounded.

So what would *I* do if presented with such an opportunity at moderate range? Try for the back of his neck, hoping to find the spinal column. If I were after meat, not antlers, I'd aim to go into the skull; the results aren't pretty, but the animal is dead and on the ground if the shot goes where intended. Should either of the above alternatives be considered too risky—say at extended range, or if the animal is moving, or if my rifle is insufficiently accurate—I'd pass up such a shot on game. I have before.

Back to an elk's imperviousness to pain and damage. Rick Jamison once pestered a bevy of Rocky Mountain elk guides with a questionnaire. Some very interesting items came to light. According to this group of 16 or 18 professionals—who not only have killed many an elk themselves, but have been there for the execution of hundreds more—the average distance traveled by an elk after taking a good solid hit in a *vital* area was 164 yards! Yep, you read it right; *one-hundred-sixty-four yards*, on the *average*. Further, the average number of hits required to put an elk down for the count was three. *Three!* Even more depressing: The consensus was that if a wapiti is hit wrong with the first shot, it is more often lost than found, *no matter where subsequent hits land!*

I don't mean to be redundant, but a synopsis of an elk's vexing traits bears repeating for emphasis. Once again: 1) they are

A big animal, tenacious of life. Big, rugged country. Those elements equate to require a powerful rifle and precision marksmanship of the would-be elk hunter.

relatively impervious to bullet shock; 2) they are large and heavy-boned, thus require more striking energy than do deer, sheep or even caribou-sized fauna, as well as bullets of great sectional density (length in relation to weight) and slower expansion than the "softer" deer-slaying projectiles; 3) their will to live is awe-inspiring; 4) they too often try to hop an express train out of town when they take a bullet (or hear a shot, or smell a hunter, or simply feel like it). In short, the elk is probably the most difficult North American ungulate to stop—not necessarily in his tracks, but at least somewhere in the vicinity—except possibly the bison. (Which doesn't count, since a buffalo is disinclined to run far under the most outrageous of circumstances unless accompanied by a multitude of his fellows, weighs as much as four elk and an aardvark, and is so dumb it would probably drop bread crumbs behind so you could find it.)

"How about moose," I hear you scream, "didn't you just say they were even larger than elk?" Indeed I did, and we'll look at the big plodding beasts later. Meanwhile, bear in mind what I said about a mountain goat's ability to absorb bullet after bullet with little apparent effect. Ditto for moose. Only more so.

Grizzlies are another story. A medium-sized bear is every bit as tough a customer as an elk, and equally hard to anchor. Unlike the wapiti, a big ol' silvertip (or even a little bitty one) can eat you to death and then micturate on your grave. But a grizzly is not an ungulate, so is excluded from this discussion. For now, we're talking about elk.

After reading the foregoing, you may be scratching your dome in confusion, wondering just what rifle and cartridge you *should* carry out West next September for a go at one of these legendary armor-plated bulls. We shall address that now, with one caveat in advance: What I'm about to relate will annoy some folks (those who don't agree), plaster a smug look on the mugs of others (who will nod in agreement) and bore many a self-styled expert to distraction (since they figure they already know everything worth knowing about killing an elk, and many even have seen one once.)

But before we toss the suet into the conflagration, let's look over the field, beginning with the ...

Magnum .30s

A .30-caliber magnum was first offered by the British firm of Holland & Holland back in 1925. Christened "Holland's Super .30," it was loaded first in this country by the Western Cartridge

Company, which later bought Winchester. Not until 1937 did a large domestic rifle producer offer the round as a factory chambering, and then it was probably due to Ben Comfort's big win at Wimbledon. Winchester added it to their catalogue first, then Remington in their Model 721, and later in the Model 700. The cartridge is renowned for its superb accuracy, moderate recoil effect for a load of its power and its uncannily smooth feeding in bolt action rifles (likely due to its long, severely tapered form). It is not quite so potent as its progeny as it comes from the factories, but when handloaded the old gentleman can really step out. The .300 Holland & Holland is my favorite among the big .30s.

Next in chronology is Roy Weatherby's most famous round, the .300 Weatherby Magnum. Based on .300 H & H brass, considerably modified in typical Weatherby fashion, it offers the most impressive factory ballistics of the magnum-.30 clan. When chronographed, it loses some of its gleam, but not so much that it doesn't still lead the pack, if only marginally. Having been used on I dare say every species of huntable game in the free world, it's proved its mettle time after time. Although accuracy is generally more than sufficient for any big-game purpose, the .300 Weatherby hasn't acquired the reputation for tight grouping enjoyed by all three of its belted siblings.

Next eldest is the .308 Norma Magnum, introduced by the Swedish firm in 1960. The cartridge is very similar in shape to the wildcat .30-338 (although *not* interchangeable), which has often been used in long-range target shooting, quite successfully I might add. So far as I know, the .308 Norma has always been available in but one bullet weight, the 180-grain, which likely limits its popularity. I'm not sure *why* it does, since the 180-grain bullet is by far the most popular among big .30s users.

The late comer, debuting in 1963, is the .300 Winchester Magnum. Such competent and seasoned hunters as Rick Jamison, Dave Petzal and Bob Hagel espouse the .300 Winchester as a serious hunting cartridge indeed, and *Outdoor Life's* Jim Carmichel has for years used it in over-the-course centerfire competition, as have many less-famous riflemen. Its accuracy is unquestioned, with Carmichel having written the following, in his book *The Modern Rifle*, published by Winchester press: "The most accurate long-range rifle I've ever owned, or used, is a .300 Winchester Magnum with Douglas barrel on a Model 70 action. Five-shot test groups fired from a bench rest have measured *as small as .300-inch* between the center or the two widest shots."

"Is it enough gun?" "Ya, it's a .300 Weatherby. It'll do the job if you do yours."

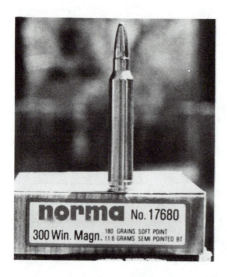

norma No. 17680
300 Win. Magn. 180 GRAINS SOFT POINT / 11.6 GRAMS SEMI POINTED BT

The .300 Winchester Magnum is used by a lot of hunters for really big game like elk and moose. The most potent 180-grain factory number is the Norma in most lots. It's often extremely accurate as well.

(Italics mine.) Jamison also applauds the .300 Win. Mag.'s precision at every turn, and recently confided that he feels any good (and properly bedded) sporter so-reamed will group around an inch or a bit less with good ammo. Not only is such a statement creditable, but credible if it comes from Rick.

Although factory ballistics vary a good bit among this puissant quartet, they all come quite close to one another when handloaded to comparable working pressures. For some reason, the .300 H & H has in later years been underloaded, perhaps due to its frequent use in the sweltering African sun. No matter; it responds to a reloader's ministrations very satisfactorily. In my Remington Model 700 Classic, my favorite 180-grain handload shows 3,052 fps at the muzzle, and with no excessive-pressure symptoms whatever. In that same 24-inch barrel, 3,250 fps is achieved with the 150 Speer soft-point boattail; 3,100 is the norm for the 165 Speer Grand Slam or the 165 Nosler Ballistic Tip with either IMR 4350 or IMR 4831. Pretty fast. Accuracy is also excellent, with most good loads falling under 1½ inches for the average, and the best ones printing right at 1¼ inches.

Factory stuff is another matter. An old lot of the discontinued 150 Winchester Silvertips clocked but 3,083 at the muzzle; the current 180 Silvertip—listed in the Olin literature at 2,880 fps—managed but 2,766; some ancient 220-grain Winchester ammo showed 2,539; a batch of long-dead Peters 180-grain Inner

Belted hit only 2,432. Remington's 180-grain soft-point Core-Lokt was the best of the factory offerings, grouping adequately while providing 2,825 fps at the nozzle.

I borrowed Chub Eastman's pre-'64 Model 70, which sports a 26-inch tube, and ran some tests. My pet 180-grain load—70.0 grains of IMR 4831 under the 180 Nosler Ballistic Tip—showed nearly 3,100 fps and grouped 1.22 inches. Speeds with the 150- and 165-grain projectiles were nigh identical to those of my shorter-barreled Model 700. Accuracy was similar as well, with only one handload—of five tested—grouping larger than 1½ inches at 100 yards. As I said, the venerable Holland round is very precise.

The .308 Norma Mag. is listed as getting a 180-grain Norma Dual Core up to 3,020 fps at the muzzle, a feat I have scant idea whether it can accomplish; I've never fired one. The Nosler loading manual mentions that one lot of factory ammo showed 2,988 in their 25-inch test rifle. I reckon that would dip to 2,950 or so in a typical 24-inch sporter barrel. As you can see, that's more than 100 fps faster than the liveliest .300 H & H factory load.

According to the Nosler book, 180-grain bullets can be cranked up to 2,984 fps with the best powder choice. Speer's current manual claims 3,011 from a 24½-inch Sako, from the zippiest load, of course. Hornady declares that they received 3,100 fps from three different propellants in a converted Springfield '03-A3, which is shown as having a 24-inch barrel. If we average all three sources, we come up with 3,032 fps for 180-grain projectiles. Doesn't look to me like the .308 Norma has any advantage on the antediluvian .300 H & H at all, except in factory guise.

Winchester's .300 Magnum is offered in a total of five bullet weights by the major producers, although none offers all five. Published speeds go like so: 3,290 for the 150-grain; 2,960 fps for the 180 stuff (except for Norma's version, shown at 3,020); 190 Hornady spire-point boattail at 2,900; 2,830 fps for Federal's Premium 200-grain bottail soft point; 2,680 for Winchester's stout 220 Silvertip. My Oehler brought to light the following, from a Winchester Model 70 Winlite: 150 Winchester Power-Point, 3,197; 180 Hornady soft point, 2,776; 180 Norma, 2,940; 180 Winchester Power-Point, 2,934; 180 Federal soft point, 2,858; 190 Hornady boattail, 2,773; 200 Federal Premium boattail, 2,590; 220 Winchester Silvertip, 2,601. In a 24-inch Parker-Hale the figures were quite similar. In that one I tried the 250 Barnes specialty item, which chronographed 2,482 fps. Thus, the average speed deficit across the board ran to 98 fps, although the 180 Winchester and Norma ammo were close to advance specs at 26 and 20 fps respectively. Pretty good compared to most magnums.

Accuracy is my Winlite was superb, especially for such a hard-kicking number. Four five-shot strings with the potent 180 Norma ammo averaged 1.18 inches. Coupling such grouping ability with its high speed makes it a whale of a hunting load for the non-handloader. Only strike against it is its semi-spitzer profile, which isn't the best for fighting wind resistance. Federal's 180-grain "red box" ammo and Hornady's 190-grain load both averaged under 1¾ inches.

In my Browning BAR, the Norma ammunition printed 1.96 inches for four groups, the best performance in that autoloading rifle. Second slot was filled by the 180 Hornady soft point, at 2.46 inches.

With handloads I reached 3,039 fps in a Model 70, using Hornady's 180 spire point and 76.0 grains of Hodgdon's H-4831. That's a very accurate combination. Rick Jamison's pet concoction features a 180 soft point and 75.0 grains of the same propellant, which he has clocked at 3,050 in "Old Ugly," his famous custom Springfield. Speer claims 3,049 fps with its fastest 180-grain load; the Hornady manual shows two propellants achieving 3,100; Nosler says it was easy to get well over 3,100 fps from their test rifle, but it had a 26-inch barrel. I suspect that 3,100 fps or a bit more would be about right if that long tube were hacked off to 24 inches. Thus the .300 Win. Mag. outruns the .308 Norma and .300 H & H by from 50 to maybe 75 fps with maximum handloads in all three. Not much of a margin, is it?

So how about the big Weatherby? Let's see. According to data from the Speer and Lyman handbooks, the 180-grain Weatherby factory load gave 3,179 (Speer) and 3,164 fps (Lyman), both in 26-inch barrels. The factory claims 3,300. The above sources show the 150 Weatherby soft point as getting 3,130 (Speer) and 3,559 (!!) in the Lyman book. (Wow, talk about a lot-to-lot variation!) Weatherby insists their 150-grain load zips along at 3,600. Lyman clocked the 220-grain factory load—shown as getting 2,905—at 2,906. (Perhaps Lyman had unusually swift lots, except for the 180-grain load.)

For dope on handloads, let's look to the manuals. In Hornady's 24-inch test gun: 3,500 fps for the 150 spire point, 3,200 for the 180, and 2,800 for the 220-grain round nose; Nosler claims 3,387 for the top 150-grain load, 3,091 for the speediest 180 and 2,962 from the 200-grain Partition, all in 24 inches; Speer's Number Eleven lists the 150 at 3,430, the 180-grain at 3,082, and the spitzer 200 as getting 2,917, all with the top powders tried in their 26-inch test gun. It looks like the .300 Weatherby, when tested in barrels of comparable length, outraces its compadres by hardly any at all in most guns. Let's give it a 25-50 fps advantage because of its slightly larger case and leave it at that.

So where does that leave us? With four belted .30-bore cartridges which will drive a 150-grain spitzer from 3,200 to 3,400 fps for long-range use on smallish big game, push 180-grain missiles to 3,050-3,150 for all-around use, and kick 200-grain Nosler Partitions to 2,900 or a so for deep digging into evil-tempered, heavy-framed animals, or simply those like elk which don't like to lie down when you sock 'em. Real hairy stuff, the big .30s. Accurate, powerful and two of the four are readily available in a panoply of rifle and ammunition selections.

Are they for you? Well, they might be if: a) you can shoot well with rifles that boot the snuff out of you, or b) you don't mind carrying a very heavy gun to tone down all that rearward thrust, or c) you are willing to exacerbate the already fearsome muzzle blast by attaching a muzzle brake out front. These last two items are notable in that they both work but have significant drawbacks.

In order for a typical .300 Magnum to be comfortable to fire—from all positions, not just offhand—it should weigh around 10 pounds or more scoped and have a well-designed stock, preferably one with a full comb and hand-filling forend and pistol grip. All those things work in concert to take the discomfort out of the shooting. (Unfortunately, they put it back in the *carrying*.)

A muzzle brake works even better, and is my personal choice for pulling a magnum's teeth. Even a six-pound .300 tiger is tamed to pussycat level when a properly-designed muzzle brake (like the one from Ultra Light Arms) is installed. The other sides of the issue involve expense (few outfits put these devices on for free) and possible hearing loss. If you happen to turn loose a fire-breathing magnum round from a muzzle-braked rifle without wearing hearing protection, you'll stagger around in a circle babbling incoherently for 15 minutes afterward. However, if you always wear good ear protection when you fire one of these cannons (including when you are *hunting!*), a muzzle brake will serve you faithfully. It removes most of the sting but retains all of the zing.

If you choose not to avail yourself of either a muzzle brake or a very hefty, well-stocked rifle, then I advise you to steer clear of the big .300s except for the Holland & Holland, which for some reason doesn't bite painfully, despite its ballistics. I cannot for the life of me figure out *why*; I just know that my Model 700 Classic does not kick uncomfortably even while slinging 180-grain Noslers to 3,050 fps, and it is neither heavy nor braked.

Lest you think I make too much of this recoil thing, let me spin you a yarn. My buddy J.R. "Rick" Jamison, about as experienced an elk slayer as I know of and a devoted fan of the .300 Winchester Magnum, once shot a nice six-point bull elk with "Old Ugly." He wrote to me of his experience, a letter from which I will now quote: "I was shooting a handloaded 180-grain bullet ahead of enough (H) 4831 to get 3,050 fps from the load at 10 feet from the muzzle. I knew that the load shot flat, and with such a rifle I don't like to hold over game. If you have to hold over, *the game is really too far* (Italics mine, and that is excellent advice.), but I had walked lots of miles in five days, and had been really discouraged, and didn't want to pass up an opportunity."

So he held high, cut loose and dropped the elk with his first shot. But the old boy kept trying to get up. Rick mortared off some more rounds. Reloaded. Fired again, repeatedly. Ran out of ammo.

Says J.R.: "I was six miles from my truck as the crow flies. I was supposed to be home by 5:00 p.m. for a late Thanksgiving dinner. It would be dark in about an hour and a half. I had little choice."

In college at the time, and in shape from running on the Northern Arizona University cross-country team, he ran the long miles back to his vehicle. Tried to drive his truck to the elk. No dice. It grew dark and he couldn't locate the critter, so he drove to town for assistance.

Rick again: "My wife was going to call the search and rescue to come look for me at 10 o'clock. Friends were already at my house, waiting for word. When I walked in, several exclaimed about the blood on my forehead and face. I had a headache that had been ignored in the excitement. *There were cuts above my eye where the scope had hit me while I was shooting prone over (a) rock. I never even noticed at the time.*" (Italics mine.)

This is a prime example of one of the reasons I seldom recommend hard-recoiling magnum rifles. Here is one of the most experienced hunters in the outdoor-writing business (or any *other* business), who has spent years firing all kinds of rifles, and who is about as recoil-sensitive as a cypress stump, getting conked on the bean repeatedly and with enough force to leave his forehead running with blood. All that thunder and lightning and the elk *still* wasn't dead when Rick first reached it!

Bear in mind when you sit down at a benchrest behind the buttpad of a .300 Mag., or when you snuggle up to one offhand, that you will probably not use those positions *in the field*. Leaning across a rock, lying prone, sitting on a sideslope ... those are the more common shooting stances when shooting at game, and the most likely to put your noggin precariously close to the scope. When that happens, as it did with Rick Jamison, you may find out real quick why the big magnums are not panaceas without costs of their own.

So, with the big .30s—or any of the other heavy-kicking ordnance we are about to discuss—here's my thoughts: Choose one with a thick, soft recoil pad; buy only a very straight stock, or possibly the Weatherby-style California design; make certain the rifle is as heavy as a forklift or equipped with a muzzle brake. Remember when shooting one of the big-cased magnums to wear ear protection. (Unless, of course, you don't care about your hearing.)

8mm Remington Magnum

Remington's hot medium bore is the 8mm Magnum, introduced in 1978 and intended to bury the .338 Winchester Magnum, which it has failed miserably to accomplish. It's certainly not because the big 8mm is lacking in voltage. The factory quotes a 185-grain Core-Lokt at 3,080 fps, for nearly 3,900 foot pounds, and a 220-grain Core-Lokt at 2,830, which yields 3,912 foot pounds. Such numbers make this round the veritable Hammer of Thor! Furthermore, achieved ballistics of the light-bullet rendition are not too wildly inflated, at least in some lots. An example is lot number H27 ND5956 of Remington's 185-grain load, which in my Remington Model 700 Safari chronographed 3,004 fps, only 76 foot-seconds below its press. The five other lots tested in that rifle were slower, with 2,876 the most sluggish of the bunch. The 220-grain load was much more uniform from lot to lot, with only a nine fps variance from three samplings. The down side is that the heavyweight item was laggard in the extreme, averaging but 2,700 fps. That's 130 shy of expectations.

The good news is that factory ammo was impressively accurate. One lot of the 220s grouped into 1.61 inches for an average; two lots of 185s went 1.60 and 1.61. Only two of the nine test lots failed to print under 2.00 inches. Unusual, that. At least in my experience.

Handloading the big 8mm is no task, either. I worked up five handloads for my portly Model 700 Safari; the entire quintet showed a mean of exactly 1½ inches after but limited developmental time, and using three different bullet weights, a trio of primers and two propellants. At the head of the class was a prudent dose of IMR 4831 pushing a 175-grain soft point; groups ran 1.28 inches. The speed averaged 3,126 fps for three five-shot test strings all fired on separate occasions. Another top load—maybe the best for all-purpose use—was 78.0 grains of IMR 4831 behind the 200 Nosler Partition, good for 2,974 fps and 1.49-inch grouping. Downrange ballistics of that load look like this: rise at 100 yards (assuming a 200-yard zero), 1.5 inches; drop at 300 yards, 6.8 inches; drop at 400 yards, 19.7 inches. Of course, if zeroed for 250 or 275 yards, the long-distance figures look much better. By the way, retained punch at 400 yards is in excess of 2,100 foot pounds, which is a bunch of foot pounds at such an extended range.

So far as I know, only Remington chambers the 8mm, or ever has, at least among the major gun companies. Their single offering is the relatively expensive Safari Grade, a product of the custom shop. I suspect that will limit the popularity of the belted 8mm considerably.

The other limiting factor is that the 8mm Magnum is an underachiever. Considering that it is built on the full-length .375 Holland & Holland case, and in an "improved" version (re, sharper shoulder, less taper, shorter neck) to boot, the big cartridge should provide better ballistics than it does. Instead, the shorter .300 Winchester Magnum is equal or superior in virtually every way. It has greater accuracy potential, is available with equally heavy bullets, can be found in a plenitude of rifles, is offered by all the major ammo makers, has a much wider range of handloading options. The .300 also comes in a handier action length, like the other "short magnums," thus is usable in turnbolt rifles designed around the .30-06. Not so the 8mm, which requires a true magnum-length bolt action or a single shot. All things considered, the 8mm just doesn't get invited to the prom.

The .338-inch 250 Nosler Partition, available not only to handloaders, but factory-ammo shooters as well thanks to Federal, is maybe the best elk hunting bullet you can use.

A Pair of .33s

Aside from such oldsters as the .33 Winchester Centerfire——popular in Winchester lever actions from around the turn of the century until the mid-1930s—the only .33 caliber cartridges that have carried much commercial weight in this country are the .338 Winchester Magnum, announced in 1958, and the slightly longer and marginally more potent .340 Weatherby Magnum, begat officially in 1962. The more popular of the pair, of course, is the .338, which hovered at the fringe of success for many years like a huge, hungry mongrel hoping for a bone. Of late, gun writers must be feeling guilty for the long period of neglect; most of them have embraced the strapping cartridge as if it were a moneyed agnate in poor health.

Its ballistics give clue to its widespread approbation. From Federal you can choose from the Premium line a 210-grain version—bulleted by Nosler—that is said to achieve 2,830 fps, which yields 3,735 serious foot pounds. There is also a 250-grain Partition at 2,660, giving 3,925 pounds feet. Winchester proffers a 200-grain Power-Point at an alleged 2,960 fps, and a 225 spire point at 2,780, both good for near-3,900 energy levels. Remington too peddles ammo, listing the selfsame 225 as Winchester (made by Steve Hornady's Grand Island outfit for both firms), and adding a 250-grain soft point at 2,660. Plenty of factory provender around for the non-reloading .338 fan.

As usual, I trotted out the trusty Oehler falsification detector. For the ammo I had on hand, here's the scoop from my Ultra Light Arms Model 28 and its 24-inch pipe: 200 Winchester Power-Point, 2,940; 210 Federal Partition, 2,851; 225 Winchester, 2,840 fps.

Fancy that! Two of these worthies exceeded published data, one by as much as 60 fps (the Winchester 225), and the single iteration that fell short missed the mark by only 20 foot-seconds. Perhaps the 30-year-old magnum medium is as good as its pontificators proclaim? Let's not jump the gun. In my M70 Winlite, this: 200 Winchester Power-Point, 2,895; 210 Federal Partition, 2,772 from Lot One, 2,779 with Lot Two; 225 Winchester soft point, 2,699. A bit short of the mark all around, but not significantly so. I guess the .338 is not just so much hot air after all.

When handloaded, I have found it small chore to better 2,800 fps with 250-grain projectiles, so long as I've a can of IMR 4831 in the larder. A fairly mild-kicking and very accurate recipe is 62.8 grains of IMR 4064 under the 200 Speer spitzer, giving a healthy 2,818 fps instrumental and 1⅜-inch grouping in my ULA. Although the recoil of that load is still a rather healthy dunch, it doesn't reduce one's deltoid to mush as do some of the heavy-bullet renderings when fired in "normal" .338 rifles. (The Ultra Light is decidedly *not* "normal," especially when it comes to recoil attenuation.)

Aside from its prodigious recoil (in most standard-configuration rifles), the .338 has but one Achilles' heel: accuracy. Not that its precision isn't sufficient for taking large beasts at normal ranges; such is not the case. It's simply that no .338 in my experience (of maybe a half-dozen fired over the years) has distinguished itself in the grouping department. Aside from the abovementioned accuracy load groomed to my Ultra Light, none has averaged in any other .338 as tight as 1½ inches. My most recent rifle—a Winchester M70 Winlite—not only pounded me to a nerveless pulp in short order, it would only by the barest of margins slip under *two inches* with its favored fodder. Better was a Model 70 I worked with a decade ago; it would usually keep five holes within 1⅝ inches of each other if I chose its feed with care and held my mouth just so.

But accuracy is not the name of the .338's game. Killing stuff is. And for that purpose it has few peers on really big stuff like elk. In fact, my buddy Dave Petzal, rifle guru-in-residence at *Field & Stream,* has opined more than once that the .338 is his personal choice as an elk-smiter if he expects to find himself in deep timber. Mister Petzal knows his elk, his rifles and his loads. If he says it, I respect it. (He also is as recoil-proof as a tractor tire and can shoot like the blazes, both of which are handy attributes that most of us are unhappily bereft of.)

An Ultra Light Arms Model 28 in .338. The muzzle brake tames the recoil to that of a normal weight .270.

If you like what the .338 offers, you'll *love* the .340 Weatherby. It hits harder, speaks louder, will loosen your bridgework more effectively, costs more to buy and shoot, and moves its owner one or two rungs farther up the ladder of peer prestige. (This latter comment might be considered by some to be a minor peccavi. Nonetheless, I'm convinced that the factor of one-upmanship has sold more than one magnum rifle.) Weatherby offers four bullet choices in factory brew: a 200 pointed-expanding at 3,260 claimed; a 210 Nosler Partition at 3,250; a 250-grain "semi-pointed" expanding at 3,000; a 250 Nosler Partition at the same speed. The A-Square Company of Madison, Indiana, catalogues three 250-grain versions, a soft-point boattail, a "Lion Load" (round nose) soft point and a Monolithic Solid, all at an alleged 2,820 fps.

In my 26-inch A-Square Hannibal, this from A-Square ammo: "Lion Load" soft point, 2,626 fps; soft-point boattail, 2,703; Monolithic Solids, 2,691. (Not much ahead of the .338, huh?) The

Weatherby ammo went like so: 3,126 fps for the 200-grain pointed-expanding; 2,925 with the 250-grain "semi-pointed." (This latter factory designation is, uh, a bit abstract for me; the bullet is as semi-pointed as the blunt end of a carrot.)

Please note that the Weatherby ammo was much faster than the A-Square versions of the same bullet weight. Still, neither load reached its published speeds, despite the Hannibal's 26-inch barrel. The increase in velocity had a marked effect on recoil, as might be surmised. However, the discomfort quotient jumped out of all proportion to what I had expected. The A-Square became unpleasant to fire from the bench, whereas with the 250-grain ammo loaded to 2,700 fps it had been as convivial as a sporter-weight .30-06, even when fired from prone. Considering the Hannibal's considerable heft, I was faintly surprised although I probably shouldn't have been. Any time a 250-grain bullet is boosted instantly to nearly 3,000 fps, something is going to happen at the aft end!

Accuracy of my A-Square .340 has been just fine, thanks. In fact, no other medium-bore (from .32 to .375 caliber) magnum I can recall has done so well for me with factory ammunition, and only a couple have shaded it with very careful handloading. So how good *is* it? Well, with 250-grain A-Square soft-point boattails, the four-group average went 1.45 inches. Quite good. Using the 200 Weatherby soft point, three fives showed a 1.50-inch aggregate, and the 250 Weatherby round nose printed 1.59. Thus, three of only five loads tested averaged under 1⅝ inches. Quite good, indeed.

The belted .33s obviously shoot well enough for any big-game hunting at any reasonable range. The .338, though of mean disposition, can be tamed easily by choosing a heavy rifle of good stock design, or installing a muzzle brake. It fits a medium-length action, giving it an advantage over the longer .340, which must be housed in a full .375 H & H-sized outfit. The .338 has the edge in ammo selection, rifle selection and cost of same. Conversely, the .340 hits harder at all ranges (and at its rear end) and shoots at least as well (maybe better, on a gun-to-gun basis). Can I make a pragmatic distinction between the two? Surely.

For most folks, monetary considerations are so heavily in favor of the .338 that the .340 isn't even in the running. Even for well-heeled nimrods, many of whom prefer standard-length turnbolts, a single shot, or an autoloader, the .338 is the cartridge of choice since the .340 Weatherby is not produced in any of these.

A friend hefts the author's long-range elk specialty rifle, an A-Square .340 Weatherby Magnum. It will shoot factory ammo under 1½ inches all day, spit out a factory 250-grainer in excess of 2,925 fps and has controllable recoil because of its considerable heft and stock design. The author's only other wish is that he could find friends to carry it in the mountains for him, too.

But for gunners who can afford the price tag attached to a Weatherby Mark V, or the even stiffer tariff of the A-Square, and who will order their Weatherby with a muzzle brake attached, I feel the .340 to be at least as good a bet as the less-powerful .338. Either way the decision goes, the hunter will be acquiring a real hell-for-leather firearm; he should remain cognizant of that fact when making his decision. These cartridges are for expert, recoil-toughened riflemen, not once-a-year, sighting-in-day shooters, not neophytes, nor yet those who believe that all that fire and brimstone will make up for a bum shot. It won't.

The Magnificent .35s

Those of you who came in at the beginning are doubtless aware that there is a whole convey of .35-caliber cartridges out there, including the modest .35 Remington, the dying .356 Winchester, the healthy but neglected .358 Winchester and some might even include the .348 Winchester since it's almost a .35. I've covered all those in earlier chapters, but saved until now three cartridges that lead the .35 power parade: the .35 Whelen, .350 Remington Magnum and the .358 Norma Magnum.

The Whelen and the .350 Remington are pretty much interchangeable ballistically, with the non-belted Whelen listed as driving a 200-grain pointed Core-Lokt at 2,675 fps, and the .350 pushing the same slug to 2,710. The Whelen is also offered in 250-grain blunt-prowed form at a claimed 2,400 fps. (The .350 used to be provided with a pointed soft point at 2,410, but the load has long been defunct.)

In a 22-inch Remington M700 Classic, my .350 Remington factory ammo showed 2,655 fps with the 200-grain stuff, 2,453 from the abovementioned 250 pointed Core-Lokt. From my 24-inch custom .35 Whelen—built on a Mark X Mauser action by ace gun surgeon Chris Latta—the 200 Remington soft point came up a bit short at 2,605 fps. The heavy-bullet loading ran 2,411. As you can see, the two are ballistic clones. So why does Remington offer both? A very astute question, that. Let's address it.

The .350 Magnum began life in the handy, homely, prescient Model 600 Remington. Intended as a tote-it-your-ownself carbine for the seeker after really big beasts (including Alaskan brown bear), it did not fare well below the Canadian border, although it was reported that residents of our 49th state fell upon it with glad cries. The sad metamorphosis of the Model 600 was chronicled in Chapter Seven, although at that time we were examining the obscure 6.5 Remington Magnum, an offspring of the .350. We need not tread that ground again. Suffice to say that the M600/.350 did not overflow the corporate coffers.

Ruger gave a hand with the Model 77, and I once read that Mossberg made up some .350s in their long-dead and unlamented Model 800. Few takers. Not long ago, Remington offered a one-time-only run of Model 700 Classics. They sold quickly, likely as not to collectors instead of hunters. Currently you can buy from their custom shop the niftiest production-line .350 ever fabricated, a sort of fourth-generation Model 600. The Model Seven KS—a Kevlar-stocked beauty—is light (maybe lighter) as the original and oh so much handsomer. Like its forebear, it's aimed at the same bear/elk/moose hunter who likes to carry his own rifle, and spends more time surrounded by woods than puffing up mountains. Barrel length is 18½ inches, so ballistics suffer a mite, but not stultifyingly so for moderate-range work on heavy game. Nice outfit.

Thus, the milieu of the stubby .350 (which is of .308 Winchester length, though much broader at its base) is best served by a short, vibrant carbine. That's a comfortable spot, since its niche is filled by no other quite so well, at least on game of this weight class.

The .35 Whelen, despite its correlative range and punch, is better suited to full-sized arms, being based on the .30-06 case necked up to accept .35-caliber bullets. Since it requires a grown-up action length, it should optimally wear a grown-up barrel, say 22 inches at minimum. With its nearly identical case capacity, the Whelen can wring impressive velocities from its 3½- to 5½-inch advantage in barrel length over its abridged cousin. Of course, the .350 can be loaded to similar speeds when housed in long-barreled rifles, but such ordnance negate its short-action advantage. In my 24-inch Mark X, 2,660 is easily reached with 220-grain Speer flat-nose bullets; better than 2,550 with the 250 Hornady round nose. Recoil is surprisingly mild for such heavy bullets and prodigious engergy levels (3,456 and 3,610 foot pounds, respectively). And that's the prime advantage the .35 Whelen enjoys over its magnum competitors: temperate recoil levels for such significant power.

Load a 250 Speer spitzer to 2,550 in the .35 Whelen (which is readily achieved with several propellants, and some rifles will come close to 2,650), and the retained energy at 300 yards is a whopping 2,206 foot pounds. Compare that to factory-quoted figures for the .338 Magnum, which is shown at only 2,025 with the same bullet weight in a barrel of identical length!

Okay, so their ballistics are laudable. But will this .35-bore duo group worth beans? You betcha. In my Whelen, I stuff a healthy dose of IMR 4895 behind the 250 Hornady round nose for deer hunting; it rewards me with groups averaging 1.35 inches at 100 yards. In my M700 .350 I like plenty of IMR 3031 under the 220 Speer flat nose, with groups running 1.69 inches. I have heard of .350 Mags that were real barn-burners; some owners of the bitty Model 600 carbines used to claim they would go an inch or a bit over when lovingly catered to. In my experience, there are no flies on the Brotherhood of .35 when it comes to poking clannish clusters into target paper, and that holds true from the .35 Remington all the way up.

Incidentally, for those hunters who value firepower—i.e. fast, fast, *fast* repeat shots—in their hunting rigs, Remington offers the quick-to-shoot Model 7400 pump chambered to .35 Whelen. If you don't mind its weight and length, such a combination would be death in the deer woods, and should work just as well on elk if 250-grain bullets are adhered to.

For those of you who are power mad, there is yet one cartridge to go, the suzerain of .35s, the whopping .358 Norma Magnum. Introduced in the U.S. in 1959, the Big Swede supposedly drove a 250-grain soft point at 2,790 fps, which is swifter than the .338 Mag. was listed at that time by nearly 100 foot-seconds. My pal Layne Simpson, of *Gun Digest*, has spent some time with an Ultra Light Arms reamed to the .358 Norma. He told me he just kept on adding powder behind the 250 Speer soft point until his chronograph read 2,800 fps. Then he stopped and went hunting. "Who needs more juice than that?" he asked me. Right.

Bullets as heavy as 275 and 300 grains can be utilized nicely in the .358 Magnum, and both weights are available from Barnes. Those bruisers can be driven to better than 2,600 in the former case, near 2,500 in the latter. Such speeds yield energies in the mid-4,100 range, more than enough for any elk or moose that ever walked, probably even a brontosaurus for that matter.

Layne's ULA really lays them in, too. The word I get is that the better recipes will put most holes so close together its scary. That's typical of Ultra Light rifles, but still speaks well of the cartridge.

No one offers .358 Norma rifles at present except for some pretty expensive outfits—like Ultra Light Arms. However, that may change soon. Federal Cartridge Company, the importer of things Norma, is bringing back the biggest .35 after a long hiatus. Maybe that will flush a rifle or two from the bushes.

The Bone-crushing .375s

When I refer to the belted .37 calibers as "bone-crushing," I'm not just referring to the *animal's* bones. Unless the rifle is as heavy as a coal barge or equipped with a muzzle brake—preferably both—it will also crush its shooter's bones. Or at least seem to.

There are those who opine that the .375 Holland & Holland (or even the horrendous .378 Weatherby!) are necessary on elk-sized

This elk was taken with a Savage 99 in .358 Winchester using Speer 250-grain soft points. This .35 caliber is a fine elk load to 200 yards or a bit beyond.

game. I've long suspected that such folks suffer from a recoil-induced lobotomy. It bothers me not in the least for fans of the excellent and revered .375 H & H to strike off into the wilderness with their trusty smokepole slung over their shoulder; I'm all for them. But I draw the line when they look me straight in the eye, adopt a serious mien, and tell me how I would do the same if I were *really* serious about elk hunting. Tain't so, folks and no amount of verbal refuse will *make* it so.

Many years ago, the *American Rifleman* reported on an experiment performed under controlled conditions. Seems a herd of elk in some Rocky Mountain state needed to be thinned. Said reduction was undertaken with two rifles, one a .375 and the other a .30-06. The former was loaded as I recall with 270-grain soft points, the latter with 220-grain bullets of similar shape. Autopsies were performed and spelled out; distances traveled by each stricken animal were listed; the number and location of each hit was right there in black and white. The consensus? As I recall, it was suggested that elk brought down with the .375 took maybe 21 fewer steps after being shot than their pals who fell to the lowly .30-06.

Every year, competent hunters kill cleanly untold numbers of elk with the .30-06 and its ilk. They always will, so long as elk habitat is maintained and the anti-hunters are held at bay. Try suggesting to one of those hunters that he'd be better off with a rifle more suited to downing a cape buffalo than a wapiti and if he doesn't deride your ancestry, intellect and social habits, I miss my guess. Now that we've got that out of the way, let's look closely at this paragon of power, the .375 Holland & Holland.

The wonderful old .375 first saw light of day in 1912. It was touted as just the load to take the starch out of Leo the Lion or *m'bogo* the buffalo. And so it proved. Current Remington factory ammo shows a 270-grain soft point at 2,690 fps, for 4,337 foot pounds, and a 300-grain FMJ at 2,530, good for 4263. Winchester offers the same duo, and adds the 300-grain Silvertip soft point to the ante. You'll note that the 270-grain rendition gets nearly the same speed as the 180-grain .30-06 as factory quoted, so shoots equally flat. Which is pretty taut, especially for a cartridge that throws slugs the size of footballs.

Are the above speeds inflated? Depends. In my 24-inch Interarms Alaskan, the 270 Winchester soft point gave 2,687 at the muzzle; the 300-grain Silvertip showed 2,525. Different lots of each went like so in my 24-inch Interarms Whitworth Express:

This Arizona elk fell to the thunder of a Winchester Model 70 in .375 H&H. Although the .375 is really unnecessary on elk, it killed this one nicely. Even so, the animal did not go down with a well-placed first shot.

270-grain, 2,550; 300-grain, 2,390. (Either slow ammo or a slow rifle!) So which is closer to what you can expect? Beats me.

With handloads, I've reached the following velocities in the Whitworth: 235-grain Speer, 2,808 fps; 285 Speer Grand Slam, 2,610; 300 Hornady round nose, 2,499. All good for more than 4100 nerve-numbing foot pounds. Of the bullets mentioned, I'd lean to the 235 Speer semi-pointed if I had to shoot an elk with the .375. It shoots pretty flat, dropping only 8.9 inches at 300 yards from a 200-yard zero, and retains 2,116 foot pounds. Plus, recoil of this loading won't actually separate your scapulae, being at about the same level as a stout .338 Mag.

The .375 is widely heralded for its accuracy, which is pretty impressive for a load of this power. My Ruger Number One averaged 1.61 inches with the 270 Winchester soft point, 1.89 with the 300 Silvertip. The Alaskan went 1.69 inches for five five-shot strings of the heavy-bullet load. Using the same 300-grain Silvertips, the Whitworth Express averaged exactly 1½ inches; its most precise handload (77.5 grains of IMR 4350 behind the 270 Hornady round nose) went 1.73 inches. Thus, I have found that the .375 shoots about like a good .338 Magnum, not quite so tight as the .340 Weatherby or 8mm Remington Magnum. But they are all within a half inch of one another, so who's quibbling?

I suppose if I had only two rifles, a .243 Winchester for deer and vermin, and a .375 H & H I'd bought at a yard sale or inherited from my Aunt Pearl or taken off a buddy's hands at a steal, I'd take the larger caliber if I found myself in a position to hunt elk. But if my "other" rifle were reamed to something on the order of the .270 Winchester or anything else in its class instead of the .243, that dusty .375 would stay in the closet.

The same goes, only doubly so, for the .378 Weatherby Magnum. I recently spoke with Layne Simpson on the horn, and among other things, the .378 Magnum drifted into the conversation.

Said Layne, "You know, I can't tell much difference between the .338 Magnum and the .340 Weatherby when I shoot 'em. But the .378 is a whole different ball game. The others aren't even in its league."

To that, three amens and a darned right!

The .378 is said to boot 270-grain slugs at 3,180 fps, and the big 300s at 2,925 fps. Energy levels are shown at 6,062 and 5,698. Awesome! I have no idea whether those numbers would hold up

Rick Jamison dropped this Colorado bull with a Remington Model 700 Mountain Rifle reamed to .30-06. He used 180-grain Winchester Silvertip factory ammo.

when pitted against the clock, since I have never chronographed a .378 and don't intend to.

I can scarcely imagine anyone choosing a .378 Mag. for elk, or even brown bear in the alders, so I will devote no more time to it. Except to say that if a bullet from one is directed into the vitals of a big bull, I expect it would kill him.

The "Best" Elk Cartridges

It's time to let the cream rise to the surface, pick out the all-time top cartridges for bushwhacking an elk. Okay. But first, let's see what a few knowledgeable hunters have to say on the subject.

A very well-known scribe who has been published in most of the outdoor journals and shooting rags once wrote that the quickest dead he ever saw an elk was when one of his relatives shot a bull with a .250-3000. Said pundit has slain elk himself with the .243 and the .25-06, seen them killed with such similarly modest rounds as the .257 Roberts. He noted no absence of punch, listed no wounded-but-lost, shed no tears of woe about the fallibility of using the small-bore numbers.

Finn Aagaard, of the *American Rifleman*, is one of the most experienced hunters alive, as well as being an honest reporter, superb writer and a gentleman the likes of which are seldom found these days. Finn spent many years as a white hunter in Africa, and guides a few folks on Texas exotics and whitetails today. In the April, 1988 issue of *American Hunter*, he penned these lines in reference to the little 6.5 X 55 Swede: ''... judging by its ... performance on medium-large African antelope, it should be fine on caribou within the same range (250 to 300 yards). I would certainly not choose it for elk, but if it was all I had I would not hesitate to hunt elk with it. I would just be very careful, and would hold my fire until I could break the beast's neck or spine, or be certain of a solid hit to the lungs and, preferably, the top of the heart.''

Note that Finn, quite rightly, emphasizes bullet placement and a specific range limitation. *All* cartridges require the same parameters, although the range will vary according to factors such as retained energy and bullet construction as it affects expansion and penetration.

Of the fine 7mm Mauser, Finn wrote the following in the November, 1986, *American Rifleman*: ''...if I were taking the little (7mm) Mauser after elk or moose (which I would not hesitate to do) or any of the larger African antelope, I would opt for the 160-grain Nosler Partition bullet, or for the 175-grain RNSP (round-nose soft point) if I was using factory ammunition. Under some circumstances the 175-grain Nosler Partition bullet hand-loaded to give near 2,600 fps might be the best of all.

''I am a subsistence hunter at heart. I have lived all my life on ranches or farms where the greater part of the meat on our table has been gathered with the rifle, so I hunt for (meat), not for horns. Consequently, I hate to blow them apart ... I like to kill cleanly but also neatly.''

There's more: ''... the 7mm Mauser ... is in my opinion the least (cartridge) that can *fully qualify as a general purpose big game cartridge*. (Italics mine.) The reason is that in order to be certain of being able to smash through heavy shoulder bones and reach the lungs on moose and elk and like-size African animals such as kudu when the occasion demands it, I want a well-constructed bullet of good sectional density that weighs at least 150 grains, and preferably more.''

Finally: "The '06 is more powerful, and may be preferable on the biggest beasties. But for 90 percent of all the big game hunting that most of us do, the 7mm Mauser is ample."

Jack O'Connor, dean of all the American firearms editors, past or present, had this to say on elk loads in his book *The Art of Hunting Big Game in North America*, published by Outdoor Life: "... the world is full of good elk cartridges. The .30-06 is the most popular of all and a good one. I have read many times that any .270 bullet bounced off of elk, but I have killed quite a few elk very dead with one shot when using that cartridge. John George of Lewiston, Idaho, who once owned a piece of a hunting lodge and did a lot of guiding, has killed a great many elk in his day. His favorite cartridge is the .270 with the 130-grain bullet."

And this: "I have also shot elk with a .30-06 and 180-grain and 220-grain bullets, and with a .300 Weatherby with the 180-grain bullet. My wife has had good luck with the 7 x 57 and a handload with 160-grain bullets driven at about 2,650.

"Les Bowman, the Cody, Wyoming, guide and outfitter, was lent a couple of 7mm Remington Magnum rifles before they hit the market. He considers the cartridge to be about as good elk medicine as one can get. He tells me he finds the 150-grain bullet to be a quicker killer than the 175-grain. That was also my impression from using the caliber on one seven-point bull and on elk-sized African antelope in Mozambique and Angola in the summer of 1962."

Further: "The big bores (.338, .375, .358 Norma Magnum, .416 and such powerful medicine) have two advantages over rifles of smaller bore with lighter bullets when used on elk and moose. First is that their strong, heavy bullets will generally break the shoulder blade whereas lighter bullets may not. This is a very academic advantage as the average elk hunter never uses the shoulder shot and couldn't locate the shoulder blade with the aid of three bloodhounds and an anatomical chart. The other very slight advantage is that the heavy bullets *may* kill or disable with a rear-end shot. However, this is questionable. Long ago I learned it was folly to shoot at the rear end of large animals. I have never seen any bullet that can be depended on to go through the heavy rump muscles of an elk, up into the abdominal cavity and on into the lungs. A round-nose solid will do it but expanding bullets generally will not."

Finally, this sage advice: "The most important pieces of equipment the elk hunter can take into the hills with him are shooting skill and common sense. Like any other game, elk are killed neatly and cleanly by putting well-constructed bullets in the right place. They are wounded by putting any bullets in the wrong place.''

Right on.

The late Warren Page, for years Gun Editor of *Field & Stream*, had this to say in the 1959 edition of *Gun Digest*, beginning on page 72: "At last count my 'Big 7' (a 7mm Mashburn Magnum wildcat) had accounted for about a 140 head of assorted big game, animals ranging from the 75-80 lbs. of the East African gerenuk to moose 20 times heavier. Its score includes most of the North American species—sheep and goat; assorted deer; all our bears except for the Alaskan brownie, which I'd take on with it any day; antelope; elk, on which its last four kills were one-shotters at 425, over 450, 300 and 75 yards."

And: "... I strenuously doubt that we have available any better multipurpose *game* cartridge, for all American animals from antelope on up to moose, than a 7mm Magnum. It won't shoot as flat as a souped-up .25, or hit as smashingly as a .375. But, it does combine at all normal game ranges, the trajectory flatness of 3000 foot-seconds-plus and the driving punch of 160- and 175-grain bullets in a fashion unrivaled by anything save the 300 Magnum(s)...minus their...greater recoil.

"Nor is the effectiveness of the load limited to mountain-country hunting and to shots at longish range, though that is where the 7mm Magnum excels. With the right bullets it bucks brush to an amazing degree. Take the last elk on my rifle's record, a gigantic British Columbia bull whose sword-pointed rack now stands (in 1959, remember) among Boone & Crockett Club North American Records. No classic long shot was possible on him. He was standing only 75 yards above me on a brushy slide, standing screened by skimpy spruces and a maze of finger-thick alders so that even with a 4X scope I could be only vaguely certain of the spot where dark neck hair merged into the cream of shoulder. But the bullet, that long semi-pointed (175-grain) Nosler, bored through and the bull slumped in his tracks. In driving through the alders, the bullet had nicked one alder branch, had cut cleanly another the size of a strong man's thumb. Yet it had entered the wapiti's hide right where I was holding. How much chance of such straight driving with a .270, for example?"

The scholarly John Wootters, a most fecund writer currently enlightening the readership of *Peterson's Hunting*, wrote in *Rifle*

A well-placed shot from a 7mm Magnum dropped this bull.

magazine, July/August, 1973, a story about his decade of experience with Remington's Big Seven. Here's John: "(A) friend of mine, Houston architect Bill Hoff, took only a beautiful Champlin 7mm Rem. Mag. on safari to Mozambique last summer and, in 11 days, killed kudu, sable, eland, waterbuck, hartebeeste, reedbuck, impala, bushbuck, zebra, nyala and a Cape buffalo with it. Nobody that I know will seriously contend that the seven mag. is an adequate buffalo rifle, of course, but, after knocking off an elephant and a couple of buffs with a rented .458 Magnum, Bill decided to see if it could be done. It could, and I know of a few other Cape buffalo which have been taken with the cartridge."

There's more: "I sprang for the first 7mm Mag. rifle I ever saw that I could afford. It was a battered old Remington Model 700 ADL which quickly displayed a propensity for shooting any sort of loading with the heavier bullets (including factory loads) under one inch for five shots at 100 yards ... Although the gun looked as though it might have seen service as a tent-peg, I used it on many great hunts and killed whitetail deer, mule deer, elk, pronghorn antelope and a fine Stone ram with it."

In 1972, Ruger brought out the long-action M77, and John took one to Mozambique. With it he slew such critters as warthogs, bushpigs, bushbuck, reedbuck, impala, duikers, oribi, nyala and baboons.

Wrote Mr. Wooters: "When it was all over, my companion, Jack Carter, and I agreed that, despite the fact that we'd fired every round of 7mm ammo we had on the trip, we'd still under-utilized the rifle, and that it *might have given quicker kills on some of the heavier game than the .375s did.*" (Italics mine.)

In summation: "There are some very knowledgeable critics in whose opinion the 7mm magnum is *not* a good all-'round big game cartridge, even for North America, and others who will state that it isn't enough more cartridge than the .270, .280, .284 or even the 7 x 57mm Mauser to be worth the additional trouble, cost and kick.

"With all due respect for these worthy and sincere opinions, I must say that a decade with the Big Seven has proven otherwise. It has been my experience and that of countless thousands of other hunters that this round, despite its shortcomings for reloaders, is the finest long-range cartridge for the average man in existence, as well as the most versatile."

Dave Petzal, Executive Editor for *Field & Stream*, and as learned a writer as is currently practicing the craft, wrote an elk piece in his magazine's April, 1988, issue. To wit: "Choose your cartridge carefully. I realize that every gun writer does a column on this subject every St. Swithin's Day, so I will dispense with the technical information and remind you of the following inescapable realities. Elk are large, heavy-boned, and thick-hided, and do not go down easily in many instances. You will likely get a shot under one of two conditions: It will be at very close range in thick timber, where you have only a part of the beast to shoot at, or it will be at extreme long range—300 yards plus. If you want to carry a heavy rifle (meaning over eight pounds), you will regret it bitterly. If you want to carry a shiny rifle, the elk will love you for it. If you can't shoot your rifle quickly and accurately, the elk will love you even more.

"Given my druthers, I like the .300 Winchester and .338 as elk cartridges. They shoot flat and knock stuff down, even big stuff. The .300 is better for long shots, while the .338 is superior at close range."

The redoubtable Elmer Keith, God bless him, wrote repeatedly that his view of a *minimum* cartridge for elk would involve a .33 caliber bullet of no less than 250 grains in weight. From there up, the sky was the limit. Elmer thought the .375 H&H was just fine, except that it wasn't quite so good as the .378 Weatherby, which in turn didn't measure up to the .416 Rigby ... and so forth.

Idaho author Bob Hagel, who does a reloading column for *Petersen's Hunting*, discussed in detail cartridges for elk and similar-sized fauna in his tome, *Game Loads and Practical Ballistics for the American Hunter*, published in 1978 by Alfred A. Knopf of New York. Bob's minimum for elk shooting at long range is the .257 Weatherby Magnum, but then only with the heaviest Nosler Partition bullets and maximum handloads, and only for picture-book shots. About the .270 he wrote: "Everything considered, my feeling after seeing many, many head of game of various sizes, and at various ranges, killed with the .270 Winchester, and some with the .264 (Magnum), is that they are marginal for heavy game *for really long range shooting at 400 yards or more.* (Italics mine.) This is not to say that they won't do the job if you are a good shot, pick your spot well and make sure the animal is in the right position when you shoot. I think Jack O'Connor has proved that point many times, but Jack has had a bit more experience than the average hunter, knows big game anatomy, is a good game shot and also knows when to hold his fire."

Hagel thinks highly of the various 7mm magnums, saying: "... the 150-grain Remington factory load with the pointed Core-Lokt bullet did very well at long range on game of all sizes, even though in hunting rifles it fell far short of the 3,260 fps muzzle velocity quoted in factory sheets. Most of the hunters who became addicted to the 7mm magnum cartridges soon started handloading for it anyway, and used the better 160-grain bullets, and the pointed 175-grain that soon appeared from most of the bullet makers as well as in Remington ammunition boxes."

Of the Big 30s, the following: "While the .30 magnum bullets mentioned will not give any more penetration than 7mm bullets in their respective sectional density levels, and do not pack much more punch at long range, and do not shoot quite as flat, they are of larger caliber. When expanded equally they form a larger frontal area and as a result, tear up a bit more tissue and deliver somewhat more shock."

Of the .33-bores, which seem to be Bob's favorites, this: "The next step up the caliber ladder as long range heavy game cartridges are the .338 Winchester and the .340 Weatherby. Either of these cartridges will give better performance on heavy animals at *all* hunting ranges than will the smaller bores, but this does not necessarily mean they are better for long-range shooting.

"For the handloader ... (the) 210 Nosler can be boosted along at about the same velocity as the 200-grain, and has a little better sectional density and ballistic coefficient. But its outstanding feature is that it does not blow up at any range even from the impact of the .340 Weatherby. I have killed a number of elk with it at various ranges, with the bulls standing in various positions, and have recovered only one bullet to show expanded form; the others made exit and may still be going."

I have spoken with other erudite elk hunters at length. Layne Simpson, who has looked through a rifle scope at more than one elk, told me that anyone who doesn't think the .30-06 and cartridges of its class will kill an elk properly should not be trusted with your mutual-fund money. Chub Eastman thinks the .338-06—a wildcat with about the punch of the .35 Whelen, but with the advantage of being able to use Nosler bullets—will work fine on elk. (Not to mention the *huge* grizzly he decked with one shot last fall!) Chub's wife likes the .280 Remington, and the last I heard had dumped two bulls with as many shots. No sweat, says Chub. In the earlier-mentioned survey conducted by Rick Jamison, several elk guides listed calibers like the .257 Roberts as their personal choices. Some of them preferred such magnums as the 7mm, but relatively few expressed any leanings toward the big .33s.

Now we'll let Jamison have his say, remembering that he's killed close to 20 elk in a relatively short time. Quoting from his letter on the subject of elk loads for close-range work: "In some instances when elk hole up in thick timber after the season opens, a quick-handling Marlin .45-70 might do the job, but that's a specialized rifle. Even in this type of hunting, you never know when another hunter is going to spook an elk across an opening several hundred yards away in mountainous country. An all-around elk rifle will do a good job even in the thick stuff."

For normal ranges, Rick likes the .30-06, as in this story: "Last fall, I tried for a shoulder/spine shot on my bull. I shot him with a .30-06 and a 180-grain Winchester Silvertip at about 200 yards. The elk was a five-pointer. The first shot *broke both shoulders* (italics mine) but left a relatively small wound channel, much like a Nosler Partition would, and I missed the spine. The elk ran off a ways and then stopped. I shot him through the opposite shoulder. That bullet exited too; the bullets crossed an inch or two apart in the chest cavity, and the elk went down about as fast as any I've taken. This one traveled about 50 yards from the first shot and dropped in his tracks at the second. (Remember, Rick used a .30-06 on that bull, not a bone-crushing magnum firing bullets the size of bran muffins!)

"Caliber size or bullet diameter doesn't seem to have as much effect on killing elk as does bullet performance and shot placement. Furthermore, shot placement should mate with bullet performance. Bullet speed and energy do make a difference regarding bullet performance and tissue destruction. Speed and bullet shape also mean that energy and bullet performance will be retained farther downrange and will be more reliable.

"Even if the elk rifle is a big belted magnum, remember it's *bullet performance* that correlates to meat destruction, and nothing has ever been killed too dead."

Here's Rick on game bullets: "Under certain circumstances, I like conventional expanding bullets like the ones from Hornady and Speer. The Speer Grand Slam is decidedly different, as is the Nosler Partition. The Nosler will almost always penetrate most.

"Contrary to common belief, the Nosler does not gain penetration by a high percentage of weight retention. There are other bullets which retain a higher average percentage of weight.

Nosler bullets, especially the old-style, expand with a very small frontal diameter. The Partition bullets usually shed most of the frontal core weight and the expanded "petals" lie close to the bullet shank by comparison with other bullets. They have a smaller frontal diameter, in other words, after they've expanded. This means they leave a smaller wound channel but penetrate more. The total wound cavity volume would be about the same as another bullet as long as both bullets do not exit, I imagine, but with the Noslers, the cavity is longer and slimmer.

"If I were expecting a shot from a difficult angle—like rear-end shots on elk running away in thick timber, the Nosler would be my choice. However, if my hunting area and my hunting style tended toward being able to place shots better, with the likely opportunity for a broadside lung shot, it's my belief that the conventional bullets with larger frontal diameters will kill quicker."

Getting to the crux, Rick offers this advice: "If you want a good elk rifle, get a .300 Win. Mag., top it with the best 4X scope you can afford, use a streamlined 180-grain bullet, load it beyond 3,000 fps, and use that same gun and load for everything from jack rabbits to moose. Shoot it a lot each month under hunting conditions, and in a couple of years you and your elk rifle will be a tough team to beat."

Well, as you can see, there seems to be a thread of commonality here. The experts agree on several points, to wit: 1) bullet placement is extremely important; 2) bullet performance (expansion and penetration, as well as accuracy and a flat trajectory) is equally critical; 3) the ability of the gunner to judge range, stay cool and cope with recoil is paramount; 4) anatomical knowledge is crucial, in that it assists with item number one above; 5) relatively heavy bullets in any given caliber are requisite, although not necessarily the *heaviest* available for each bore diameter; 6) a cartridge's long-range abilities are considered to be of utmost import, and to make matters more difficult, its capacity for close-in bashing is scrutinized; 7) magnum cartridges are heavily stressed, for all ranges.

Time for me to jump into the fray. I plan to consider more than one aspect of elk hunting, since—as with whitetail deer—I believe that sometimes a specialized rifle is in order if a hunter is to be *ideally* prepared. And away we go.

First off, geographical considerations. For the hunter who works, eats, sleeps, plays and maintains his home on the range, most any old rifle is an elk rifle. Such a gent knows elk, elk habits, elk habitat and can come back next week if he isn't offered a good shot today. More often than not, he keeps his shootin' eye sharp on coyotes during the off season, and guns down antelope, mule deer, black bear and whatnot when the seasons are open. In short, he can shoot, knows game, is an outdoorsman by praxis, and need be in no hurry to fill his larder. Guys and gals like that need no advice from me or anyone else when it comes to armament for beasts found in their bailiwick.

Unless of course they are new to the game, or live in one of our Western metropolises like Denver or Portland, close to elk country but not out working in it every day. And then there are the Midwestern and Eastern sportsmen who salt away their simoleons, planning for a Rocky Mountain elk trip. It's these folks to whom I address the bulk of my thoughts.

First, the specialized rifles and cartridges, beginning with outfits for close range. For those gunners who like to locate an elk hidey hole, then sneak in to set up an ambush while the residents are off tending to elk business, a long-distance rig isn't called for. Neither is it needed by the still hunter, who tip-toes along, stopping regularly for a look around—nor yet for the proficient bugler, who can pull in a lovelorn bull like a bass on a line. For such work, I like a short, quick-on-the-shoot rifle chambered for something big enough to make bone meal out of a wapiti's shoulder blades or spinal column.

For the handloader specifically, I would recommend a Marlin lever action .444 or .45-70, since no ammo house makes entirely suitable elk medicine in either of these chamberings, so far as I'm aware. Closest to it would be Remington's 265-grain soft point .444. When hand-fed, the .444 can go all the way up to 300 grains (from Barnes and Freedom Arms); such a load would get a bull's attention. The .45-70 can handle any weight from 350-grains (the 300s are too light for elk) on up to 500 if you like to roll bowling balls. I'd likely suffer anguish for weeks trying to choose between the 350 Hornady round nose and the 400-grain Speer flat nose. I suspect either would serve, so probably would try both and let my rifle decide.

If limited to factory ammo only, I would pick a Marlin 336 or Winchester 94 in .356 Winchester (if I could find one), and stuff it with 250-grain Power-Points. All the Marlin big bores come with sling swivels and recoil pad, which makes them doubly desirable.

Fine form with the author's first choice as a brush gun for elk, the .45-70 Government Marlin. The .45-70 is a handloader's proposition on elk, since the factory 300-grain loads are too lightly constructed, and the 405-grain too slow.

Next best would be a Browning BLR reamed to .358 Winchester. Only two flies on the BLR so chambered. First, the .358 is factory loaded with 200-grain bullets only, which may not have the sectional density necessary to drive through sufficient elk sinew from all angles. (Then again, it might. I once shoved one from sternum to stern on a 215-pound whitetail, and the bullet not only tunneled all that way, but did so while expanding to .62 caliber.) Second, trigger pull on every BLR I have examined has been pretty grim. Not so the Marlins and the Model 94, and both of those can be tuned easily by a competent 'smith. (I am told it's pretty tough to improve the BLR's pull.)

For the bolt-action fan, it would be hard to improve on a Remington Model Seven KS in .350 Rem. Mag. These guns aren't cheap, but neither is an elk hunt; perhaps one could be worked into the budget. Besides, it'd be a doozy as a bear and deer rifle, thus could earn its keep outside of elk habitat.

My own first pick for an elk rifle to be used at arm's length would be my Ultra Light Arms Model 20 in .358. With its heft of less than six pounds—scoped—I can sling it and forget it while wending my way into a bedding ground, or carry it all day at port arms when still hunting. Its stubby 20-inch barrel would be a decided aid in dodging the greenery. Loaded with either 250 Hornady round-nose soft points or Speer's fine spitzer of the same weight, it will put an elk's four hooves in the air. The 100-yard energy number with the Speer bullet reads 2,715 when started at 2,400 fps, more than most factory .30-06 loads show at the muzzle when actually chronographed, plus it offers all that bullet weight to add authority.

Make no mistake about it, the .358 is a serious elk cartridge. Linda Jamison clipped a big bull with her Savage M99, using the Speer pointed projectile. It did a fine job, downing the elk in short order, expanding well and retaining a high percentage of its original weight.

Although this business of short-range elk gunning is scoffed at by many who claim that most hunters can't get close enough to an elk to use a brush rifle, such is not always the case. I wonder how black powder hunters take their elk. And handgunners. Said harvesting seldom occurs at ranges past 125 yards, and usually *much* less. During the rut, elk are not especially difficult to creep up on, or call in.

On a Western hunt last autumn, I found out just how chummy one can get with elk when the rutting moon is full. I was deer hunting in mixed cover, and had been worried by a couple of bulls bugling and grunting at each other for about an hour. First they'd be over east, then several hundred yards to the north. Then the sounds of their brouhaha would swing in on a westerly wind. I tried to steer clear of them, since I figured a battle was imminent. But they out-foxed me. They went silent for a spell, then suddenly crashed down the wooded slope, catching me with my pants down, literally and metaphorically.

Caught at the edge of a draw near a little copse of trees, I hitched up my habiliments, shagged it over to the nearest tree and tried to permeate its bark. The bulls, a five point and a really big six pointer, had me stuck neatly between them, like a pig on a skewer. One circled my protective grove of trees at my right, the other to my left. Then they'd change places. They snorted and pawed. Circled and blew foam. Hooted and feinted. No more than 50 yards separated the would-be combatants, with me on the 25-yard line. I could have killed them both stone dead with a .44 Magnum revolver!

After a month or two, the smaller bull decided discretion was the better part of valor and hoofed it back upslope. I watched the big boy amble off; he looked disappointed. Reckon he figured he'd gotten all worked up for nothing.

Alas, having only a deer license, I could but watch them go, one in each direction, before returning to the pressing urge that had been interrupted. While I was thus engaged, a fat three-point (Western count) buck sashayed by at maybe 40 yards. No, I didn't manage to drop what I was doing and pick up my rifle. He trotted blissfully away, totally unaware of my existence. I cussed those two bulls for hours afterward.

Moving away from the close-range encounter, we'll now examine another specialist, the long-distance operator. Some elk hunters like to settle themselves on a rocky promontory where they can oversee a wide expanse of real estate, watching for horny bulls or elk that other hunters push out of the bushes. It works, but it involves a true long-range howitzer, an excellent judge of range, a sensitive trigger finger and a steady hand.

Since such tactics seldom involve much walking, a long, heavy, accurate rifle is no burden. Indeed, it is practically requisite. My idea of such an arm is epitomized by my A-Square Hannibal .340 Weatherby, which is what I had in mind when I ordered it. It weighs around 12 pounds field-ready, wears a high-powered variable scope boasting click adjustments and an adjustable objective. With a 250-grain pointed soft-point boattail starting out at 2,900 fps, it will provide the following trajectory when zeroed for 300 yards: at 100 yards, the bullet is 3.8 inches high; it's 4½ inches up at 200; at 400 yards, the drop is only 10.3 inches, and the retained energy is 2947 foot-pounds! Let me put that in perspective for you. My rifle and load will show virtually identical drop at *400* yards when so zeroed as a 180-grain Winchester Silvertip .308 Winchester factory load exhibits at *300*! It hits harder at 400 yards than any .30-06 Springfield factory load does *at the muzzle*! If that isn't a reach-out-and-touch-something tool, I dunno what is.

If I wanted the advantages of a Nosler 250 Partition, I'd lose only 335 foot-pounds at 400 yards. Then I would worry not about bullet break-up should a big bull rush right up on me in lustful exuberance. I could have the best of both worlds by sticking a few Nosler handloads in an accessible pocket while keeping the boattail spitzers in my rifle's magazine to cover my original intent.

For those who must use factory ammo in their .340, I recommend the Weatherby offering that features the 250 Nosler

Partition. If it's as fast as that firm's 250-grain round nose, it might perform better than my handloads!

To negate the .340's fearsome recoil, the A-Square features—in addition to its considerable heft—a wide, thick, soft-rubber buttplate, a hand-filling stock with very little drop and longer-than-average length of pull and a wide comb. All the above do not totally wash out the discomfort, so as soon as I refill my piggy bank I intend to ship the rifle to Mel Forbes up at Ultra Light Arms, for one of his spiffy muzzle brakes. That'll convert the punch to a shove, although it will increase the roar out front.

Of course, there are other cartridges that will stretch out to 400 yards to handle an elk, but the .340 is likely the best of the bunch so far as factory rounds are concerned. If you can cope with its backthrust, either by choosing a heavy rifle or one with a muzzle brake, it's the way to go. If not, then such lesser rounds as the .300 Winchester Magnum, .300 Weatherby, or the .338 might be preferable, though all those kick up a ruckus at their rear ends as well. But for the long-range specialist, heavy recoil is a fact of life, at least on elk.

Most of us, however, are not only content to hold our fire past 300 yards or so, but will unquestionably do so except under the most extreme circumstance. Many very experienced hunters prefer to stay within 200 yards, to be as certain as possible of a telling shot. Such attempts constitute the majority of *successful* efforts on wapiti. Let's address the guns and loads that will do a workmanlike job under normal conditions.

With 200 yards as a rough outer limit, plenty of cartridges will work well on elk if a good bullet is stuck in the heart, lungs or spine. I'd place the .25-06 Remington as minimum, using as hot a handload as my rifle would handle safely, and then only with 120-grain Nosler Partition bullets. If forced to use factory ammo, I'd consider only one: Remington's 120-grain pointed Core-Lokt.

The 6.5 X 55mm is next up the list. Either of the two Norma factory loads will do. Although the 139-grain hollow point shoots flatter and retains more energy, the 156-grain round nose digs deeper into flesh and bone. Better yet would be a 140 Nosler Partition at 2,750 fps or so. Shoots flatter than a 180-grain .30-06 factory load and carries over 1700 foot pounds to 200 yards.

In the 7mm-08 or 7 X 57, I'd handload the 154 Hornady Interlock, the 160-grain Speer or 160 Nosler Partition; all can be pushed to better than 2,700 with the right powders. If the 160s are started at such a speed, their 200-yard energy runs close to 2,000

On non-trophy bulls at woods ranges, any good cartridge with stout bullets will work on elk. The .270 is a good example.

foot-pounds, which is more than a 220-grain Silvertip retains at 300 yards when fired from a .300 Win. Mag.! That's enough for elk if the shooter does his part.

The .270 Winchester, .280 Remington and .284 all offer more than is necessary in a 200-yard gun when used with stout 150-grain bullets, either handloaded or factory. Ditto the .300 Savage, .308 Winchester, .30-40 Krag, .303 British and, of course, the .30-06, all with properly streamlined bullets of at least 180 grains in weight. The 8 X 57 is just as good with the heavy-bullet Norma loading or handloads featuring the 200 Nosler or Speer spitzers. I'd not hesitate to use my Marlin .356 with 220-grain Speer handloads; the .358 is even better. As I said, a profusion of cartridges have all it takes to make elk meat when shots are limited to 200 yards or a bit beyond. (How *much* beyond depends on the cartridge and the gunner.)

At ranges to 300 yards, such cartridges as the .280 Remington—shown here in one of the limited-edition Model 70 Featherweights—works fine on elk and moose with good bullets.

When the distance marker approaches 300 yards, the field tends to thin out a mite. Except for the most careful shot, who might get by with lesser loads, I'd recommend only a few cartridges for true 300-yard elk gunning. In factory guise, the .270, .280 and .284 all have what it takes so long as heavy bullets are utilized. For the .270, I'd want the Federal Premium 150 Partition. In the .280, the 150-grain Remington pointed Core-Lokt would do nicely if from a fast lot. There is only one version of the .284, Winchester's 150-grain, so that's what I would use.

In the two 7mms particularly, I'd be much happier with handloads. I'd stick with the 160-grain items from Speer and Nosler, or the 154 Hornady spire point, and goose them right along. But none of the foregoing would be my first choice as a 300-yard elk demolisher.

The .308 Winchester is in the same 300-yard energy class as the previous threesome, and with the 165 Federal Premium boattail beats them all by a slender margin. However, except under ideal conditions, I wouldn't want to use such a light, quick-expanding bullet on elk. Better would be the 180 Remington pointed Core-Lokt, which according to the factory sheet retains over 1,550

foot pounds at 300. Handloaded with a 180 Nosler Partition, the
.308 shows 1,669 foot pounds at 300, with the 180-grain Solid
Base even better at 1753. I used the latter on a really big bull, and
at longer range than we're discussing. Worked perfectly,
expanding to double its original diameter while penetrating from
one side of his tremendous rib box to the other, where it lodged
'neath the skin.

When handloaded, the 8 X 57 Mauser is fine, too. Shove a 200
Nosler Partition to 2,500 (easily accomplished), and it retains
1,720 foot pounds after sailing the length of three football fields,
and drops about 10 inches from a 200-yard zero. Let no one tell
you the 8 X 57 is anemic.

If I were suggesting the optimum cartridge for the non-
reloader, it would be the .30-06, no question about it. Available
from Federal is a 180-grain Nosler Partition that hits with a
1,600-foot-pound punch at 300 yards, drops only 10 inches or so
from a 200-yard zero, won't deafen a mule with its muzzle blast
and offers recoil that can be handled by experienced, *practiced*
riflemen. All that spells death to a wapiti.

For the handloader, it becomes a toss-up between the .30-06
and the .35 Whelen. In the 'ought-six, a 200-grain Nosler Partition
can be started at from 2,600 to maybe 2,650 in most rifles. So
boosted, it hangs on to about 2,150 foot-pounds at 300 yards, fully
as much as any domestic 180-grain .300 Win. Mag. factory load *at
the same range*. Let me say it again: A .30-06 loaded properly with
200 Nosler Partition bullets is the *full* equal of any 180-grain .300
Win. Mag. factory load produced in this country, and may equal
the hot Norma rendition as well when both are chronographed side
by side and used in barrels of similar length.

The good old .30-06 shoots plenty flat, too, showing only an
8.4 inch drop at 300 yards when zeroed for 200. Move the zero
range out to 250 and you can forget bullet drop on a 300-yard elk,
or a deer for that matter.

The Whelen, although offered in two excellent factory
permutations, is not a 300-yard elk load unless handloaded. The
Remington bullet that would likely work best when applied to a big
bull's rib cage is the 250-grain item, which unfortunately is too
blunt of nose to hold its initial impetus. All the handloader needs to
do is purchase a box of 250-grain Speer spitzers and stick 'em in
his brass atop a goodly portion of one of the medium burners such
as IMR 4895. When he does, he'll find that those beefy Speer
spitzers will zip out his barrel at about 2,600 fps. When one arrives

at the 300 mark, it still fetches along 2,302 foot pounds according to Speer data, which is more than the abovementioned 200-grain .30-06 handload. Trajectory is adequately taut, the 300-yard dip being but 9.4 inches, only an inch more than the .30-06 provides.

Rick Jamison has dug 250 Speer spitzers out of elk and bear meat, and he says the performance is excellent, with no tendency to blow up even at point-blank range. That's good enough for me.

I refuse to choose between them. The .30-06 kicks a bit less, comes in a wider selection of rifles and action types, has the advantage of several good elk loads in factory trim. Some folks will think its adaptability to Nosler bullets about cinches the argument. But the Whelen has its own advantages. It transmits more energy at all ranges, cuts a wider swath through tissue, and gets more of its power from bullet weight than velocity. To reiterate: it's a coin toss. For 300-yard elk gunning, nothing more is needed than either or this pair. And nothing less is quite as good.

All Purpose Elk Cartridges

And now let's look at all-purpose elk rifles and loads, ones I consider the real gems of the group. These outfits will handle all elk hunting chores, from hard-off-the-muzzle to a full 400 yards. They aren't magic, being only as efficient as their operators, but for those folks who can cope with the noise and backthrust sufficiently to hit a basketball-sized target nearly a quarter-mile away, the following rigs are the proper tools for the job.

If I had more dust than cash in my wallet, and my accounts payable resembled the national deficit, I'd be forced to choose very wisely indeed, looking for a no-frills rifle. No matter how deeply in penury I wallowed, I would buy only a synthetic-stocked rifle for my once-in-a-decade hunt out West. The three I'd select from are the Browning A-Bolt Stainless Stalker, Winchester's Model 70 Winlite, and the Remington Model 700 KS. That might well be my order of preference, since it's the order in price. I'd have the best four-power scope I could afford mounted securely by a gunsmith, who I'd also have adjust the trigger to my liking.

The caliber? No question about it, Remington's 7mm Magnum. Recoil is acceptable, even in such reasonably light rifles, and its accuracy is unquestioned. If I loaded a 160 Nosler ahead of 80.0 grains of H-870, as I have in my Browning, I'd get over 3,200 fps at the muzzle and 2123 foot pounds of smash way over there at 400 yards. Almost but not quite as good would be the 175 Nosler and 78.0 grains of the same powder, for 3,035 or so foot-seconds at the muzzle and nearly 2,000 foot pounds remaining at 400.

If forced to shoot factory ammo in a Big Seven, I would prefer the Weatherby cartridge if it came in any of the abovementioned rigs. Since it doesn't, I'd likely choose Federal's 160 Partition Premium, or the 175 pointed Core-Lokt 7mm Rem. Mag. Better yet, I'd try to con a reliable handloader into letting me use his equipment, then stoke my own.

Now, let's say my Uncle Mannie dropped a bundle on a ball game. Further, let's pretend it was me to whom he lost it. I'd take my loot, choose a Winlite M70 or Browning Composite Stalker, only this time I'd go for a .300 Win. Mag. or a .338. Then, not only would I have its trigger worked on and the scope mounted permanently, I'd ship my rifle off to have a muzzle brake affixed to its snoot. I'd fill its cupboard with top handloads featuring the 200 Nosler Partition if it were a .300, the 210 or 250 Nosler Partitions were it a .338. Among factory loads, I would be happy with the 180 Federal Premium Partition in the .300 chambering, the 210 Federal Premium in .338.

So why did I abandon the 7mm Magnum? Simply because the .300 and .338 cut a little wider wound channel, carry a modicum more energy, spit out slightly heavier projectiles and all without any attendant facility for maiming me with recoil *so long as I have a muzzle brake*. However, if I were so hard-headed as not to use hearing protection while shooting—particularly in the hunting fields—I wouldn't shoot a muzzle-braked rifle on a *bet*, but would stick to a Seven Magnum and be forever content.

What if, you ask, I won the door prize at a Tupperware party and carried home under guard in excess of a thousand clams? Wow! I'd order a Weatherby .340—Fibermark persuasion, thank you—and make sure it either left South Gate with a muzzle brake or was promptly treated to an aftermarket unit. While I was at it, I'd insist on having it finished in matte blue, and have a trigger job performed unless I'd had the foresight to order it with a Canjar single set.

If my ship came in, or better yet if my brother-in-law paid me all the money he owes me, I would let Melvin Forbes up at Ultra Light provide me with a Model 28. I'd want it fitted with a 4X Leupold scope in Ultra Light's ultra-light mounts—mated to the receiver so's they'd never work loose under the stresses of recoil, having a horse roll on the rifle or dropping it out of a tree stand. I'd ask for a 13¼-inch pull (no extra charge), and three-pound trigger, a steel trigger guard, a blue camo stock (no additional cost), and then I'd agonize for weeks over caliber choice.

The candidates? Two: the .338 Mag. and the .358 Norma Magnum. If Nosler would bring out a 250-grain .35-caliber Partition, my indecision would be effaced. I'd take the .358 Norma and run.

And now let's take a cursory look at...

Moose and Grizzlies

Although moose are much bigger than elk, and grizzly bears more aggressive, mean-tempered and at least as hard to stop, the rifles most useful for all-around elk hunting are equally suitable for this duo. I can hear you shaking your head now, so let's talk about it.

Moose, though as big and heavy and strong and solidly constructed as a cement mixer, aren't especially hard to kill. It just takes them a while to get the message that they're dead. They are worse than hogs in that respect. When they finally do, they tip right over. What's more, a wounded moose is too dumb to know he's hurt, and too phlegmatic to do anything about it anyway. So he simply stands around, like a huge, dark, taciturn mountain goat, and waxes philosophical until the lights go out. In short, a bull moose is as impervious to shock as a 2,000-pound sack of Jello.

Bob Hagel once shot a middling-sized Shiras bull that he caught standing in a beaver pond. Bob was toting a .375 H&H Magnum. He got comfortable, put his crosswires on the moose, and slid one into its ribcage. The bull walked slowly to the edge of the pond, put his chin over the dam, backed up, and stood once again in the center. Mr. Hagel put one more in the boiler room, whereupon the animal repeated the performance, ending up once again at the pond's middle. Once more a hollow *boom*! rent the stillness. The moose trundled over to shore again, and died. That proves the .375 Magnum ain't enough for moose, right? Sure it does.

Trappers in the far North still subsist on moose meat slain with a .30-30. Indians routinely kill them with .22 Hornets, or once did, simply because ammo is cheap and the rifles easy to shoot accurately.

Bob Petersen, ramrod of Petersen Publishing Company, took on a big bull with a .44 Magnum Smith & Wesson revolver. He popped the beast once, twice, thrice, with the moose all the while just standing there looking bewildered and beleaguered. At the

A moose is a big critter, and none too bright. Although it takes a lot to down one quickly, they don't often travel far when wounded. Any elk cartridge stuffed with heavy, stout bullets is a good bet for moose.

third hit, he fell like a brick. Proves the .22 Hornet, .30-30 and .44 Magnum sixgun are super moose arms, right? Sure it does.

Hagel wrote a piece on the .378 Weatherby Magnum in *Handloader* magazine, issue No. 42, March-April, 1973. In it he had this to say: ''.. for whatever it's worth, I did clobber a pretty husky bull with it and a 270-grain Nosler that started on its way at 3,130 fps. The huge old bull was standing quartering to the gun at what proved to be 175 yards, and had no idea anyone was around. I laid the crosshair on the big shoulder joint and touched the .378 off. The slap of the bullet came back almost as loud as the rifle shot. The bull shuddered from the end of this big nose to the tip of his stubby tail, but he didn't even sag. He just stood there as though he had suddenly frozen solid. I could see that the bullet had landed exactly where it should have gone, so there was no reason to give him another. It took that moose about the usual one minute and 53 seconds to discover he was dead, and he didn't know it then until he tried to take a step.

''The Nosler had pulverized the shoulder, passed through the ribs and the full length of the top of the lungs. It had entered the paunch and stopped somewhere inside ... it had penetrated nearly three feet of heavy bone, lung tissue and soggy paunch.

''Why didn't the bull drop at the shot after absorbing all of the energy kicked up by the big bullet? A good question. But this is normal moose behavior, no matter what you clobber him with unless you break the spine or penetrate the brain. Moose aren't given to fast thinking, and it just takes them a couple of minutes to discover they are on the other side of the Great Divide.''

Believe it, folks. If a .378 Weatherby won't flatten a moose on the spot, *nothing* will!

In the book, *Jack O'Connor's Big Game Hunts*, published by Outdoor Life and E.P. Dutton and Company, Jack told of a bull he and Doc DuComb collaborated on in British Columbia. The moose was about 200 yards away, browsing along, thinking moose thoughts, when O'Connor busted him with his .270. Wrote Jack: ''The bull humped up, took a couple of steps, and stood there with his head hanging down. I shot again, and heard the bullet strike. Still the moose was on his feet, so I shot once more.''

''He'll go down!'' opined one of Jack's companions. The bull was like a fighter out on his feet, and was making no attempt to quit the scene.

Ducomb asked if he could shoot. O'Connor said okay.

''Doc hoisted up his .30/06 and touched her off. I heard the

This hunter took a big cow with a Ruger Model 77 .30-06 and Norma factory ammo.

bullet strike. For a moment the bull stood there weaving, then collapsed like the side of a building.

"When we skinned him out we found that all four shots had slammed into the lungs, literally tearing them to shreds. I have seen a fair number of moose killed myself, but I have never seen one knocked down in his tracks unless he was struck in the brain or spine. I have never seen a moose killed with one shot ....

"... I think the answer to why one of these animals is so hard to stop with a single shot is that there is simply too much moose. The bigger an animal is the harder he is to kill, and a bullet that will kill a mule deer or a ram in his tracks instantly simply won't do it to the moose that weighs four or five times as much ..."

So a .270 and .30-06 are poor moose medicine, right. Sure they are.

I'm going to let Craig Boddington, author of *Campfires and Game Trails*, published by Winchester Press, close the discussion on moose: "In terms of size, moose should rate the heaviest artillery a hunter could carry. However, they're not particularly difficult to kill. One the other hand, they are inordinately hard to put down. They seem to have a phlegmatic disposition that is fairly impervious to bullet shock, and it seems that if the first shot doesn't do the job immediately, the next three or four might not either.

"Because of their sheer size, a rifle of adequate caliber with a stout bullet designed to offer good penetration is certainly called for. A .30-06 with 180- or 200-grain bullet is a sensible minimum, and is probably quite adequate. A .300 or .338 magnum might yield quicker results, *but I'm not altogether certain about that* ...(Italics mine.)

"Typically a bull hit (in the heart/lung region) will remain where he is or amble off a few yards before dropping over ...

"Bullet effect on moose seems to defy all the laws. I've shot moose with a .375 H&H, a pretty decent moose gun, only to see absolutely nothing happen, and have to shoot again. On the other hand, my dad once shot a moose with a 180-grain Silvertip from a .308 Winchester—a bit on the light side. The shot was to the heart, and that moose dropped in his tracks as if struck by lightning ..."

So the .308 is better than the .375 on moose, right? No it isn't. But it may well be just as good. And that's my point: Shoot moose with whatever you want, so long as you use a bullet of controlled expansion and good sectional density, and stick it in the right spot. Any load that will kill an elk will likewise do in a moose. It'll just take longer.

I hesitate to tell anyone what load to use on big bears, just as I am loathe to advise the average person about a home-defense handgun. Someday *their* life might depend on the validity of *my* counsel, and that makes me a bit nervous. So I'll simply relate what *my* choice would be if I were going one-on-one with a big, nasty bruin.

Hosea Sarber, legendary Alaskan game warden, is said to have slain the bulk of his considerable lifetime bag of brown bear (which are merely fish-fed grizzlies) with a .270 Winchester. Grancil Fitz, in hunting all the big game on this continent, used only one rifle—a .30-06. Jack O'Connor, who killed more than one big bear, wrote that the minimum cartridge he'd want to tackle a mountain grizzly with is a 7 X 57. When Jack went to Alaska after coastal browns, let it be known, he chose a .375 Holland & Holland. The .300 Weatherby Magnum has sent many a sofa-sized bruin to the happy hunting ground, and quite neatly too. As I recall, Warren Page felt that his 7mm magnum was more than adequate for grizzlies, and had no compunction about facing a brown with Old Betsy in tow.

So, what does all this indicate? Bob Hagel puts it succinctly in his tome, *Game Loads and Practical Ballistics for the American Hunter*. Here's Bob, answering the foregoing question: "Maybe more than you think. While it is obvious that all these hunters can't be right, it does show that if you use the right load, are a good shot, keep cool when the time comes to shoot and know where to place the bullet you are using in the right spot to do the most good, you can get by with any good cartridge and load. It does *not* mean, however, that any one of these cartridges, or any other cartridge, stands bullet, neck and shoulder above all other cartridges, and that it will perform feats that no other cartridge will."

I suggest emphatically that you read that passage over again. It is as wise an apothegm as you will come across. And quite true.

Before going into my personal choices, let's reiterate what Bob and every other writer worth his salt has said time and time again, especially since it has such serious meaning when applied to the taking of potentially dangerous animals like big bears. A hunter must know his rifle, have it zeroed properly, choose the right ammunition, be cool under pressure, know big-game anatomy like his own and practice, practice, practice. Anyone who does not meet *all* these criteria has no business shooting at *anything*, but especially a grizzly. Doing so unprepared is not only a fool's errand, it is totally irresponsible, since a wounded bear might very well vent its spleen on unwary (and unarmed) citizens who happen along its path.

Now, if I were sheep hunting and got into an argument with a grizzly, I'd go for his brain and use most anything I had along, from the 6.5 X 55 Swede up. If I were moose hunting and got jumped by ol' *ursus horribilis*, I'd likely be carrying a .30-06 or something of that nature, loaded with heavy (for the caliber) Nosler bullets. Under such a circumstance, the bear would be in more trouble than I unless he caught me unaware at very close range.

For grizzly hunting specifically, with the chance of digging a wounded one out with the end of my gun barrel, I'd want a minimum of the .30-06/200 Nosler, and a 175-grain Partition in a 7mm Magnum would be better still. Actually, I might prefer the .300 Winchester Magnum to a .30-06, although the additional recoil would slow down repeat shots, and one bullet is often insufficient on a big bruin.

Use the .375 on big bear if it gives you confidence, but pick a different iteration. This Ruger Number One is beautiful, but it will likely belt you from beneath your beanie when you squeeze one off. Besides, you'll feel more confident with faster follow-up shots.

So I reckon I'd flip a coin again, between the .35 Whelen/250 Speer and the .338 Win. Mag./250 Nosler. I'd want either of them in an Ultra Light Arms rifle, because lighter is faster, always. I'd have a muzzle brake, a shorter-than-standard stock (to obviate the probability of snagging the butt on my clothing when I tossed the gun to shoulder), a light crisp trigger, and I'd practice rapid bolt manipulation *from the shoulder* until my right hand became a calloused blur. Further, I'd study bruin anatomy as if my life depended on it, as indeed it might.

For that once-in-a-lifetime chance at a brown bear, I'd likely stay with the same choices, although I would consider the .358 Norma as well. If I wanted something bigger, I'd bypass the .375

and jump to one of the short .41-caliber magnum wildcats in order to gain a *noticeable* increase in punch. But I doubt I'd need it, or at least that I would *feel* that I did.

In the January, 1988, issue of *American Hunter*, my pal Finn Aagaard wrote of the .35 Whelen. He had this to relate: "A friend of mine named Joe Phillips, who lives in Alaska, has some experience with the .35 Whelen on large animals. Besides moose and caribou, he has taken four Roosevelt elk and four brown bear with it, mostly with the 250-grain Speer bullet at 2,500 fps. He claims that no beast he has hit with it has ever traveled more than 50 yards. One of the Speer bullets that penetrated both shoulders of a bear was recovered from just under the hide. It still weighed 204 grains and had expanded to a diameter of about .61 inch.''

Finn's friend wrote that he'd recently shot a brown at maybe 65 yards, using the Speer bullet. The angle was steep and downhill, with the bullet entering behind the left shoulder, tearing up both lungs and maybe the top of the heart, ending up lodged in the bear's right leg. The bear fell down, tried to regain its feet, then died. Pretty good performance.

And a pretty good shot, by an experienced hunter using an excellent bullet fired from an adequate cartridge.

That's what gets the game.

9

Cartridges For
Varmints And Predators

In many ways, varmint gunners get the sweet end of the hunting stick. Not only are bag limits liberal—in some cases unlimited—but their quarry is often huntable year-round, or pretty close to it. Most nimrods live within driving distance of some type of vermin shooting, frequently within walking distance. No special type of equipment is necessary, though the way some varmint seekers outfit themselves you'd never know it. Varmint extermination does not require the use of hard-recoiling rifles that uncap your teeth, nor is it expensive. Finally, vermin hunting is a gregarious pursuit—as my buddy Bob O'Connor says,..."a team sport." You and your pals can spend an enjoyable day afield in each other's company, not spread out over 600 acres ... all alone ... no one to lie to. A fie on elk hunting, deer bustin', bear baiting! Varminting's for me!

So what, exactly, constitutes a varmint? (Aside from your neighbor's pet ferret, of course.) Such little critters as ground squirrels, prairie dogs, rock chucks, groundhogs, badgers and crows all fit the varmint mold. Landowners in parts of Texas include the little piglike javelina, but in other Southwestern states the imitation porkers are considered game animals. Although such animals as bobcats, foxes, coyotes and mountain lions are sometimes thought of as vermin, they are in actuality predators,

There's no doubt about it. Of the rifleman's hunting opportunities, varminting is the most social.

albeit pesky ones. For the nonce, we'll cover true varmints; later we'll take a gander at predators.

Varmints

There are varmint rifles and cartridges; then there are rifles and cartridges *used* for varmints. The former is nearly always the latter, but the latter is not always the former. Got that? As an example, take Bob O'Connor's *varmint rifle*, a heavy, superbly accurate rifle built by famed gunsmith Kenny Jarrett and reamed to a super-hot wildcat .22 centerfire cartridge that will transform a hapless whistlepig into a red mist. The rig is the very apotheosis of a varmint rifle/cartridge combo.

On the other hand, consider the gun Mike Holloway *uses* to eradicate groundhogs, a Remington Model 700 ADL chambered to the deer-slayin' .270 Winchester. Last time we went after the over-sized rodents, Mike dumped one offhand at maybe 35 yards, using a 130-grain Nosler Ballistic Tip. He then drooped his belly o'er a rock and smote one at about 225, all in a space of two minutes and without uprooting himself from one spot.

The point of the two preceding paragraphs was to illustrate the polarity of varmint armament. Died-in-the-wool vermin chasers

This happy lady has just killed her first chuck. Her rifle is a Ruger Model 77 International in .250-3000. Shot was a measured 200 yards.

often utilize very specialized equipment, and hie off to the field at every opportunity. Fellows like Master Holloway sojourn to the chuck hills but once or twice each annum, thus having no burning need for such limited-purpose ordnance. They can simply tote along their deer or pronghorn rifle, so long as it is not chambered to one of the "brush-country" loads. (Actually, the .30-30 will work on vermin out to 200 yards or better in an accurate rifle, and there are factory loads intended specifically for that purpose. Not the case with most close-range cartridges, though.)

The true varmint cartridges are—with one exception—.22-caliber centerfires, beginning with the .22 Hornet and running through the mighty .220 Swift. Each cartridge is loaded to a velocity level that is range-limiting, and several commercial loads are so close together ballistically that they are nigh interchangeable.

The .22 Hornet, .218 Bee and .221 Remington Fireball make up the entry-level cartridges, offering adequate speed and precision for 175-yard certainty (assuming a good shot and little wind), and

Friends gathered again to hunt varmints. The members of this trio all used Kimber rifles to collect this bag in a few minutes.

maybe stretching to a full 225 in the case of the Fireball. The Hornet is factory-quoted as booting a 45-grain hollow- or soft-pointed bullet along at 2,690 fps, and the little guy will more often than not manage that feat in domestic trim. Alas, the precision of most factory loads leaves a bit to be desired, with groups running in the 1¾-to 2¼-inch neighborhood, which ain't the high-rent district. However, given its modest speed and paltry retained energy (only 225 foot pounds at 200 yards), the Hornet's accuracy is obviously not the sole factor limiting its use.

Norma once offered a 45-grain soft point, but the current catalog fails to list it. A pity. In virtually every Hornet I ever tested, it was far and away the most accurate fodder. My Anschutz M1700 Bavarian, for example, printed five five-shot strings under a minute of angle at 100 yards; American-made stuff can only dream of such grouping. On the downside, the Norma ammo was slow, slow, slow—in the low-2,400 foot-second range. I guess the factory-ammo Hornet shooter had to choose either speed and far-apart bullet holes, or tiny shot clusters at rock-throwing velocities.

Handloading helps a little, but not so much as you might surmise. It is difficult to exceed Hornet factory speed with bullets of the same weight, but generally simple to improve accuracy. (Except in the case of the Norma stuff.) If I kept a Hornet in the cabinet, I'd definitely handfeed it.

The .218 Bee, almost defunct but still around in the Kimber bolt-action single shot, is shown as getting 2,760 fps from a 46-grain hollow point. My Kimber shaded that a tad, clocking 2,777 with the Winchester offering, which is the *only* offering. Groups ran to 1.84 on the average, which is Hornet territory. As one can see, the Bee offers little more sting than the Hornet in factory guise.

The clouds part when a reloader gets in on the action. In my Kimber .218, it was no trick to beat 2,900 fps using Hercules 2400 beneath a 45-grain Nosler soft point, although accuracy was a sometimes thing. Better was 13.0 grains of IMR 4227, giving 2,825 fps with the same bullet, and groups running 1.31 inches for the aggregate. Not bad. Most accurate load was 17.8 grains of Hodgdon's BL-C(2) and the 50-grain Nosler Expander, at 1.23 inches for four strings. A bit laggard, though, at 2,351 fps. I reckon the Bee might be a 200-yard varminter under windless conditions, but only with the better reloads. For the factory product, shorten the distance by 25 yards.

The .221 Fireball, originally chambered in the Remington XP-100 "handgun," was added to the Kimber queue a few years ago in a blatant attempt to oust the often intractable Hornet, which was keeping the Oregon-based firm abuzz with customer complaints. The plan went like so: First, Kimber would announce to one and all their intention of being the first manufacturer to produce rifles chambered for the Fireball. When that news hit the streets, it was averred, the disreputable old Hornet would be forced to abdicate due to shooter apathy. Into the resulting interregnum would step the .221 Fireball; then it—and Kimber—would reside happily ever after. The strategy was excellent, its execution timely, its vehicle (the Lilliputian Mauser-like Model 84) a marvelous piece of equipment. The plot fell flat on its beezer.

Not only did the heir apparent fail to ignite public fancy, but the hoary old Hornet—recalcitrant and doddering though it was—declined to wither and die. In fact, it was reinstated! The plebiscite had been conducted; the *Fireball* was the also-ran, and none too well admired for having attempted a coup. (Which probably should teach the firearms industry something about which tail wags which dog, but likely won't.)

Now the .221 is no slouch ballistically, at least when compared to the above-discussed duo. As the factory stokes it, a 50-grain soft point kicks its heels up to 2,840 fps or so, which is roughly 100 foot-seconds over the heads of its elders, give or take a few fps. And the Fireball uses bullets that are 10 percent heavier, yielding nearly 900 foot pounds at the muzzle. (The Bee can muster similar levels of energy when handloaded, but is in arrears by a hundred or so as factory baked. The Hornet runs aft of that by another 60 foot pounds, whether factory or home-brewed.)

Handloaded, the .221 Fireball nips at the heels of factory-load ballistics provided by the bigger .222 Remington, which was also offered in the Kimber 84, as well as many, many other rifles over the years. So why buy a .221 when you can have a .222? Because, some say, the .221 serves the same purpose the Hornet and Bee have since the Depression era: Adequate 175-200 yard varminting capability with a quiet voice. As juiced by the ammo companies, this is a valid point.

However, Fireball fans on the one hand tout to the heavens the miniscule bark of their Hornet-level handloads, then objurgate the selfsame Hornet's piddling ballistic reach, claiming that their hero will nearly match the larger (and *louder*) .222. What happens to those vaunted low decibel levels when the .221 is so loaded? It smells of fish, here; one can't have it both ways. Either the .221 Fireball is a Hornet-quiet 200-yard load, or its a 250-yard .222-strident fire-breather. Maybe the point is that it can be both. If so, here's a bulletin: So can the .222!

Bottom line: Why should you buy the .221 Fireball instead of a Hornet or a .222 Remington? You shouldn't, except maybe as an investment. (I strongly suspect that the Hornet will be tossing dirt in the Fireball's face before we all get much older. Which means that Kimber Fireballs will become dusty-but-valuable collectors' items.)

That covers the 175- to 200-or-so crowd. The next step up is to another trio, the .222 Remington, .222 Remington Magnum and the .223 Remington.

The .222 is said to achieve 3,140 fps from its 50-grain soft- or hollow-pointed factory bullets. I recently averaged up the speeds provided by five different factory loads, all chronographed in rifles having 22- or 24-inch barrels. The mean was 3,078 fps. Not shabby. Two loads—one lot of Remington's Power-Lokt hollow point and Norma's full-metal-jacket number—managed to surpass factory data, with the former making it to 3,175, the latter seeing 3,181.

Handloads will improve things perhaps 125 fps in some rifles, which is not noticeable in the field. Accuracy from factory ammunition is usually quite acceptable; often impressive in the extreme. Ditto for handloads. The .222 is a 225-yard cartridge under most conditions, and will stretch to 250 or so when guided by a knowing hand.

The .222 Magnum—which is not a magnum in any way except name, is not especially fast, not unusually accurate, not commonly available and wears no belt—was born out of military trials in the mid '50s. The Army spurned the cartridge, perhaps because it was a wee bit long for the Armalite rifle then the apple of Uncle Sam's eye. Remington offered it to the populace in 1958, whereupon it was largely ignored for years. And well it might be; it was certainly no giant step beyond the excellent and well-established .222. When the .223 Remington came on stage a few years later, under the government's avuncular largesse as well as in civilian form, the .222 Mag.'s fate was sealed. It began its long slide into the boneyard.

Still loaded by Remington with a 55-grain soft point or Power-Lokt hollow nose, the factory list claims 3,240 fps, exactly the same as is shown for the .223. Will it make it? In a word, no. I tested four lots of Remington's finest, using two Sako rifles with barrels at least 23 inches long. The average for the four samplings was 3,139, about 100 foot seconds shy of a load. (The .223 averaged out at 3,175 fps, for 23 separate tests involving eight factory loads in several rifles, all having barrels of 22 or 24 inches in length.)

The .222 Magnum and the .223 are ballistic clones when handloaded as well, with both managing around 3,300 fps at their best using just the right propellants. Although I've had much better luck with the .223 in the precision department, my intellect tells me that the two should be equal in grouping ability. So let's leave it at that.

The .222 Mag. and the .223 are often thought of as 250-yard cartridges, with some authorities allowing as how they can reach out to maybe 275 under ideal conditions. My view is that they serve best at 250, but can handle a chuck clear out to 300 if everything is right. Retained energy at 300 is around 500

This hunter takes a shot at a distant whistlepig with a Remington .223. For shots to 275 yards, the .223's all you need.

foot-pounds with the right bullets, which is more than the Hornet offers at 75!

One of the most thoroughly smushed groundhogs I ever saw shot was hit at a paced 235 yards with a 52-grain Speer hollow point. The little speedster was launched from a Remington 788 .222 by my chucking partner Mike Nelson. Taking the hog in the paunch as it quartered away, the bullet ranged forward into the lungs and blew up. That whistlepig looked as if it had been unzipped from stern to sternum. I believe that the deadly Speer 52-grainer will thoroughly wreck a chuck's boiler room clear out to 300 yards if the shooter does his part.

The .223's ace in the hole—and it's a *big* ace—is its military heritage. Government sponsorship of a cartridge usually guarantees its commercial success, regardless of ballistic merit. So it is with the .223. In any kind of impartial test, it can hold its own against its two siblings, regardless of the parameters, so its military record is only part of the reason for its approbation.

The fact that every arms maker in the free world chambers it, that it is available in most action types (including one lever action) and in a variety of price ranges is mere frosting on the pastry.

Taking a quick count of the .222 Mag.'s factory-load options, I come up with the number two. That's all. For the .223, make that 22, and that doesn't include the generic stuff offered at a pittance by most of the ammo manufacturers. Sounds like the .223 is the better bet, right? Right.

When hunting shank's mare, often a steady sitting position is the best a hunter can hope for. This hunter shows his form with a Model 70 Sporter-Varmint .223 while gunning prairie dogs in Montana.

So how far have we come here? We've looked at what I'll refer to as the Hornet class of .22-caliber varminters, those offering bullets of either 45 or 50 grains at speeds from 2,700 to around 2,850. Then we canvassed the .222 Remington crowd, all moving 50- or 55-grain bullets at roughly 3,100 to 3,200 fps (although the .223 comes from various factories with bullets as light as Federal's 40-grain Blitz at 3,500 fps-plus and as heavy as Winchester's 64-grain Power-Point). We decided that the Hornet and its ilk were 175-yard loads ideally, with 200 yards feasible when things were really perking. The .222 class were judged as 250-to 275-yard items under normal conditions, with 300 at the far end if the breezes laid low. Our next move upward is not such a momentous one.

The .225 Winchester, another nearly-dead cartridge, drives a 55-grain spitzer at a claimed 3,570 fps. Ha! I've clocked four lots in two rifles, and the swiftest ran 3,356 fps, with the average of all four lots at 3,329. Talk about factory hype!

Handloads help a bunch. Saddle a 38.5-grain dose of Hodgdon's H-414 with Nosler's excellent 50-grain Solid Base and you can get 3,750 fps without breaking anything. Fifty-two-grain bullets will reach from 3,500 to about 3,540; the 55s will make it to 3,430 under the impetus of 35.5 grains of H-380, giving fine accuracy all the while. Why Winchester so underloads the .225 is a mystery. Not many folks really care; it has been nearly 20 years since Winchester turned out rifles chambered to it. Most shooters are only vaguely aware of its existence.

The .224 Weatherby Magnum is in the ballistic ball park with the .225, at least when both are properly handloaded. As put up by Weatherby, the .224 leaves the .225 for dead. In my 24-inch light-barreled Mark V, I received 3,470 fps from one lot of the now-gone 50-grain factory soft point, 3,471 from a second. The current 55-grain iteration (listed in the catalogue at 3,650) showed 3,567 from one batch, 3,583 with a second. I've clocked several .22-250 factory loads that were much slower, only one or two that were quicker, despite the ammo companies' claims to the contrary.

Handloading will push 50-grain Hornadys to 3,635, 52 Speer hollow points past 3,600 and a 55-grain soft-point boattail at roughly 3,400 with no excessive-pressure indicators. Best accuracy comes with 31.0 grains of IMR 3031 and the 52 Speer in my Weatherby. Four groups averaged .94 inch, and the speed hit 3,602 instrumental, about 3,615 fps when converted to muzzle velocity. Anything that needs to be done to a varmint within 300 yards—maybe 325—can be handled nicely by such a load.

The .224 has as its albatross the same problems that plague all the Weatherby rounds—expense in both rifles and ammo; difficulty in finding such reloading essentials as brass, dies and shell holders in local gunshops; a lack of published load data. Let not the latter items stand in your way. Weatherby or RCBS can provide you with dies and a shell holder forthwith; a dealer can order all the brass you want; Hornady and Lyman offer reloading information in their manuals. So, if you can stand the tariff and like the little Mark V varmint rifle, I suggest you consider the .224 as open-mindedly as you would its other chambering, the .22-250. It's doubtful you'd ever notice a difference in the field.

The .22-250 Remington was discussed in some detail in Chapter Four, so there's little need to expound on it further. It propels 55-grain factory loads of various configurations at anywhere from 3,400 fps to as much as 3,800-plus in some lots, with the norm in the 3,550 to 3,600 area. There is also a 40-grain Blitz from Federal at a listed 4,000, which runs to 3,900 or so in most rifles, though some—like my 24-inch Weatherby Mark V—barely manage to hit 3,800 fps.

The .224 Weatherby Magnum will bust a groundhog good. Note Redfield 10X binoculars, a must for the serious varminter.

Rick Jamison used a .22-250 to take this Colorado coyote with a handload featuring Rick's own fluid core bullet.

Handloads reach 3,850 with the 50-grain spitzers, 3,825 with the 52/53-grain match hollow points, and more than 3,700 with the 55-grain jobs. The highest muzzle speeds are provided by Hodgdon's H-414 in my rifles, with H-380 yielding the best accuracy.

In my Browning BBR heavy barrel, which is the most accurate production rifle I have ever owned, 37.0 grains of H-380 under the 52-grain Watson benchrest bullet averages under one-half inch consistently, and has on several occasions printed in the low .40s when conditions were good. The same load averaged .544 in my five-pound Ultra Light Arms M20, with one group miking .234 inch!

Up until a couple of years ago, I had been underwhelmed by the .22-250. Now the reverse is true. I like it as well as the .220 Swift, although the latter is a bit faster.

The Swift, incidentally, (also examined in Chapter Four) is the King of the Hill among varmint cartridges. If any .22 centerfire is a genuine 400-yard number, the Swift is it. I don't know how many 400-yard varmint *shooters* are out there, but for those rare individuals who are capable of such feats, the Swift can carry the ball. It will kick little 45-grain pointy bullets along in excess of 4,100 fps, boost 50-grain soft points to around 4,000, and surpass the 3,800 mark with 55-grain streamlined spitzers.

Want to talk flat shooting? Zero a Swift just 2.2 inches high at 100 yards, and it will be 3.0 inches up at 200, on point of aim at 300, only 8.1 inches low at 400 yards, where it retains 556 foot pounds according to Speer data for the 50-grain spitzer. Choose a 50 Nosler Solid Base and you get a slightly flatter trajectory and another 50 foot pounds at 400.

For shots to 300 yards, either the .225 or the .224 Weatherby is preferable to the Swift or the .22-250. Both are less asperous to barrel steel, easier on the ear drums, massage one's shoulder with less vigor and shoot quite well in good rifles. For the gent who feels that any rodent within 350 yards is fair game, I can think of nothing better under most conditions than a .22-250 loaded properly. And for the long-reaching rifleman, the Swift is the top of the .224-bore heap of factory cartridges.

I might as well mention the tiny .17 Remington. Produced only by Remington—both guns and ammo—it is said to provide 4,040 fps from a 25-grain hollow point. At 300 yards, it retains about as much energy as the Hornet does at 200, so I suppose it would be effective at that range if all else stood in its favor. Such as? No wind, primarily; the .17 is *very* wind sensitive. Accuracy can be another problem. The .17 Remington fouls its bore quite readily, so must be cleaned more often than, say, a .223. And cleaning it is no picnic, since its tight bore requires a special rod and little bitty patches. Further, there is only one factory load and one component bullet; if your rifle doesn't respond well to one or the other, you're out of luck.

On its plus side are a mild voice and almost nonexistent recoil. Advocates of the petite round claim they can see a chuck disintegrate through the scope as the bullet strikes home, there is so little muzzle jump. Perhaps that is addictive, but I'm not sure why.

So what's the best choice among the .22s? If I sought an all-around varmint rifle, for everything from groundhogs at long range to come-what-may coyotes and long-distance sniping at crows and prairie poodles, I'd buy a .22-250 as first choice, with a Swift as my featured alternate. However, if I felt that ranges from 275 to 300 yards would encompass the bulk of my shots on chucks, that I'd reserve coyotes for my deer rifle and that I'd spend more time gunning prairie dogs and ground squirrels than the preceding, I'd choose the .223 in a medium-weight sporter. Its barrel would last far longer than it would if chambered for one of the large-cased hotrods, ammo and brass are both plenteous and inexpensive and there's a much broader selection of rifles available. (Of course, the .222 Remington and .222 Mag. would serve as well ballistically, but no better. Besides, they aren't nearly so easy to find, especially the latter. Hence my vote for the .223.)

The varminting purist might decide he can't live without a battery of rifles, selecting them like golf clubs for specific situations. For such a sport, I would suggest the following trio of .22s.

On those days when the terrain dictates modest distances, or when the hunting area is so heavily populated that a quiet cartridge is in order, or for those times when one's stalking skills are being honed, I would opt for the Hornet. Remember, though, that the .223 can be loaded down to Hornet speeds with some of the faster powders, and at such levels wouldn't be stentorian. To the factory-load user, this point is, of course, irrelevant.

For the gent who wants a lightweight rig with enough reach so that a 300-yard crow can't feed along unconcernedly, a fat chuck sun itself superciliously, a family of prairie pups scurry around above ground with nary a care, the .223 is unbeatable.

One of the best varmint rigs around is the Remington Model 700-Varmint. Author has tried more than a half dozen; all but one grouped under .7 inch at 100 yards, and that lone specimen went into .75 inch with a split stock!

Finally, for the occasional 350- to 400-yard opportunities that are too tempting to pass up, the cartridge in your chamber should bear the headstamp ''.220 Swift.'' Then if you judge the range correctly, read the wind with a practiced eye, manage to coax that trigger into breaking at *just* the right instant, you just might bring off one of those braggin' shots your buddies claim they make *all* the time.

Now that we've scrutinized the true varmint loads, let's look at cartridges larger than .22, those labeled ''varmint/deer,'' and even bigger ones. Many seasoned varmint hunters prefer these heavier loads; their reasoning is not always specious.

For one thing, the bigger calibers usually carry higher energy numbers than their small-bore brethren. On game the size of groundhogs, sometimes (*not* always) the increased power can make up for a marginal hit. Second, depending on the specific cartridge used, larger, heftier bullets sometimes display less wind sensitivity than the flea-weight projectiles. (Remember, this is *not* an absolute. A good .220 Swift handload, for instance, is less affected by wind than, say, a 130-grain .270 flat-based spitzer factory

The hunter in the foreground looks at a prairie dog the author shot. That speck in the back is another of the author's buddies standing 250 yards away, at the point from which the shot was fired. Gives you an idea of prairie ranges for varminting.

When loaded with a good bullet a .243 will take the wind out of a whistlepig's sails.

load.) Third, a heavy bullet kicks up a more pronounced divot than a little 55-grain slug, enabling you to make a correction in your hold on subsequent shots, especially if you have a spotter along to view the strike with binoculars. If you hunt alone, the heavier chamberings can work against you; their increased thrust may cause you momentarily to lose sight of your quarry under recoil. Unless your shot is at extreme range, by the time you pull the gun back down and regain your sight picture, the result of your bullet's impact may have dissipated. (Which is another good reason to hunt with a partner.)

One final advantage in using a big bore on chucks and stuff: It enables you to hunt with your big game rifle year round. The familiarity gained through constant use will stand you in good stead come autumn.

Remember to use the lighter weight bullets in a given caliber. Why? For one thing, it theoretically cuts down on ricochets, although I would *not* count on it. Be certain of your backstop when firing any rifle at anything any time! Secondly, the lighter bullets shoot flatter than the more portly items, in most instances at least.

Lastly, the lightweight renderings are designed to open quickly, which is what you need to anchor a tough ol' badger when he eases out of this den for a postprandial stroll.

Among the deer-capable calibers, several stand out for use on faraway creatures of diminutive size. The .243 Winchester, 6mm Remington and .250-3000 are particular favorites of mine. With 75-grain handloads, all of them will shoot into an inch or less in a properly-adjusted rifle. In factory persuasion, the 75-grain Hornady hollow point .243, the 80-grain Remington Power-Lokt in the same chambering and the 80-grain .243 and 6mm soft points from Federal are always acceptable, often eye-popping.

In the .270, I like 90- and 100-grain hollow points, handloaded of course. The 130 Nosler Ballistic Tip works well too, but isn't quite as destructive. And man, will it buck the wind! Amongst the factory offerings, only the 100 Winchester soft point has ever worked for me.

Remington makes a 120-grain hollow point for the 7mm-08 and .280 Remington, designed especially for varmints. In the .30-30, .308 Winchester and .30-06, the same firm offers the sabot-encased 55-grain Accelerator .22-caliber soft point. In guns that handle them accurately, they'll do a good job in the field.

When handloading for a 7mm, I use only one bullet for vermin: Speer's 115-grain hollow point, the slug I have long referred to as the "magic bullet." Not only is it nearly always the most accurate hunting bullet you can shoot in your 7mm (regardless of *which* cartridge it is), it'll detonate a woodchuck as if he'd swallowed gelignite.

For home-assembling the .30-bores, I'd choose a 130 Speer hollow point, or perhaps the new 125-grain Ballistic Tip from Nosler. This latter is intended for the little 7.62 X 39 Russian, in which it is launched at about 2,400 fps or so. Imagine what such a thin-skinned bullet would do if pumped out of a .308 Winchester at 3,200, or a bit faster from a .30-06 ... groundhog hash!

Were I an habitue of the chuck pastures, I would buy two rifles. The first would be a good lightweight sporter reamed to .223 Remington. I'd stuff its closet with handloads featuring the 52 Speer hollow point and 25.5 grains of Hodgdon or IMR 4895. If I did my part on calm days, such an outfit would be shambolic to any critter I spotted under 300 yards. Further, it would be the berries as a ground squirrel/prairie dog rifle; one can shoot a goodly number of rounds before barrel heat mandates a cessation

Out West, this is typical shooting position in a prairie dog town. It works!

of hostilities. Not so a .22-250 or Swift, nor even the mid-sized .225 Winchester.

My second rig would be chambered to the 6mm Remington, and of medium-sporter heft. I would insist on a 24-inch barrel if given a choice, maybe even if I weren't. Plugged with handloads built around a good 75-grain hollow point, or maybe the beautiful Speer 85-grain spitzer boattail, the whistlepigs would tremble in their dens when Old Charon was uncased.

A possible alternative to the 6mm would be a 7mm-08. It would likely be as accurate, although it would belt me harder and wouldn't shoot as flat. But I dearly *love* that magic 115 Speer crater-point; when it hits something—*whop!*—you *know* it. (The recipe is 46.0 grains of IMR 4064.)

We've touched all the varmint bases. It's time to peruse the taking of...

Predators

Woodchucks, prairie dogs and jack rabbits are pests. Predators are pests with sharp teeth and glossy fur and unsavory reputations. Mostly deserved in the case of coyotes, I might add, although the cat family takes it on the chin without so much cause.

A spotter is a big asset in shooting varmints at long range. He can immediately tell the shooter where the bullet went. (The sign is no gag or set-up! The Montana government makes it easy for the inexperienced nimrod to find game!)

Four factors in the taking of predators dictate to some extent the arms best used. Those factors: 1) their uncommon (for their size) tenacity of life; 2) the fact that they are larger than most "varmints," though a big woodchuck or badger is often heavier and of stouter construction than, say, a fox; 3) their tendency to stay on the move, which means that often as not any shots taken on their behalf will be at a running animal; 4) their pelts are valuable.

Hunters who gun predators for their fur are separated into two schools of thought. One group believes in an extremely frangible bullet at high speeds, hoping that the projectile will get inside the critter, disintegrate amidst the plumbing and never again see

Hunter looks over typical Colorado coyote country.

daylight. That way there is but one hole to sew up. These hunters tell me that even in the rare event of bullet exit, the exit wound is usually small enough to be of little import so far as damage to the hide is concerned.

Popular among this claque are such zipsters as the .17 Remington, .22-250, .220 Swift and even the 6mms when loaded with very light slugs started very fast. Wildcat numbers such as the .22 CHeetah and the .220 Jay Bird, which can move little bullets at near Mach IV speeds, are viewed with favor among the handloading predator callers.

The dissenting view is that since one cannot always be certain that any bullet will *not* completely penetrate an animal, and that the result of said departure is not only unsightly but time-consuming and expensive if not expertly repaired, a non-expanding, full-jacketed bullet should be used. Such a round almost always sails right on through whatever gets in its way, flesh or bone. In its favor is that the back door is usually the same size as the front, unless the slug tumbles as it leaves or carries with it secondary bone fragments. That *really* makes a mess.

I find it impossible to condone such inhumane conduct. Certainly a bullet that merely bores a tunnel through an animal will do little damage to its pelt; it doesn't leave much destructive reconstruction in its wake, either! Consequently, too many animals escape to die a lingering, painful death, all for the sake of $$$$$. It smacks too much of market hunting to me. *Any* animal deserves an expeditious death, even one that kills for a living. (How many *humans* are vegetarians...?)

Taking all things into consideration, the best predator loads for those who don't care to blow gaping holes in the fabric are the above mentioned high-speed items loaded with explosively expanding projectiles. The Swift is the best of the factory cartridges, simply because it's the fastest. However, the 40-grain Federal Blitz might be a fine choice for the .22-250. It is always accurate, sometimes incredibly so, and in my experience is pretty destructive without an attendant facility for over-penetration. Good load.

For specialization on such diminutive game as foxes, the .222 or .223 Remington with fragile bullets are all that is needed. The larger-cased cartridges are better left to coyotes, and maybe bobcats, both of which require more killing power.

Now, for those of you who don't care a whit about fur damage, the best loads for taking coyotes start at the .243 and slant upward. I've spoken with several professional coyote slayers; to a man they relate horror stories of ones that got away even when hard hit by a hotshot .22. The 6mm is well thought of and widely recommended. One government coyote hunter swears by his .25-06, and swears *at* anything less.

My view is that unless one is a serious coyote hunter—which usually means he is after pelts or employed by someone to keep the population in check—the best rifle is the same one used in the fall for deer-sized game. As with varmint hunting, using one gun all year long can't help but make its owner more proficient in its use. It enables the gunner to memorize trajectory, requisite lead on running animals and to some degree inures him to recoil. All in all, quite a dividend.

Some years ago, I was enroute to Wyoming for a mule deer foray. Making a slight detour through Arizona, I cast my sleeping bag on Rick Jamison's doorstep. (When it rained, he let me sleep inside.) Rick took me coyotein'.

After a fruitless morning—for *me*; Jamison had already killed several right out from under my nose—I finally got my chance. Rick was upslope from me on the lip of an arroyo, honking his rabbit squall, when a prairie wolf popped into view. He was cantering straight toward me, using the arroyo for cover. When I

Although not necessary for critters the size of this fox, the .257 Roberts will manage. This one dropped while its slayer was deer hunting. Many vermin are taken incidental to such hunting.

maneuvered my carcass for a better view, he spotted the movement and swapped ends. I brought up my 7mm Magnum, sought him in its scope. There! All he presented was a rear view, which meant I'd have to go up his flue. So I did. Boom! He dropped as if broadsided by a truck.

Feeling smug about it, since I'd never heard Jamison fire and was certain he hadn't even *seen* the coyote, I sashayed forward in a manner I hoped Rick would divine as mock humility. Instead he ran down the side of the arroyo, his countenance split with mirth, and said exuberantly, "I got him!"

"What the hell you mean, *you* got him?"

"Din'cha see it? Man, I really busted him."

At this point my face had undoubtedly assumed a mauve hue, strangled as I was by the audacity of this bodacious interloper claiming my one and only coyote! It got worse. He had indeed shot the critter, right through both shoulders as it galloped away broadside, exactly simultaneous with my shot!

Rick Jamison soaked this coyote when it came nosing around a gut pile where the author had killed a mule deer the day before. Rifle is a .300 Win. Mag.

This unlucky coyote was bumped off in Colorado, too. Today, almost every state has a pesky coyote population. As a hunting resource, they are way under utilized.

I did note one discordant item regarding the defunct yodel dog: The top of its head was in disarray, still attached to the prognathous skull by only a thin scrap of hide, not unlike a hinged box lid. My bullet had traversed the beast from fanny to funnel, removing his pate in passing. Deadest coyote I ever saw.

Javelina and Cougar

Although, as mentioned before, javelina are considered vermin in some areas of Texas, more often they are looked upon as big game. Not very big, but then neither are turkeys, which are also accorded the same status.

If you are interested in hunting the little porcine lookalikes, simply tote whatever gun you want so long as it's a centerfire. Peccaries are not especially hard to stalk, so close-in shots are the rule if a hunter will adopt the slightest degree of furtiveness. Most hunters I have spoken with figure the .357 Magnum revolver to be a gracious plenty for the biggest of javelina boars. Said monarch might run to 50 pounds if he's lived to a ripe old age and waxed fat.

The stress is on short, light and handy when it comes to armament. Of course, many peccaries are taken by deer hunters who spot a pack rooting its way along a *sendero*. Under such conditions, they naturally use whatever they brought along for deer. (Or perhaps a secondary handgun, carried for just such an eventuality.)

Cougars—a.k.a. pumas, painters, catamounts and mountain lions—are most often shot out of a tree, to which they are clinging laconically after having been chased up it by a pack of boisterous hounds. The sport is in the chase, not the kill. Most guides recommend a .357 or .44 Magnum revolver for the *coup de grace*, or a .30-30 carbine if the executioner can't hit beans with a shortgun.

I'll go along with that.

And thus we draw the curtain on the wee fauna, the beasts of ill repute, and those that soar and caw and seek in the night.

10

The Minimum
North American Battery

One of the most common questions in hunting circles is: Can I buy just one centerfire rifle for all types of hunting in North America?

Sure, you can. You just won't be as well prepared for a ground squirrel foray as you might be for a mule deer hunt.

Other prospective nimrods figure they can stretch the old budget to include *two* rifles. What should they choose?

Finally, the really thorough types seek advice on what the minimum North American battery might consist of, to cover every basic type of hunting they are likely to encounter. This latter is the best approach, in my view, and would include four rifles. However, let's look at this ideal battery situation in detail, beginning with the gent who wants only one gun.

One Rifle

There are good and poor reasons for keeping your arsenal to a minimum. One is that the shooter is apt to become a fine shot when using only one gun, or so the theory goes. The theory *is* true if the one-gun person shoots a lot. Just *having* one gun won't make anyone a Dead-eye Dick.

A second advantage in owning one gun is that you become very familiar with it, always cognizant of where the safety is located and what the trigger pull feels like. A third advantage is simply economics: it costs more to buy two or three rifles than it does only one. And these three items, my friend, are all I can think up in favor of the one-gun solution.

There are some folks who cite the necessity of learning only one set of trajectory data as a prime advantage of the one-gun shooter. I disagree. The single-rifle man should know the numbers for at least two different loads, assuming he hunts both vermin and cud-chewing critters with that one gun. Besides, someone who favors one cartridge has the same benefit as one who has but one rifle.

The cartridge and its bullet determine external ballistics, not the rifle. Thus, a hunter who seeks pronghorn out West might carry his 26-inch-barreled Ruger Number One, reamed to .30-06 Springfield. Back home in South Carolina, he might tote an 18½-inch Remington Model 7400 carbine into the whitetail thickets, chambered again in .30-06. Although each gun fills a distinctly different function, and each wears the same caliber marking on its barrel, neither is well suited to the other's task. However, trajectory data for each *could* be made to jibe closely, assuming careful selection to bullet weight and profile.

Reloading hunters like to claim that having only one rifle simplifies the logistical problem attendant to having several cartridges for which to load. One has to stock but two or three bullet weights and powders, and to purchase only one set of loading dies, they cite. I'll simply refer them to the preceding paragraph; having *ten* guns in one chambering would yield the same result; or even having different rifles chambered for several cartridges of the same *bore* size, for that matter.

But there *are* distinct disadvantages in having only one rifle, assuming you intend to hunt a myriad of game. If your only gun is a .280 Remington or .30-06, try shooting 200 rounds at prairie dogs in one day. You'll feel like you just took a spin in an industrial washing machine! Conversely, try digging a wounded grizzly out of the alders with a .243 Winchester, assuming that modest cartridge to be your singular choice. Neither would be much fun.

Further, if you take a pack hunt into the wilds of Canada after bull elk and your extractor breaks while verifying your zero the day before the hunt, what do you do then? Use the guide's gun, an unfamiliar military retiree reamed to .303 British? Right.

Maybe you can fix the extractor? I once watched a master gunsmith try to jury-rig an extractor on a hunter's rifle, one designed and made by a top-notch tradesman. Miles from civilization, only basic tools like a mallet and chainsaw in camp. Didn't work. Fortunately, the hunter had a spare, which would have been difficult if he had owned but one rifle.

Nonetheless, suppose you're convinced that you need only one centerfire rifle in your stash, and you want to know what caliber to buy. Ask yourself this question: Am I likely to hunt any animal larger than an eating-size elk (say, up through 450-500 pounds, maximum) on a reasonably regular basis? If the answer is no, then I'd suggest you choose any chambering you want from the following list: 6.5 X 55, .270 Winchester, 7 X 57, 7mm-08 Remington, .284 Winchester, .280 Remington, .308 Winchester, .30-06 Springfield or 8mm Mauser. All of them can and do drive bullets of 120 up to 200 grains (depending on the caliber) at muzzle speeds from 2,615 feet per second to about 3,000. When zeroed at 200 yards, all of them will—if bullets are chosen correctly—show a 300-yard drop of nine inches or less. That is as far as most of us need to shoot, as I have mentioned repeatedly. Retained energy out to the 300 mark is sufficient for game up to the size aforementioned, assuming a good bullet, of course.

I wouldn't turn around for the difference in field performance between any of these loads; I would, however, choose from the larger bores if most of my hunting was for smallish elk and caribou, or maybe black bear and boar. If the bulk of my game centered around varmints and deer-sized creatures, with only an occasional hunt for bigger game, I'd choose a mild cartridge from the above list.

If I were selecting one gun for game to include trophy elk and moose on a regular basis, say every other year at least, then I'd do two things: I'd buy a good 24-inch-barreled boltgun reamed to the 7mm Remington Magnum; I would never hunt ground squirrels or prairie dogs unless I used a .22 rimfire. As a close second choice, I would suggest a .30-06 for the non-handloader. Personally— since I *do* reload—I might try to find a gunsmith who would cobble me up a .30-06 Improved or .30 Gibbs for a reasonable price. Then again, I doubt I'd go to the trouble; the 7mm Magnum will do everything ballistically that I need to have done on this continent. Except kill prairie dogs.

Two Rifles

Now, all a two-gun hunter has to do is add a .22-250 Remington to either of the above choices and he's in good shape.

With a pre-'64 Model 70 cradled in his lap, this hunter searches for Colorado mule deer bucks. A good .30-06 will reach out as well as many modern cartridges if loaded correctly. It's a good choice for the one-gun man.

In fact, for the fellow who can afford two rifles, I'd bypass the lesser calibers—such as the .270 or 7 X 57—mentioned above, and suggest the 7mm Mag again. For anything up to coyotes and small deer (where legal), the .22-250 will work OK; and you can shoot at crows and suchlike without causing your bursitis to act up. The Big Seven will take care of any long-range gunning on sheep, muledeer and whatnot, plus send a 175-grain Nosler deep, deep, *deep* into elk or moose sinew. A tough combo to beat.

In fact, I'm not certain any further increase in battery accumulation is necessary, especially if our hunter owns a .22 rimfire. There are certain relatively specialized persuits at which a two-gun man might find himself disadvantaged, but a rimfire back-up rifle and a change in his light caliber would cover several bases.

For example, let's assume that on occasion our hunter will seek whitetails in the brush. If so, he can buy a lightweight

For long-range work from these Colorado bluffs, a good 7mm Magnum is all a hunter needs, for any sized game, if he chooses a good bullet.

22-inch-barreled turnbolt reamed to 6mm Remington. Such a firearm, while not *ideal* for close-range whitetail jumping, is at least acceptable in proper hands. Thus, our gunner could use his little rimfire on ground squirrels and prairie dogs up to 100 yards or so—(a bit farther if he chooses the .22 Winchester Magnum Rimfire)— relegating his 6mm to long-range use on same, plus woodchucks, coyotes and other vermin. The .22-250 could handle similar chores, but would be a bit light on deer to be ideal.

The point is that a hunter who owns a rimfire might well choose a 6mm Remington instead of the .22-250 to go with his 7mm Magnum. Alas, this is a bit like cheating since the .22 rimfire constitutes a third rifle, although not a third *centerfire* rifle.

Thus, I'll stick to my original recommendation of a .22-250 and a 7mm Magnum for the two-rifle hunter. Whether said hunter owns a rimfire is beyond the scope of this discussion.

For the bulk of North American hunting, the two-gun nimrod is well prepared. Only in brush-country shooting, small-varmint gunning, close-in handling of semi-dangerous game, (black bear and boar) and other equally esoteric endeavors would he be less than properly armed. Going to three rifles would alleviate the problem, right? Let's see.

An accurate .223 like this Kimber Model 84 will handle all varminting chores clear out to 300 yards in good hands.

Three Rifles

For the three-gun battery, I'd abandon the .22-250; too much cartridge for a day's shooting at wee fauna, a bit underpowered for come-what-may shots at buck deer. In the .22-250's stead I'd pick two items. First, a medium-weight, 24-inch turnbolt or single shot .223 Remington. Why not a .222 or .222 Remington Mag.? We'll get to that in a minute.

Secondly, I'd buy a lightweight 6mm Remington of modest barrel length, to handle all my real long-range varminting and predator chores, plus tackle deer and pronghorns to 300 yards. Even in the Southeastern brush, a 22-inch 6mm would not be out of place.

My pick for the third cartridge/rifle pairing would remain the

This pronghorn was taken at long range with the help of a Harris bipod on this 6mm Remington. It's a good cartridge for game in this class out to 300 yards.

7mm Magnum. However, if someone opined that it might make good sense to go to a .338 Magnum or .340 Weatherby for the big stuff—trophy moose, bull elk, grizzly bears—I'd not argue long. The 6mm could handle everything up to 250 pounds or so, with the big magnum reserved for the 800-pound class. Sound good? How about mule deer, black bear, wild boar, caribou and normal-sized elk? That's a good question. And it's why I personally would stick with the 7mm Magnum. Clearly, a .338 or .340 Weatherby is not *needed* on animals under 800 pounds live weight. Further, most hunters simply cannot handle the recoil of a heavy-kicking rifle well enough to hit the kill zone regularly and accurately.

Now, many a hairy-chested gunner is confident of his ability to handle a big hairy-chested cartridge with precision. Maybe some can. Most can't. (Unless, of course, the big magnum cartridge is chambered in a heavy rifle of 10 or 11 pounds, or sports an expensive muzzle brake, or both. That's another story.)

Use a Big Seven; shoot a long, heavy Nosler bullet; practice a lot. You'll be well armed.

Four Rifles: The Best Choice

And now...drum roll...what you've been anxiously awaiting: the ideal do-it-all North American battery! In case you're tired, here's the list of cartridges: .223 Remington, 6mm Remington, .308 Winchester, and the 7mm Remington (or Weatherby if you intend to purchase a Mark V rifle) Magnum. You can turn the light off now.

For those of you curious about the whys, stick around. Not only will I attempt to justify my cartridge selection, I'll list exactly what rifle configuration I'd want for each one. Onward.

The .223 is the obvious choice on the bottom end. For any and all varmint hunting out to perhaps 300 yards, there are no better loads. There *are* some just as good ballistically, perhaps, but "just as good" ain't "better." I would have no quarrel, for example, with the .222 Remington in and of itself. It is so close to the .223 in accuracy, punch and trajectory that no quantifiable difference exists. Ditto the .222 Magnum.

But, the .222 is dying off; every year, fewer and fewer rifles are so-chambered. The .222 Mag. is even less popular. Remember, when there are no *practical* reasons to choose one cartridge over another, always go with the more popular choice. Besides, the .223 has several distinct advantages over its two brethren.

It is available in every action type made except for the pump. Virtually every manufacturer offers it, so you can remain loyal to a marque if you feel the need. Ammo is turned out by every munitions maker, in a suitable variety. The little cartridge has all it needs to do its job, so there is no reason to eye longingly a .22 centerfire that boasts a bit more bullet speed. Military surplus ammo is cheap and plentiful; special loadings from several domestic ammunition producers are sold nigh as cheaply. And finally, the .223 is as accurate in a good rifle as either of its competitors, ballyhoo about the .222 notwithstanding.

Thus, for a marathon shooting session in the "dog" towns, a killing shot at yon coyote, a plinking contest with bargain-basement ammo, or to take that big, fat, grizzled groundhog at the far edge of the back 40, the .223 has exactly what it takes. Nothing else has.

So what rifle? I'd want a Remington Model 78 Sportsman if I had to watch by pennies. If my wallet was thick with green, the Kimber Model 84 would be my choice, in its heavy-barrel iteration. And if cost was no object, I'd ask Melvin Forbes to stick a 24-inch Number Two-contour Douglas Premium barrel onto one of his super little Model 20-S actions. Then I'd have the ultimate .223—light enough to carry, so accurate it'd make my teeth hurt and equipped with a trigger I could adjust for everything but treble and bass.

The 6mm, again, is the obvious choice as a long-range varmint, moderately long-range deer and antelope cartridge. The big-cased .25's are a bit abusive to both ear and shoulder to be ideal for long-range work, and I've never found them to be quite as accurate as the smaller rounds—although in the case of the .25-06, the difference is not pronounced. Such larger cartridges as the .270 or the .284 Winchester are oriented too much toward big game to make flawless vermin busters. No, the 6mm's direct competitors are three: the .243 Winchester, .250-3000, and .257 Roberts. So why didn't I choose one of those?

The .250-3000 is out simply because it isn't as popular as the others, so factory ammo availability is limited. Rifle selection is sparse as well. But the deciding factor is this: the little Savage round isn't quite as potent as the 6mm Remington. Nor is the .243. Good as it is, *popular* as it is, the .243 is and always will be a bit downstream of the 6mm ballistically. What's more, it has never been quite as accurate in my test rifles.

Which leaves the .257 Roberts. The good ol' Roberts is as good—maybe a tad better—on deer as the 6mm. The 6mm, conversely, is superior by a tiny margin for vermin. Explain? Well, the .257 will handle a bit heavier and deeper penetrating bullets than the 6mm, while the .24-bore shoots a tad faster and flatter than its elder sibling. The advantage is small in each instance, but real. But, you say, since each has only a minor advantage, isn't it a toss-up between them? No. The .257 loses the ball game because of one factor: accuracy.

The average 6mm will, in my experience, shoot rings around the average .257 Roberts. As I have mentioned, only one .257 that I know of will group five shots consistently into one inch at 100 yards. Most good 6mm's will better the inch mark decisively. And for long shots at small animals, a one-MOA rifle is requisite. The 6mm Remington wins.

Several companies turn out 6mm bolt-actions, and Ruger makes the Number One. Rifle availability is no problem; neither is ammo if you don't reload. In addition to the three loads Remington catalogues, Winchester, Federal and Hornady offer factory loads. Brass and components are easy to come by, a decided plus for the reloader.

A short-barreled .308 will handle its end of the job in mixed terrain, assuming proper bullet selection for the task at hand.

And which guns? The Remington 700 ADL would get my vote at the low-price end, with that same firm's synthetic M-700 Custom as my mid-range choice. At the top of the heap would be the Ultra Light Model 20 again, with the same Number Two-contour 24-inch Douglas air-gauged barrel that I designated for the .223, to get as much of the 6mm's speed and accuracy as I could squeeze out.

That brings us to the .308. This rifle-and-cartridge combo will handle the bulk of big-game hunting at distances up to 300 yards or so. Although one of the primary reasons I chose the .308 is identical to that for the .223—inexpensive and readily-available ammunition—the short .30 caliber can stand on its own merit.

A good bullet in the .308, such as this 180 Nosler Solid Base, will enable that mild cartridge to take game out of its normal weight class. The expanded slug was taken from an elk.

It is one of the most accurate cartridges ever designed, comes in all action types, is loaded by every munitions factory in the free world and is as pleasant to fire as any cartridge in its power range.

Being of modest length, the .308 will work through short bolt actions quite nicely. It offers scant room for legitimate complaints. Out to the 300-yard mark, it shows within an inch or two of the drop attainable from the very flattest-shooting cartridges in its class, such as the .270 Winchester or .30-06. While it yields a few paltry foot-pounds of energy to such as the .284 Winchester and .30-06, it still carries plenty of steam to deck cleanly any game for which the foregoing pair is suited. What does that include? Mule deer, black bear, caribou, sheep, eatin'-sized elk. The .308's all that's necessary for a quick dispatch. Bullet weights up through 200 grains can be handled at sufficient velocities to enable sure hitting at all reasonable ranges.

It is light on such game as bull elk and moose, but so are the .270 and ought-six, at least in many hunters' eyes. That's why we have a four-gun battery in mind; the .308 is not the powerhouse of the quartet, but the jack-of-all-trades.

Since I spend more time east of the Mississippi than west of it, I would lean toward a 20-inch, super-flyweight .308. When persuing black bear, whitetails and boar in dense brush, such an outfit would be virtually ideal. Should I have an opportunity to seek sheep in the Western mountains, the same rifle would be slung across my shoulders. If I lived out West, I would likely opt

When loaded with a good 175-grain bullet, in factory or handloads, the 7mm Mag will handle anything in the lower 48 states with aplomb, and probably wouldn't bounce off a brown bear if it ran into one.

for a two-inch increase in barrel length; my choice of caliber would remain the same.

Although the .308 Winchester is not one whit superior in the game fields to the 7 X 57, 7mm-08, .270, .284 or .30-06, it is just as good for all practical purposes. Its other virtues are what makes it my first choice.

In the popular-priced arena, the Remington Model 7 and Ruger Model 77 International or Ultra-Light would be my favorites. The Sako Handy might find its way into my cabinet if I could afford its higher tab. Once again, the ULA Model 20 would win out if price were no object. I'd request a 20-inch lightweight tube and 13¼-inch length of pull for snap shooting. If a better whitetail rig can be had, I don't know about it.

There is little need to justify the 7mm Remington Magnum; I've covered most of it. When you have a gun/cartridge duo that will safely propel from its maw a 175-grain Nosler bullet in excess of 3,000 fps, carrying better than 3,500 foot-pounds of muzzle energy, anyone can see that little more could be desired for any North American game. Retained smash clear out to 400 yards is in the 2,000 foot-pound neighborhood with either the 160 or 175 Nosler Partition bullets, all with good handloads, naturally. The 160-grain Nosler can be had in factory-loaded form from Federal, and will hit about 2,850 fps in most 24-inch barrels. That's good for nearly 2,900 foot-pounds.

The .300 Winchester Magnum, 8mm Remington Magnum and

If cost were no object, the author would choose for his four-gun battery a quartet from Ultra Light Arms. Calibers would be: top left, .223 Remington; top right, 6mm Remington; lower right, .308; and 7mm Remington Magnum.

the .338 Mag. can equal or better those numbers, but any ballistic advantage they'd show would be negated by a decreased "hittability quotient." And even if these three actually did evince a demonstrable increase in tissue damage, such would do no good if said damage were in a non-lethal spot.

John Wootters once wrote that he could not tell any difference in recoil between a 7mm Magnum and a sporter-weight .30-06. I agree 100 percent. Such can *not* be said for the .300 Magnum, I emphatically assure you, let alone such fierce ordnance as the 8mm Magnum or .338. It is my feeling that the 7mm Magnum and the .30-06 form the upper limit of recoil tolerance for 99 percent of all gunners. Go beyond that limit and shooting skill invariably suffers. Muzzle brakes, thick recoil pads and portly rifles can assuage the kick to a marked degree, but *all* magnums have recoil pads and those other two items present problems of their own. Besides, neither excessive tonnage nor braking is needed with the 7mm Magnum. So why bother with anything else? Why, indeed. I don't.

Give me an accurate .223, a good 6mm Remington, a portable .308 Winchester and a 7mm Magnum of moderate heft. With such a battery, I can do anything that needs to be done on this continent, assuming I direct my bullets to the vitals of my quarry. If there's a hunting task in North America for which one of these four is not well suited, I can't envision it. Owning additional centerfire rifles would be based on whim or curiosity, not need.

11

Custom Rifles

The word "custom" when applied to rifles means different things to different shooters. Perhaps most often brought to mind is the type of arm depicted each year in the "Custom Gun" section of *Gun Digest*. All are very expensive, one-of-a-kind renditions artfully crafted by the likes of Dave Tally, Jere Eggleston, Vic Olson, Maurice Ottmar, Dale Goens, Joe Balickie, Earl Milliron and Keith Stegall. As much as I admire such fine *objets d'art*, I will not cover them in this treatment. And I'll tell you why.

First, I can't afford one. And if I could I would never be able to rationalize their exorbitant cost against the practical aspects of being able to buy 10 or so "normal" rifles that would likely work as well, shoot as well and that wouldn't make my wallet ache each time one acquired a dent. Second, rifles by the above mentioned artisans are not *intended* to be used at those tasks rifles do best; they're meant to be the finest examples of artistic craftsmanship human hands can fabricate. And they are. But, except for the very rich or those who are provided with these guns at nominal charge (for whatever reason), they are not suitable for tough, hard use. In fact, to do so borders on sacrilege.

Don't misunderstand; such rifles will do the job all right. But to subject them to the rigors of the hunt is ludicrous, and insulting to the skills of their makers. Such arms are best relegated to

Author is shown with Missouri whitetail killed with his pet custom rifle. It is a .35 Whelen built on a Mauser Mark X action by craftsman Chris Latta. Chris specializes in this kind of fine work.

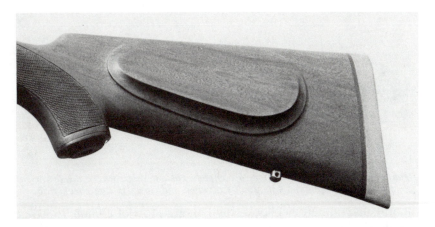

A sculptured undercut cheekpiece like this one is the mark of a skilled craftsman, and a skilled 'smith can handle the job. Note also the cut checkering and fine fit of the recoil pad.

display, with maybe an occasional outing at the rifle range to insure their owners they can indeed earn their keep if called upon. You are free to disagree, of course.

I know well a gentleman who once bought a mint-condition late-'50s Corvette with less than 10,000 actual miles on its rare, full-injected engine. As soon as he had remunerated its owner—who admonished him to push it gently since it hadn't been driven in some time and wanted warming up—he jumped behind the wheel and took off at high speed across a plowed field. After the car had been in his possession for a few days, it resembled a Conestoga wagon that had barely survived an Indian attack, and was worth about as much! Taking a true custom rifle into the game fields is similar folly in my view. And since this is a book about tools, not voluptuous devices intended to be admired for their looks instead of their abilities, I shall now abandon their discourse.

For those of you who are not hopeless sybarites, but who still admire a nicely turned heel, an ample curve against your cheek, a hand-filling swell in your palm, a retrousse tilt where it gladdens the eye, fret not. There are rifles available that will not only fulfill these desires, but won't set you back six months on the mortgage while sating them.

Remington has a custom shop with a reasonable waiting list, moderate prices when compared to the hand-built items, excellent quality and a fairly lengthy catalogue of indulgences. Such as? Various grades of wood, tasteful engraving, hinged-steel

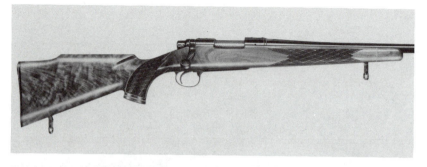

Remington Arms Company offers a complete custom shop, where the buyer can select from many options. Note quality of wood and fine skip-line checkering.

floorplates, numerous checkering patterns, lots of chamberings, ad infinitum.

Weatherby, too, will make all manner of modifications to their famed Mark V, from inletting the stock with exotic woods to checkering patterns you never dreamed existed. They'll jewel the bolt and follower, install a single-set trigger that is pure joy to use, hand lap the action to velvety smoothness, give you a modest choice in barrel length and configuration.

Such arms makers as A-Square, Dubiel, KDF and Shilen will bake you up a bolt-action sporter in almost any chambering. Ultra Light Arms will build for you a rifle on one of four action lengths, all of which are the lightest for their size in the industry, and in most any caliber you can conjure up, including wildcats.

However, none of these is a true custom gun, but merely *modified* production or semi-production permutations. If you want something really personalized, you'll have to turn to one of a small coterie of gunsmiths who'll do their best to mix your yearning with their learning.

I've dealt with four of these; the results of their labors have been pleasant in the extreme. Here they are in alphabetical order, beginning with...

Kenny Jarrett:

Jarrett Rifles, Inc., (Route 1, Box 411, Dept. NAH, Jackson, SC 29831, (803) 471-3616) is owned and directed by one of the most successful benchrest competitors of all time, Kenny Jarrett. Jarrett is opinionated, skillful, knowledgeable, irascible, abrasive, honest, an amateur ballistician and a Southern gentleman of the old school. The rifles he builds are as accurate as money can buy.

Kenny likes to do things his way. If you have other views, go

Weatherby offers some customizing in-house. Note select wood on this sample Mark V. Various inlays are available, special checkering, barrel lengths, et al.

to someone else. His idea revolves around tolerances that won't let air through, let alone light. His conception of proper metal-to-metal fit is as if there were no joint. Jarrett's notion of bolt-to-receiver alignment, barrel-to-receiver rigidity and breech-to-boltface perpendicularity is simple: as close to perfection as his practiced hands and eyes will allow. And that is damned close!

Kenny's rifles are built for the hunter who likes to stay put, meaning they are usually long and weighty. That way, he maintains, they shoot straighter. How straight?

Well, the Jarrett-built .280 Ackley Improved I hunted with a couple years ago would print 10 shots into .875 inch, all day, every day, and with full-bore hunting loads, not milquetoast stuff.

My hunting pard Bob O'Connor owns a Jarret switch-barrel rifle—meaning that his gun came with two barrels, each chambered to a different cartridge of the same head size; the barrels are easy-on, easy-off. One is reamed to the wildcat .220 Jay Bird, which Kenny devised and named after his son. That combination in O'Connor's rifle will group five shots time after time into .300

inch at 100 yards, often under that, and with 52-grain bullets sailing along at 4,150 fps!

Bob's second barrel is a .280 Imp like the one I used. The last time he had it out it put three five-shot strings into .718, and he claims it will go around .625 with its pet fodder. Not bad, huh?

Jarrett rifles are normally built on modified Remington Model 700 actions, although I have seen a few turned out on the Japanese Howa turnbolt as offered currently by Interarms. The stocks are always synthetic, supplied by an outside vendor and finished up by Jarrett. The end result is not a thing of beauty, but it sure *shoots* beautifully.

Kenny charges somewhere in the $1500 to $2000 neighborhood, which is not inexpensive. But he offers superior accuracy at a price anyone who really *wants* to can afford, though admittedly with some belt tightening for most of us. And that's one of the things a custom rifle is *for*: shooting tighter groups than over-the-counter hardware is generally capable of.

Chris Latta:

The Base Camp (2407 West 5th St., Dept. NAH, Washington, NC 27889, (919) 946-3113) is the hunting enthusiast's hotspot in Eastern North Carolina. Its owner, Chris Latta, not only does a booming retail business, he turns out custom rifles at affordable prices.

Chris builds most of his hunting guns on commercial Mauser Mark X actions, but he will use a suitable military Mauser if he can find one or if his customer provides same. One of his specialties is color-case-hardening, which has lit my wick since I saw my first Colt Single Action Army.

Latta and I collaborated on a project last year. I specified a Douglas barrel chambered to the then-wildcat .35 Whelen, a 13⅜-inch length of pull, a color-case-hardened action (which included everything—the bolt, trigger-guard/floorplate assembly, receiver, and as an added touch, the Redfield mounting system as well), and let him decide the rest.

He produced one of the finest rifles I've ever hunted with, and the most accurate .35-caliber arm I've tested, of *many*. He selected a 24-inch barrel, to squeeze all the juice out of the cartridge we could, topping it at the muzzle with a banded front-sight ramp permanently affixed. A Remington rear sight complemented the front, with both of them intended only as backup equipment in case of a (admittedly rare) scope failure in the field.

Gunsmiths put much handwork into their wares, which is why the factories can't do so and sell their rifles inexpensively.

The trigger is a Timney unit, adjusted to three crisp pounds. Chris hand lapped the action, glass bedded the works, not only for a perfect fit but to prevent, as much as possible, any point-of-impact shift due to the hygroscopic nature of wood.

A fine hunk of American walnut was provided, fiddle-backed in grain structure and very handsome. It was fitted with a rosewood forend tip, sling swivel studs, a black rubber recoil pad and a checkered steel grip cap. The stock was left uncheckered to keep costs down, although Chris can provide the service if a customer wants. But it ain't cheap.

The result of all these ministrations is one of the best-fitting rifles I've ever owned. The forend is very slender; the buttstock wears a sculpted cheekpiece but no unsightly Monte Carlo. Comb height and thickness are perfect for me; when I toss the rifle to shoulder, the scope is right in front of my shootin' eye, like magic.

My Whelen will print under 1⅜ inches with its best handload, which was arrived at quickly, in preparation for a hunt, not labored over for weeks to see just how tight the rifle would group. The new Remington 250-grain factory ammo prints even better than my handloads, around 1¼ inches for five shots at the 100-yard mark.

An exemplary achievement, my Latta rifle, one I intend to tote after game far and wide for many years, God willing. The whole outfit retailed for a few bucks under a grand, including the 4X Redfield scope. A bargain!

Butch Searcy:

Butch Searcy (15 Road 3804, Dept NAH, Farmington, NM, 87401, (505) 327-3419) builds all kinds of rifles, in all price ranges. One of his specialties, and not an unusually expensive one at that, is modifying current-production Model 70 Winchester actions to resemble closely the hallowed pre-1964 configurations. For years, various foozles have prated on about the superiority of the discontinued M70's controlled-round feed system, Mauser-style extraction and ejection, and coned-breech feeding smoothness. Such die-hards go to gun shows cash in hand in search of pre-'64s to gobble up.

Butch has ameliorated that necessity. For a chunk of green, he will take any new Model 70 and machine its bolt to accept a long side-spring extractor. He'll then install the old Model 70 pivoting ejector in the bridge, and funnel the breech end of the barrel to accept the reshaped bolt nose. About the only things then missing are the unduplicatable "feel" of the original and its guide rib.

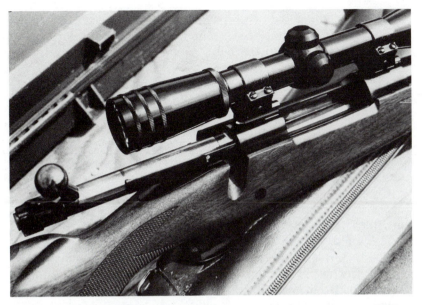

This post-1964 (current model) Winchester Model 70 has been modified to controlled-round feed by New Mexican Butch Searcy. Note long side-spring extractor at right of bolt body.

Butch sent me a worked-over new-issue Model 70 .30-06 Sporter to have fun with. I did. Rounds fed from its belly with oily slickness; the extractor yanked empties out with alacrity; cases were ejected in a fashion dictated by the shooter's whim, just as on the originals. So far as I could tell, accuracy was unaffected one way or the other. The rifle shot like I expect all Model 70s to shoot.

I'm uncertain of the going rate for the conversion, but if the customer provides the rifle, I suspect the whole outfit would set him back around a thousand bucks, depending on how much he paid for the gun to begin with.

Brian Zappia:

At the helm of Greensboro Gunworks, Inc. (3304 Edgefield Road, Dept. NAH, Greensboro, NC, 27409, (919) 668-2809) is Brian Zappia, a young fellow with an unerring eye for detail, pronounced or subtle.

As you undoubtedly know if you have been following along in this tome, one of my favorite hunting pieces is a Marlin 336-ER reamed to .356 Winchester. There were only three things about this handy little carbine that ill-suited me: its trigger was acceptable but not bragworthy; it reflected sunlight like a pier glass; it was a quarter-inch too long in the butt. Zappia volunteered to alleviate my complaints.

First he disassembled the little rifle and matte-blued the whole rig, including all the small parts. While reconstruction was in progress, he soldered the front-sight in place, removed the factory blade and replaced it with a Burris square-faced bead angled 45 degrees skyward to gather as much light as possible. A Lyman aperture sight was conjoined to the slab-sided receiver with Lok-tited screws.

Considerable time was allotted to getting the trigger just like I wanted it, a creep-free 3¼ pounds. It snaps like a pretzel and is consistent from tug to tug.

A Michaels of Oregon gray rubber buttpad was appended, and the stock abridged the amount I'd specified. Marlin's original white spacer was trash-canned by the dictates of good taste.

Finally, Brian spent much time with fine-grain sandpaper and linseed oil, reducing the stock shine to a muted sheen. I don't know how many hours of hand rubbing went into this aspect of my Marlin's transmutation, but the effects were worth it.

What I have now is a gleamless rifle that snaps to shoulder with a mind of its own, sends off a bullet exactly when I tell it to, and which warms my cockles like no other lever action I've given room and board. All work for less than $175 at Zappia's conventional rates, no discount for my rugged good looks or tennis prowess. A bargain!

The foregoing foursome offer a perfect microcosm of typical reasons rifle aficionados seek the expertise of a custom gunsmith. One was built to be as accurate as possible, regardless of aesthetics and damn portability. Another was tailored just for me, and was the embodiment of my notion of what an all-purpose wood-stocked hunting rifle should be. The third was intended to provide the reactionary individual with an action type that is getting harder and harder to find, and do so at an affordable tariff. Finally, we have a rifle that was almost but not *quite* right for its owner, that was thus molded to his conception of how it should have been when it left the factory, and all at a price that was affordable, even when done by a master hand like Brian Zappia's.

That is what a ''custom'' rifle means. To me.

12

Sighting In Your Rifle

The single most important aspect of shooter/rifle field performance is the ability of the gunner to direct his projectile where it is supposed to go. (Aside, of course, from being certain that the gun will actually *fire* when its trigger is tugged!) Several factors conspire to make such a task difficult. A few of them are range, range estimation, trajectory, bullet yaw, the effects of wind—both in lateral deflection and actual lift—the quality of the projectile, the accuracy of the load itself (bullet/powder/case/-primer match-up), the accuracy of the rifle, mirage and the ability of the shooter. But none of these is as oppugnent to sticking a bullet where it belongs as is an improperly zeroed rifle, or worse yet, one that has never been zeroed at all.

Not too many years ago, shooters were a more naive lot than they are today. Many—if not most—of them hunted with open, iron sights, which were provided by the factories on new guns. It was often assumed that such ordnance had been sighted-in at the factory, and in some instances they had indeed. But by someone other than the end user, with an unspecified bullet weight and brand, from an undetermined type of rest and at an unknown distance.

For normal woods ranges, such a rudimentary approach to riflery often sufficed. After all, a whitetail's chest is a large target at 60 yards. But alas, many a fine game animal has undergone a

To test a rifle for accuracy and zero, some shooters feel that one needs a pedestal-type stand and leather bags filled with sand. A spotting scope helps, and ear and eye protection are a must.

most unpleasant demise due to the ignorance and naivete of its assailant.

For some unfathomable reason, many hunters still misunderstand the mechanical aspects of sighting-in their own rifles. Worse, some consider doing so to be merely the abstruse vagaries of fussy old women, not really requisite for the descendants of Old Dan'l Boone hisself. The very thought of spending time and money and effort on such an unnecessary errand is an execration to them! Such hunters should be barred from the woods.

Admittedly, sighting-in a rifle is time consuming, moderately expensive and often frustrating. But the time is well spent, enabling a better understanding of and familiarity with one's armament; the expense will not reduce anyone to penury; and if you stay with me, I'll try to alleviate as much of the frustration as possible.

Sighting a gun in is not an extemporaneous task, although it is often treated as such. Quite the contrary; it must be fastidiously planned, performed correctly and meticulously, and repeated periodically to make certain naught has gone awry. Let's take it step by step.

How To Do It

First, make certain that your sighting system is properly and *securely* installed. If you don't know how to do it *right*, yield the project to someone who *does*. Period. No alternatives. Do not let your cousin Lou attach your expensive scope and mounts just because he owns two mallets and a screwdriver and can adjust the valves on your 1966 Volvo with panache.

Your scope (or iron sights if such are your preference) must be mounted with solidity and permanence. Furthermore, the sighting system must be appended at the right height for *your* rifle comb and *your* face, not those of your gunsmith. Eye relief is critical, and also dictated by the physical characteristics of both you and your rifle. And it must be perfect, or sooner or later it will cost you game. Believe it.

The crosswires within the scope should be absolutely vertical and horizontal, not leaning two or three degrees east or west. If you hold your gun with a pronounced cant, you may want to tilt the reticle a bit to counter your aberration, but I think it better that you learn to hold correctly instead. Why? Because it is exceedingly unlikely that you will exhibit the exact same degree of list in each of the several field positions you will find yourself using. It's better simply to ascertain that the vertical element of the crosshairs runs straight up and down and make your own physical adjustments accordingly.

All of your mount screws—especially those for the *bases*— should be sealed in place with something like Lok-Tite. Many gunners opt to have the bases soldered or sweated in place; I vote for that. If the scope is to be removed from time to time, then the large screws that attend to that withdrawal should be snug but not arm-wrenchingly so. (Actually, if you use too much force on these screw heads, they may shear off.) The screws that mate the ring halves should be as steadfast as the base screws, and sealed in place chemically.

Some type of adhesive or roughened tape (as provided by the Burris scope company) can be placed between the scope tube and the inside surfaces of the rings. I don't feel this is an absolute necessity with rifles of moderate recoil (say .30-06 level or under), but on heavy hitters, it is a fine idea. Few things are more atrabilious in the field than noting that your rifle scope has slipped forward under the stress of recoil. Your confidence factor will slide down around your shoes, right when you need it most!

When installing a scope, a gun cradle is invaluable. The gun is held securely and the requisite tools rest in the base, keeping them from rolling off the bench.

What type of mounts are best? Tough ones. Secure ones. Sturdy ones. Quick-detachable ones. I've used them all, and tend toward Weaver or the Burris/Leupold/Redfield systems. These latter have windage adjustments in the base, which can be a distinct advantage if the scope of your choice is limited in its lateral deflection. The Weaver, on the other hand, is better at returning to zero should you desire to remove and replace it for any number of viable reasons.

Incidentally, the Ruger mounting system, which comes at no extra charge on many of their models, is excellent in every way. I highly recommend it.

Before going into the details of aligning your aiming point with your impact point, a cursory word about scopes. My own preference in brands is not particularly biased; I've used most of them. From every marque I can recall, I've had both satisfactory results and an occasional problem area. With glass sights, a good rule of thumb is that the more money you spend, the better the product. Etch this in granite: I would rather hunt with an inexpensive rifle wearing a high-tariff scope secured by good-quality mounts than with the most expensive rifle ever built under a cheap scope, or one with unreliable mounts.

Scope magnification is a personal thing, but there are elements of a scope sight that are even more important. Examples are lens quality, light "gathering" ability, retention of zero, dependability of adjustments, eye relief, field of view, moisture proofing, resistance to recoil (both in lens movement as well as reticle integrity), size, weight, sturdiness of the scope tube and resistance to point-of-impact shift (in variables). Such factors are beyond the scope (excuse me) of this treatise. My thoughts are that the hunter can't go wrong with a 2½- to three-power scope for moderate ranges, say to 250 yards or so. If more of my time were spent in the woods than out in the open, I'd lean to the 2½.

For all-around use, at all ranges which big game shots should be attempted, a straight four-power is tough to beat. I like also such low-end variables as the various 1½ to 5X models, and similar items. For dangerous game, those are the ticket.

When I tote a dual-purpose rifle, such as a .243 or .25-06, I lean to a variable on the order of 2-7X or 3-9X. However, when zeroing the rifle for vermin, I do so at a relatively high power—say 7X or 9X—*and leave the dial set on that magnification throughout the varmint season.* When fall comes and I rezero with my big-game load, I rotate the power ring down to 4X, where it usually stays. I have had such bad luck with variables shifting their points of impact when the power-selection ring is changed, that I no longer vacillate back and forth like a pendulum.

Further, I have noted that my abilities to judge range through a rifle scope diminish in direct relation to how often I change powers. I like to acquire a mental image of what a groundhog or whitetail looks like through a scope of a specific power at a given range. Then, when I'm looking one over, I can come closer to guessing its proximity.

Also, please be aware that variables are more expensive than fixed-power scopes, more critical of eye relief and more difficult to seal against moisture; they are heavier, usually bulkier and are without doubt more fragile. Nope, I'm not exactly dithyrambic about variables. Sorry.

I decry even more the use of "see-through" scope mounts. It is patently impossible to have a scope sight mounted at the proper height for quick, accurate use when shackled by such a ridiculous device. The alleged purposes for see-through mounts are two. First, they enable an instant choice of either iron sights or scope. Thus, if yon bighorn is standing placidly awaiting his death, one can set the scope at nine power to dial him up with such clarity his mouth can be examined for ecthyma, let alone making it appear easy to hit the right button. Conversely, it is averred, should a big old buck go smoking out of his bed when a nimrod soft-shoes up on him one morning, said hunter can simply peer beneath the scope, align the iron sights, and smite him hip and thigh. Sure he can.

Problem: Said bighorn might decide he doesn't like the cut of your jib and hie himself off to safer climes. When he's tooling along at a good clip 250 yards away, which sighting system do you use to bust him? The answer is probably neither. He's too far away for anyone but the most experienced even to consider a shot with irons, and since your scope is mounted so high on the bridge, you'll never attain the proper cheek weld to enable a telling shot with the scope. Result: The sheep lives to a ripe old age and you wrap your rifle around a fencepost.

The second reason expounded for choosing see-through mounts is equally ludicrous: When your scope lens fog up, get covered with mist or crusted with snow, you merely have to peep through the tunnel at your trusty open sights. There is a nugget of common sense here, albeit a small one. All the above visual hindrances do happen to riflescopes; unfortunately, too often. Which is why manufacturers offer quick-detachable mounts. Better to remove your scope altogether and sequester it in a dry pocket; then you'll have an unobstructed view of those back-up iron sights. Further, should you be offered a long shot at an unwary critter, you can replace the scope, torque the screws to a predetermined spot, and gaze through a crystal-clear, unbesmirched lens system. Better all around.

Forget see-through scope mounts.

So, now we have our rifle ready to go. The scope, as expensive as we can afford, is mounted at a height commensurate with our own cheek as it mates to the rifle's comb. Our mounts are well-designed, solid, attached so that only a nuclear device will remove them from the rifle, and no one can "see" through them.

Next Step

Go to the store and purchase at least two boxes of the ammo you intend to hunt with. Three are better, but two will probably do. Make *certain* that not only are both boxes of the same bullet weight, not only from the same manufacturer, but of *the same lot number*. Read that last sentence again. *It is imperative*, and cannot be emphasized too strongly!

If you plan to use handloaded ammo, ascertain that you have a good supply of all four components on hand, and that all are from the same lot, *especially the powder and primers*. When loading your ammo for the hunt, utilize only those components you used when sighting in. If you exhaust your stock and have to resupply *any* component, verify your zero before going into the field!

This is proper position when one shoots for accuracy from the bench. Once the rifle is close to perfect zero, then a slightly different position should be assumed —preferable with the front hand holding the forend—for final adjustments.

OK, we've got our ammunition supply awaiting our pleasure. Our rifle's chomping at the bit. Are we ready, or what? Not quite. More items are requisite. Indispensable is a *good* set of muff-type ear protectors, or at least a highly-rated pair of plugs. If you neglect these on the premise that you don't plan to fire many rounds, you will undergo a tintinnabular experience you will not soon forget. Nor probably ever recover from. Buy the muffs!

More equipment. Some type of rest is needed, the softer the better. Two or three sofa pillows will work if you can spirit them out of the house and back again without fomenting familial discord. A stack of worn-out towels will do, or a couple of shot bags filled with kitty litter, or a daypack stuffed with underwear. It matters little.

If your range does not have a suitable benchrest, and you have no access to one that does, try to locate some kind of portable support like a card table. Sturdiness is not a key issue, just so long as it will stand by itself. If neither of the foregoing is practicable, then plan to use the hood of your car. Even better if you own a pickup is to stand in its bed and rest your rifle across the cab. (If you have a camper on your truck, this is probably not a good idea.)

Synthetic stocks—like this Bell & Carlson, on a Ruger Model 77—are taking over the game fields. They are impervious to moisture and warpage that can throw off wood-stocked rifles.

Into a paper poke, toss a small coin or screw driver that will fit your scope-turret adjustments and the windage screws in your mount bases if present. Add a batch of targets, home-made ones will do. Enclose a large sheet (three or four feet square) of any cheap, light-colored paper. Take along either a staple gun (make sure it's full!) or a handful of tacks. Include a couple of felt-tipped markers, preferably in different colors.

If your shooting spot is not equipped with a target frame, then either nail one together yourself from scrap wood, or go to an appliance store and purloin a high, wide cardboard box. Do *not* settle for a short, small carton; it will be all but useless.

It won't hurt to take along a large screw driver to fit your rifle's action screws, or a couple of smaller ones if your gun is a lever action. Ofttimes those screws tend to loosen under the stresses of firing; you don't want to discover that fact two days after you arrive in deer camp. Check the screws often; generally, once a rifle has been fired 40 or 50 times and the screws retightened, they take a set and will not loosen again. Of course, a wooden stock can warp, changing the tension on the action screws, and not often for the better. That's one reason why many serious hunters are switching to synthetics.

Now you're ready. When you arrive at the range, or out on the prairie, or at the local garbage dump, make certain of your backstop. Be sure that you will shoot *into* it, not over, around, or through it. Check it out! (And be sure to check up on local laws relative to where and when you can shoot your rifle!)

Although some shooters feel it is unnecessary to don shooting glasses, and don't mind letting you know of the disenchantment, it is a good idea. Note author's wife reaching for hers, however unhappily.

Staple the large sheet of light-colored paper to the target frame or cardboard box. The result should be a generous expanse of bullet-holeless background. Now affix a target at the exact center of the frame, atop the sheet of clean paper.

Remove your rifle from its case. Disengage the scope turret caps and put them in your pocket. If you don't, you'll lose them. Get out your small coin or a suitable screw driver. Put it in your shirt pocket so it'll be handy. Protect your ears now, and don a pair of glasses. If you don't wear corrective lenses, stick a pair of sunglasses astride your proboscis. Whichever, *protect your eyes as well as your ears*.

Poke a cartridge into your rifle's magazine, leaving its bolt open. Walk over to the target, keeping your gun pointed in a safe direction at all times. Pace off 10 feet from the target, face it, chamber the round, and fire one careful shot at the center of the bull. Open the bolt, remove the spent casing. Examine the target.

Assuming that your squeeze was a good one, that you neither jerked the trigger nor flinched wildly, you will now make adjustments according to the location of your bullet hole. If it is below the spot at which you aimed, move the elevation turret screw in the direction marked "up." If your bullet went high, make your adjustment accordingly. Ditto left or right.

Should you be using iron sights, drift the *rear* element in the direction you desire the bullet location on the target to move. For

A good shot can do his preliminary zeroing (at 10-20 feet) from an offhand position. Less steady gunners should try sitting or prone, even at this stage of zeroing.

example, if your bullet hole is high and right of center, then you must lower your rear sight and shift it to the left.

If, as on some military rifles, the adjustments must be made to the *front* element, reverse the above directions. When moving the front sight, always move it in the direction the shots *impact*. Thus, in the above example of shots hitting high and right, the front blade would need to be displaced higher and to the right. Clear?

Now, mark the hole in the target with a felt-tipped pin by drawing a circle around it, close to the edge of the hole. Place another cartridge in your magazine. Move 20 feet away from the target and repeat all the above. If for some reason you are not steady enough to do sufficiently precise shooting offhand, then sit down, or rest your elbows on your vehicle, or lie prone. Whatever is most expeditious for you.

Check the location of your second shot. Make any adjustments necessary. Draw a circle around the bullet hole; load one round. If your bullet holes are fairly close to the aiming point, move out to 25 or 30 yards and fire once again. If your shots have impacted off the target, or way out of the bullseye, then continue to shoot at 20 feet until your bullets strike near center.

A good view of proper bench technique. Note where the non-trigger hand goes. When so placed, it can manipulate the rear bag for both elevation and minor deflection adjustments. Stay relaxed. Grip the wrist of the stock with the thumb opposite the bolt-side. This gives better control.

At 25 yards, your shots should be going in just below the exact center of your target, perhaps an inch or so. If they are, you can move to 100 yards and set up your benchrest, table or what-have-you. Before doing so, put up a clean target. If any bullet holes are present in the larger backdrop paper, circle them in ink.

Fire a sand-bagged group of three shots from 100 yards. Walk down and check it out unless you have a spotting scope or a very high-powered scope on your rifle. If your shots are very far from dead-center, make the proper corrections and fire a deliberate *five*-shot string after letting your barrel cool a few moments.

After firing the second group, either replace the target or go downrange to mark the bullet holes. That way, you won't get confused as to which holes belong to which group.

Assuming the foregoing operations have gone smoothly, and that now your shots are hitting nigh dead center at 100 yards, it's time to establish your hunting zero.

If you are shooting a very short-range woods cartridge, such as the .44 Magnum, then I suggest you zero an inch high at 100 yards and leave it at that. You'll be dead on the money at about 125 yards, which is stretching the little cartridge pretty thin.

With the .30-30 class of cartridges, I like to zero a scope-mounted rifle from 1½ to two inches high at 100 yards. The latter number would yield a 150-yard zero range, and put the bullets less than five inches low at 200. However, a lot of .30-30s and .35 Remingtons are never encumbered with glass sights. Because their iron-sightline is lower than that of a scope by around three-quarters of an inch, their trajectory doesn't appear to be as flat, thus shows a tad more drop at long range. On a deer, the difference would not matter much. I wouldn't fret it.

If you have access to a 200-yard range, that's where you move next. Most cartridges like the 7mm-08, .270 Winchester, .280 Remington, .308 or .30-06 should be zeroed for 200 yards when used by the average hunter. Depending on the exact load and bullet configuration selected, such a zero would put the bullets between 1½ and two inches up at 100 yards, between seven and 10 inches low at 300. That's a very useful trajectory, and undoubtedly the best compromise for all but the most expert gunners. If you have access only to a 100-yard range, make certain bullet impact is set at the height above mentioned.

Why not zero for longer range? Several reasons. First, it promotes attempts at game that are beyond the capabilities of most shooters, and many gun/cartridge combinations. Second, there are many times—especially in woods or "edge" hunting—when only a small portion of an animal can be seen, such as its neck. Trying to guess exactly how low to hold on a 120-yard neck shot when using a rifle zeroed for 275 yards is tough sledding indeed. And since most game is brought to bag at ranges much under 200 yards, a long-range zero is of no assistance.

The real *bona fide* long-range shooter can zero his magnum rifle for 300 yards if he likes, so long as he memorizes the bullet rise at mid ranges and knows how to compensate for same. Most of these gents will be handloaders anyway, and can peruse ballistics charts in the loading manuals at their leisure.

One further point about zeroing. Some rifles shoot to differing points of impact when they are fired from a rest than when handheld. The difference can be quite pronounced, and can very well cause an animal to be wounded and lost, even when the hunter makes a good squeeze. The only way to find out is to fire your rifle

When zero verification is required in the field, this is about as steady a position as can be wished for. Note that Rick Jamison has placed a pair of gloves between the log and his rifle; otherwise the rifle might well kick away from the hard surface, giving a different point of impact than it would when hand held in a common field position.

from a variety of positions and compare the points of impact.

I am currently testing an Israeli GALIL .308 assault rifle, complete with bipod. When fired from prone using the bipod, the rifle not only groups wonderfully—around 1.8 inches with Samson 168-grain match ammunition—but hits exactly on point of aim at 100 yards with the sights set as they came from the factory. However, when I shoot the rifle from sandbag rest on a bench, the same ammo prints 10 inches *high* and groups around 8½ inches! Shot from the sitting or offhand positions (with no sling), it clusters its shots *low*. That rifle might work fine on groundhogs or plains game, where many shots can be made from prone. But for hunting come-what-may, it would be frustrating in the extreme.

The moral is to try your rifle from various shooting positions when establishing its hunting zero. Despite the fact that a benchrest is obviously the steadiest way to test a rifle for *accuracy*, it does not follow that it's the right method for ascertaining a hunting zero. In many instances, the opposite is correct.

Incidentally, varmint hunters need to keep their bullets closer to point of aim than big game gunners, due to the diminutive size of their targets. I usually zero my .22 centerfires from one to 1½ inches up at 100 yards, and use the click elevation adjustments in my varmint scopes to allow for long-range drop.

Trouble Shooting

If your rifle is not grouping like you think it ought to, there are several things to check. First and foremost, are *you* grouping like you oughta? If you have any doubt at all about your shooting ability, then ask a good shot to try your rifle for you. If he gets it to perk nicely, then you'll know where the fault lies. So don't traduce your armament until you're certain *you* are up to snuff.

Next thing to do is screw around. With your rifle's action screws. If they have remained snug, check your scope mounts, particularly the bases. (If you followed my advice about scope installation, then you will likely find no problems here. If you didn't, shame on you.) Finding all is well with those items that bind your gun and mounts, you'll have to look elsewhere.

Ammunition is the next item to undergo close scrutiny. If a panoply of choices is available in your rifle's chambering, try a different brand or two of the same bullet weight. I suggest Federal or Hornady ammo; both are often uncommonly accurate. If your load is not a popular one, you may have a problem. Which is why I repeatedly advise choosing a cartridge for which a plenitude of factory offerings is available.

If you have tried several good loads in your rifle and it still refuses to group as you think it should, some remedy must be sought. First, let's decide just how well your trusty game slayer should group, lest you have a false and unreasonable goal for it to fulfill.

A good sporter-weight turnbolt should print five shots under two inches, and 1½ inches is not an unreasonable expectation. I'd not be satisfied with groups larger than 2¼ inches from a Remington pump, and in the sub-.30 calibers (or the .308), I'd want 1¾ inches or better. Marlin leverguns are normally good for 2½ inches, although I would not balk at anything that stayed under three. The Model 94 usually runs around an inch or so larger, though not always, especially in the case of the 7-30 Waters. Single shots from Browning, Ruger and Thompson/Center should stay inside two inches, and 1¾ is not hard to come by. I must opine in all probity that only the Browning BAR (among *sporting* autos) is capable of sub-two-inch precision on a gun-after-gun

This is the kind of group most hunters strive for, but few rifles deliver. It measures 1.03 inches, just under true minute of angle (1.047 inches), and was fired from Remington 700 Classic .350 Remington Magnum from the bench at 100 yards with factory ammo!

basis, although a good example of the Ruger Mini-Thirty will go 2½ inches, as should the better Remingtons.

Should your rifle turn in groups larger than this, and you have no screw loose, have tried several loads and either are an accomplished gunner or have had someone test the rifle who is, then here's the scoop. If your rifle is a Remington pump or auto, trade it off or learn to live with its limited accuracy. There is little that can be done to improve things, even by a gunsmith. Ditto the Browning BAR. Sometimes, glass-bedding the forend on a lever action will work wonders, as will relieving any pressure provided by the barrel bands (if present). Generally a job for a 'smith. Savage 99s can often be "tuned" by adjusting the tension of the forend screw, as can such single shots as the TCR '87 and to a lesser extent the Ruger Number One and Browning 1885.

The most remediable of the rifle types is the turnbolt. Several things to check. First, see if the barrel is bearing evenly along both sides of its channel. If it isn't, get some sandpaper and see that it does. Or maybe better yet, remove all contact betwixt barrel and forend (called free-floating) and test the gun again. If it shoots *worse* than before, simply glue a thickness of business card into the barrel mortise near its tip, which should provide some upward pressure. You can experiment along these lines indefinitely.

Next, run a *thin* sheet of paper into the stock cutout for the bolt handle. Close the bolt. Does it impinge on the paper? If it touches it, remove wood until it doesn't. I fixed a poor-grouping Mauser 7mm Mag. that way, cutting its average by maybe 40 percent.

Check guard screw tension. If the action is of the three-screw design, such as the Winchester M70 and Ruger M77, make certain that you are not bowing the action by torquing the middle screw too tightly; it should be snug, but not knuckle-whiteningly so.

On two-screw actions, try removing the rear screw. As you loosen it, hold your fingers at the tang/wrist juncture. During that first half-turn of the screw, does the tang spring away from the wood? If so, rebedding is in order. Should nothing be amiss at the tang, shift your mitt to the forend. With your fingers at a location where you can feel both the wood and the barrel, loosen the forward action screw. If the stock jumps away from the metal as if it were alive, things are not as they should be. Unless you are pretty handy with wood, take your rifle to a gunsmith.

Most of the foregoing will probably not beset you. Generally, bolt-action rifles provide all the precision the average hunter needs if he'll spend some time testing ammo. Even if his rifle's bedding isn't perfect, two-MOA grouping is normally easy to acquire. Except for varmint hunting, no more precision than that is needed. Spend your time *practicing* with your rifle, not fooling with it, gooping it up with bedding compounds, carking over minutiae.

But make *sure* that it's zeroed!

13

The Budding Hunter

Quite often when I am loafing in gun shops, kibitzing campfire dissertations or merely eavesdropping at the firing range, I am subjected to much verbal excreta relative to the proper arming of a newcomer to big game hunting. Fathers of adolescent would-be nimrods, husbands to wives tired of sitting at home whilst hubby prowls the forest, girlfriends eager to make "your" thing into "our" thing, all have in common the need to make an intelligent choice. The advice commonly proffered is well-meaning but vague, and often based merely on conjecture, or worse yet, memories of their own first experiences.

For some abstruse reason, many long-time hunters await with eager anticipation the day when young Sally or Sammy walks over, all wide-eyed and innocent, and asks, "Next time you go shootin', Pop, can I come along?"

Little devil's horns poke through Dad's hairline as he suppresses a snicker of delight. A couple days later, he drags out Gran'pa's old L.C. Smith 12-bore double, selects a box of four-dram equivalent 2¾-inch magnum shells, installs his off-spring in the station wagon.

Upon arriving at the range, where his pals have convened to see the show, he retrieves the shotgun, fills one of its barrels, hands it smilingly to his child, then stands aside, eyes brimming with merriment. After all, this is the way he was introduced to the centerfire shooting sport by *his* father. Besides, the "joke" about to be perpetrated on the unsuspecting youngster won't *really* hurt, or at least not much. And the guys expect it. After all, there'll be no *permanent* damage. Sure there won't, physically anyway.

So little Sal or Sam, with absolute trust and eager anticipation, shoulders the gun, squints down its barrels, yanks one of the triggers.

Instantly a horrendous roar assaults their ear drums, someone slugs them painfully in the shoulder with a baseball bat and the ground rushes up to meet their rear end. They sit there, dazed but more than a little proud; after all, they've been allowed to enter the grownups' world.

Then they notice that instead of rushing over to congratulate them, the milling crowd is guffawing and pointing and slapping knees in mirth. Two things happen now in the mind of that child: He (or she) is forever programmed to fear centerfire shoulder arms, and has almost certainly acquired a built-in flinch that may never be conquered; she (or he) will never again trust fully the parent responsible for their ignominy.

That, my friends, is no way to begin a lasting and fruitful relationship. Try it on a wife or girlfriend and you may well lose more than just their trust and respect.

Best to start them off right, so that the hunting world might gain another steadfast adherent, not a disillusioned enemy.

The Right Rifle/Cartridge Combination

Of all the cartridges in the hunting spectrum, only a few are truly applicable to the beginning shooter. Naturally, all initial shooting should be done with a rimfire, since it allows the learning of such fundamentals as trigger control, sight picture, proper breathing and correct stance without a concomitant tendency to bankrupt the household. But should the neophyte ultimately express a desire to go hunting—specifically for something large (such as deer), or that must be taken at ranges beyond the reach of a rimfire (such as groundhogs)—an apropos selection of cartridge must be essayed.

The list would run like so (including most everything except the real esoterica) for various types of hunting: .22 Hornet, .221 Fireball, .222 Rem., .222 Rem. Mag., .225 Win., .224 Wthby Mag., .22-250 Rem., .220 Swift, .243 Win., 6mm Rem., .240 Wthby, .25-20 Win., .250-3000 Sav., .257 Roberts, .25-06 Rem., 6.5 X 55 Swede, 7-30 Waters, 7 X 57 Mauser, 7mm-08 Rem., .30

The beginner should always be started with a rimfire, so they can grasp the basics. Here's a youngster shooting with a specially built Kimber .22 Long Rifle. It was made to his size. Note short barrel to keep balance rearward.

Carbine, 7.62 X 39 Russian, .30-30 Win., .32-20 Win., .32 Win. Sp., .357 Mag., .41 Mag., .44-40 Win., .44 Mag. Let's look at varmint loads first.

If your would-be hunter is content to try their hand on such little creatures as ground squirrels, prairie dogs, groundhogs, jack rabbits, foxes and the like, I can recommend the following from the above list: .22 Hornet, .223 Rem., .22-250, .25-20 WCF, 7.62 X 39, .32-20 WCF and the .357 Mag. Why did I leave out so many? Either because none has any advantage on the ones listed, or because I feel that the cartridge in question is more suitable to big-game than varmints at the ranges to which a beginner should be restricted.

Now, among the above mentioned eight loads, which are best? Depends on two factors: range and rifle selection.

The newcomer should always be tended to carefully during their initial outings, and held to ranges at which they are reasonably certain to make clean, swift kills. This is to everyone's benefit: The game doesn't suffer from its assailant's lack of expertise; the new hunter doesn't have to witness a noble animal's painful demise.

In light of the foregoing, I feel that the neophyte should be limited to 100 yards on game the size of foxes and groundhogs, and then only when firing from a solid position, under good light conditions, at a fully visible, stationary animal. Bear in mind that the heart/lung area of a 12-pound animal is small indeed, and that's what needs to be hit.

Critters the size of jack rabbits and smaller should be considered 75-yard game until the new gunner becomes adept at hitting from quickly-assumed field positions under the stresses of time and excitement. Although practice at the range is necessary and helpful, it will *not* duplicate the adrenalin-charged atmosphere of the hunt.

Considering the foregoing range limitations, I would choose for the younger beginner a .22 Hornet turnbolt or single shot if they are of sufficient stature to handle a rifle of that size. For the smaller person—such as an average 10- or 12-year old—I would choose a Marlin .25-20 or .32-20, possibly a Browning B-92 in .357 Magnum, or a Ruger Mini-14 or Mini-Thirty in .223 Remington or 7.62 X 39 respectively.

My reasoning goes as follows. If our pilgrim can handle the length, weight, length of pull and forward balance of a normal-sized bolt action, then a Hornet will stand them in good stead even when they become capable of shots as far as 175 yards. Recoil is nil, muzzle blast the merest whisper, ammo inexpensive and accuracy more than sufficient. If one can afford a Kimber or Anschutz, then an excellent trigger pull is assured without having to seek a gunsmith.

For the diminutive youngster, a short carbine of exiguous heft is the ticket. Thus my preference for a Marlin levergun if said trainee is not emotionally mature enough for an autoloader. The .25-20 or .32-20 has all that is needed in a 100-yard fox or groundhog load; when handloaded, they're impressive indeed. Bullet drop is more pronounced with this duo than is the case with more modern loads, but the beginner must learn to cope with holdover sooner or later; why not now? Additional advantages to the Marlin 1894 carbines are their affinity to providing good trigger pulls and their easy scoping.

The .357 Magnum is faster and more powerful than either or the foregoing, but not enough to take it much out of the varmint-only class. It is adequately precise in the little B-92. The

This distaff hunter took her Blue Ridge Mountain porker with one shot from her Savage over/under .357 Magnum/20 gauge. She used a 180-grain Federal hollow point .357 loading.

Browning is somewhat kid-sized—short of stock, handy in overall length and light enough for a pre-teen. Iron sights are requisite unless a side-mounted scope suits you. This increased difficulty in precise aiming is somewhat obviated by the .357's flatter trajectory when compared to the .25-20 and .32-20. Of course, its recoil is sharper too, and the bark, so if your particular aspirant is extremely recoil or noise shy, you might by-pass the .357.

I like the Ruger Minis for four reasons. One, they are easy for the hunter of very small stature to handle. Two, both come in chamberings that under very specific, stringently-observed conditions will take deer-sized game. Three, their sights are rudimentary but fully adjustable aperture units, not the step-elevator, drift-punch items indigenous to many rifles in their price category. Four, the Rugers are readily scoped; in fact the Ranch Rifle iterations come from the factory with rings.

Now, if our neophyte is an adult, a scoped, bolt-action .223 or .22-250 makes a crackerjack varmint rifle. I'd have a gunsmith affix a recoil pad, and while he was at it adjust the length of pull to match milady's torso perfectly. A trigger job would be a cardinal addition, in my view. The result of these attentions to detail would be an outfit that could handle all basal gunning chores with dispatch, and if chosen wisely wouldn't require a king's ransom.

The .22-250 is plenty powerful for such fauna as groundhogs, but is light of recoil.

An alternative for the strapping teenager or normal-sized adult would be a rifle reamed to one of the varmint/deer numbers, like the .243, 6mm Remington or .250 Savage. If only one gun is planned, that's the way to go. A handloader can stoke his rifle's furnace with but a modicum of coal, providing fodder as meek as deemed necessary at first. As time passes, experience accumulates and shoulders toughen, the tinder can be fanned a bit without much likelihood of promoting an accuracy-destroying flinch. Ultimately, full-power loads will be handled impassively, and likely without cognizance of the increased amperage.

My wife, Barbara, can handle a .44 Magnum revolver with such precision that in certain circles her accuracy would be applauded by *riflemen*. Its ghastly recoil levels do not fill her with trepidation, merely serve to harden her resolve. Since she *always* wears ear protection, the Maggie's horrendous muzzle bark fails to render her aphasic from concussion. But Barb's frontal shoulder muscles are as tender as lightly breaded veal. Rifle recoil annoys her, puts her off her feed, causes her normally extraverted manner to become obvolute. Yet even she can handle recoil levels up through that of the .257 Roberts with aplomb, displaying precision that embarrasses her not, in any company. My point is that if my

Barbara Harvey, author's Storm & Strife, is not comfortable with much recoil from a rifle. This 6mm Ultra Light Arms gives her no trouble, despite its six-pound heft, scoped. That costume is her usual groundhog-hunting outfit. Note ear plugs in place, shooting glasses on.

wife can shoot a 6mm Remington or .257 Roberts without shrieking in pain, any adult can.

Lest you suspect that she might lean toward the bulky side, the better to absorb all that recoil, let me disabuse you of that notion. Her fightin' weight is 110 pounds. After a meal. A big meal. She stands five feet, seven-and-a-half inches tall, barefoot. No Amazon, my Barb.

OK, our distaff adult or mature teenager can handle .243-level recoil. Unless the intent is to shoot a *lot* at very small vermin like prairie dogs, I'd simply let them use the same ordnance on deer and pronghorn. I'd insist they hold their fire if an animal was out past 200 yards or so. But up to that distance, the 6mms and mid-sized .25s will haul the freight.

Our smaller, younger set can stick to the .223 and 7.62 X 39 if that is what they've been using on varmints. Abandoned are the .25-20, .32-20 and the .357 Magnum; not enough sauce for deer. The .223 is best used at 100 yards or under; the little .30-caliber

The adult distaff gunner can often handle a full-sized rifle, but not full bore recoil. A moderately heavy, gas-operated auto like the BAR is a good bet, especially in .243.

Russian round can go on to 125 or a step more under a tyro's direction.

At this point, someone will raise his hand to point out that I haven't espoused the .30-30 class. Reason: Most .30-30s, .32 Specials and the like are found in lever-action Marlin and Winchester rifles. These handy carbines weigh little, so are easy to maneuver. But that very lack of heft gives them unpleasant recoil, which is exacerbated by stock design. No, I'll pass on such loads for a youngster.

The older teen or lady gunner can manage a .30-30 quite nicely if they lean to the traditional lever action. Better I think is the 7-30 Waters. It's a bit flatter shooting than the .30-30, comes back with less vigor. Even better would be a Savage 99 or Browning BLR chambered to .243, maybe even the 7mm-08 if our fledgling hunter can cope with man-sized recoil levels.

Actually, if our novice is strong enough to handle an eight-pound rifle, but is still not exactly enamored of recoil, a gas-operated semi-auto might well be the answer. In .243 chambering, a Browning BAR hardly kicks at all due to its heft and the recoil-assuaging properties of its gas operation. Such semi-military carbines as the Heckler & Koch SL-7, while not gas

The Ruger .44 Carbine, a gas-operated auto, is not only short and light enough for a youngster to handle easily, but it kicks little and has plenty of punch for deer.

operated, have actions whose cycling reduces the comeback noticeably.

If an autoloader is considered off limits for a beginner, then a moderately heavy turnbolt is the best choice. Its trigger can be tuned; its stock design allays kick somewhat if it is chosen with an eye toward that purpose. I strongly recommend that the length of pull be fitted exactly to the shooter, and a thick, soft rubber recoil pad be installed. Such will be much appreciated, and reward the user by enabling better marksmanship.

Small fry need to stick to a short-coupled rig, to keep the balance point as far to the rear as possible. Hence my proclivity for the Ruger family of self-feeders. I trained 10-year-old Alan Reaves

Ten-year-old Alan Reaves slew this big tusker with a Ruger Mini-14 in .223. The pig weighed more than three times as much as Alan.

on a Mini-14, in two days. Then we went off to the North Carolina mountains where he shot a 250-pound wild boar.

Young Bob Newsome used a military 6.5 X 55 cut down to his tidy proportions on the same hunt. Got his hog, too. The 6.5 is perhaps the finest neophyte cartridge in existence. It hits hard, recoils at a noticeable but not inhibiting level, and is not particularly loud mouthed. Its only blemish is limited availability of new guns, although many importers are bringing in military cast-offs in good shape. They are not expensive, and can be transformed into a serviceable if homely sporter with little cash outlay.

For undersized nimrods whose short arms have difficulty reaching a bolt knob, and whose benefactors don't feel comfortable with an auto in their hands, the Marlin .41 Magnum Model 1894 is a good bet. Loaded with 175-grain Silvertip hollow points, recoil is quite moderate and killing power sufficient for 75- to 100-yard shots at deer.

If buying from the used-gun market is deemed acceptable, such arms as the Savage 99 chambered for the old .250 Savage would be

The used-gun market will yield such fine and mild-recoiling ordnance as this Savage 99 in .250-3000. Easy on the shoulder, tough on whistlepigs and buck deer!

a fine outfit for the smaller folk. The same gun reamed to .300 Savage is suitable for growed-up distaff gunners, or well-developed teens, but recoil could hinder precision unless the shooter intends to practice a lot.

Remember the key points: Start the beginner off with a rimfire until the basics are mastered; move up to a varmint-level centerfire, preferably one that can be used at close range on deer-sized game so that the skill and familiarity gained in the varmint pastures can carry over to the deer woods; finally, the now-experienced hunter will graduate to cartridges useful for deer at all normal ranges, and even black bear and elk in the timber. At that point, you'll have gained a full-fledged hunting *partner*, not merely a protege.

Index Of Rifle Calibers

Index